Television Image Quality

Television Image Quality

Basic Concepts and Perspectives
New Recording Technologies
New Distribution Technologies
New Display Technologies

A collection of papers on television technology presented during the 18th Annual SMPTE Television Conference in Montreal, Canada, February 10-11, 1984.

Foreword
Papers Program Chairman
Stanley F. Quinn
Canadian Broadcasting Corp.

Preface
Maurice L. French
Canadian Broadcasting Corp.

Editor
Jeffrey B. Friedman

Cover Design
Mathew V. Kuriakose

Published by the Society of Motion Picture and Television Engineers
862 Scarsdale Ave., Scarsdale, NY 10583

The Society of Motion Picture and Television Engineers,
Scarsdale, NY 10583

© 1984 by the Society of Motion Picture and Television Engineers

Library of Congress Catalog Card Number: 84-50346

ISBN 0-940690-09-8

CONTENTS

New Display Technologies

FOREWORD

Television engineers face a period of great change. Decisions are required in the next year or two to establish new standards and a new generation of equipment for program making, distribution, and reception/display. For example, new digital video tape recorders of impeccable performance are needed for program making; new signal standards are required for direct-to-home broadcast satellite services with improved picture quality; new "smart" receivers are expected in the home. Further in the future is the likelihood of standards for a new high definition television service. Driving these changes, of course, are the ongoing developments in solid-state technology.

The benefits from these changes are that television audiences will be able to get much better picture quality, including larger and wider screens, and more choice of programs. Of course, television audiences have already become accustomed to a remarkable progress in picture quality and program choice since the NTSC standards were first adopted. Today's home TV receivers are a far cry from the early ones. There is considerable choice of programs since cable TV and home video cassette recorders became popular in recent years. So far as picture quality is concerned, what we have seen has been equipment design and performance catching-up with the capabilities of the NTSC system. In the future we can expect a break-away from the NTSC system, and its limitations, to television systems of superior performance. Such superior systems are expected to live alongside the older NTSC system, each satisfying particular markets. For example, there is a need to provide a superior delivery system for wide-screen movies in the home.

The 18th Annual Television Conference has been dedicated to exploring the new technologies with particular emphasis on the decisions now facing television engineers. This has been done by dividing the conference into four sessions; the first is concerned with basic concepts and perspectives of image quality, the second with new video recording technologies, the third with new distribution technologies, and the fourth with new reception/display technologies.

It is hoped that the Conference will contribute, on the one hand, to educating the international family of television engineers in the new technologies and the nature of the decisions to be made, and, on the other hand, to making the decisions needed.

Stanley F. Quinn
Papers Program Chairman

Stanley F. Quinn, Director of Engineering for the Canadian Broadcasting Corporation, joined the SMPTE in 1962 and was made a Fellow in 1970. He joined EMI in 1951, where he designed switches for the BBC, and in 1957 he went to CBC as a spcialist in broadcast engineering. He has published a number of technical papers, several of which appeared in the SMPTE Journal. He has served on a number of SMPTE committees including the New Technology Committee and the Public Relations Advisory Committee. Mr. Quinn is a member of the SMPTE Board of Editors and a former SMPTE governor of the Canadian Region.

PREFACE

The Society of Motion Picture and Television Engineers is pleased to publish, for the ninth consecutive year, selected papers from its annual television conference.

As a Canadian, this volume, *Television Image Quality,* is one that is of particular significance to me personally because the 1984 Television Conference was held in Montreal, Canada. This book will serve to document what I believe was the finest collection of international technical papers ever presented at a television conference.

New technology is being developed at an accelerating rate. To insure that new information is disseminated as quickly as possible, we have bypassed conventional typesetting methods and have published the original transcripts as provided by the authors.

On behalf of the Society, I would like to thank the authors of the papers, who, by their contributions, helped to provide the insight needed in this "time for decisions." Many of these highly respected authors traveled from various parts of the world to present news of their exciting technical discoveries and developments.

The excellence of this book was made possible through the efforts of the Program Chairman Stanley F. Quinn, Canadian Broadcasting Corp.; the Deputy Program Chairman Janet A. West-Cyr, Canadian Broadcasting Corp.; and members of the Papers Program Committee. They are to be commended for their superb organization, dedication, and commitment to the 18th Annual SMPTE Television Conference: "Image Quality — A Time for Decisions."

Maurice L. French
Editorial Vice-President

Maurice L. French is the SMPTE Editorial Vice-President. A founding member of the Society in Canada, he was Chairman of the Toronto Section for three terms and served consecutively for 20 years on the Section Board of Managers. He is a recipient of the SMPTE's Outstanding Service Citation. Mr. French was Program Chairman of the 116th Technical Conference and General Arrangements Chairman of the 14th Annual SMPTE Television Conference. He has served two terms as Governor of the Canadian Region. He is an SMPTE Fellow. He received the Centennial Medal of Canada in recognition of valuable service to the nation. Mr. French is with the Canadian Broadcasting Corporation in Toronto.

Image Quality From A Non-Engineering Viewpoint

Harry Mathias
Consultant
Los Angeles, CA

When asked to do this paper, I tried to decide whether the title suggested that I confine my remarks to non-engineering issues or simply limit my remarks to a non-engineering point of view on engineering issues. I also thought, given the title of this paper, that everyone who was involved in the very complex engineering problems of the new video imaging technology would think "I can relax and tune this paper out, he is just talking about non-engineering considerations." Meaning, I suppose, what color a high definition camera should be painted, or should a large screen display be done in a high tech or traditional walnut motif to blend in with a modern living room. While these are, of course, all weighty questions we shall not, however, consider them here.

If we assume everyone on the engineering end of the new imaging technologies executes designs with the same brilliance and imagination as has been used in proposing new system configurations and in attacking problems of noise, compatibility, and band-width thus far. I for one feel confident that although all of these problems are not yet solved, they soon will be. When we are to the point of producing a practical, well engineered, advanced video production system or more likely several advanced video production systems in an "A","B", and "C" format, which will slug it out in the marketplace, (until everyone forgets that the original intention was to drain the swamp of alligators and not introduce new ones into it).

But, anyway, if all this comes about then the resulting enhanced or high definition systems will live or die on the basis of non-engineering considerations. Or, to put it another way, when all the engineering obstacles have been met, we will not, as a production industry, have a useable, advanced video production system until the non-engineering obstacles are overcome.

The non-engineering difficulties that a new technology faces are generally the final obstacles which it must overcome before being accepted and put into practical use. Unlike the engineering obstacles, however, the non-engineering ones are rarely planned for in advance, rarely even researched until they are encountered. Problems of application and acceptance of a new technology catch everyone by surprise even though they could have been foreseen with a little advance research or even a conversation or two with the people who will apply the production technology that will result from all of the careful study and thoughtful discussion that we are participating in here today.

Any new production technology redefines the production process, and it has always been a mystery to me that designers of production equipment spend so little time studying the production process before designing and producing equipment which will impact and change that process. It almost seems as if practitioners of film and video production are constantly attempting to understand the impact of new technology on their art and craft while the makers of this technology do not seem to understand the art and craft which the products of their technology are impacting.

All film and video productions regardless of budget and regardless of production quality consist of creative work and decision making under moderate to severe time and budget pressures. Equipment designed for this industry, format, and image quality decisions made for this industry, must be undertaken in such a way as to alleviate this time and budget pressure rather than intensify it. Practicality and flexibility are the cornerstones of our non-engineering considerations.

We were, of course, asked to discuss image quality from a non-engineering point of view. While image quality is certainly of paramount importance, in the minds of the production industry practicality, flexibility, and usefulness are frequently traded for considerations of image quality. One need only look at the evening news for occasionally overwhelming examples of this trade.

So now that we have come this far in our discussion, and in the true high definition study group tradition, let's redefine this paper's title. We will change it to "If It Works, Why Fix It". Because, seriously, that is the question most often being asked these days by film producers, studios, directors, and cinematographers, even television network executives. In short, the customers whose equipment purchases will ultimately pay for all the research and development which is now going into advanced television imaging systems.

As we continue this discussion on image quality, I suggest all of you bear in mind the question "if it works, why fix it"? In other words, NOT will this or that proposed standard or encoding method do the job of encoding, producing, and editing quality images, but will it do the job SO MUCH BETTER than what is currently being used as a production standard so as to justify the change. Will the improvement convince a pragmatic, deliver-the-goods-on-a-budget-type producer at 2:00 A.M. standing out on a New York street in the rain when the director just told him that the next set up will be down a sewer manhole cover that the new technology will be worth the additional problems that new technologies always create.

Or will the subtle improvement in image artifacts that some of the extended or enhanced definition systems promise be of importance only to an engineer in a control room studying a high resolution test monitor. Because if that is the case, if we toss out the technology we have, in favor of some barely noticeable measure of image improvement for the sake of bandwidth conservation and compatability, then we may never get another chance to toss that system out in favor of REAL image improvement.

Let's consider first the most volatile proving ground of new technology. Namely dramatic, feature length production for big screen display. If you're concerned about the proposed advanced imaging systems' appropriateness for large screen display, if you are a member of the "we can produce quality pictures, but we can't put them on a theatre screen" society, then stay with us through this discussion, but omit the large screen display. The problems are really the same in all areas of consideration except resolution, whether the end product is displayed on a theatre screen or a quality television screen.

Despite its tinsel-town, fantasy land image, motion picture production is very much the art of the possible, the art of the practical. Although the motion picture industry has the reputation in the popular media of being financially irresponsible, it is actually fiscally and technologically conservative.

The upright moviola in the editing room, for example, is a classic mechanical contraption existing almost unchanged in style or function from the 1930's version though today's. It is a fixture in the Hollywood editing suites. Although it is known to consume film and tear sprocket holes with alarming regularity, and although the improved horizontal flatbed-type editors have existed since the mid 1960's, the changeover is slow and my prediction is that at least in the Hollywood area, upright moviola editing machines will exist and be used daily to edit film until the turn of the century.

This conservative streak is not to say that the motion picture industry is not without its pioneers. There are certainly those within the feature production community with a considerable taste and daring to innovate. However, in an industry where computers are being used to keep track of pages shot per day and set ups completed per hour with daily reports sent to accountants and producers; and, when a director's job security is based on a computer projection of the completion date of the project based on an extrapolation of current page counts, directors in this climate are understandably leery of technological innovations on the set.

The rewards for being the first director or producer to utilize new technology are media attention and notoriety for the innovators. The penalty for experimenting with new technology on a production can be set delays and the most expensive kind of research and development. The type which goes on while the cast and crew stand around waiting. It is the fear that any form of innovation applied to a production will interfere with the creative process or such intangibles as pace, working rhythms, or production styles that has tended to keep production innovations from being applied in the production industry thus far.

Any casual observer within or outside the production community is certainly well aware how difficult it is to predict the success of a script, a production concept, a production style, or even the blending of selected artists and technicians into a working community. Since no one can guarantee the success of a production approach, no one can guarantee with certainty which aspects of the production process can be successfully modified.

The reason I feel it is so essential to concentrate on the applicability of new imaging technology to the theatrical production field is that by studying the most demanding application we can learn a great deal about the other applications of this technology. There is an analogy here in the way the automobile industry has utilized the sport of racing to test, modify, and refine their car designs. The motion picture industry has always been used in much the same way by the television production community. Motion pictures set the standard in the areas of photographic effects, visual moods, and image styles, not to mention photographic quality.

So what then are the design priorities for a high definition video system to possess in order to successfully compete with motion picture film in the production of feature length dramatic films. These priorities listed in order of importance to the production community are:

1. Practicality, flexibility, and ruggedness.
2. Aspect ratio.
3. Sensitivity.
4. Gamma or Transfer characteristics.
5. Resolution. I don't believe resolution is number 1 in priority although resolution has figured heavily into the debates on system configurations.
6. Standards acceptance.

Or, failing to find a consensus for one standard, then the second choice for our number 6 priority would be standards conversion.

The ranking of these priorities may seem odd and indefensible to you, but this list is prioritized according to the "if it works, why fix it" imperative. In other words, these priorities meet the needs of box office, common sense, and bottom line--the three golden yardsticks against which all production decisions are measured. This is a list of the priorities of the producer, of the director, and cinematographer. This is not necessarily the way a distributor or broadcasting network would prioritize its needs. But we are assuming that if production priorities are met, standards conversion could be used to alter these priorities for distributors, or television networks' use.   Let's discuss these system considerations one a a time.

PRACTICALITY would seem to be obvious, but is probably the consideration that merits the most discussion precisely because it is the one which is least often discussed in any debate of new technology. We must not fall into the trap of thinking that the dramatic production industry has problems that need to be solved simply because those who advocate new technology have an idea that they want to try out on this industry.

The benefit most often promised to dramatic producers by advocators of new production technology is cost savings. The minute one mentions cost savings to a producer one immediately has his undivided attention. The argument that video technology will save a producer money would be more convincing if experiments with single camera video use in the production of a traditionally film-type dramatic show had ever resulted insignificant cost savings.

It would even be more convincing if a cost-effective, single camera production had received critical, in addition to fiscal, rave reviews. But, dating back from Universal's experiments with single camera video on "Harper Valley", where a projected $17,000 budget savings turned out to be only $3,000 because of post production overruns; to Universal's experience with "Invisible Woman" which resulted in only a $4,000 difference between the video and the film budget, this has not been the case. Matt Herman, of Comworld, remarked after producing three feature length television movies on video tape exclusively, that "video tape technology results in little cost savings if the same time and quality is spent on the video, as would be on a film production."

There is certainly a more important consideration than the cost saving aspects of dramatic production on video. It's quite reasonable to argue that any new technology in its infancy may not be cost effective, and possibly not even artistically effective and that with practice greater success in both areas will be possible. The truth is, that the motion picture production community already possesses a flexible, versatile, adaptable production method, one in which changes come slowly through a process of evolution over a period of years.

Take, for example, a piece of production equipment called an "apple box." Apple boxes are frequently used for raising people and production equipment to desired heights, sort of like large building blocks. Several years ago, for example, a grip discovered that by cutting the handles of an apple box in an off-center, rather than a centered position, they could be carried two at a time with one hand, instead of one at a time as was previously done.

This idea was debated for a while and is slowly coming into acceptance, but the moving of handles on apple boxes from the traditional position was not a change accepted lightly. The film industry unlike the video or computer industry does not possess a "Gee Whiz" attitude towards new technology, but more of a "give me one good reason to change" attitude. When you pick up apple boxes a thousand times a day during the long working conditions of a dramatic production, you want to know that the movement of a handle from its traditional position is not going to create more problems than it will solve.

Likewise, when Universal decided to produce a televison pilot and six episodes for a series called "Fitz and Bones," in which video would be used in addition to film, they were reluctant to undertake the experiment. The story of "Fitz and Bones" concerned a news ENG camera crew and the concept was that, while the show would be shot on 35mm film, the video news cameramen's pictures would be shot with an ENG camera modified for 24-frame recording and screened on 24-frame 3/4 inch video tape playback. The working method used is that after a motion picture sequence was shot in which the actor was video taping a scene, a video crew separate from the film crew would step in, video tape that sequence, and that video tape would later be played on monitors in editing room sets and control room sets of the dramatic show.

The shooting progressed smoothly enough and the video experienced no technical difficulties or performance problems, but the video crew experienced a great deal of difficulty fitting into the working rhythms and pacing of the show's film crew. The result was that after a sequence was filmed and it was time to video tape the additional sequences, the film crew frequently experienced delays and breaks in its working rhythm while the video crew shot its sequences. These problems were not technical, they were more procedural and interpersonal. The result is that at the end of the first week, Universal determined that the video production crew had resulted in a $20,000 cost in terms of crew and cast delays and the video crew was simply replaced with a film crew and the inserts that were intended to be video taped, were filmed and transferred to video tape.

This story illustrates, in some small measure, how despite the successful solution of technical problems, the failure to be equally successful at solving practical problems can be terminal for any new production system. The use of video tape on the Universal show "Invisible Woman," for example, was considered by all measures of performance, to be successful, but, apparently not sufficiently successful, not overwhelming successful enough, for Universal to plan at this time, other single camera television episodic shows. It seems for a new production system to gain industry acceptance, it must not only be practical and cost effective, it must also be connected with the production of an artistically and financially successful project.

Image vision, the Image Transform system of producing video tape for transfer to 35mm motion picture film, for example, is an artistically and cost effectively viable production system. Many observers in the industry have not been able to understand why it has not found greater industry-wide acceptance, and the only conclusion that many of us who have looked with sympathy at the development of Image Vision, have come to, is that it has been Image Vision's misfortune to never have been identified with a film which was succcessful artistically and in the box office. It seems as you discuss Image Vision with the motion picture production industry that everyone wants to be the second person to produce a successful Image Vision feature; nobody wants to be the first.

What then is the relationship between design considerations and box office success? Well this is certainly a tenuous connection to be made, but two factors can be discussed:

1. If a production system advocates itself and promotes its use as a means of saving money, then it certainly increases its chances of being identified with quick and dirty exploitive production where quality and artistic effectiveness are not a primary concern.

2. If a new production technology is awkward to use or inflexible, it interferes with artistic options. By being limited in lens selection or photographic options, it threatens to disrupt working methods and such intangibles as artistic pace and mood. These limitations will make the production of an artistically successful project more difficult. If one advocates a production system solely on the basis of cost savings, then one is condemned to constantly justify the money saving aspects of its use. In the case of video, this is frequently done through the use of smaller crews, lower lighting budgets, and the use of a more hectic shooting schedule. None of which are conducive to quality production.

Current video production equipment is designed for three camera, live-switched shows or news. Although recent modifications to camera designs have been made for field production, none of these go far enough to produce a full-featured location production camera for quality imaging, with the possible exceptions of the Panacam and Ikegami EC-35. It remains to be seen whether any of the cameras developed for high definition, will even go this far towards meeting the needs of the production community.

Our second priority, ASPECT RATIO, has certainly been greatly debated, and everyone with even a casual interest in high definition systems, is aware of the bandwidth dilemma. The bandwidth required for wide aspect ratio has argued persuasively in favor of moderate aspect ratio systems. Five to three is often discussed, and a ratio of 1.85 to 1, or 2.35 to 1, quite common in the motion picture industry, is considered wasteful or even radical as a proposal to make for high definition broadcast systems.

This may be true, but as Kerns Powers once pointed out, the history of the motion picture industry shows, that when given a choice between wide aspect ratio and resolution, the industry has chosen wide screen and wide aspect ratios on every occasion. The motion picture industry has done this based on the most conclusive, most immediate, type of audience preference poll-- that of whether or not they will pay at the box office. It seems a shame when we are on the verge of new imaging technologies, we would consider taking a step backwards in terms of aspect ratio, especially since our entire motion picture heritage exists on films predominantly shot on a 2 to 1 or wider image format.

One possible alternative to the bandwidth conservation issue which, in my opinion, has not been adequately explored is the application of anamorphic lens systems in the original photography of high definition video pictures. The subsequent de-anamorphosing could be accomplished through the use of frame store technology at the receiver or projection end. This could also be accomplished, in an even simpler fashion, by modifying the receivers' vertical height with a switch and fixed resister to change the vertical size for de-anamorphosing.

This system has been used in motion picture production video monitors for some time. While this may produce the dreaded, underscanned screen that the FCC, at least in the U.S., has such a phobia towards, there are precedents of, for example, the feature "Manhattan" being shown in the New York area with black bands top and bottom in the original wide screen format. Certainly, with all the discussion of wide screen display systems, it is probable that display systems of the future will have sufficient area that the shrinking of vertical height will not pose an image size problem. The advantages of this system should be obvious in terms of increased vertical resolution at no additional cost in terms of transmission broadcast bandwidth usage.

Our third priority is SENSITIVITY. Some of you may have been puzzled that I placed sensitivity above resolution as a priority. I felt justified in doing this because camera sensitivity translates directly into production costs, whereas resolution does not. To realize the impact of increased sensitivity on a production one must study what has occurred in film production with the advent of 5293, 5294, and other high speed motion picture stocks. To be responsible about this investigation, one must realize that high speed motion picture stocks did not begin with 5293, and that even 5247, which is now considered to be a normal speed motion picture stock, was once itself considered a high speed motion picture stock.

Sensitivity in a motion picture stock, or indeed in a video production camera, directly translates into man-power hours required to light a set. Other hidden costs of low sensitivity are: electrical power consumption, caused by increased lighting and air conditioning needs on the stage, fatigue factor on the part of actors, expensive production delays caused by the need to reapply make-up that has faded from heat and perspiration, as well as the length of time required to set up and strike a location of heavyweight compared to lightweight lighting instruments.

It has certainly not been lost on the advocates of motion picture technology that high sensitivity in relation to signal-to-noise ratio figures is currently a major advantage of motion picture stock over video technology. This advantage will increase, rather than decrease as video technology progresses farther in the direction of high definition video systems.

Number 4, GAMMA. The ability to reproduce extremes of contrast is a critical requirement for any film or video camera. It is a difficult variable to quantify. In practical terms, a camera's ability to reproduce images of wide scene brightness range often is of primary importance to its photographic usefulness. Since lighting contrast ranges occurring in nature exceed the ability of both film and video to reproduce adequately, in professional photographic situations it is usually necessary to reduce the existing contrast range through the use of fill lighting. Put simplistically, the narrower the dynamic range which can be safely reproduced by a camera the more fill lighting is required to reproduce a scene.

Dynamic range limitations have always occurred in video cameras that do not occur in film cameras. In current state of the art equipment, the video camera is at a disadvantage over a corresponding film camera only to the extent of a stop and three quarters in latitude. This generally translates as a seven stop range from opaque blacks to transparent whites in film and a five and a quarter stop range for the equivalent exposure levels in video.

While gamma compression devices on current electronic cinematography cameras are incapable of increasing the camera's actual photographic latitude, they nevertheless, simulate a filmic appearance in the reproduction of high-key contrasty scenes. The current contrast reproduction differences between film and video are certainly workable, if somewhat problematic, but if the dynamic range of a high definition camera tube were to prove limited, even by today's standards, this would definitely be a very serious problem.

The ideal, of course, would be a high definition production camera with dynamic range beyond what is currently available approximating or surpassing that of film. It is conceivable that CCD technology may make this possible although it would, of course, be necessary to overcome first some of the CCD's other technical limitations.

Our fifth item on our priority list is RESOLUTION. This may surprise some, because resolution is the first item on most engineering lists of priorities where HDTV or other advanced imaging systems are concerned. I think this is partially the case, because when designing a video system to compete with film, many engineers are perhaps overly defensive about matters of resolution. Many cinematographers feel it is not the superiority of film over video, in terms of absolute sharpness, which is the problem. A relatively small area of the picture, in any given frame, is critically sharp. The resolution characteristic of film, which is most difficult to imitate with electronic cameras, is the gradual transition from sharp areas of the image to soft-focus areas of the image.

Due to the optical nature of this transition in film, it seems natural to our eyes, compared to the aperture-corrected, electronic appearance of video contours. This same transition in video, from an in focus enhanced portion of the image to an out of focus and thus unenhanced portion, is most objectionable.

Mr. Dee Pourciau's paper called "High Resolution TV for the Production of Motion Pictures", which was given at the fall 83' SMPTE conference, was a very interesting comparison between the resolution of film systems and video systems. While Mr. Pourciau is the first to say that he is still in the process of verifying his work, the paper strongly suggested that the resolution of theoretically possible high definition systems were competitive with currently available film resolution figures.

When discussing resolution in motion picture film, two very important practical considerations must be kept in mind:

1. That the motion picture industry has never proven a correlation between image sharpness and box office success, or even between image sharpness and artistic success. "The Concert for Bangladesh," for example, utilized 16mm film blown up to 70mm and whatever measure of success that production met with was not limited by its lack of sharpness. A feature film called "Signal Seven," directed by Rob Neilson, was shot on three-quarter inch video cassette. Photographed entirely under low light conditions, in car interiors, and on city streets at night. It was blown up to 35mm by Image Transform, and met with critical acclaim at the Telluride Film Festival.

No one is suggesting, of course, that the resolution limits, inherent in three-quarter inch video tape, are adequate for large screen projection, but the point must nevertheless be taken that the audience did not throw tomatoes at the screen and run out of the film festival shouting. As a matter of fact, it seems quite clear from all accounts that a large percentage of the audience did not know they were viewing a film that was originally shot on video tape.

The second practical consideration of resolution is that sufficient motion picture sharpness for professional theatrical applications can be defined as follows: that amount of resolution which allows the cinematographer to put diffusion or nets in front of the lens, and deliberately toss away a large portion of the available resolution. That also allows the assistant, working with high speed lenses, to miss his critical focus once in while and still provide a result that can be screened to a large audience, on a projection system that is rarely in focus, without that audience stamping its feet and complaining. If this seems to imply that motion picture resolution requires a reserve of sharpness to handle a certain amount of accidental or intentional abuse in the hands of cinematographers, then that was my point exactly.

As a cinematographer, I have learned that discussions of resolution cannot be separated from discussions of lens design and quality. The selection or design of a high resolution camera tube is something that generally takes time and careful attention. But, the design of a lens appropriate for use with that tube is an equally difficult, if not more difficult, undertaking.

A specific high definition camera needs only three quality pick up tubes at any given time, but it may require dozens of lenses of resolution equal to that pick up tube throughout its production life. Too frequently in the design of video production equipment are lens specifications given to lens designers too late in the design process. Too frequently are video lenses hastily produced and with too limited a focal length diversity for professional production applications. Many video cameras that theoretically promise great resolution, actually deliver poor resolution, because of the limitations of the corresponding lenses which were produced for that camera.

This takes us back to our central theme of the high priority of flexibility and practicality in a dramatic production camera. It's worth touching on at least the subject of registration in a high definition camera. Obviously, any situation but perfect registration would produce major resolution limitations in the final high definition picture, but it should be remembered that a high definition video camera must be more than capable of superior registration, it must capable of achieving that registration in a short time period, consistently, and hold it under adverse conditions, and extremes of temperature and vibration.

Our sixth point on our list of priorities is STANDARDS ACCEPTANCE. Certainly the dramatic production industry can be counted among the supporters of one worldwide standard at least for production if not for distribution. Producers who invest a great deal of money in a dramatic production want to know that the standard in which it was photographed will continue, and be universally accepted for some time to come. That the production standard of a given project is so superior to distribution standards that if need be it can be standards converted without a great deal of loss in image quality.

It's interesting to note, however, that while broadcasters are interested in standards compatibility and/or simplicity of standards conversion, producers as a group, are more interested in standards complexity and less interested in convenient standards conversion. The primary reason for this is that piracy or unauthorized duplication of motion picture products, according to Variety, is an industry whose profits reached one billion dollars last year. Complex encoding schemes and the use of encription devices promise to make motion picture piracy a more difficult undertaking.

This has great appeal for producers and certainly is a tangible argument for high definition video production of dramatic subjects. Simultaneous worldwide distribution via direct broadcast satellite also promises the producer a sizeable immediate income from his product. More importantly, it is a profit that can be realized before motion picture piracy can significantly errode into the box office earnings of his production. This short turn around between completion of a production and the box office return on its investment, promises to stimulate production in a era of high interest rates, and in some small measure stem the tide of rising production costs. And don't think the promise of a world-wide release before the reviews can come out, is lost on the production community, either.

Can all of these design requirements and goals be met in the production of an advanced video imaging system. I think they can be. Will they be? I'm not sure. Remember as the debate goes on during these sessions that we are not simply designing hardware, we are designing a creative tool to be used in the production of art and communication.

The answer to the question we posed at the beginning of this paper "if it works, why fix it," is that you fix something to improve it, but any attempt to improve an existing system must start with an understanding of the methods currently used to produce dramatic production and a realistic assessment of actual needs, not imagined needs. We must ask ourselves are we designing equipment to solve problems that don't exist. Equipment to improve production methods must first possess basic system flexibility and image resources that current equipment and methods provide, and build from there.

Harry Mathias has been a motion picture director of photography for 19 years with experience on 19 major feature films, 39 network television dramatic shows and comedies, an Academy Award nomination, many national commercials and 235 documentaries, in both film and video. He has also been a consultant and designed production equipment for Arriflex, Cinema Products, Photo Research, and is president of Mathias Designs Inc. He is the author of numerous articles for SMPTE, On Location, Video Systems, Millimeter, and an upcoming book on the subject of electronic cinematography for Wadsworth Publishing. He has taught classes in Cinematography, Video, Lighting, and New Production Technology for UCLA, San Francisco State University, AFI, and five years of national lecture tours speaking to the production industry. Mathias graduated from San Francisco State University with a B.A. degree in Radio, Television, Film and an M.A. degree in Creative Arts with a minor in Electronic Engineering. In addition to his cinematography activities, Mathias is currently Senior Consultant to Panavision Inc.

Perceptual Considerations for High-Definition Television Systems

Curtis R. Carlson and James R. Bergen
RCA Laboratories
Princeton, NJ 08540

Abstract

The perceptual impact of various high definition television (HDTV) systems is evaluated using just-noticeable difference analysis. The major conclusion of this analysis is that foreseeable cameras and displays do not permit effective utilization of luminance bandwidths beyond roughly 10 MHz in a 4x3 aspect ratio format. Furthermore, by exploiting the eye's reduced temporal capabilities for both high spatial-frequency luminance and for chrominance information, and by utilizing subcarrier quadrature modulation, a HDTV system seems possible whose total bandwidth is less than 10 MHz in a 5x3 format.

I. Introduction

The merit of any new high-definition television (HDTV) system must be judged by a number of perceptual and practical criteria. It is our purpose to outline several of these criteria and show that they point toward a HDTV system requiring substantially less bandwidth than the 30 MHz HDTV system proposed by NHK[1].

We will begin by stating briefly some of the essential practical issues to be considered in the design of any HDTV system. Then we will use a form of perceptual analysis, called "just-noticeable difference" (jnd) analysis, to evaluate several different HDTV systems. It will be shown that the practical considerations and the perceptual analysis suggest a HDTV system whose luminance bandwidth is less than 10 MHz in a 4x3 format.

II. Practical Considerations

The list that follows summarizes some of the issues that must be addressed by advocates of any new HDTV system:

1. Perceptual Impact: In order to justify the expense of HDTV, it should be as visibly distinctive from current NTSC as color television was from black and white. We will show shortly that this distinction will be difficult to achieve by changing bandwidth standards only.

2. Aspect Ratio: An increased aspect ratio would provide a better match between the display and the requirements of the eye, and would provide new opportunities for programing sports, theater, music, etc. However, the initial advantage of the increased aspect ratio would be that it is unmistakable: It provides the required distinction between HDTV and NTSC.

Since a change of only around 4% in the shape of an image can be seen, any of the proposed HDTV aspect ratios would be easily discriminable from our current 4x3 aspect ratio. The NHK suggestion of 5x3 is reasonable, but either slightly smaller or larger aspect ratios would also be suitable. Large aspect ratio formats, of say 2x1, are undesirable, since they require displays that are difficult to build with the required spatial frequency response at the screen edges. Thus, much of the transmitted bandwidth associated with such systems would be wasted. One possible solution to this quandary would be to adopt a flexible format, such as the E-MAC proposal of Philips[2]. This system allows signals with different aspect ratios to be transmitted and then properly configured within the receiver with the aid of control information. Conceivably a system could be designed, suitable for either dramatic presentations or sports, with a wide aspect ratio and with variable resolution over image space. The left and right sides of the displayed image could have low resolution while the center could have high resolution. Such a system is well matched to the eye[3]. For alpha-numeric information the E-MAC signal could be reconfigured to give uniform resolution over a smaller aspect ratio image space. These ideas are intriguing, but further discussion is beyond the scope of this paper.

3. Bandwidth: We consider the total 30 MHz bandwidth required by the NHK system to be uneconomical. It is inconceivable that any U.S. broadcaster would willingly allocate this much bandwidth to one channel. Although such bandwidths are inappropriate for transmission standards, they might be appropriate for production standards. Also, in general, studio standards require somewhat higher total bandwidths than do transmission standards. In a practical system, the production, studio, and transmission standards should be easily convertible to each others formats.

4. Human Visual System: The spatio-temporal frequency volume of the HDTV signal should match the requirements of the human visual system. Although the static, spatial properties of the visual system are reasonably well understood for the purposes of designing a new HDTV system, the temporal properties are not. Thus, in determining the required temporal properties we will resort to previously accepted practice. However, we note that the current 30 Hz frame rate of the NTSC system may provide excessive temporal bandwidth for both the highest spatial frequencies and for the chrominance information. William Glenn of NYIT has constructed a HDTV system where the high frequency luminance signals are sent at a 5 Hz frame rate[4]. Our impression, after viewing his system, is that a 5 Hz frame rate is too slow but that 10 Hz may be adequate. A 10 Hz rate would be in better agreement with the spatial-temporal properties of the human visual system[5,6] at the appropriate HDTV spatial frequencies between roughly 10 to 20 cycles per degree.

5. Kell Factor: The Kell factor is an empirically determined ratio relating the number of samples to the maximum displayable spatial frequency. Measured Kell factors between 0.5 to 0.7 indicate that nonoptimal pre- and post-filtering in the camera and display results in inefficient use of bandwidth in sampled systems[7]. Any HDTV system must reduce the bandwidth losses associated with the Kell factor.

6. Cameras and Displays: The spatio-temporal standards for any HDTV system should match the performance of cameras and displays likely to be available over the next 10 to 20 years. Thus, the bandwidth allocated for the HDTV system should not exceed the capabilities of forseeable cameras and displays. We assume that high brightness,

practical displays will be capable of fully resolving and converging no more than 1125 lines. We assume similar limitations on cameras. We believe these assumptions are reasonable since demonstrated laboratory cameras and displays just match these requirements. Projection display systems are potentially capable of higher resolution, but suffer from poor brightness, large size, and high cost. Only the RCA flat panel[8] seems capable of overcoming these objections. However, even this system would be limited to roughly 1000 lines in a 30x50 inch format.

7. Signal Processing: Sophisticated signal processing will be an essential feature of the HDTV receiver. Frame stores and microcomputer based signal processing will be utilized to improve the displayed signal-to-noise ratio, increase the displayed image sharpness, provide deghosting, etc. Such processing is necessary to exploit the full HDTV bandwidth. We refer to such processing as "computer enhanced video" (CEV).

8. Compatibility: The HDTV signal should be easily convertable to NTSC and other signal formats; it should be easily derived from production and studio standards; and it should degrade sympathetically, as well as be suitable for additional future extentions. For these reasons it is necessary to be able to recover undistorted component signals from whatever camposite format is used. Multiplex Analog Component (MAC) type formats have ben proposed to meet this requirement, accepting their less efficient use of signal bandwidth. Advanced signal processing techniques applied to the more efficient subcarrier type formats such as NTSC or PAL may make this sacrifice unnecessary, however. The techniques for providing compatibility between the various alternatives are beyond the scope of this paper; emphasis here will be on the perceptual effects that result from bandwidth changes. We assume that the performance outlined below can be achieved by a number of different transmission standards.

III. Perceptual Analysis of Different Systems

With the considerations listed above we will now evaluate the perceptual impact of various television systems. The analysis is primarly concerned with transmission and display of luminance information. We will start with our current NTSC system and then move toward higher bandwidth systems, ending with the NHK system.

In the analysis that follows we will make the following assumptions: (1) The viewing distance is taken as either 2 or 4 picture-heights, since the advantages of HDTV are not realized at the more conventional viewing distances of 6 to 10 picture-heights. (2) We assume a limit of 1125 line displays with peak luminances near 300 fl. The sharpness advantages of HDTV are rapidly lost if the peak display luminance drops much below 100 fl.[10]. (3) We assume cameras with maximum line numbers of 1125. (For consistency we have selected 1125 lines as our reference in this analysis. If we were considering only the NTSC system, however, we would select 1049 lines.) (4) All systems are based on frame rates of 30 per second, and (5) all the bandwidths listed are nominal values, intended primarily for comparative purposes.

In evaluating these systems we will use just-noticeable-difference (jnd) analysis [10]. This type of analysis has been used previously to evaluate a wide range of display characteristics [10-13]. It is appropriate here because it converts the objective parameters of the various television systems into perceptual units that quantify how strikingly one system differs from another. Thus, using this analysis we can assess the perceptual impact seen by the viewer resulting from differences between the systems.

A jnd is defined to be the change in an image required for an observer to correctly see that change 75% of the time. Clearly 1 jnd improvements represent insignificant perceptual effects. However, 10, or more, jnd changes represent significant effects that can be seen almost 100% of the time. We consider improvements of 40 jnd's to be the absolute minimum required to justify any new HDTV system. For comparison, we have estimated that the distinction in going from monochrome to color television was equivalent to several hundred jnd's[14]. We will show shortly that such large perceptual changes are unlikely to result only from an increase in bandwidth. Consequently we believe that a change in aspect ratio, which provides a striking distinction between systems, is an essential feature of HDTV.

In Table I we list the television systems to be compared along with some critical system parameters. For each system we show as an inset a schematic of its spatial frequency response, f_y versus f_x. Also listed in the Table are the nominal aspect ratios for each system; their luminance bandwidths; four orientations (H = horizontal, V = vertical, and D = diagonal); the number of active lines per picture height; a "Filter factor" that accounts for systems losses other than those due to sampling processes, such as spot size; the Kell factor; and the resulting number of lines seen by the observer given by multiplying the Filter factor, Kell factor, and the number of active lines. In all cases, as stated earlier, we will assume that the maximum number of lines that can be scanned out in the camera and also presented on the display is 1125. Also listed in the table are "comments" that briefly describe how each system is configured.

The entry to the far right in Table 1 lists the number of jnd's, ΔJ, by which each system differs from perfection along the horizontal, vertical, and diagonal directions. In our analysis we take the test image to be 100% contrast edge transitions aligned along each of the four orientations. This test image has been shown to give results similar to those obtained with natural scenes [10,12]. We assume that there are four orientation specific channels in the human visual system, which reflect the known anisotropy of the system. In the model the visual anisotropy is obtained by reducing the contrast sensitivity of the visual system by $\sqrt{2}$ along the diagonals. This estimate of four channels may be low[15], and the assumption about the distribution of information in scenes questionable. Also, we are fully aware that the Kell factor reflects both spatial and temporal sampling artifacts: Simple multiplication of Kell factors and Filter factors is a rough approximation to reality. Nevertheless, for our purposes these uncertainties are relatively unimportant. The general conclusions of this analysis are invariant with respect to reasonable assumptions about the anisotropy of the scenes displayed, the details of the visual model, and the assumptions about the quality of the filtering achieved.

We begin in Table 1 with Case I, which represents the NTSC system as typically experienced at the present time. The inset figure roughly shows the transmitted spatial frequency spectrum of the NTSC system. The number of active vertical lines transmitted is 483; the number of active horizontal lines transmitted is 328. In this example we assume: (1) a line-comb filter, which removes some diagonal bandwidth, and (2) an overall horizontal bandwidth of 3.5 MHz (i.e., a Filter factor of .8 due to spot size and amplifier limitations). We assume no vertical interpolation in either the camera or the display to overcome the Kell factor. Estimates on the value of the Kell factor vary between 0.5 and 0.8: Here we conservatively take the Kell factor to be 0.7 [16]. The viewing distance is taken as four picture heights. For this situation the number of jnd's lost when compared to a perfect imaging system is significant in all directions, with a total loss, summed over all directions, of over 100 jnds. At this viewing distance it is obvious to all viewers that the displayed images are significantly degraded.

In Case II almost all of the bandwidth of the NTSC signal is recovered using both a frame comb and vertical interpolation to 1125 lines. The 1125 line display helps to minimize the Kell factor, removes the visible raster line structure, and allows the full diagonal resolution to be realized. We also assume a 1125 line camera whose output is filtered and them subsampled to 525 lines. Overscanning in the camera has two positive effects: (1) it reduces vertical aliasing and (2) it allows close to the full diagonal resolution of the system to be realized. (It should be noted that the full effects of a 1125 line display cannot be realized unless it is used in conjunction with a 1125 line camera.) Thus, along the diagonals we have included a Filter factor of only 0.8 to represent the roll-off in the corners of the f_y versus f_x plane due to the camera spot, etc. If these changes are made then significant perceptual improvements can be realized, as indicated by the drop in total jnd's lost from 108 to 51.

Next, in Case III, we consider a hypothetical MAC system with 525 vertical lines (i.e., still 483 active lines) and a transmitted bandwidth of 5.6 MHz. As above, we assume filtering from 1125 lines to 525 lines in the camera and then interpolation back to 1125 lines in the display to get the Kell factor up to 0.9. In this case the resulting perceived horizonal and vertical performances are approximately equal. The increased bandwidth of this system results in an 11 jnd improvement over the fully realized NTSC system (Case II). At the expense of additional bandwidth this MAC system would also have better temporal and chrominance performance, which are not included in our analysis. As noted earlier, however, these advantages would generally be perceptually insignificant when compared against fully realized NTSC images.

In Case IV we next consider a system that has its horizontal and vertical resolutions increased by $\sqrt{2}$ by rotation of the "square" frequency response shown in Case III. Since the bandwidth area, f_y versus f_x, is the same as the MAC system, we call this system MAC-D, where the D stands for a diamond shaped frequency plane. It is well appreciated that producing a clean diamond shaped spectrum requires sophisticated diagonal filtering. However, we have assumed the same values for the Filter factor and Kell factor as used in Case III. In effect, we are assuming rather idealized filtering in both the camera and the display. This diamond shaped frequency response is slightly better matched to the characteristics of the eye, which is reflected in the jnd results. Each orientation is now degraded more equally, which represents a perceptual advantage. Overall, however, this system is not significantly better than the conventional MAC system. We have performed simulations of Cases III and IV that confirm this conclusion.

In Case V we have now increased the overall transmitted bandwidth to 11.2 MHz. Because the area in the spatial frequency plane is again diamond shaped and because we have doubled the bandwidth, we call this system 2MAC-D. As above, this case is somewhat difficult to analyze. If we assume no interpolation to line numbers greater than 1125 in the vertical direction, then the vertical Kell factor will remain at roughly 0.7. The additional diagonal Kell factors of 0.8 and 0.9 reflect the difficulty of producing and displaying an image of this type on a 1125 line display. Nevertheless, overall this system would produce excellent images. However, given the complexity associated with producing a clean diamond shaped spectrum, there is some doubt that in practice this high quality could be realized. Case VI shows a second simple possibility for a 11.2 MHz system. This system has twice the bandwidth of the MAC system but the same shape in the spatial frequency plane. Thus, we call it a 2MAC system. Now the vertical resolution is 742 lines, but, as before, we assume down sampling from 1125 lines in the camera and interpolation in the display to our limit of 1125 lines to help overcome the Kell factor. This increases the Kell factor to roughly 0.85. The jnd results also indicate that this system would produce excellent images although the diagonals are, as expected, overresolved when compared to the horizontal and vertical directions.

Case VII, representing the 1125 line NHK system, requires 20 MHz of luminance bandwidth in a 5x3 format[1]. We show the bandwidth of the NHK system as 16 MHz in Fig. 2, which is appropriate for a 4x3 aspect ratio system. Here we assume no interpolation to overcome the Kell factor, since we have reached the limit assumed in this analysis of 1125 lines in the camera and display. A Kell factor of 0.7 was used, which results in a significant reduction in peformance. As a result we see that this system, requiring 40% more bandwidth, is not significantly perceptually improved over Case VI. Of course, if we assume roughly 1687 line cameras and displays the Kell factor could be significantly overcome and the image would look almost perfect vertically. However, in the horizontal direction this system is still somewhat deficient. It would be desirable to exchange some of the diagonal bandwidth to increase the horizontal bandwidth to make an almost perceptually perfect image.

IV. Summary of Perceptual Results

In summary, these results indicate that either a fully realized NTSC system or a 5.6 MHz MAC type system would produce excellent pictures, particularily when compared to our present day NTSC system. Given the potential excellence of these systems, we feel that a true HDTV system should be accompanied by a change in aspect ratio to set it apart. That is, a change in aspect ratio is perceptually more significant than a 20 or 30% change in bandwidth. This point is emphasized in Fig. 1, which shows the number of jnd's from a perfect image plotted as a function of the transmitted luminance bandwidth in MHz. The cases listed in Table I are shown as the points, "x", on the figure. The vertical lines about each point represent the range of performance expected depending on the quality of the filtering achieved to overcome the Kell and Filter factors. Although the actual achievable performance is difficult to estimate accurately, the important inferences about relative perceptual quality of the different systems are robust. We note, again, that the MAC type systems have slightly better temporal and chrominance performance than does fully realized NTSC: These additional virtues are not included in Fig. 1. However, the addition of chrominance information in the MAC systems requires additional bandwidth.

Figure 1 also shows that the potential improvement in going from either the fully realized NTSC or MAC system to one of the 11.2 MHz systems would be worthwhile, but not as striking as one might wish for such a costly new system. The perceptual differences indicated will be even less after including the degradations introduced by the source material and by transmission. Finally, we see that while the NHK system could produce almost perceptually perfect images under the most favorable conditions, the additional improvement over the 11.2 MHz systems is negligible. This is because with a limit of 1125 line cameras and displays the total bandwidth cannot be effectively used. Of the two 11.2 MHz systems the diamond shaped one (2MAC-D) is attractive because it is so well matched to the eye. If fully realized it could produce perceptually perfect images at a viewing distance of 4 picture heights. However, in practice the difficult filtering required by such a system significantly reduces its overall practical effectiveness. Also, as we have assumed throughout this paper, we doubt that in the future it will be possible to build high brightness displays with the spot size and convergence required to do justice to such large vertical and horizontal bandwidths.

Figure 2 shows calculated results similar to those of Fig. 1, but now at a viewing distance of 2 picture heights. Even at this close viewing distance the general conclusions listed above are maintained.

V.   Conclusions

The major result of this analysis is that forseeable camera and display technology does not permit effective utilization of luminance signal bandwiths beyond roughly 10 MHz in a 4x3 format. This bandwidth is matched to the capabilities of 1125 line cameras and receivers and, with interpolation, overcomes the large bandwidth losses associated with the Kell factor. Such systems can produce excellent images. Increase of luminance bandwidth beyond 10 MHz produces small perceptual improvements unless corresponding improvements are made in cameras and displays. Finally, this analysis did not attempt to exploit the eye's tolerance of reduced temporal resolution for both high-frequency luminance and chrominance information. It seems likely that inclusion of these factors could result in a HDTV system whose total bandwidth is less than 10 MHz in a 5x3 format.

REFERENCES

1. Fujio, T., et al., "High Definition Television System - Signal Standard and Transmission," SMPTE Journal, 89, pp. 579-584 (1980).

2. Philips Laboratories, Demonstration at the 1983 Montreux Television Symposium, June, 1983.

3. Yuyama, I., and Fujio, T., "Transmission System Using Eye Movement and Visual Power of Peripheral Fovea, Nat. Conv. of ITE, Japan (in Japanese) pp. 1-5 (1978).

4. Glenn, W., Personal communication, May, 1983.

5. Robson, J.G., "Spatial and Temporal Constrast Sensitivity Functions of the Visual System," J. Opt. Soc. Am., 56, pp. 1141-1142 (1966).

6. Kelly, D.H., "Motion and Vision. II. Stabilized Spatio-Temporal Threshold Surface," J. Opt. Soc. Am., 69, pp. 1340-1349 (1979).

7. Wendland, B., "Picture Scanning for Future HDTV Systems," Proceedings of the International Broadcasting Convention, pp. 144-147, Sept. 1982.

8. Credelle, T.L., "Large-Screen Flat-Panel Television: A New Approach," RCA Engineer, 26, pp. 75-81 (1981).

9. Windram, M.D., Tonge, G., and Morcom, R., "MAC - A Television System for High-Quality Satellite Broadcasting," IBA Report No. 118/82 (1982).

10. Carlson, C.R. and Cohen, R.W., "Visibility of Displayed Information," Office of Naval Research Report, No. CR213-120-4F, July, 1978.

11. Carlson, C.R., "Thresholds for Perceived Image Sharpness," Photographic Science and Engineering, 22, pp. 69-71 (1978).

12. Carlson, C.R. and Cohen, R.W., "A Simple Psychophysical Model for Predicting the Visibility of Displayed Information," Proceedings of the SID, 21, pp. 229-246 (1980).

13. Carlson, C.R., "Application of Psychophysics to the Evaluation of Imaging Systems," Proc. 1982 Inter. Display Research Conf., Cherry Hill, NJ, pp. 1-15, Oct. 1982.

14. Mezrich, J.J., Carlson, C.R., and Cohen, R.W., "Image Descriptiors for Displays", Office of Naval Research Report, No. N00014-74-C-0184, p. 115, Feb. 1977.

15. Campbell, F.W., and Kulikowski, J.J., "Orientation Selectivity of the Human Visual System," J. Physiol. (London)., 187, pp. 437-445 (1966).

16. Pearson, D.E. Transmission and Display of Pictorial information (John Wiley and Sons, New York, NY) 1975.

TABLE I

System	Aspect Ratio	Band-Width (MHz)	Orientation	Active Lines/P-H	Filter Factor	Kell Factor	Effective Lines/P-H	JND's Lost, ΔJ
I. NTSC TODAY	3x4	4.2	H	328	0.8	1.0	262	−32
			V	483	1.0	0.7	338	−22
			D	584	0.5	0.7	213	−27
			D	584	0.5	0.7	213	−27
								Σ −108
II. FULL NTSC	3x4	4.2	H	328	1.0	1.0	328	−22
			V	483	1.0	0.9	435	−15
			D	584	0.8	0.9	435	− 7
			D	584	0.8	0.9	435	− 7
								Σ −51
III. MAC	3x4	5.6	H	437	1.0	1.0	437	−15
			V	483	1.0	0.9	435	−15
			D	651	0.8	0.9	493	− 5
			D	651	0.8	0.9	493	− 5
								Σ −40
IV. MAC-D	3x5	5.6	H	618	0.8	0.9	445	−14
			V	683	0.8	0.9	492	−12
			D	461	1.0	0.9	415	− 8
			D	461	1.0	1.0	461	− 6
								Σ −40

Comments (I):
- Includes a line comb in the receiver.
- 525 line camera and display.

Comments (II):
- Includes a frame comb in the receiver.
- Camera filtered from 1125 to 525 lines.
- Display filtered from 525 to 1125 lines.

Comments (III):
- Camera filtered from 1125 to 525 lines.
- Display filtered from 525 to 1125 lines.

Comments (IV):
- Camera is scanned diagonally and filtered from 1125 to 525 lines.
- Display is scanned horizontally, and filtered from 742 to 1125 lines.

TABLE I (cont.)

System	Aspect Ratio	Band-Width (MHz)	Orientation	Active Lines/ P-H	Filter Factor	Kell Factor	Effective Lines/P-H	JND's Lost, ΔJ
V. 2MAC-D	3x4	11.2	H	874	0.9	0.8	629	– 7
			V	966	0.9	0.7	609	– 8
			D	651	1.0	0.8	520	– 3
			D	651	1.0	0.85	553	– 2
								Σ –20

Comments:
- Camera is scanned diagonally with 1125 lines and filtered to 742 lines.
- Display is scanned horizontally with 1125 lines.

System	Aspect Ratio	Band-Width (MHz)	Orientation	Active Lines/ P-H	Filter Factor	Kell Factor	Effective Lines/P-H	JND's Lost, ΔJ
VI. 2MAC	3x4	11.2	H	618	1.0	1.0	618	– 7
			V	683	1.0	0.85	580	– 9
			D	921	0.75	0.85	636	– 1
			D	921	0.75	0.85	636	– 1
								Σ –18

Comments:
- Camera filtered from 1125 to 742 lines.
- Display filtered from 742 to 1125 lines.

System	Aspect Ratio	Band-Width (MHz)	Orientation	Active Lines/ P-H	Filter Factor	Kell Factor	Effective Lines/P-H	JND's Lost, ΔJ
VII. NHK	3x5	20 MHz:	H	618	1.00	1.0	618	– 7
		16 MHz in	V	1035	.95	0.7	686	– 5
		a 3x4	D	1205	0.7	0.7	646	– 1
		format	D	1205	0.7	0.7	646	– 1
								Σ –14

NOTES APPLICABLE TO ALL SYSTEMS:

- Viewing Distance is 4 Picture-Heights.

- Assume High Brightness Displays:
  Mean Brightness, $\bar{I}$, Above 100 FL.,
  Peak Brightness, I_p, Above 300 FL.

- Frame Rate is 30 per second.

- Kell Factors: 0.7 with No Interpolation
  0.85 for Interpolation from 742 to 1125 lines.
  0.90 for Interpolation from 525 to 1125 lines.

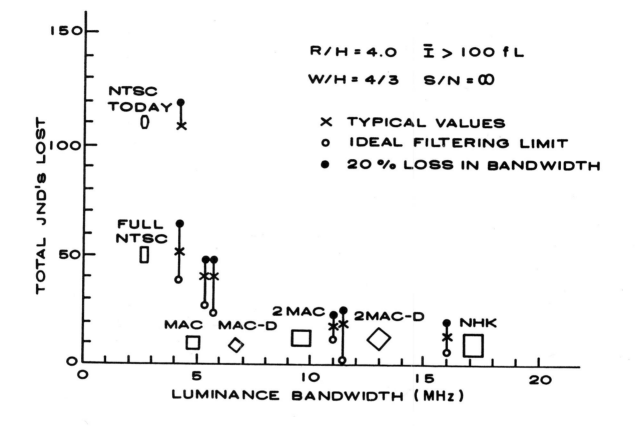

Fig. 1. Plot of the total number of jnd's of signal lost when compared to a perfect image as a function of transmitted luminance bandwidth. All systems have 30 Hz frame rates and are viewed from 4 picture heights away. The small figure beneath the name of each system gives a rough indication of the spatial frequency shape of that system. Note that the general results of this figure are maintained over reasonable assumptions about the quality of the filtering used. The points marked "x" represent the assumed values from Table I.

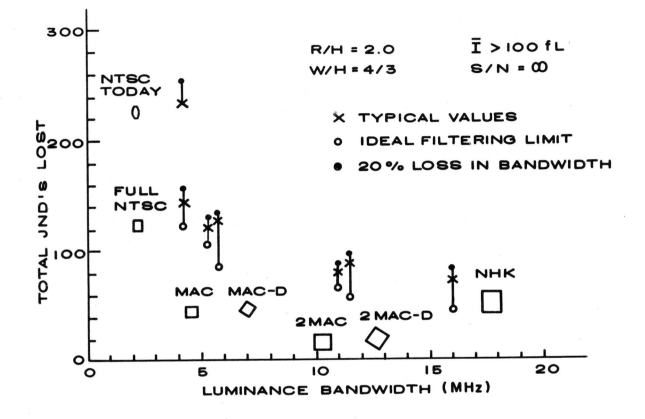

Fig. 2. Same as Fig. 1, but at a viewing distance of 2 picture heights.

Curtis R. Carlson received the BS degree in Physics, with honors, from Worcester Polytechnic Institute in 1967. He received the MS and PhD degrees from Rutgers University in 1969 and 1972, respectively. His thesis work was primarily concerned with problems in coherent optics.

Since joining the Technical Staff of RCA Laboratories, Princeton, NJ, in 1973, Dr. Carlson's research has centered on visual processing in both human and machine visual systems. This includes basic research in psychophysics, signal processing, imaging analysis and artificial intelligence, with applications to NTSC television, high-definition television, and robotic vision. In 1982, he became Head of Advanced Image Processing Research at RCA Laboratories. Dr. Carlson was an NDEA Title IV Fellow and is a member of Sigma Xi, Tau Beta Pi, the Optical Society of America, the Society for Information Display (SID), and the Association for Research Vision and Ophthalmology. He is a member of the SMPTE Committee on HDTV. He was recently a Special Editor of an issue of the SID Proceedings on "Recent Advances in Visual Information Processing." Dr. Carlson has won two RCA Achievement Awards for his research in vision and image processing. He has published or presented over 50 technical reports and publications and holds four U.S. patents, with many more pending, in his fields of interest.

James R. Bergen received the B.A. degree in mathematics and psychology from the University of California, Berkeley, in 1975 and the Ph.D. in biophysics and theoretical biology from the University of Chicago, Chicago, IL, in 1981.

His work concerns the quantitative analysis of information processing in the human visual system. At the University of Chicago he was involved in the development of a model of the spatial and temporal processing that occurs in the early stages of the system. From 1981 to 1982 he was with Bell Laboratories, Murray Hill, NJ. His work concentrates on the effect of visual system structure on the extraction of information from a visual image. He is currently with RCA Laboratories in Princeton, NJ.

His current work includes basic studies of visual perception as well as perceptual considerations for design of imaging systems.

Psychophysics and the Improvement of TV Image Quality

William F. Schreiber
Massachusetts Institute of Technology
Cambridge, Massachusetts 02139

Summary

The motivation for contemporary efforts towards the development of improved television systems is presented. The impossibility of obtaining substantial improvements by straight-forward means, such as increasing the line and frame rates, without excessive bandwidth expansion, is discussed. The television process is described as a linear system whose task is the transmission of a "video function", which is continuous in x,y, and t. The fidelity requirements for the transmission of the video function are related to the psychophysical properties of the human visual system, which are reviewed. Making use of the prospects of quite complicated signal processing through developments in semiconductor technology, a series of possibilities for improved systems is explored. Some of these proposed methods take advantage of the spatio-temporal characteristics of the video function which are inherent in its role as the conveyor of picture information to human viewers. Others deal with the special characteristics of TV cameras and displays as perceptual information processors and make use of signal processing to improve their performance.

1. Introduction

1.1 Motivation

Thirty years' experience with the NTSC and PAL systems have demonstrated the general soundness of the original concepts and the appropriateness of the chosen parameters. In spite of the stringent constraints of compatibility with the then-existing monochrome system, picture quality has proven acceptable, the hardware sufficiently inexpensive and reliable, and a large industry has arisen based on this technology.

A number of forces have developed for changes in these systems with a view toward improving picture quality. One is the rapid increase in the variety and capability of semiconductor devices, especially memory, and the accompanying decrease in cost. Much more sophisticated signal processing is thus becoming feasible. It appears that frame memories will become practical in receivers before the end of the decade. Many other improvements such as comb filters and digital demodulation are already practical. A second set of possibilities arises from digitization of post-production, which promises greater convenience and flexibility for the producer, more complicated effects, higher SNR, and perhaps precorrection for certain degradations likely to be produced by channel and receiver. The strongest impetus for improvement, however, has undoubtedly come from the demonstration of the Japanese (NHK) HDTV system. [1] While it is not surprising that better pictures can be obtained with 4 to 5 times the bandwidth, impressive technological virtuosity was exhibited by the development of the system components, particularly the camera and picture tubes. The sight of vastly improved images, comparable to 35 mm theatre quality, on real TV equipment, has whetted everyone's appetite for more improvements, preferably with less increase of bandwidth.

The path to the practical application of these potential improvements is hardly clear. There are few channels suitable for the NHK system* and there is a serious question as to whether, or by what means, a new system ought to be made compatible. Many possibilities for improvement have been demonstrated which do not require so much bandwidth. [2] Digitization for such a system would be considerably more difficult and expensive than in the case of NTSC. The principal purpose of this paper is the discussion of methods, based on visual psychophysics, by which maximum picture quality can be obtained for whatever channel capacity is provided. It is recognized that there are many other important considerations in the design of new TV systems, such as removing the defects of NTSC, but they are not discussed here.

1.2 TV as Visual Representation

In a sense, the TV system substitutes for directly viewing the original scene; hence its success in that role can be used as a measure of its performance. It is clear, however, that true "presence" is unattainable with any currently proposed system, not only because of the limited spatial and temporal bandwidth and field of view, but because of the two-dimensional (2-d) representation of a three-dimensional (3-d) scene. The use of a single monocular camera of fixed gaze, or even panning to track a single moving object, whereas the viewers who are many are constantly moving their eyes over the scene, is a truly serious limitation. Finally, although the large-area color reproduction is often excellent, the dynamic range of a cathode ray tube (crt) is far below that of most outdoor and many indoor scenes. The increased definition and field of view of the NHK system are certainly steps in the right direction. However it should be noted that its motion rendition is bound to be poorer than at present since the field of view is larger and the frame rate is the same.

1.3 The Potential Contributions of Psychophysics

Psychophysical principles were of course appealed to in both the monochrome and color NTSC proposed standards. [3] The relative horizontal and vertical resolution, the frame rate, the use of interlace, and the overall image quality goal were all selected in this manner in 1941 for the monochrome system. In the color deliberations, the primary pyschophysical contributions concerned the representation of the color signal as luminance plus lower resolution chrominance. The supposed non-visibility of the color subcarrier was more a hope than a fact, and the desired non-interference between chrominance and luminance never did exist, in general. There was no justification in psychophysics for the gross disparity between vertical and horizontal chrominance resolution. It is true that a number of

---

*Some examples are direct broadcasting from satellites (DBS), cable TV, and fiberoptics.

the color-related problems of NTSC were less visible because of the properties of the then-existing transducers. In any event, virtually all contemporary proposals abandon the non-reversible mixing of chrominance and luminance and no more will be said here.

One hope for future improvements rests on the considerable body of evidence that neither NTSC nor the NHK system makes maximum use of the luminance bandwidth. The sampling theorem tells us that a certain 3-d bandwidth (the Nyquist bandwidth) should be recoverable "exactly", given the vertical and temporal sampling frequencies and the signal bandwidth. Yet, through a combination of factors, the system throughput, at the upper (3-d) limits of the Nyquist bandwidth, is much less than 100%. Furthermore, in many cases simply increasing the response would not increase perceived quality, since certain defects would become more obvious. A number of demonstrations [4] have been made which show that much better pictures can be produced from the existing transmitted signal simply by up-converting the line and/or frame rate, thereby decreasing flicker and the visibility of the line structure. Wendland [5] has proposed the use of spatially interlaced sampling to accord more closely with the angular dependence of visual acuity, and Glenn [6] has proposed making use of spatio-temporal interactions for much the same purpose.

In this paper, we shall first describe the television process from the viewpoint of linear signal transmission theory, the input being the collection of illuminated objects before the camera, and the output the picture display as perceived by the viewer. We shall then review some psychophysical data which characterize visual response under controlled (and, unfortunately, rather artificial) conditions. With this background, we shall calculate the required channel capacity for a variety of idealized systems, and show that no straightforward system can give greatly improved quality without unreasonable bandwidth expansion. Finally, we shall discuss a number of alternatives to current TV system designs which exploit more thoroughly what is known about human vision. Most of these proposals involve signal processing considerably more complex than now used and thus may not become economically feasible for a number of years. When they do become practical, however, they promise a much better quality/bandwidth ratio than now achievable. We shall not discuss the additional improvement which might be attained by statistical coding.

2. The TV Chain as a Linear System

2.1 A Generalized TV System

As shown in Fig. 1, light from the scene before the camera is caused to form an image $i(x,y,t)$ in the focal plane. We call this image the "video function", and note that the function is a vector for colored images. It is the task of the system to produce a (modified) version $i'(x,y,t)$ on the display device for viewing.

The video function is converted to a video signal, $v(t)$, by a scanning process operating on the charge image developed by the camera. A simple view of this process is that the signal produced from each point of the focal plane is proportional to the integrated light power which falls on the point in between sampling times. The video signal is further processed by the channel (modulation, filtering, digitization, transmission, etc.) producing a modified signal v'(t) to be applied to the display device. In another simplified view, the display process can be thought of as tracing out, on the viewing surface, a scanning pattern (raster) like that in the camera, in which an amount of energy is emitted at each point of the raster proportional to the light energy collected at the corresponding element of the camera focal plane. In practice the emitted energy is spread out over some time interval, almost always much shorter than one frame time.

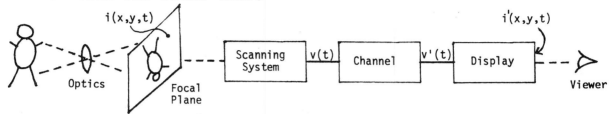

Fig. 1. A Generalized TV System.

This description reveals a highly significant difference between the original and reproduced video functions. The former is continuous in space and time, while the latter is not. If it were, the system could be characterized simply by its spatio-temporal frequency response which could be compared with the corresponding sensitivity of the human visual system (HVS). The fact that i'(x,y,t) is highly discontinuous in space and time is the cause of much of the inefficiency in utilization of the channel capacity. Simple-minded elimination of the sampling structure by blurring, the use of long persistence phosphors, or by viewing from afar, attenuate important components of the transmitted signal as well as the structure.

2.2. The Special Problem of Interlace

Since 30 frames per second (f/s), progressively scanned, would produce totally unacceptable large-area flicker, the stratagem of interlace was introduced very early in the history of TV development, doubling the flicker rate to 60 Hz while preserving the full number of lines in the frame. The only condition under which 30 Hz large-area flicker can result with interlace is when the average brightness of odd and even fields is significantly unequal, a rare event. It was recognized that with phosphors of persistence short enough not to cause inter-frame blurring, vertical motion could sometimes produce a display with half the number of scan lines, which it does distressingly often. Likewise, horizontal motion can produce serrated vertical edges, which it does not ordinarily do because of camera integration. What was not generally recognized, however, is that for viewing distances at which the lines can be clearly resolved, the interline flicker rate is 30 Hz and is easily seen as a shimmer. A side-by-side comparison of interlaced and non-interlaced images (the latter takes twice the bandwidth, of course) makes this difference very obvious.

Even at longer viewing distances, at which the line structure can not be resolved, in areas having significant vertical detail substantial 30 Hz flicker is clearly visible in interlaced pictures under certain conditions. The flicker occurs when odd and even lines are sufficiently different at any resolvable spatial frequency. This flicker can be eliminated either by reducing the vertical resolution of the camera and/or the display, or by integrating over a full frame by some kind of temporal averaging device. With any such method, spatio-temporal resolution is reduced.

In the light of these considerations, the subjective effect of interlace has never been fully investigated, since the vertical resolution, whose role has only been appreciated recently, was not adequately controlled. Even so, Brown's early study [7] concluded that for a 225 line TV image viewed at 8 times picture height, interlace produced a subjective increase in vertical resolution of only 24%* in the line number compared with a progressively scanned image at 60Hz. A similar NHK study in 1982 [8] gave an increase of 20% for a 1500 line picture viewed at two times picture height. These numbers are so much lower than 100% , which would be obtained if interlace "worked", it makes us wonder why it has so long been thought to be so effective. It is quite clear that for present-day scanning standards, interlace produces troubling artifacts which become more obvious as the vertical resolution is increased and as the image is more closely viewed, while the vertical resolution is increased only slightly.

2.3. Special Properties of the Camera

In most camera tubes, the target, which effectively integrates the incident light at each point between successive visits of the scanning beam, is nearly completely discharged each field. Of necessity, the integration area, in the vertical direction, comprises at least two of the 525 nominal scan lines. Thus a vertical pattern of 262 1/2 cycles per picture height (p.h.) is rendered with zero response, and a frequency of even half that is substantially attenuated, to a degree which depends on its phase. Yet the sampling theorem tells us that we ought to be able to use the full bandwidth of 262.5 c/p.h. If, however, the vertical response of the camera is increased, as it readily can be, for example, in laser scanners, we find disturbing interline flicker.

In some modern CCD cameras which have one row of detectors for each scan line, the pairing of two lines of data for each output line is done deliberately. [9] In cathode ray camera tubes the process is considerably more complex due to the physics of target discharge and the shape of the electron beam. [10] In this case, dark areas are completely discharged by the leading edge of the beam, while bright areas are not fully discharged until passed over by the trailing edge. The resulting geometrical distortion and small-area tone-scale distortion are not so serious. More important is the fact that, as ordinarily operated, the vertical resolution of camera tubes is very much less than the horizontal resolution (expressed as lines/mm on the target). To some extent this is fortuitous, since higher vertical resolution would make interlace even less acceptable. However, it means that by employing interlace, we have sacrificed a significant portion of the theoretically available

----

* at 50 ft-lamberts, 36% at 40 ft-lamberts, and only 6% at 100 ft-lamberts.

vertical definition, and with it, much of the supposed benefit.

2.4. The Picture Tube

Cathode ray display tubes are essentially linear, so that the integrated light output at each point can be found by convolving an ideal (zero spot diameter) raster with the beam cross-section, which is generally Gaussian. With such a shape, the elimination of line structure by defocussing (or by blurring in the eye) also blurs the image. In color tubes, an additional factor is the structure of small phosphor spots. In a 19" diagonal shadow mask tube with .31mm triad spacing, only about four triads are available for each picture element in the NTSC system. This is bound to introduce a great deal of spatial high frequency noise, to which, fortunately, we are not very sensitive. However, the channel SNR for AM transmission is uniform with bandwidth and therefore does not take advantage of this phenomenon.

2.5. The Channel

In present day systems, the purpose of the channel is to reproduce at the picture tube the output of the camera tube with perhaps some minor amount of processing. Of course, noise is invariably added in the process and there may be some loss of bandwidth. As one shall see, the most probable source of major improvement is to introduce substantial signal processing betweeen camera and channel and between channel and display. Since the second processor must be cheap, that is the location of the real technological challenge.

3. The Psychophysical Background

3.1. Normal Seeing

The HVS, presumably as a result of evolution, is very well adapted to rapidly deriving a large amount of useful information from the scene before the observer. This scene - 3-d, variously illuminated, moving, produces slightly different 2-d images on retinas of both eyes. The latter are in constant voluntary motion over the scene, both by head motion and by rotation in their sockets, and also execute small involuntary motions which have been found to have an important, even essential, role in vision. [11]

The retina consists of a matrix of receptors of two kinds - cone cells which exclusively cover the central 2^{O} (the fovea) and whose density decreases away from the axis, and rod cells whose density is maximum 15° from the center. Cones are responsible for the high visual acuity on axis and for color vision at normal (photopic) levels, while rod cells, which are much more sensitive, provide off-axis low light level (scotopic) sensitivity but have much lower spatial resolution.

Each cell is characterized by a certain sensitivity which depends on its state of adaption and on the excitation of its neighbors. The sensitivity is characterized both by a static (input-output) function and a frequency response. Spatial resolution of point objects is roughly equal to the cell spacing but because of cooperation of retinal receptors, resolution of long parallel lines is much finer than the cell spacing. The discrete nature of the retinal mosaic is never obvious in normal vision. Much visual processing is carried out on the retina itself, but additional processing occurs at higher levels of the visual nervous system. [12]

3.2. Characterization of Visual Response

Although all aspects of the visual sense are remarkably interdependent, it is customary to begin by discussing its performance along separate axes. This is a frustrating study, since the vast literature would take years to master, yet data is lacking on many points which are vital for the design of efficient systems.

3.2.1. Contrast Sensitivity

By this we mean the visual response as a function of luminance, although what is usually measured is the just noticeable difference between near-equal luminances, displayed side-by-side or one after the other. It is quite clear that temporal or spatial separation is essential to measure contrast thresholds, so that it is quite impossible to separate contrast sensitivity completely from these other variables.

With the usual test field as in Fig. 2, the observer is allowed to adapt to the surround, L, and then the smallest discernable ΔL is found. [13] The results are as in Fig. 3, showing that $\Delta L/L$ is nearly constant over five decades, so that we can see over an enormous luminance range, given time to adapt. The constancy of $\Delta L/L$ is called the Weber-Fechner law, the fraction being as small as 1% under optimum viewing conditions.

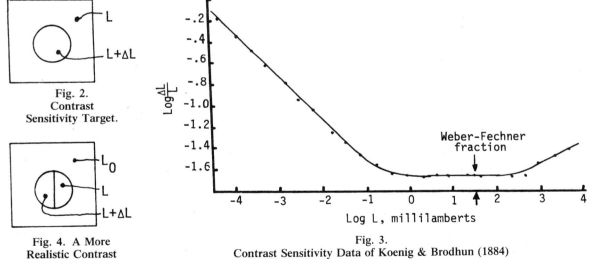

Fig. 2.
Contrast
Sensitivity Target.

Fig. 4. A More
Realistic Contrast
Sensitivity Target.

Fig. 3.
Contrast Sensitivity Data of Koenig & Brodhun (1884)
(Quoted by Hecht, *J. Gen. Physiol.* 7.1924.421).

In the more normal situation of observing actual scenes or their reproductions, the degree of adaptation is much less. If we now measure $\Delta L/L$ as a function of the adapting luminance L_0, using a target such as that of Fig. 4, we find that the operating dynamic range is much less. More significant is the appearance of the central patches as a function of the relative brightness. When the surround is about 100 times brighter than the central area, the latter looks black, no matter what its actual luminance, while in the reverse case it looks white. [14] When the central area is sufficiently intense, it appears to be a light source, rather than an illuminated surface.

The meaning of all this for picture reproduction is that nearly four decades of dynamic range are required to give the impression of seeing a real high contrast scene, such as out-doors on a clear day. This condition is approximated by optical projection from film with good equipment in a perfectly dark room. Under all other conditions, such as TV displays, the dynamic range must be compressed. While this can be done in such a way as to give pleasing results in terms of brightness and contrast as those terms are normally used, it is very hard to impart realism.

3.2.2. Temporal Frequency Response

Flicker and motion rendition are associated with this factor, so it is of great importance and has had the attention of psychologists for many years. The "purest" method, i.e., least contaminated by other factors, is to superimpose a sinusoidally fluctuating component on a constant luminance and use a very wide field with defocussed edges. The definitive measurement has been made by Kelly. [15] The most interesting aspect is that over a significant range of temporal frequencies, the HVS is a differentiator, as shown in Fig. 5, not an integrator. Flicker in this range is very noticeable. In addition, it is quite evident that at 25 or 30 Hz, flicker is almost always present, at 50 or 60 Hz, it is present in very bright images, and that to avoid flicker in the worst case, which is at the edges of a bright, wide-field display, 80 or 90 Hz might be needed. One notes that peripheral flicker is sometimes seen in wide screen motion pictures, where the flicker rate is usually 72/sec.

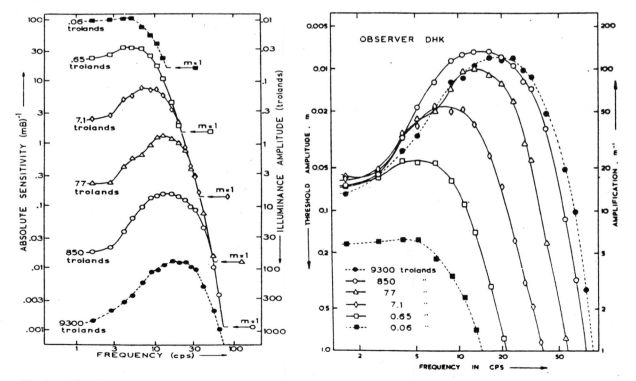

Fig. 5. Kelly's Temporal Data, Plotted Two Ways. (From D.H. Kelly, "Visual Response to Time Dependent Stimuli. I. Amplitude Sensitivity Measurements," *J. Opt. Soc. Am.*, Vol. 51, No. 4, 1961, pp. 422-429.)

3.2.3. Spatial Frequency Response

Visual acuity - the ability to see sharply and resolve small details - is one of the most obvious aspects of vision. While threshold contrast is often measured as a function of spatial frequency using square-wave gratings at various angles, the results are easier to interpret if sine-wave gratings are used. [16] A variety of indirect methods have also been used, in which transient response [17] or response to filtered random noise [18] has been measured. In spite of the hazards of applying linear analysis to such a non-linear system, all the results are similar to those shown in Fig. 6. Remarkably enough, the spatial characteristic also shows a differentiation region, one of the effects of which is to sharpen images a great deal. It is thought that this effect is principally due to neural interaction on the retina. Note that there is some response up to 30 or more cycles/degree. For a 90° display, 2700 cycles, or 5400 picture elements, would be required for absolute invisibility of the scanning structure. For the lines in an NTSC picture to disappear completely, only a 16° field can be covered.

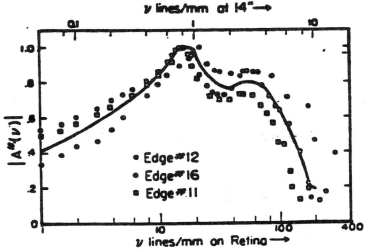

Fig. 6. Spatial Frequency Data of Ref. 17. (E.M. Lowry and J.J. DePalma, "Sine Wave Response of the Visual System," *J. Opt. Soc. Am.*, Vol. 51, No. 4, 1961, p. 474.)

In the vertical and horizontal directions, the spatial frequency response is about equal, but at 45° it goes down by a factor of 2 or more. This is the main reason why half-tone patterns are usually at 45°. It is also the basis of proposals for interleaved sampling. [19] Whether this is significant is hard to say. For example, Baldwin [20] carried out a very careful experiment to determine the effect on picture quality of varying the relative horizontal and vertical resolution. For pictures of 56in² area with a total of about 36,000 resolvable elements viewed at 30", the just noticeable degree of asymmetry was 2.5:1! This is in spite of the equal horizontal and vertical limiting resolution of the eye. Thus it is not at all clear that interleaved sampling would help image quality, although it might be used to make structure less visible.

3.2.4. Spatio-temporal Interactions

Measuring the combined effect of spatial and temporal fluctuations is more difficult and a much wider variety of methods can be used. Nevertheless, there is reasonable agreement which shows a peak sensitivity at about 2 Hz and 2 cpd, with integration at higher frequencies and differentiation at lower frequencies. This has been modelled [21] as the difference between an excitatory and an inhibitory response, which is interesting but not of direct value to the system designer. There is some evidence that the shape is somewhat more complicated, but in any case, the essential result is that the derived baseband in three-dimensional frequency space is certainly not cubical, but more nearly ellipsoidal. No one seems to have repeated Baldwin's experiment for spatio-temporal resolutions. Just because the limiting spatial and temporal frequencies have been shown to be inversely related, for example, does not prove that in a system where the signal components are well below the limiting frequencies, that the system bandwidths ought to be so related.

3.2.5. Masking

Of great interest to the psychophysicist, and in this case of equal interest and value to the system designer, is the phenomenon of masking. It seems that in all sense modalities, response to particular kinds of stimuli is reduced significantly by the presence, in the immediate spatio-temporal neighborhood, of similar stimuli. In the case of large uniform slowly changing scenes, we ordinarily call the phenomenon adaptation. It is of great value because it enables us to see well under a wide variety of conditions. A similar phenomenon occurs for stimuli of similar spatio-temporal content. Exposure to a spatial grating reduces sensitivity to gratings of similar spatial frequency seen just afterwards or even just before. [22] Exposure to a temporal sinusoid reduces sensitivity to sinusoidal flicker of like frequency. [23] The presence of "activity" (sharp edges or fine detail) reduces noise sensitivity in nearby areas. [24] A well-known example of the latter in the space domain is the much lower visibility of additive random noise in detailed or "busy" image areas and its much higher visibility in relatively blank areas. For this reason SNR, even weighted according to the variation of visibility with frequency, is a very poor indicator of image quality. Simple images require a much higher SNR than complicated ones for the same visual quality.

A related phenomenon is the masking of detail in a new scene by the presence of a previous scene. Repeating an earlier experiment of Seyler's [25], in our own laboratory we found that a new scene could be radically defocussed, and then refocussed with a time constant of .5 sec, without visible effect. Recently Glenn [26] has demonstrated that it takes about .2 sec to perceive higher spatial frequencies in newly-revealed areas. This effect is nature's gift to temporal differential transmission systems, as it allows new scenes to be built up over a period much longer than a frame.

3.2.6. Motion Rendition

Americans believe that it was Edison* who discovered that the illusion (sic) of motion could be produced by viewing a rapid sequence of slightly different images. This is the "phi motion" of psychology, in which the successive flashing of two

---

* No doubt other countries have their own favorite inventors of motion pictures.

small lights with the appropriate time and space separation, makes it appear that the light moves from the first position to the second. [27] Should the angular jump be too large or the interval too long, the motion effect is discontinuous, and in extreme cases, can even be retrograde. We have all seen wheels standing still or even moving backward. This stroboscopic effect, which has its uses, of course, is an example of temporal aliasing. Like other kinds of aliasing, it is but one possible defect which should be traded off against others for optimum image quality. The smoothness of motion is directly related to filling the gaps between successive positions. The degree of temporal bandlimiting which can absolutely preclude temporal aliasing has the effect of blurring moving objects. [28] Especially in low frame-rate systems, it may be preferable to show a sequence of sharp still images rather than a continuously moving image so blurred as to be useless.

Careful observation will show that motion is generally smoother in TV than in motion pictures. This is because the TV system actually takes 60 pictures per second, as compared to 24 for film. In addition, most TV cameras integrate for the full 1/60 sec. while all motion picture cameras use exposure times of less than (and sometimes very much less than) 1/24 sec.

Objects which move across the retina while our eyes are fixated elsewhere are blurred by the temporal upper frequency limit of the HVS. The same thing happens in TV cameras, which is perfectly all right unless the observer happens to be tracking the object in question, in which case the TV (or motion picture) representation will be disappointing. In fact, there is no simple way the TV camera can satisfy the entire audience when the scene contains two or more important moving objects.

3.2.7. Color

Color is not a principal preoccupation of this paper. Colorimetry is quite satisfactory in existing systems. In a new system design not constrained by the requirement of compatibility, there are several simple ways of adding color to a monochrome signal, based on the lower required spatial color resolution, which increase the channel capacity by 20%, or even less. [29] More complicated systems [30] decrease the color penalty even more. At these incremental levels, it is almost invariably the case that the color picture, with slightly lower luminance resolution, is far superior in perceived quality, almost however measured, to the monochrome picture with the slightly higher luminance resolution. [31] Looked at this way, the addition of color can be viewed as a valuable way to _decrease_ the total channel capacity for a given subjective quality.

It is also possible but not yet demonstrated, as far as we know, that the required temporal bandwidth for color is less than for luminance, in which case an additional possibility for compression would be available. [32]

4. Performance Goals for TV Systems

4.1. Perfection

A perfect system can be defined as one which gives a convincing illusion of reality. This probably does not require three-dimensional reconstruction, as might be done holographically. It appears that a very wide field of view is quite effective. [33] Assume that 90° vertically and 180° horizontally might be enough. The question, then, is the required resolution. A frame rate of 100/sec. would certainly prevent flicker, but even that would not be sufficient to keep rapidly moving objects in focus. Using 50 cpd as the upper perceptual limit, a raster about 9,000 x 18,000, or 162×10^{6} samples/frame would do, for a total rate of 1.6×10^{10} samples/sec. Of course such a signal would have very high redundancy and could be compressed a great deal. Nevertheless, the obstacles to constructing such a system are insurmountable at present.

4.2. Idealism

An ideal system, for our purpose, is based on the use of resolution parameters so high that raising them would not materially improve quality. We would, however, accept a more limited field of view and the motion rendition obtainable at 60 f/s. For a 45 x 90° field of view and a sampling density of 12/mm at normal viewing distance (30cm), which is considered excellent quality for continuous tone color prints, we have a more modest 3,000 x 6,000 raster - a mere 18×10^{6} samples/frame or 10^{9} samples/sec. Actually, to do full justice to this resolution, we would probably want to raise the frame rate somewhat - perhaps to 80/sec. for a rate of 1.25×10^{9} samples/sec. These pictures would give the effect of looking at the real world through a fairly large window, except that if we were to track rapidly moving objects (say those that move across the screen in less than four seconds or so) we would see a definite loss of resolution.

4.3. Theatre Quality

This is a very poorly defined term, particularly as film is getting better and better [34] and we now know how to make essentially diffraction-limited optics. For the sake of discussion, for 35mm film with a frame height of 18mm and 30 to 50 lp/mm assumed for the effective resolution limit, 1080 to 1800 lines and 1.5 to 4.3×10^{6} samples/frame would be required. This is in accordance with the NHK experience.

Equating TV and film quality is not simple and certainly requires careful subjective testing. The spatial frequency response of film and optical systems tends to fall monotonically, starting at quite a low spatial frequency, as shown in Fig. 7. Television systems have a rather well defined upper frequency limit, but within the passband we are free to use almost any characteristic we wish. A considerable degree of sharpening is possible and is routinely used in electronics-based graphic arts systems. [35]

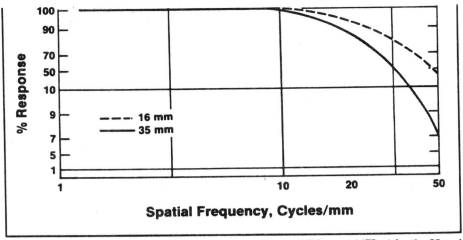

Cascaded MTF Curves (MTF$_{camera}$·MTF$_{7291}$·MTF$_{printer}$·MT F$_{projector}$·MTF$_{eye}$) for the 35-and 16-mm stretched visual response.

Fig. 7. Overall Response of Film System (from R. C. Sehlin, et al, *SMPTE Journal*, 12/83).

5. Vision-based Design

5.1. Spatial Filtering, Sampling, and Interpolation

Input and output still images are inherently spatially continuous. When represented at some point by an array of numbers, the continuous-discrete and discrete-continuous conversions can have a significant effect on image quality. Since analog TV is sampled only in the vertical direction, this section applies principally to processing designed to give maximum vertical sharpness without artifacts.

A basic problem with discrete imaging systems, as mentioned earlier, lies with the sampling theorem, which states that the recoverable signal bandwidth (Nyquist bandwidth) is one-half the sampling frequency.

At the transmitter, the bandwidth should be limited to the Nyquist value to prevent aliasing. There is no obvious mechanism for accomplishing this in a TV camera. Furthermore, if we somehow did implement such a filter, the ringing associated with sharp horizontal edges would be unacceptable. There *is* an optimum filter and its implementation will be discussed shortly.

At the display, it clearly would be desirable to eliminate the scan lines. They are obtrusive and, due to the masking effect, suppress to some extent the high frequency structure. Achieving this result by defocussing the more-or-less Gaussian scanning beam causes noticeable loss of sharpness, while relying on the filter of the HVS produces a similar effect, although with less loss of sharpness. In any event, the effect of the HVS is strongly dependent on the angular subtense of the scan lines at the eye, as can be seen by examining Fig. 6. When viewing an NTSC picture at 4H, the line structure is 34 cpd. At these spatial frequencies, visual response drops about 18 db per octave, so that the line structure is attenuated 18 db compared to the signal components at the upper end of the Nyquist band. However, to achieve this separation, the signal components are also attenuated substantially. Viewed at 2H, the relative attenuation is only about 12 db.

A method by which vertical filtering can be done effectively is to operate both camera and display at a substantially higher line rate, and to interpose processing elements between camera and channel and channel and display, as shown in Fig. 8. At both camera and display, this could give enough vertical samples to implement the appropriate digital filter, while at the display, such up-conversion would also raise the line rate to a point where the HVS would more easily separate the structure from the image. Incidentally, but perhaps importantly, high line-rate operation of the camera might very well ameliorate the problems discussed above due to the non-linear target discharge, especially with progressive scanning.

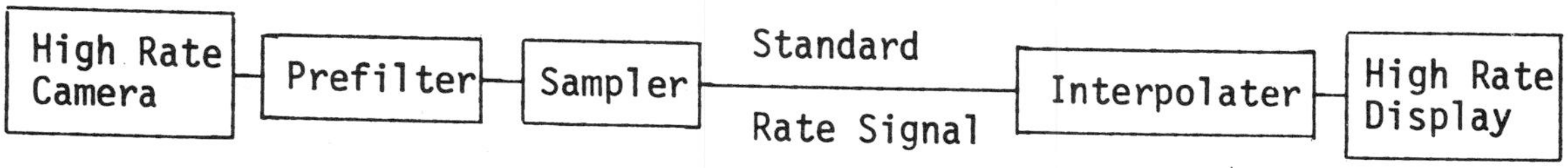

```
+-----------+   +-----------+   +---------+   Standard    +---------------+   +-----------+
| High Rate |---| Prefilter |---| Sampler |               | Interpolater  |---| High Rate |
| Camera    |   |           |   |         |  Rate Signal  |               |   | Display   |
+-----------+   +-----------+   +---------+               +---------------+   +-----------+
```

Fig. 8. The Modified TV Chain.

The application of similar methods to still pictures has resulted in a channel capacity saving of as much as 40% for the same perceived quality, as compared with simple-minded methods. [36]

5.2. Temporal Filtering, Sampling, and Interpolation

The situation here is analogous to that caused by spatial sampling. Again, the sampling theorem tells us that 30f/s gives a 15Hz Nyquist bandwidth. To avoid aliasing (jerky or stroboscopic motion), we should low-pass filter before sampling. Since a camera which integrates perfectly for the frame (or field) time is hardly an ideal filter, we could tailor pre-sampling filters much more accurately if the camera operated at four or five times the frame rate. At the display, the extra samples would have a similar effect but in addition, as in the spatial case, would raise the flicker rate so that it can more easily be separated by the HVS from the baseband.

5.3. Three-dimensional Processing

Naturally, the spatial and temporal processing discussed above could be combined so that the filters of Fig. 8 would be 3-d. As such they would involve frame and line stores and therefore digital techniques. Thus we must deal with a completely digital TV system, discrete in all three dimensions. This raises the question of the sampling pattern in the channel signal, and the corresponding three-dimensional Nyquist bandwidth.* The Cartesian pattern of Fig. 9 gives the Cartesian spectrum of Fig. 10, while the interleaved pattern of Fig. 11 gives the odd-looking pattern of Fig. 12.* This pattern trades off spatial and temporal bandwidth in a manner which probably is better than the Cartesian pattern, although observer tests are necessary to be sure. It has higher spatial response at low temporal frequencies and vice versa, and higher vertical and horizontal resolutions than diagonal.

----

* The sampling patterns of the camera tube and display are of little importance since they will not be detected by the viewers.

* Other 3-d patterns are possible.

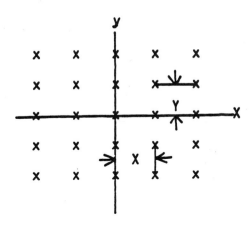

Fig. 9.
Cartesian Sampling.

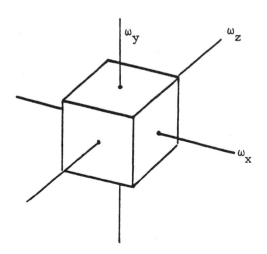

Fig. 10.
Cartesian Spectrum.

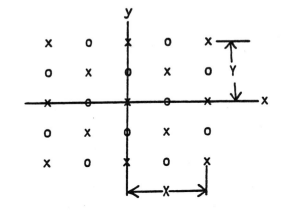

Fig. 11.
Temporal Interleaving.
x = even fields.
o = odd fields.

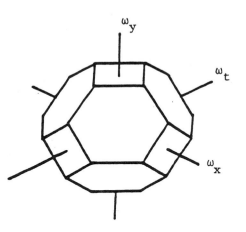

Fig. 12.
Alias-Free Bandwidth for
Temporal/Spatial Interleaving.

Interleaved sampling bears some relationship to present-day interlace. Interlace is primarily motivated by the need to double the flicker rate. However, we can think of the vertically offset sampling as a means to raise the time-averaged vertical resolution for a given vertical scan rate. In this endeavor it mostly fails, for the reasons cited. Interleaved sampling as described here, however, when used in connection with the three-dimensional pre-sampling and interpolation filter has none of the defects of ordinary interlace. It gets no "free" expansion of bandwidth. In fact, the volume of the three-dimensional Nyquist baseband is identical for all sampling patterns which have the same number of samples per unit (x,y,t) volume. What it does do is to change the shape of the Nyquist baseband from Cartesian to something else which may be better.

It would be quite difficult to implement a filter with the response as shown in Fig. 12. However, an ellipsoidal impulse response would clearly approximate it and, if Gaussian, would be separable and therefore practical. Since a form of Gaussian filter was found optimum in the studies cited [20], it is quite likely to work well in this case.

5.4. Multi-Channel Systems

There is a certain amount of evidence that the HVS treats various spatial frequency components of the visual stimulus quite differently, so much so that some advantage is to be gained by separating the signal into two or more channels and using different transmission parameters on each component. This is quite in accord with widely-held theories [37] that the visual system is organized in this manner. A number of such systems quantize low and high spatial frequencies differently, using a rather coarse quantization in the highs channel. [38] The quantization noise, preferably randomized [39], tends to be masked by the high frequency detail.

Glenn [6] has suggested that the high frequencies can be transmitted at a lower frame rate. While a certain amount of trade-off between spatial and temporal response is possible by offset sampling, Glenn does much more, in that the highs are transmitted only at 5f/s. In the case of newly uncovered stationary detail (a new scene, or newly-revealed background which emerges from behind a moving foreground object) this seems to work rather well. In the case of detailed objects moving in the scene, it would appear that the blurring would be much worse than at 30f/s. Clearly more work needs to be done on this technique, since, if successful, a very considerable saving would be possible.

6. Conclusion and Acknowledgement

We have described TV transmission as a problem in the analysis of linear systems. A review of the literature on visual psychophysics as it applies to this formulation has revealed a number of possibilities for the improvement of picture quality in relation to the channel bandwidth. These involve three-dimensional processing at the transmitter and receiver, and in the latter case would be practical only with a high degree of circuit integration.

Specific visual problems due to the characteristics of camera and display devices and to the use of interlace have been pointed out. The amelioration of these effects by operating these devices at very high line and frame rates again implies rather complicated signal processing, but presents the prospect of substantial improvement in the utilization of transmission channel capacity.

The literature in this field is large and growing rapidly, so the list of references should be considered representative and not exhaustive. Of the ideas presented, many have grown out of discussions with friends, colleagues, and students. I have had the assistance of G. Saussy in collecting psychological references. S. Sabri motivated me to write this paper.

BIBLIOGRAPHY

1. E.C. Cartarette, et al., ed., Handbook of Perception, Vol. V, "Seeing," Academic Press, 1975.
2. T.N. Cornsweet, Visual Perception, Academic Press, 1970.
3. Handbook of Sensory Physiology, Springer-Verlag, 1973.
4. D.E. Pearson, Transmission and Display of Visual Information, Pentech Press, 1975.
5. C.G. Mueller, Sensory Psychology, Prentice-Hall, 1965.
6. G.J. Tonge, "Signal Processing for HDTV," IBA Report E8D 7/83 USA.

REFERENCES

1. Fujio, T., et al., "HDTV," NHK Tech. Monograph #32, 6/82.
2. Lucas, K., et al., "Direct TV Broadcasts by Satellite," IBA Report 116/81.
3. Fink, D.G, "TV Standards and Practice" (1941 NTSC), McGraw Hill, 1943, Proc. IRE Jan. 1954 entire issue (1953 NTSC).
4. Sandbank, C.P., and M.E.B. Moffatt, "HDTV and Compatibility with Existing Standards," SMPTE Journal, 5/83, pp. 552-561.
5. Wendland, B., "Extended Definition TV with High Picture Quality," SMPTE Journal, 10/83, pp. 1028-1035.
6. Glenn, W.E., et al., "Compatible Transmission of HDTV Using Bandwidth Reduction," IGC paper, unpublished.
7. Brown, E.F., "Low-Resolution TV: Subjective Comparison of Interlaced and Non-interlaced Pictures," BSTJ, Vol. 46, Jan. 1967, pp. 199-232.
8. Mitsukashi, T., "Scanning Specifications and Picture Quality," in NHK Tech. Monograph No. 32, 6/82.
9. Murata, N., et al., "Development of a 3-MOS Color Camera," SMPTE Journal, 12/83, pp. 1270-1273.
10. Schut, T.G., "Resolution Measurements in Camera Tubes," SMPTE Journal, 12/83, pp. 1287-1293.
11. Riggs, L.A., et al., "The Disappearance of Steadily Fixated Test Objects," JOSA, 1953, Vol. 43, pp. 495-501.
12. Cornsweet, T.N., Visual Perception, Academic Press, 1970.
13. Data of Koenig and Brodhun (1884) quoted by S. Hecht, Journal of General Physiology, Vol. 7, 1924, p. 421 ff.
14. Heinemann, E.G., "Simultaneous Brightness Induction," Journal of Experimental Psychology, 1955, Vol. 50, pp. 89-96.
15. Kelly, D.H., "Visual Responses to Time Dependent Stimuli.I. Amplitude Sensitivity Measurements," JOSA, 1961, Vol. 51, No. 4, pp. 422-429.
16. Campbell, F.W., and J.G. Robson, "Application of Fourier Analysis to the Visibility of Gratings," Journal of Physiology, 1968, No. 187.
17. Lowry, E.M., and J.J DePalma, "Sine Wave Response of the Visual System," JOSA, 1961, Vol. 51, No. 4, p. 474.
18. Mitchell, O.R., Ph.D. Thesis, MIT EECS Dept., 1972.
19. Wendland, B., "On Picture Scanning for Future HDTV Systems," IBC, 1982.
20. Baldwin, M.W., "The Subjective Sharpness of Simulated TV Pictures," Proc. IRE, 10/40, pp. 458-468.
21. Burbeck, C.A., and D.H. Kelly, "Spatio-Temporal Characteristics of Visual

Systems," JOSA, 1980, Vol. 70, No. 9; and Van Nes, F.L., et al., "Spatio-temporal Modulation Transfer in the Human Eye," JOSA, 1967, Vol. 57, pp. 1082-1088.

22. Sperling, G., "Temporal and Spatial Visual Masking," JOSA, 1965, Vol. 55, pp. 541-559.

23. Braddick, O., F.W. Campbell, and J. Atkinson, "Channels in Vision: Basic Aspects," in Handbook of Sensory Physiology, Vol. VIII, 1978, Springer-Verlag, New York.

24. Netravali, A.N., and B. Prasada, "Adaptive Quantization of Picture Signals using Spatial Masking," Proc. IEEE, Vol. 65, No. 4, pp. 536-548.

25. Seyler, A.J., et al., "Digital Perception After Scene Changes in TV," IEEE Trans. Information Theory, Vol. IT-11, 1/65, pp. 31-43.

26. Glenn, W.E., "Compatible Transmission of HDTV Using Bandwidth Reduction," National Association of Broadcasters, Las Vegas, 4/12/83, videotape demonstration.

27. Kinchla, R.A., et al., "A Theory of Visual Movement Perception," Psychological Review, 1969, Vol. 76, pp. 537-558.

28. Korein, J. et al., "Temporal Anti-aliasing in Computer Generated Animation," Computer Graphics, Vol. 17, No. 3, July 1983, pp. 377-388.

29. Schreiber, W.F., and R.R. Buckley, "A Two-Channel Picture Coding System: II - Adaptive Companding and Color Coding," IEEE Trans. on Communications, Vol. COM-29, No. 12, 12/81, pp. 1849-1858.

30. Buckley, R.R., Ph.D. Thesis, MIT EECS Dept., 1982.

31. Gronemann, U., Ph.D. Thesis, MIT EE Dept., 1964.

32. de Lange, H., "Research into the Dynamic Nature of the Human Fovea-Cortex System," JOSA, 1958, Vol. 48, pp. 777-784.

33. Shaw, W.C., et al., "IMAX and OMNIMAX Theatre Design," SMPTE Journal, 3/83, pp. 284-290.

34. Kriss, M.A., et al., "Photographic Imaging Technology for HDTV," SMPTE Journal, 8/83, pp. 804-818.

35. Schreiber, W.F., "Wirephoto Quality Improvement by Unsharp Masking," Pattern Recognition, Vol. 2, pp. 117-121, 3/70. See also W.F. Schreiber and D.E. Troxel, USP 4,268,861, May 1981.

36. Ratzel, J.R., Sc.D. Thesis, MIT EECS Dept., 1983. See also W.F. Schreiber and D.E. Troxel, "Transformation between Continuous and Discrete Representations of Images: A Perceptual Approach," MIT Report, submitted for publication.

37. Maffei, L., "Spatial Frequency Channels: Neural Mechanisms," in Handbook of Sensory Physiology, Vol. VIII, 1978, Springer-Verlag, New York.

38. Troxel, D.E., et al., "A Two-Channel Picture Coding System: I - Real-Time Implementation," IEEE Trans. on Communications, Vol. COM-29, No. 12, 12/81, pp. 1841-1848.

39. Roberts, L.G., "Picture Coding Using Pseudo-Random Noise," IRE Trans. on Information Theory," Vol. IT-8, pp. 145-154, 2/62.

William F. Schreiber was born in New York City in 1925. He received the B.S. and M.S. degrees in Electrical Engineering from Columbia and the Ph.D. in Applied Physics in 1953 from Harvard University. Dr. Schreiber was a junior engineer at Sylvania from 1947—1949. From 1953 to 1959 he directed electronics research at Technicolor Corp. Since 1959 he has been with MIT, where he is Professor of Electrical Engineering. From 1964 to 1966 he was Visiting Professor of Electrical Engineering at the Indian Institute of Technology, Kanpur, India, and in 1980—1981 he was half-time Visiting Professor at the University of Quebec, Montreal, Canada.

Since 1948 Dr. Schreiber's major professional interest has been in picture coding and transmission systems. He is associated with the Cognitive Information Processing Group of the Research Laboratory of Electronics at MIT where an active program in this field is under way. He has also served as consultant on image transmission systems to a number of industrial and government laboratories.

A Producer's View of Quality

Norman Campbell
Producer-Director
TV Arts, Music and Science
Canadian Broadcasting Corp.
Toronto, Ontario, Canada

In a technological world in which information is stored on magnetic disks, it is refreshing to be asked to deliver a "paper." A "paper" is a term as comforting as a fireside, as quaint as a quill pen and India ink.

My "paper" is titled "A Producer's View of Quality," a title chosen <u>for</u> me, and one which has intrigued me in the few minutes of a busy season which I've had time to think of it. As a producer and director, I could save you a lot of time by saying simply, "Yeah, I think quality is a good thing--gimme some of it and I'll use it!"

You see, as a producer I've been spoiled because in 32 years of television, I've been given quality by you people every day of the year. Quality always meant the best you could do, and you delivered.

Now, although I had a background in university math and physics, when I became a director I was dependent on you engineers to give me picture and sound--"You take care of the line-up charts and I'll line up the dancers and musicians." And it's worked, a happy collaboration. And that's how we're going to achieve quality in the 80's and 90's, through happy collaborations.

When I address the subject of quality, which hat do I wear? Does a producer of a ballet want a different kind of quality than the producer of a football game, or is quality an elusive kind of Holy Grail that we all are seeking--something almost indefinable, a quest that may never be realized, but that will absorb us and our children's children forever.

Because I'm sure my children's children will be watching television in the 21st century, what will it be? Video, or film, or Pizzascope, some totally unheard of and wonderful system that your descendents will discuss the merits of in this very room, with the same kind of charts and diagrams you entertained me with this morning. Now here's where, as a non-technical producer, I feel intimidated. So I have brought a chart which we will call Fig. 1. It's an organizational chart of the sort used in dispelling the mysteries of modern corporations. This should make everything clear.

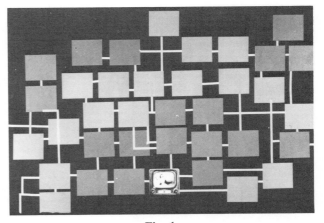

Fig. 1

54

Now this typical chart has a head honcho and underneath a bunch of vice honchos, and here are some executive supervisers, and here are some supervisory executives, and away down here is a producer, and here, away down here would be a television program.

I knew this chart was upside down.

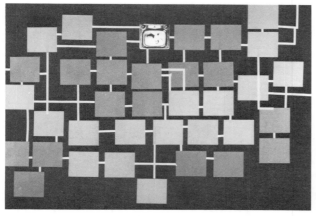

Fig. 2

Now this is more like it. The head of this organizational chart is the television set-- it's why we're all here. Millions of people, mostly only one or two at a time, sit in front of this set waiting to be astonished, delighted, informed, moved, or entertained.

Here is the set. What's going to be on it? Well, what

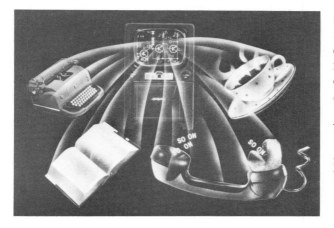

Fig. 3

it had better have is ideas. So right next to the set we put writers, and nourishing them in turn we need newspapers, magazines, so let's put in a library, and over here let's have a coffee shop where people can meet and generate more ideas, and so on (Fig.3).

Our chart is much different when you put the program first.

I don't know what this picture is (Fig. 4), but you have to admit the image quality is terrific. Maybe these are the inventors of quadraphonic.

Fig. 4

Now when you come to talk about image quality, perhaps you could use the same sort of chart--a TV set with a screen, maybe as big as a house, and as flat as a pancake, but a picture of a quality better than we have ever seen.

You will have achieved splendid definition, a full range of color, and now comes the question -- What is going to nourish this instrument of quality? What do we put on our organizational chart next to the screen? Well, sound. There have been many marginal movies that have seemed ever so much more engrossing when viewed in a big cinema with Dolby and stereo surround. A mere picture of a fern can evoke a whole forest if the atmospheric sound track is right. But, when screens get flattened for a wall installation, what happens to the speakers? There must be development in new ways of emitting sound from small sources. If Paverotti can thrill an opera house from a larynx this big, there is hope for miniaturizing speakers. (Perhaps I should have used a smaller tenor to make my point.)

I directed a feature film with the Canadian magician Doug Henning, called "The Magic Show," and all the way through we were dealing with illusion. In most of our entertainment television we are dealing with illusion--we work on the mind of the viewer to make him feel emotion and wonder. With large image television we need new thrusts in lighting techniques, sophisticated and quick ways to put beauty on the screen. There are some real artists in video lighting, but there need to be more. I believe we must support training programs that acknowledge lighting as an art as well as a technical skill, to be able to support our forthcoming "Image of Quality." I think it's in your interest also to see better training programs for the directors of the future so they won't regard cameras as screwed down to the floor, but will devise élegant movement to give a three-dimensional effect to your already superb picture.

The studio floor! If you had a knob on your set which could increase the vitality of the performers on your wonderful new screen, would you use it? Of course you would. Well, an important part of the well-being, even survival, of dancers on television is the floor. They can't be bouncy on concrete. The performers' unions these days demand wooden floors to put spring in the step of singers and dancers, and so they should.

But now, as a director, I find my heavy camera mounts can't do the kind of elegant moves they used to--on a wooden floor they wallow unevenly, and the crane, once a poetic tool in the camerawork, must be curtailed in its usefulness. Mundane though it may be, new floor structures with resilience need to be researched along with lightweight camera mounts, and I assure you, it will show up as quality on your screen.

Image size is very important to me as a producer. As director of the aforementioned feature, "The Magic Show," I edited the 35 millimeter film on a Steenbeck with a screen the size of a TV set. Then we would screen portions of the show in a theater. Because of screen size, the dynamics were so different that I had to re-edit looser shots to maintain the mystery of the magic. It's very important to know the screen size of the major audience you are aiming for, and I hope the acceptance of large screen will be universal and swift when it is introduced.

There is another area you must not stay out of as technicians. You must be very concerned with where this image of quality is placed. You may have to become interior decorators or architects, for if there is a way to defeat your quest, Mr. Average Viewer will do it. He will place his set by a window, and he'll turn up the brightness knob so there are no blacks in the picture, so don't give him a brightness knob! Real estate futurists are predicting the shrinkage of our living space in the next decade, so while your screen is getting bigger, albeit thinner, the space is getting smaller. I plead with you to be concerned about the ambiance, more than what we look at, how we look at it.

Let me say something else about our viewing future. The superb craftmanship which gave us the Sony Walkman has alienated some of us from each other--wearing earphones, we live in an isolated world unto ourselves. Those of you in film will corroborate--there's nothing like enjoying a movie with a good audience. Our perceptions increase and our enjoyment is transmitted in unexplainable ways. Please, as you develop Superscreen, don't give us a 3-D system with glasses or sound with earphones. Let us have family viewing where we can comment, laugh, or watch in silent communion a work of quality.

Storytelling, which is our main use of the new screen, is often the art of not telling too much. We receive information from the screen and interpret it. If that information is too literal, we can't participate imaginatively. No amount of computer enhancement can really sharpen a soft image, but you can always diffuse a sharp one. Give us an incredibly brilliant and detailed picture, but then give us controls to modify the image. Let us, if we choose, have a screen full of purest black with one red dot in the middle, but let that black be black, as black as in a modern motion picture screening room. Give us controls to produce by computer what we now have to do physically.

Suppose I have two cameras in the field, one film and one video. The scene comes through the lens, impacts the film, and chemistry and physics renders the image onto celluloid. Filters are employed and a work print is made, exposed to a TV camera in a telecine chain, and ends as an electronic image on my TV set. The video camera shoots the same scene, but there is no chemistry; it's electronics all the way. There is no denying the final image quality of these alternatives on the same monitor is very different. It's a question of taste which is better. Film people will argue only film has "such a patina," and video folk may say their image is "today" and "real" But I'm just a producer. I like them both for their individuality.

Give me controls so that a computer will take the image coming through the lens and render it "as if" it had gone through a chemical and physical process. Let me have on your new screen "film quality" or "tape quality"--whichever will express the mood I want to convey.

When I direct in tape, I love tape.

When I direct film, it is the only medium in the world. But being vain, as a director I crave immortality, and so far only film seems to have prestige and long life associated with it. If I create an epic on tape, can I be sure drop-out and print-through will not diminish my work of art? Give me permanence along with those other goodies I've asked for.

And one last thing. When I create the show of my dreams on the screen of my dreams I know the viewer is extremely unlikely to watch it in real time. He will play it at his own sweet pleasure over whatever VCRs will have become by then. Don't let down those standards, or we're all lost. Convince the industry and the public of our quest for, and the rewards of, quality.

When I saw my first television set 35 years ago, it was a furniture salesman who was responsible for the brightness being turned up. He was an expert on mahogany, but not on electronics. I'm afraid that furniture salesman is still with us, misleading we viewers into what quality is. I think we have to all tell our story. The producer's role is changing--we now have to be co-production experts and public relations wizards merely to survive. And I think you members of the SMPTE cannot be content merely to build a bigger and better mousetrap, but to make sure we know it's coming. Be activists!

It took decades for AM listeners to discover the joys of FM. Surely, in this sophisticated age, we can shorten that time and turn our addicts of the "boob tube" into connoisseurs of an image of quality.

Norman Campbell is a television producer and director for the Canadian Broadcasting Corporation in Toronto. He has directed productions for the major networks in the U.S.A. and in Great Britain. In 1979, he was awarded the Order of Canada, and his productions have won many awards including two Emmys. He is the composer of the musical "Anne of Green Gables," which has played in London, Tokyo, and for twenty years, in the Charlottetown Festival in Canada.

The Scanning Process

G. J. Tonge
Independent Broadcasting Authority
United Kingdom

1   INTRODUCTION

The scanning process is fundamental in television. It is the means by which two-dimensional images are converted into a continuous 'one-dimensional' electrical signal. Similarly scanning is used in the subsequent reconversion of the electrical signal into an image for display. Scanning can be represented as a sampling procedure. The electron-beam scanning of a scene imaged onto a television camera target, for example, provides information about the scene centred at the discrete positions in the vertical direction which were scanned. Thus a scan which has 483 active lines gives rise to a sampled image with a vertical sampling frequency of 483 cycles per picture height (c/ph). If the same vertical position on the photoconductive layer is rescanned every 1/30second then this represents sampling in time with a frequency of 30Hz. The sampling action of scanning is clearly not ideal, since the scanning aperture is not infinitely small in either the vertical or the temporal direction, but it is nevertheless a sampling process.

With the emergence of digital signal processing for television, it is becoming more common to consider the television signal as an array of picture elements, or pixels. The scanning and analogue-to-digital conversion procedures can then be combined conceptually as a means of converting a continuous real image into a discretely sampled electrical version of the image. Digital-to-analogue conversion and rescanning for display then provide the means for reconversion to a continuous image. This 'pixel array' approach highlights the sampling nature of the scanning process. Fig. 1 illustrates this idea showing only two dimensions (horizontal and vertical space). In practice there is a third dimension, namely time, in each of the three stages in the figure and the pixel array becomes three-dimensional. This pixel approach is especially relevant also to solid state imagers or displays in which the scanning process itself involves addressing a pixel array.

The pixel, or sampled, approach is useful also when contemplating the resolution capabilities of the television system. There is a direct relation between the pixel density and the resolution available, assuming of course that the optical /electro-mechanical resolution of the scanning process is adequate. The frequency bandwidth which can be supported is reciprocally related to the 'distance' between the samples, via Fourier theory. In one-dimension this results in the well known 'Nyquist criterion' that frequencies up to half the sampling frequency can be supported. In two or more dimensions analogous criteria can be defined. This is explored in the Appendix.

It appears that the allocation of 'bandwidth' or 'resolution' capability in television can exactly and in a straightforward manner be specified by the scanning/sampling procedure. However, there are usually physical constraints involved in the scanning process itself which preclude the full effective use of the limiting resolution capabilities. These physical constraints have, along with other parameters, given rise to the Kell factor concept affecting vertical resolution and hence image quality. The Kell factor has been used to quantify the effects of imperfect scanning. It therefore forms a useful focal point for a discussion of the scanning process and its imperfections. After briefly reviewing the use of the Kell factor historically we shall attempt to outline the various scanning effects which give rise to it. This will then enable a discussion on methods for overcoming these scanning deficiencies and making the fullest use of particular scanning standards.

2   THE KELL FACTOR

2.1   Its Historical Use

It was recognised early on in television that a practical system could not usefully resolve as many horizontal black and white bars (on static pictures) as might first be expected. A straightforward 'Nyquist' limitation would indicate that for a scan of, say, 240 lines, up to 120 black/white sinusoidal transitions (ie a vertical frequency of 120 c/ph) could be resolved unambiguously. Kell, Bedford and Trainer (1) were among the first to discuss this matter. A factor K (subsequently known as the 'Kell factor') was introduced indicating the extent to which practical systems fall short of their theoretical capabilities in this regard. A Kell factor of unity would correspond to a 'perfect' system while in a system with K = 0.5, for example, only half the theoretical number of bars could be resolved.

Early tests using a tapered wedge of black and white bars (having 'square', rather than sinusoidal, transitions) provided in subjective evaluation a figure which has been quoted as 0.64 (1, 3) or as in the range 0.65 - 0.75 (2). It was appreciated in these tests that this figure could not be precisely and rigorously defined since it was based on purely subjective impressions. A number of bars beyond that suggested by the Kell factor could be resolved, it was a matter of deciding at which point other spurious effects sufficiently detracted from this resolution capability (2). Subsequent to these tests both Kell (3) and others (4, 5) attempted to put the concept of this factor on a firmer footing by some analytical work based on un-bandlimited edges or single fine lines, in an original scene. The value of the factor which emerged had again a significant spread owing to the various different assumptions made.

In all cases the Kell factor concept was employed in the context of comparing vertical and horizontal resolution in television systems. Hence it is not surprising that an alternative, slightly modified, use of the Kell factor emerged. In this definition the Kell factor is the ratio of the number of half-cycles per line at the highest video frequency to the number of lines in a system for equal subjective horizontal and vertical resolution and normalised for a unity aspect ratio. The major difference between this definition and the first (in terms of resolvable horizontal bars) is that the concept of video bandwidth has now been introduced. It was pointed out by Lewis (6) that this introduces yet more ambiguity since horizontal bandwidth, or 'the highest video frequency', can itself be defined in a number of different ways according to the precise filter characteristics etc. A further drawback with this definition is that it has the implicit assumption that equal horizontal and vertical resolution is a primary target for a television system. This is not necessarily the case since in extensive subjective tests Baldwin (7) found that the human observer is rather insensitive to equality in horizontal and vertical resolution.

A particularly important scanning parameter in Kell factor considerations is the use of interlace. For this reason some workers (8) have preferred to introduce a separate 'interlace factor' in addition to a non-interlaced Kell factor, even though both factors are used to quantify a similar phenomenon – namely the influence of line-scanning on effective vertical resolution.

Work by Jesty [9] attributed a factor of 0.6 to interlace and 0.7 to other effects resulting in an overall Kell factor of 0.42. Interlace effects are very subjective and such figures would be highly dependent on precise test procedures.

One thing which is evident even from these discussions is that the Kell factor is <u>not a universal constant</u> for television systems. Instead it is highly dependent on various system and test parameters. For this reason Lewis [6] has argued that a more appropriate term is the 'Kell effect' since a single factor does not sufficiently well convey the various processes involved.

2.2   Frequency Characteristics

Before considering the various parameters which give rise to the Kell factor, or 'Kell effect', it would be useful to review the frequency characteristics of the scanning process.

Consider a scene with a vertical frequency spectrum as illustrated in Fig. 2. The scene is then sampled by scanning. For simplicity we shall first ignore the time dimension and consider a purely vertical scan. This is then a one-dimensional sampling process. The uncertainty introduced by sampling is represented in the frequency domain by repeats of the image frequency spectrum centred on multiples of the sampling frequency. This is illustrated in Fig. 3 for a sampling frequency of f_v (ie for a TV system with f_v active lines, if f_v is measured in c/ph). In this example there is very significant overlap between the 'baseband' image spectrum and its repeats introduced by sampling. This is an 'aliasing' problem where high frequency components of the original scene have become indistinguishable from low frequencies. This confusion can be avoided by <u>prefiltering</u> the original image spectrum so that no frequencies above $f_{v/2}$ are present. The situation as in Fig. 4 then emerges with no spectral overlap. Thus any frequency component in the sampled signal has a unique interpretation. If the sampled signal with the spectrum of Fig. 4 were now displayed directly, it would nevertheless fall short of a true representation of the original image in two ways. Firstly it has been prefiltered. The prefiltering which has been applied will affect the image sharpness. This is an irreversible effect: the lost sharpness cannot be correctly restored. Secondly there is a further 'aliasing' problem in that shifted versions of the prefiltered image spectrum are present. This will give rise to spurious effects such as a visible line structure and a false 'sharpness'. This impairment can be removed however by the use of appropriate <u>postfiltering</u>. A suitable postfilter would also have a zero response beyond $\pm f_{v/2}$ and the prefiltered image could then be displayed accurately from the resulting 'clean' spectrum as illustrated in Fig. 5.

The consideration of the time dimension for a non-interlaced signal does not significantly influence this simple model. It means that whatever happens on the vertical frequency axis is itself repeated at multiples of the field sampling frequency. This is illustrated in Fig. 6 for a system with 242 active lines and a field-rate of 60Hz. The resulting two-dimensional frequency model is of no significance to Kell factor considerations (which apply to static pictures) except in as much as the display flicker frequency might affect subjective resolution evaluation. If <u>interlace</u> is used however then the model does need amending. Suppose for example that we consider a conventional 525/60 system which has 483 active lines with 2:1 interlace and a 60Hz field rate. The simple temporal effect illustrated in Fig. 6 no longer applies. There is instead a different temporal frequency displacement applying to alternate repeats of the vertical spectrum, as illustrated in Fig. 7. If pre- or postfiltering is inadequate a <u>frame-rate</u> flickering effect (at 30Hz in this example) occurs with a high vertical frequency component. With inadequate prefiltering the effect is <u>interline flicker</u>. This can be explained as being a high vertical frequency component in the scene aliased by the scanning as a lower frequency component flickering at the frame rate. With inadequate postfiltering the main effect is <u>line-crawl</u>. Here the temporal frequency offset of the repeat spectra results in a line-structure which appears to move vertically. These interlace effects are significant when discussing the Kell factor.

2.3   <u>Discussion of Parameters Influencing the Kell Factor</u>

Having outlined the general frequency characteristics of scanning, we can now consider various parameters in the light of these. The parameters in question are summarised in Table 1 and will be discussed briefly in turn:-

(i)   <u>Scene content</u>

The value of the Kell factor will depend on the type of scene or test pattern for which the factor is defined. Ideally it should be provided by subjective test results on a wide variety of scenes. Specific test patterns have been used however such as frequency gratings or single sharp edges. With gratings it is a matter of how fine a pattern can be resolved. With edges it is a matter of interpreting the influence on resolution of the uncertainty in edge position resulting from scanning (3). The effect being measured by these approaches is not identical and therefore the results will be dependent on the test pattern or scene assumed.

(ii)   <u>Resolution of optics and imaging device at source</u>

Since in general the image passes through optics and onto an imaging device <u>before</u> scanning, these items can perform a <u>prefiltering</u> procedure. Indeed this prefiltering is necessary if aliasing is to be avoided as discussed in section 2.2 above. With practical systems the frequency characteristics of this filtering action tend to have a slow roll-off. Thus a balance needs to be found between insufficient resolution and excessive aliasing. In general the optical resolution of systems is such as to allow some aliasing along with some in-band loss of modulation depth. The effect of this aliasing on the Kell factor again depends on scene content. If frequency gratings are considered then this type of alias effect will not restrict the Kell factor. If edges are considered then an uncertainty in position will result and the Kell factor will be affected. With real images a small degradation is likely to result.

(iii)   <u>Scanning line profile at source</u>

The finite vertical aperture of the source scanning line acts as a vertical low-pass filter on the image. This also constitutes a prefiltering procedure. In practice this cannot be sufficiently well defined to provide an optimised response. Indeed for this negative excursions would be required. With some sources, such as television cameras, the resolution loss tends to be excessive (and hence aperture correction is required) while with others, such as flying spot telecines, alias rejection can be inadequate.

(iv)   <u>Scanning line profile at display</u>

In the same way as at the source, the line profile at display has the effect of a low-pass filter on the image. This filtering action is in fact that desired of a postfilter. Thus if methods were available of precisely defining this profile, allowing both positive and negative excursions, then the effect could be put to very good use (10). In general the postfiltering action is inadequate and some of the repeat spectra indicated in Fig. 4 produce visible results. These significantly affect Kell factor measurements and result in a visible line structure. More severe postfiltering, resulting from a wider line profile, will tend to lead to a loss in resolution.

(v)   Display phosphor resolution

Depending on the method of construction, the display phosphor itself can independently sample and filter the image. A resolution loss with a consequent effect on the Kell factor can again result.

(vi)   Display frame-rate and persistence

With a non-interlaced display, this should not significantly influence the Kell factor, although if flicker is severe then subjective evaluation will be impaired. With interlace however, display frame-rate is an important feature. This is because the 'annoyance' factor associated with the temporal effects illustrated in Fig. 7 depend heavily on the frame-rate. This usually gives rise to perceptible interline flicker, being at 30Hz in 525-line countries in 25Hz in 625-line countries. The precise frequency of this flicker is very important in determining the effect of interlace on the Kell factor. With the current systems, the flicker is such that it is typically the most significant factor which limits vertical resolution. If the frame-rate is increased then interline flicker becomes much less significant.

Related closely to this are the persistence characteristics of the display device. These can affect the Kell factor if flicker visibility is influenced.

(vii)   Non-linearity of display

Although it is not a first-order effect, the display tube non linearity (gamma) can influence the interpretation of the Kell factor. This is true particularly for systems which use electronic processing to modify the vertical image spectrum. Suppose for example that prefiltering is performed electronically by first scanning the image with a very high line number and subsequently downconverting to the required number of lines. If the filtering is implemented on a gamma-corrected signal then the non-linear display procedure will introduce harmonics which will cause alias effects. These inhibit resolving ability and hence affect the Kell factor. This effect is evident at present when using electronic test signals for investigating vertical resolution. Second-order alias effects due to display non-linearity are very evident when using sinusoidal patterns at large depths of modulation, such as in the zone plate. Thus image prefiltering should be performed in the linear domain, as it is when performed optically.

(viii)   Viewing distance and line standard

The most significant interface in these considerations is that with the eye. The eye itself will act as a postfilter, the properties of which will greatly affect the Kell factor. Thus the actual vertical frequencies involved as seen at the eye are very significant. These depend on the line-standard used and the viewing distance relative to the display height.

It is apparent from the above that there are many possible sources of a 'Kell effect' which gives rise to a specific Kell factor. Therefore it is not wise to apply Kell factor results obtained with one system to another. It is undisputed that the Kell factor describes a real effect. Care must be taken in its use however since a single factor cannot possibly do justice to the complex combination of effects giving rise to it. The above discussion of parameters also serves to highlight the various aspects of scanning in which future developments could lead to improved resolution.

3   A SYSTEM WITH IDEAL SCANNING

It is possible to envisage an ideal system for the future in which the Kell factor has no place. The straightforward constraints of sampling as discussed in the Introduction and in the Appendix could then be applied. Referring to the frequency characteritics of section 2.2, what is required is a maximum bandwidth 'clean spectrum' as shown in Fig. 5. An optical/electro-mechanical approach would require an imaging device which acted as an optimised prefilter and a display device which acted as an optimised postfilter. Such goals are not practically realisable.

There is an alternative approach which is now becoming a more feasible proposition. Interpolation techniques can be used at source and display to ease the requirements on the 'analogue' pre- and post-filtering. This method requires a source and display which scan at a higher line-rate than that required in the intervening television signal. Professor Wendland from Dortmund University has described an approach similar to this in some detail in a number of recent publications (11). The method is outlined in general terms in Fig. 8, with an examination of the frequency characteristics given in Fig. 9. The optics and imaging device are chosen to provide the required resolution. The source scanning is then performed with a sufficiently high number of lines f_s to avoid spectral overlap into the frequency region of interest (Fig. 9a). Electronic vertical filtering is then applied to bandlimit the signal in a way suitable for scanning with the desired number of lines f_v (Fig. 9b). Down-conversion to the desired line-standard then takes place (Fig. 9c) without undesirable spectral overlap. For display the signal is postfiltered and interpolated (or 'upconverted') to a sufficiently high line standard f_d (Fig. 9d) to make the combined effect of the eye and the line profile a suitable postfilter for the required viewing distance. In this way the desired 'clean spectrum' of Fig. 5 can be obtained. As mentioned in section 2.3 the electronic filtering needs to be applied on a linear (rather than gamma-corrected) signal to achieve best results.

If the Kell factor is defined in terms of resolvable gratings then even in an 'ideal' system its value is unlikely to be unity. This is because for any sampling there is a trade-off which needs to be optimised in the anti-aliasing filtering which is applied. If the filter cut-off is too sharp then the ringing on sharp edges becomes objectionable. Thus even in such an 'ideal' system a Kell factor of around 0.9 may apply. In this case however, the Kell factor is not a necessary concept for scanning since identical constraints will apply to the horizontal sampling for digitisation.

This concept of an 'ideal' system applies especially to a non-interlaced scan in the desired transmission path. If the line-scan is interlaced, then in order to realise a resolution improvement on static pictures the filtering applied will need to introduce a motion degradation. An example of this is illustrated in Fig. 10 for a 525/60/2:1 scanning standard with 483 active lines. This figure shows two-dimensional spectra which are repeated in a way appropriate for 2:1 interlaced scanning, on axes of vertical and temporal frequency (see the Appendix). Prefiltering has been applied in order to avoid spectral overlap. This figure thus represents a two-dimensional equivalent to Fig. 9c for interlaced scanning. The curves are contours (for example they could be -6dB contours) of a suitable electronic bandlimiting filter. A gap is shown in between the contours to allow for practical filter cut-off transitions.

Such a filter contour shape would allow as much vertical resolution on static pictures as that offered by a 483 active line non-interlaced signal. The price paid for interlace however, would be a loss in vertical resolution with motion. This is evident in Fig. 10 by noting how the vertical frequency bandwidth reduces with increasing temporal frequency. The only way in which this effect could be avoided altogether would be to filter vertically to less than 121c/ph, independent of temporal frequency. In this case no resolution advantage would be offered by using 483 lines interlaced in preference to 242 lines non-interlaced. In order to minimise motion defects Wendland (12) has suggested the use of motion adaptive electronic prefilters for 'ideal' interlaced transmission.

4   AN ALTERNATIVE APPROACH

The system just described is complete and deals with each of the Kell factor effects. This is achieved at the cost of an extremely high quality source and display and some fairly complex signal processing. One could envisage however, a system which deals with only the most significant of the Kell factor effects but which yields worthwhile improvements in picture quality. It is likely that such a simplified system would be practically feasible (in both professional and domestic environments) in a much shorter timescale. Such a system will now be described on the basis of compatibility with currently used broadcast line-standards.

The essential elements of this approach are outlined in Fig. 11. A high quality source of conventional line-standard (such as 525/60/2:1 or 625/50/2:1) provides television signals for the transmission medium, also of conventional line-standard. The source may be derived from a higher line-rate source (as discussed later in section 4.2), but this is not an essential feature of the system. The important feature is that there is some upconversion processing prior to display with a higher line-rate.

4.1   Display Processing

With current 525 and 625 line standards and high quality sources and displays the major effect limiting the perceived vertical resolution is the interline flicker resulting from interlace. Sharp edges as used in text, or fine detail and texture (as often present in clothing), can give rise to a visible 'edge twitter' or flicker. This detracts from the legibility of small text and from the perception of detail. This interline flicker occurs due to the use of interlace not at source or transmission, but rather at the display. Indeed the effect can be removed without departing from the use of interlace at source or transmission, but only at display. The potential of picture improvement by display processing has been recognised widely and at present this area is one of active research worldwide (13-18). In particular scan conversion for non-interlaced (or otherwise called 'progressive' or 'sequential') display has received attention. If interpolation is used to provide additional display lines for 525/60 non-interlaced, or 625/50 non-interlaced, display then a significant picture quality improvement can result on static pictures. Subjective tests in Japan (13) have shown improvements in the range +2.6 to + 1.4 on a 7-grade comparison scale for scenes with little or no movement. In our own laboratories many have commented on the 'high definition' appearance resulting from such scan conversion using component-coded television signals. Not only is interline flicker removed but there is also a noticeable absence of 'busyness' in the line-structure of the non-interlaced display.

An improvement in perceived resolution is not achieved however in scene areas containing significant motion. The use of interlace in transmission does imply some trade-off between vertical and temporal resolution. Indeed if a fixed interpolation algorithm for scan conversion is used then an improvement in static picture quality is offset by a degradation with motion. For this reason most of the research has pursued the option of a motion-adaptive interpolation procedure. The purpose of this is to achieve the improvement for static pictures described above while maintaining the conventional motion portrayal capabilities of interlace. Some of the interesting difficulties encountered in the motion detection processing for such systems are discussed in references 16 and 19.

Such display processing in itself is not able to yield an ideal situation with the absence of a Kell factor, but it does deal with the main source of Kell factor degradation in conventional interlaced systems. Very close scrutiny of a scan converted scene of high detail derived from a high resolution source (such as a flying-spot telecine) does reveal some 'alias' patterning resulting from incomplete prefiltering. In addition the visible line structure effect of incomplete postfiltering is evident with close viewing distances. It is found however, that these effects do not have a significant detrimental influence on picture quality. Indeed in countries using a 50Hz field rate the major remaining detrimental feature of the display is probably the large area flicker. This tends to be noticeable especially with peripheral vision and bright pictures. The significance of this effect on home viewing is not yet fully clear. Nevertheless consideration is being given to a further upconversion procedure for 100Hz field rate display in order to overcome this effect. With a 60Hz field rate it is generally regarded that the large area flicker is sufficiently imperceptible so as to make further upconversion unnecessary.

4.2   Source Processing

Given the fact that adaptive display processing goes much of the way towards alleviating Kell factor effects, the question arises as to whether source processing is worthwhile for a compatible higher definition television system. The answer from a signal prefiltering point of view is probably no. This is because the adaptive display processing is particularly efficient in its interpretation of scene content, even if some aliasing is present. It is possible however that some limited amount of prefiltering (not true 'anti-aliasing' filtering) may be beneficial (16), although this is not proven. Other considerations may also influence this choice however, and there may be a need to derive sources from a higher line-rate standard for other reasons. One factor is that considerations of high definition television standards may result in the widespread use of higher line-rate sources in any case. Source processing would then be required in order to interface with conventional line-rates. If the high definition standard is not ideally matched to the transmission standard, however, then a quality loss, rather than improvement, may result from source processing. With television cameras there can be some motivations for an increase in line-scanning rate. Firstly a greater line density can itself provide a desirable improvement in vertical resolution (smaller spot size). Secondly, more suitable vertical aperture correction can be applied on a camera signal with more lines per field. These advantages need to be offset of course with the attendant increase in noise resulting from the higher video bandwidths necessary and a substantial increase in cost.

Fig. 11 therefore does not include source prefiltering since this is not a fundamental element of the approach being presented.

66

4.3 Implementation for Direct Broadcasting by Satellite

Direct Broadcasting by Satellite (DBS) presents an opportunity to envisage the provision of a television service which would put to full use the display processing discussed here. In Europe the MAC (Multiplexed Analogue Components) approach to vision coding has been recommended for DBS services. This provides two significant features in this context. Firstly component-coding is employed. This bypasses the familiar cross-effects common with composite colour coding and enables wider luminance and chrominance bandwidths to be considered. The resulting high picture quality is all the more suited to display improvement techniques. Secondly, the nature of the sound/vision/data coding system (known as 'C-MAC/packets') as a whole is such that a wider aspect ratio can be envisaged. It is possible to arrange the provision of this in a compatible manner (20, 21) such that conventional receivers with a 4:3 aspect ratio are unaffected. Thus one can consider a compatible higher definition television service as illustrated in Fig. 12. A high-quality 625 line source with wide aspect ratio (eg 5:3) is coded in such a way that the picture 'edges' (ie those parts outside of a 4:3 window) are 'hidden' as far as a conventional decoder is concerned. The conventional DBS viewer then uses a small screen to display high-quality component-coded pictures in a 4:3 aspect ratio. The higher definition viewer has a large-screen wide aspect ratio (eg 5:3) display which employs the scan conversion techniques discussed in section 4.1 and signal processing techniques to restore the picture edges. It is likely that in 625 line countries the picture quality obtained in this way will not be far off that already demonstrated using an 1125 line HDTV (High Definition Television) system (16, 20).

The fact that source pre-processing is not viewed as essential may have important implications. It opens up the possibility of an intermediate 'extended definition' standard for sources in which the line-scan rate remains the same, while the aspect ratio is changed and perhaps the horozontal resolution is improved. This would present fewer technological problems than a change to 'high-definition' sources with increased line-rates.

5 CONCLUSIONS

The scanning process can be viewed as a sampling procedure. The Kell factor - a measure of scanning imperfections - can then be broken down into its constituent effects according to the way in which these influence the sampling and reconstruction of the image. The Kell factor is by no means a universal constant in television systems. It is highly dependent on the television system parameters and the tests for which it is defined.

Having highlighted the various 'Kell Factor effects' a system has been proposed which would alleviate these and provide an 'ideally scanned' system. In addition to this a simplified approach has been suggested which deals with the most significant of these effects in conventional television systems by applying scan conversion techniques at display. The resulting system provides an improvement in picture quality without the need of changing source or transmission line-scan rates. In this way the same transmission can be used to serve both 'conventional' viewers and 'higher definition' viewers having a large-screen display (with wider aspect ratio). The fact that the source line-rate need not be changed may have significant implications, for example, in television camera technology. It implies that an 'extended definition' standard could emerge requiring high resolution and wide aspect ratio but without a change in scanning rates.

6   ACKNOWLEDGEMENT

The author wishes to thank the Director of Engineering of the Independent Broadcasting Authority for permission to publish this paper. I would also like to thank collegaues within the Authority for helpful suggestions on the manuscript.

7   REFERENCES

1   Kell R D, Bedford A V and Trainer M A, 'An Experimental Television System', Proc. IRE, 22 (11), 1246-1265 (November 1934).

2   Bedford A V, 'Figure of Merit for Television Performance', RCA Rev., 3, 36-44 (1938).

3   Kell R D, Bedford A V and Fredendall G L, 'A Determination of Optimum Number of Lines in a Television System', RCA Rev., 5, 8-30 (1940).

4   Wheeler H A and Loughren A V, 'The Fine Structure of Television Images', Proc. IRE, 26 (15), 540-575 (May 1938).

5   Wilson J C, 'Channel Width and Resolving Power in Television Systems', Journal Television Society, 2 (Part 2), 397-420 (June 1939).

6   Lewis N W, 'Television Bandwidth and the Kell Factor', Electronic Technology, 39, 44-47 (February 1962).

7   Baldwin M W, 'The Subjective Sharpness of Simulated Television Images', Proc. IRE, 28, 458-468 (October 1940).

8   For example, Fujio T, 'A Study of High-Definition TV System in the Future', IEEE Trans. Broadcasting, BC-24, 92-100 (1978).

9   Jesty L C, 'The Relation between Picture Size, Viewing Distance and Picture Quality', Proc. IEE, 105 (Part B), 425-434 (1958).

10   Monteath G D, 'Vertical Resolution and Line Broadening', BBC Engineering Monograph No 45, December 1962.

11   See for example, Wendland B, 'High Definition Television Studies on Compatible Basis with Present Standards' in Television Technology in the 80's, SMPTE, Scarsdale, New York, 1981, p 151-165.

12   Wendland B, 'High Quality Television by Signal Processing', Second International Conference on New Systems and Services in Telecommunications, Liege, Belgium, November 1983.

13   Nishizawa T and Tanaka Y, 'New Approach to Research and Development of High-Definition Television', NHK Technical Monograph No 32, 98-101, 1982.

14   Kraus U E, 'Avoidance of Large-Area Flicker in Home TV Receivers', Rundfunktech Mitteilungen, 25, 264-269 (1981). In German.

15   Achiha M, Ishikura K and Fukinuki T, 'A Motion Adaptive High Definition Converter for NTSC Color TV Signals', 13th International Television Symposium, Montreux, 1983.

16   Tonge G, 'Signal Processing for Higher Definition Television', IBA Technical Review No 21, 13-26, 1983.

17   Roberts A, 'The Improved Display of 625-line Television Pictures', BBC Research Department Report 1983/8.

18   Uhlenkamp D and Guttner E, 'Improved Reproduction by Standard Television Signals', NTZ Archiv 4, 313-321 (1982). In German.

19   Nishizawa T, 'Investigation of Interpolation Filters for Conversion of Interlace Scanning to Non-Interlace Scanning', Japanese TV Inst. Tech. Report TEBS 83-4, September 1982. In Japanese.

20   Long T, 'Why Non-Compatible High-Definition Television?', IBA Technical Review No 21, 4-12, 1983.

21   Windram M D , Morcom R and Hurley T, 'Extended Definition MAC', IBA Technical Review No 21, 27-41, 1983.

22   Miyakawa H, 'Sampling Theorem of Stationary Stochastic Variables in Multi-Dimensional Space', Journal of IECE Japan, 42, 139-145 (1959). In Japanese.

23   Petersen D P and Middleton D, 'Sampling and Reconstruction of Wave-Number-Limited Functions in N-Dimensional Euclidean Spaces', Information and Control, 5, 279-323 (1962).

24   Tonge G, 'The Sampling of Television Images', IBA Experimental and Development Report No 112/81.

25   Nyquist H, 'Certain Topics in Telegraph Transmission Theory', Trans. AIEE, 47, 617-644 (1928).

APPENDIX

NYQUIST CONSTRAINTS FOR SAMPLING IN TWO OR MORE DIMENSIONS

The scanning process in television involves sampling in two dimensions, namely the vertical space dimension and the time dimension. Often in television signal processing sampling in a third dimension (horizontal space) is also introduced. An understanding of this multi-dimensional sampling is benefited by the investigation of multi-dimensional frequency constraints (22-24). A brief introduction to this field is given in this Appendix.

The frequency constraints of one-dimensional sampling are well known and are often expressed as 'Nyquist Limitations' after early work on pulse transmission by Nyquist (25). The result is that the frequency components which can be reconstructed in an unambiguous manner after sampling are less than half the sampling frequency. In practice frequencies up to perhaps 90% of this limit are resolved in order to allow headroom for filter characteristics. The amount of headroom required depends on the precise application and has to do with the visibility of 'ringing' in the frequency region of interest and the filter complexity available. Since this headroom is not strictly defined, it is still common to refer to the theoretical Nyquist limitations of sampling.

In two or more dimensions the 'sampling frequency' cannot be defined so simply. A two-dimensional sampling frequency can best be thought of as a grid or 'lattice' of sampling positions. The frequency of sampling then has two levels of application. In a general sense it defines the density of sampling points per unit area in the plane of sampling. In a specific sense it defines the precise pattern of these sampling points. In a similar way it is found that a 'Nyquist' frequency limitation can be defined on these two levels. In a general sense it describes the area in the frequency domain which can be supported. In a specific sense it describes the shape of this area.

Let us consider two simple examples; an orthogonal sampling grid and a quincunx sampling grid. These are illustrated in Figs. 13a and 13b respectively. The density of each grid is the same. Thus in the general sense the sampling frequency is the same. Indeed, in a scanning implementation both patterns would result in the same practical sampling rates. Specifically, however, the sampling frequencies in Figs. 13a and 13b are different because of the different patterns used. In the frequency domain a pattern of 'reciprocal lattice' points results, indicating centres of the repeat spectra introduced by sampling. These are shown for orthogonal and for quincunx sampling in Figs. 14a and 14b respectively. A 'Nyquist limiting region' can be defined for each as indicated by the shaded regions in Fig. 14. As expected, the areas of the two shapes are the same, but the shapes themselves are different. These shapes are a representation in two dimensions of frequency components which are less than half the (two-dimensional) sampling frequency. The regions are thus defined to contain all frequency which are closer to the 'baseband' spectrum than they are to any of the repeat spectra. Defined in this way, these 'Nyquist regions' are exactly analoguous to Brillouin Zones used in solid state theory.

In practical terms however, these Nyquist regions are not unique options for anti-aliasing filter properties. Because of the second dimension in the sampling, a degree of freedom exists in choosing the frequency region to be defined by an anti-aliasing filter. For example a filter which defines the Nyquist region for orthogonal sampling (Fig. 14a) could be used, if so desired, as an anti-aliasing filter for <u>quincunx</u> sampling (Fig. 14b) but not vice-versa. The validity of this can be seen by noting that the region will not overlap when repeated on each point of the lattice of repeat spectra, as shown in Fig. 15. Indeed, a filter which defines any region having this property is an admissible anti-aliasing filter. Thus it is also evident that a filter defining the region of Fig. 14b for quincunx sampling is <u>not</u> suitable for the orthorgonal sampling of Fig. 14a.

This freedom of choice for anti-aliasing filters is an important facet of multi-dimensional sampling and filtering. Although the strictly defined 'Nyquist region' portrays the inherent symmetry properties of the sampling, and any naturally favoured frequency directions, practical constraints often make alternative filter characteristics more suitable.

The extension of the above concepts to three dimensions is straightforward and is discussed in Reference 24. Area becomes <u>volume</u> and Nyquist regions become three-dimensional solid shapes. The freedom of choice in anti-aliasing filter properties also exists, and is in fact greater due to the extra frequency dimension.

The application of these concepts to scanning needs to be considered with some care. This is because one dimension is in <u>space</u> and the other is in <u>time</u>. Nevertheless the quincunx sampling pattern of Fig. 13b, for example, can be used to represent 2:1 <u>interlaced</u> scanning. The frequency characteristics can then be discussed with reference to the repeat spectra as illustrated in Fig. 14b, with an appropriate change of frequency axes. Similarly the orthogonal sampling of Fig. 13a and 14a can be discussed in the context of <u>non-interlaced</u> scanning.

Gary Tonge received his B.Sc from the Electronics Department of Southampton University in 1977. He went on to the Applied Mathematics Department of the same university to research into theoretical aspects of energy conversion for his Ph.D. In 1980 he joined the Independent Broadcasting Authority to work on digital television. Initial work on video data-rate reduction led to an interest in sampling theory and multidimensional filter design. More recently his efforts have been directed towards signal processing for higher definition television. He is currently a Senior Engineer in the Video and Colour Section of the IBA.

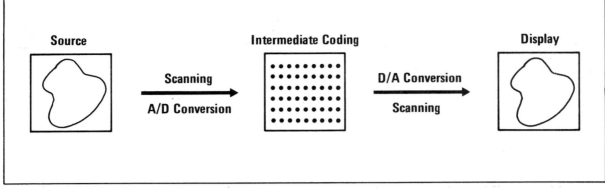

Fig.1   Scanning and analogue-to-digital-conversion as a means of converting a scene into an array of picture elements, or "pixels", and back again.

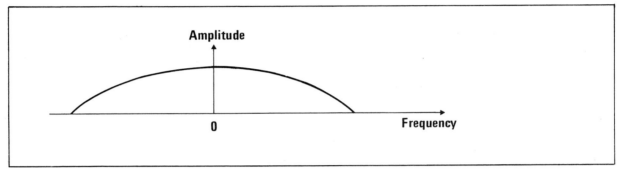

Fig.2   Vertical frequency spectrum of a scene prior to scanning.

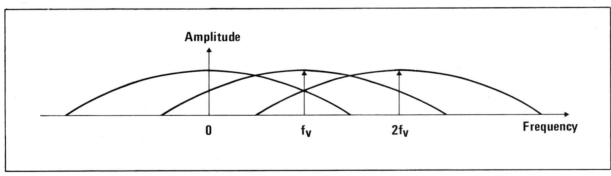

Fig.3   Vertical frequency spectrum of a scene after scanning with f_v active lines showing spectral overlap.

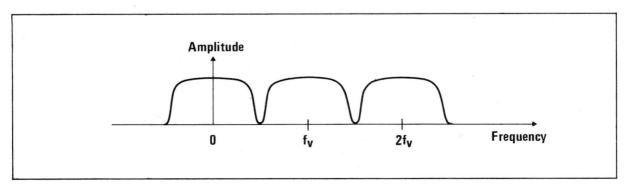

Fig.4   Vertical frequency spectrum of a scanned scene which has been suitably prefiltered showing no spectral overlap.

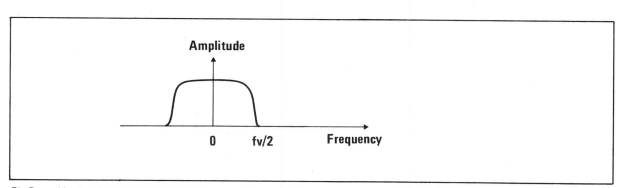

Fig.5   Vertical frequency spectrum of a scene after prefiltering, scanning and suitable postfiltering.

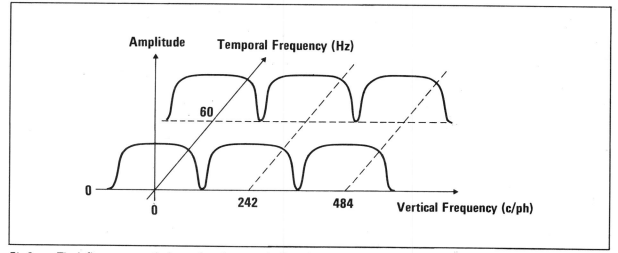

Fig.6   The influence on vertical scanning of temporal effects for a non-interlaced scan with 242 active lines per frame and 60 frames per second. The vertical frequency spectrum of the scanned scene is seen to repeat at multiples of the frame rate.

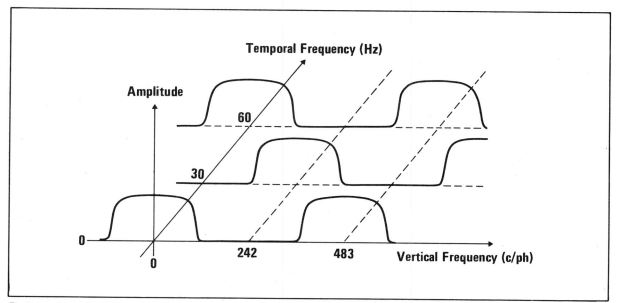

Fig.7   As for Fig.6 but with a 2:1 interlaced scan with 483 active lines per frame and a 60Hz field rate. A temporal frequency offset between adjacent vertical spectral repeats is evident.

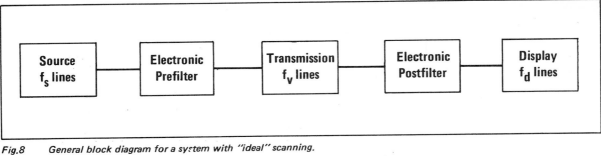

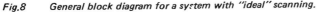

Fig.8   General block diagram for a system with "ideal" scanning.

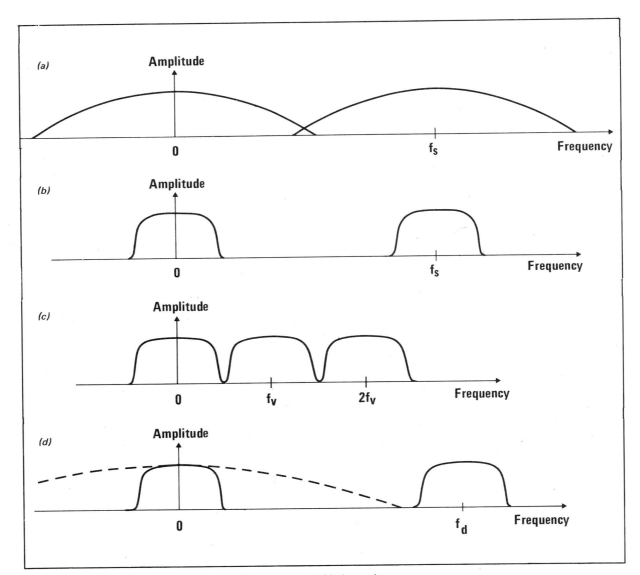

Fig.9   Vertical frequency spectra for a television system with ideal scanning:

a)   Initial scan with f_s lines sufficient to avoid spectral overlap into the region of interest.

b)   Electronic prefiltering to enable downconversion to a transmission standard of f_v lines.

c)   The effect of the downconversion.

d)   Upconversion for display with f_d lines such that the eye and the line profile act as a suitable postfilter.

74

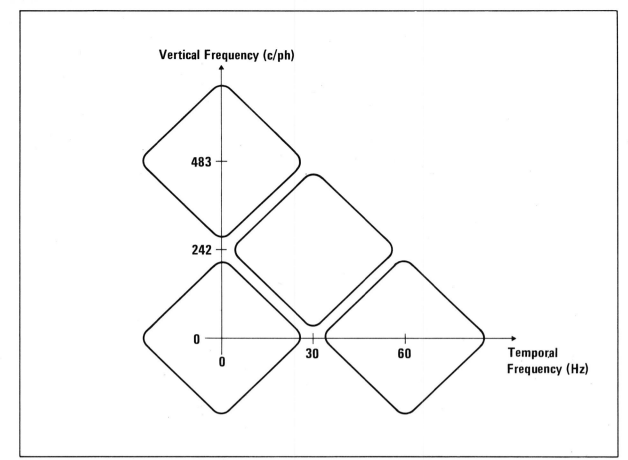

Fig.10   An example of a two-dimensional frequency response contour of a filter suitable for interlaced scanning with 483 active lines per frame and a 60Hz field rate.

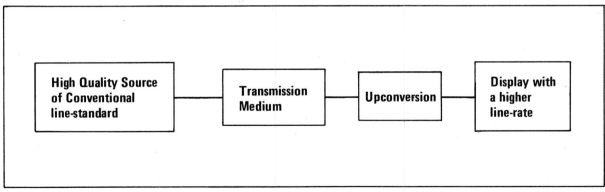

Fig.11   The essential elements of a simplified approach towards vertical resolution enhancement.

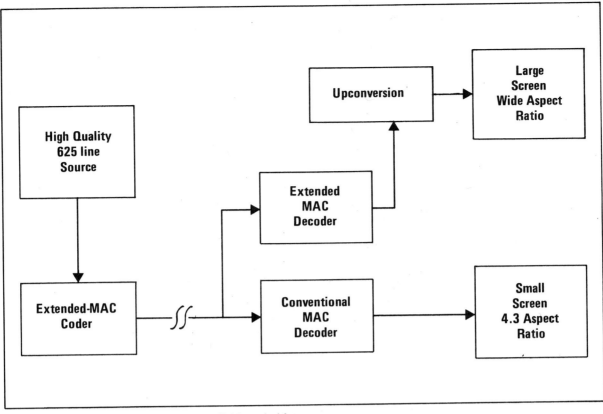

Fig.12   *A compatible approach to higher definition television.*

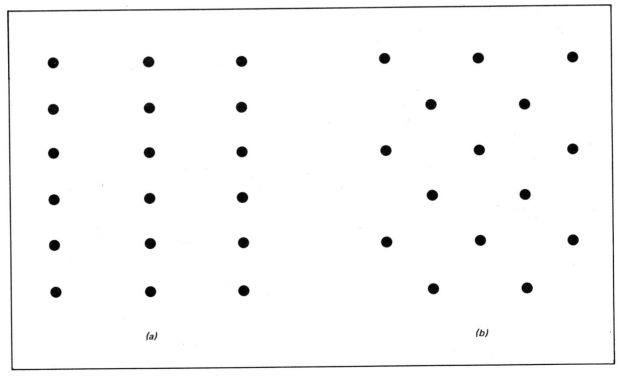

Fig.13   *Sampling patterns for two-dimensions:*

    a)   Orthogonal sampling

    b)   Quincunx sampling

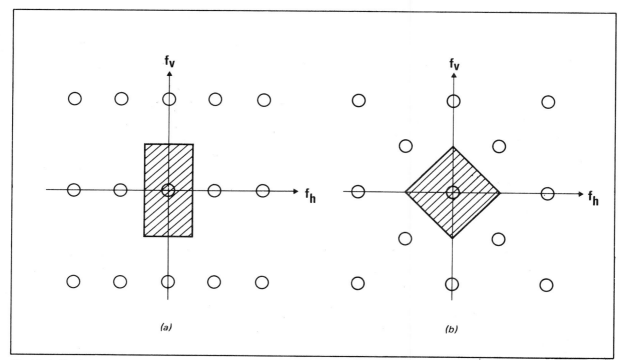

Fig.14 The "lattices" of repeat spectra in the frequency domain associated with the sampling patterns of Fig.13a and 13b
(a&b) respectively on nominal axes of horizontal frequency f_h and vertical frequency f_v. The shaded regions represent
"Nyquist limitations" on the sampling.

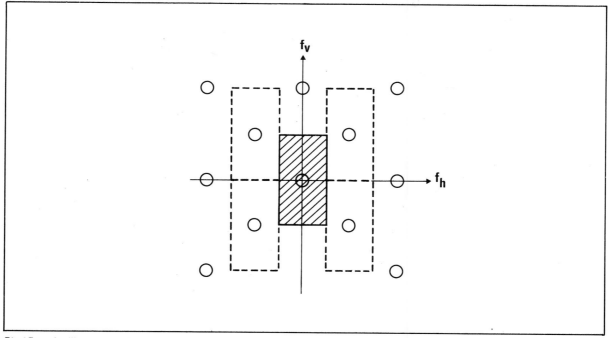

Fig.15 An illustration of how the Nyquist region of Fig.14a can be applied by filtering to the sampling of Fig.14b and still
lead to an absence of spectral overlap (aliasing).

Scene content

Optical resolution at source
Imaging device resolution
Line profile at source
Line profile at display
Display phosphor resolution
Display frame rate
Display persistence
Display non-linearity
Viewing distance
Line scanning standard

} The Kell Factor: a single measure of effective vertical resolution

TABLE 1 : Some of the parameters which can influence the Kell Factor in television systems.

Some Factors in the Evaluation of Image Quality: A British View

Christopher P. Daubney
Independent Broadcasting Authority
Winchester, Hampshire, United Kingdom

INTRODUCTION

The Romans worshipped a number of gods; one of them was Janus. It will be remembered that Janus was a two-headed god with faces looking in opposite directions. Of course, January acquired its name from Janus as, in that context, the god is seen as looking back over the old year and forward into the new.

Perhaps broadcasting engineers have - but hopefully not to worship - a Janus-like situation in television at this time. For much more than a decade, the world's colour television systems have operated on fairly clearly defined, and well-accepted, principles. Within the last year or two, the broadcasting world has suddenly found itself at one of those great watersheds when it has the chance to keep its present practices or to make a significant change. These opportunities do not occur very often.

This paper considers some factors in the evaluation of image quality, both in terms of where the present system has reached and also with one eye on where it is, or may be, going. Inevitably, therefore, it is a mixture of the author's personal views and those of the post which he holds within the Independent Broadcasting Authority (IBA) in the United Kingdom. There, as its Head of Quality Control, he is responsible for overseeing the technical standards which prevail in the independent part of broadcasting in the United Kingdom - a system consisting of seventeen programme companies, with more than sixty studios, providing programmes for the IBA's two television networks and 1,000 transmitters. Accordingly, the author lives very much with the problems of today.

SUBJECTIVE OR OBJECTIVE EVALUATIONS

Now presumably everybody who watches television does so entirely subjectively - i.e. the aural and pictorial images carry all the information which the broadcaster wishes to convey. It would, therefore, be delightful if all evaluations of picture quality could be made purely subjectively. However, it is a well-known fact that even professional broadcasting engineers are rather variable in their assessment of the seriousness of impairments. As a consequence, they resort to objective evaluation techniques; if such evaluations are to be fully meaningful, it is vital that "the objective measurements should always relate to the subjective effect or defect".

THE PRESENT STANDARDS

The IBA networks operate to widely publicised technical standards - set out in its Code of Practice. Essentially, these are analogue-based with a composite coding system for transmission, and with the viewing expected to be on a screen having a diagonal between perhaps 20 and 26 inches, i.e. between one-half and two-thirds of a metre - a small screen therefore. The

United Kingdom broadcasters have established operating tolerances for the studio equipment, the transmission links and the transmitters themselves, all of which are as near transparent as the present balance in broadcasting economics will allow them to be. Table 1 lists the day-to-day operating tolerances for various signal paths in and around a studio centre. Table 2 extends the details of Table 1 by including the distribution network and various transmitter configurations. Until recently, these standards have been sensibly met for some 90% of the broadcasting time. Before considering the 90% concept further, it is important briefly to consider the front end of the system as well - the place where the studio scene is turned, by one means or another, into an electronic signal.

In this journal, it is not necessary to rehearse all the pros and cons of electronic cameras versus film cameras. In objective measurement terms, tolerances exist within the IBA's network for the lens and electronic camera combination. These are illustrated in Table 3.

It is harder to find the equivalent lens and film camera details. However, there is a much more tortuous electronic versus film debate. Suffice it to say that, certainly in the United Kingdom and presumably in North America as well, there is a definite school of directors that prefers "the film look".

ELECTRONIC LOOK VERSUS FILM LOOK

From the purely engineering standpoint, quantifying that statement is a nearly impossible task - but perhaps it is one to which the electronic camera devotees have not paid enough attention. Variations in transfer characteristic, colorimetric performance, picture repetition rate in movement portrayal, and definition are obviously significant factors - though the last is only indirectly related to the electronic camera per se.

(i) Transfer Characteristics

It is notable that, in some recent television camera designs, new variations in transfer characteristics are becoming a reality. These will allow a closer emulation of this apparently desirable film look by allowing a knee in the highlight area. One of the "failings" of electronic cameras is "burnt-out" whites - when the contrast range is too great and highlights have to be clipped in order to expose flesh tones correctly. But why is the highly non-linear transfer characteristic of the film chain deemed to be preferable to the more linear electronic, when both are viewed via a television system - or is that only true for certain types of programme production? Whatever the reason, it has a marked effect on the next point.

(ii) Colorimetry

Work going on, particularly within the United Kingdom Independent Broadcasting Authority, on an analysis of colorimetric problems is also starting to produce fruit. A spectrophotometric analysis system for cameras and monitors, based on the use of a desk top computer and suitable transducers, etc., has been developed - Figure 1; work is now starting on the equivalent system for film and telecines.

(iii) <u>Movement Portrayal</u>

Perhaps the least contentious difference between the two looks is the effect of picture repetition rate on movement portrayal. There are fundamental differences in the way movements in scenes are portrayed by film and by electronic systems, although the basic picture repetition rate can be the same. Does the staggering of the temporal sampling due to interlace in the electronic picture produce a more pleasing movement portrayal than film?

(iv) <u>Exposure Settings</u>

Considering the whole business of resolution, there is an interesting Janus-like effect again. In general, electronic cameras, working with 30mm tubes and with zoom lenses operating at around f4, have a far greater depth of field than that used and desired by film makers. This appears to be exacerbated by the rather poor "best focus" of a zoom lens compared to a prime lens. As a result, in order to achieve the film resolution look of the precisely sharp main subject of the picture and the quite definitely defocussed surroundings, programme makers are resorting to gauze and gelatine on television camera lenses - which also blurs the <u>main</u> subject as well! - instead of taking the more logical - and humanitarian - course of action - to turn the light level down and force the iris in the lens wider open. Some of the reasons for not doing that are clear. The IBA's regular testing of electronic cameras and lenses shows quite clearly that the zoom lens has, in general, some rather serious failings over parts of the zoom range if the lens is opened up much beyond f4. Shading, vignetting and lack of resolution in the corners become serious problems. It is, of course, even more ironical that this general desire, certainly in entertainment programmes, for a reduced depth of field is actually being made <u>worse</u> with the advent of the lightweight cameras using 17mm tubes. The depth of field has become even greater with these lightweight cameras - which are otherwise so desirable, since they can be made to emulate film cameras in operational convenience terms. That makes the irony yet greater still!

(v) <u>Modulation Transfer Functions</u>

The rather poor "best focus" of a zoom lens compared to a prime lens was mentioned above. This is a factor in the other great difference in resolution performance. It is clear that the modulation transfer function of a lens and electronic camera is different from a lens/film combination. The lack of fine detail in the television system, coupled with the poor vertical resolution due to interlaced scanning, does need compensation. Within the constraints of the system bandwidth, this is partially provided by the correction for scanning spot size. In addition, the use of mid-band horizontal and vertical correction - as a way of allegedly improving the sharpness of the picture - has become an accepted practice. However, one can have too much of a good thing! The "cardboard cut-out" or "bags under the eyes" effects, and magnified skin imperfections, will be familiar to the reader! Too much fine detail correction leads to the well-known problems of "cross-colour" - and that raises the whole subject of luminance bandwidth - to which further reference will be made.

OPERATIONAL CONSIDERATIONS

Some of the effects in engineering terms of the differences between zoom and prime lenses have already been discussed. Because the evaluation of picture quality is, in the end, entirely subjective, and because television is concerned with moving, rather than static, pictures in the main, operational and production factors must count - albeit in a less than easily quantifiable way.

Prime lenses, combined with the tracking of cameras, produce a much greater and realistic sensation of depth in movement than does zooming. Of course, the zoom lens, when considered as a turret with an infinite set of fixed lenses, is another matter.

PRODUCTION REQUIREMENTS VERSUS TECHNICAL QUALITY

It may be just a vogue but there does seem to have been a recent tendency to blame poor technical quality on "producers' requirements". Surely producers do not actually want poor quality. Are not both the engineer and the producer to blame? The engineer shuts himself away in his corner, taking no interest in the artistic requirements, and the producer almost prides himself on knowing nothing about modern technology. Of course, that is an extreme view - but it has more than an element of truth about it. It needs both parties to apply themselves to the optimum solution. Broadcasting engineers have a lot of technology available to them - it is incumbent upon them to take the time to apply it so as to achieve what it is that the producer wants. Likewise, the producer must take the trouble to try and quantify his desires in a way which the engineer can interpret.

On the whole, well aligned television cameras, pointed at well lit scenes (and how important lighting, of whatever style, is to good pictures), are already capable of providing a good start to television pictures. How long will it be before the new television camera is capable of producing pictures very akin to the old favourite, film, but with even more latitude? That sounds like Janus again!

SIGNAL PROCESSING

That thought leads conveniently to another area of interest - the subsequent processing of signals. Table 2 listed the day-to-day operating tolerances in the United Kingdom television networks. These tolerances are met for some 90% of the time. The use of "special effects" - in the widest sense - has traditionally been regarded as only happening for less than 10% of the time. Times have changed.

The types of technique, previously used solely for those special effects, are now finding their way into circuits used for much greater periods of time.

The spin-off from the computer technology is having its effect on the television industry. Synchronisers, time base correctors, special effects (including electronic scenery) and stills stores, to name but four items, are now coming into regular use. Most of them would not have been sensibly possible before digital processing. Whilst there is undoubtedly an earnest looking forward to the day when the whole signal chain will be digital, there is going to be a long period with those famous digital "islands" in an analogue "sea" and, perhaps later, analogue "islands" in a digital "sea". Broadcasting engineers are spending considerable amounts of time on establishing digital standards for the different parts of the chain - or else on how to construct equipment based on those standards. However, it must not be forgotten that these digital islands each involve a transcoding process from analogue to digital and back again. That in itself requires very careful thought, the need for which is yet further stressed by the fact that the world digital standard is a component and not composite based standard. Broadcasters are therefore facing not only analogue-digital codecs, but composite-component ones as well.

One of the great problems, which is taxing the minds of the engineers in Independent Broadcasting in the United Kingdom, is the increasing use of both forms of transcoding. The present analogue composite standards were chosen on the assumption that there would be one and only one decoder - in the receiver. Since three of those four processing systems mentioned above effectively demand signals in component form - and presumably more and more will as further digital equipment, based on the world digital standard, comes into use - a start is having to be made on assessing the effect of cascaded composite/component coders and decoders. Traditionally, no-one has paid a lot of attention to the bandwidth of the chrominance signal; these successive processes are focussing attention marvellously on this problem.

Within the IBA network, a lot of consideration is being given to how to modify the existing measurement techniques to cope with these new processes. So far, reliance has been placed, certainly for signal path evaluation, on one-dimensional test signals - pulses and bars, staircases, etc. Problems have already been experienced with non-linearity testing of equipment employing PAL delay-line decoders when using the CCIR 1 in 4 staircase - where one line carries the staircase and the next three a pedestal of either 0% or 100% luminance amplitude. Since television signals convey moving information, should the test signals move over the picture area so that any integrating/averaging effects are also taken into account - or will such temporal variations make it too difficult to determine the results?

Janus is back again because the ultimate quality available from a full digital system - operating in its component form - should clearly be better than any of the present analogue systems. After all, the digital standard is such that more than 5.5MHz of luminance and 2.5MHz of chrominance bandwidth are available. Yet, in the process of getting there, the present system is apparently becoming worse and worse. Great care is needed in the engineering considerations if the highly desirable features, which synchronisers, effects units, etc., offer, are not to allow such a poor technical standard to become accepted in the interim, that the motivation to go to the higher quality full digital system is partially or completely eroded. The amazing spread of home VCRs ought to convey a warning to everybody!

A STEP IN THE RIGHT DIRECTION?

A personal thought - on, perhaps, a better compromise path to the all-digital system than allowing the present problems to continue - might be appropriate. Experience of working on the operational side of the IBA's MAC experiments provided a forceful reminder of how good analogue component pictures can be. If the opportunity arises within a studio centre, could not an analogue component studio system be tried - as a stepping stone?

Vision mixers, capable of handling full 5.5MHz component signals, are soon to be available. Television cameras are already capable of that sort of performance. The one weak link in the chain is the video recorder. Although they do not have the full luminance bandwidth, the evidence of the first ½" component recorders suggests that broadcasters could do far worse than to allow such recorders to be used for a limited period - so as to allow a complete component studio system to be tried. The overall advantages in picture quality of operating a studio in component form - albeit analogue - and only coding to composite for final transmission, seem to outweigh - even with the limits of present ½" VTRs - some of the other distortions from which composite signals suffer - cross luminance, cross colour and chrominance noise particularly in FM systems. If such a scheme was tried, the "weak link" of the ½" VTR could be replaced by a full bandwidth analogue component machine when one is available - or, of course, by that elusive pimpernel - the digital VTR. The opportunity is unlikely to arise very rapidly in the United Kingdom because most of the independent studios there have recently re-equipped with composite equipment. However, the future is unknown - and this suggestion could be one safe route to the digital component studio centre.

WHAT WILL IT LOOK LIKE ON A BIG SCREEN?

So far, no mention has been made of the differences between evaluations on small screens and on big ones. As was stated at the beginning, the present picture quality evaluations have been based on viewing distances from the screen of between four and six times the picture height. Indeed, within the IBA, critical assessments are made under viewing conditions which conform as closely as possible to the international standard set out in CCIR Recommendation 500. Under those conditions, it does seem that some of the most objectionable impairments with the present system are produced by the moving artifacts due to cross colour, cross luminance and interlace. How much more disturbing will they be on a big screen where the viewing distance is between two and a half and three times the picture height? How will the mind accept larger screen displays of scenes in an environment where the surroundings against which to judge size, etc., can easily be seen? An analogy from the IBA's surround-sound research may be useful. A similar difficulty was experienced with people accepting the realism of the sound image - which was undoubtedly there under certain conditions - when heard in their living rooms. Unlike stereophony which can never produce a sound-filled which envelops the listener, surround-sound can "transform" the living room very effectively into a large reverberant concert hall, with the sound truly enveloping the listener. Yet the mind is always struggling to accept that large concert hall in a much smaller, familiar room. Will the same problem arise with large faces - much larger than life size - looking at us at the much closer viewing distances - or will production techniques change to encompass this? In his vision of the future, aptly called 1984, George Orwell commented "Big Brother is watching you"!!

ACKNOWLEDGEMENT

The author gratefully acknowledges the help of many colleagues within Independent Broadcasting in the United Kingdom for help in preparing this article, and to Messrs. J.L.E. Baldwin and P.A. King in particular - and to the Director of Engineering of the Independent Broadcasting Authority for permission to publish it.

Christopher P. Daubney was educated at Clifton College, Bristol, and St. John's College, Cambridge. He joined the BBC in 1964 and worked in various departments including Studio and Outside Broadcast Operations, as a Lecturer in Engineering Training, and as a Planning and Installation Engineer in Capital Projects. In 1973, he joined the IBA as the Principal Engineer in Quality Control Section and is now Head of Quality Control. In April, 1984, he will become head of the IBA's Engineering Information Service.

TABLE 1

	Direct Path	Worst Path	Studio Path
SIGNAL LEVELS			
(a) Signal Level Adjustment Error	0.7v $\pm$0.2dB	0.7v $\pm$0.2dB	0.7v $\pm$0.2dB
(b) Signal Level Gain Stability	$\pm$0.2dB	$\pm$0.2dB	$\pm$0.2dB
LINEAR WAVEFORM DISTORTION			
(a) 2T Pulse-to-Bar Ratio	$\frac{1}{2}$%K	1%K	$\frac{1}{2}$%K
(b) 2T Pulse Response	$\frac{1}{2}$%K	1%K	$\frac{1}{2}$%K
(c) 2T Bar Response	$\frac{1}{2}$%K	1%K	$\frac{1}{2}$%K
(d) 50Hz Square Wave Response	$\frac{1}{2}$%K	1%K	$\frac{1}{2}$%K
(e) Chrominance/Luminance Gain Inequality	$\pm$3%	$\pm$4%	$\pm$3%
(f) Chrominance/Luminance Delay Inequality	$\pm$20ns	$\pm$40ns	$\pm$20ns
NON-LINEARITY DISTORTION			
(a) Luminance Line Time Non-Linearity	3%	5%	3%
(b) Differential Phase	$\pm$2°	$\pm$5°	$\pm$2°
(c) Burst/Chroma Phase	$\pm$2°	$\pm$5°	$\pm$2°
(d) Differential Gain	$\pm$3%	$\pm$5%	$\pm$3%
(e) Transient Gain Change, Luminance	2%	5%	$\pm$2%
(f) Transient Gain Change, Chrominance	2%	5%	2%
(g) Transient Gain Change, Sync	2%	5%	2%
(h) Chrominance/ Luminance Crosstalk	-	-	-

Cont'd

TABLE 1 Cont'd

	Direct Path	Worst Path	Studio Path
INPUT/OUTPUT IMPEDANCE-RETURN LOSS			
(a) Luminance	-30dB	-30dB	-30dB
(b) Chrominance	-30dB	-30dB	-30dB
(c) Low Frequency	-30dB	-30dB	-30dB
VLF RESPONSE			
(a) First Overshoot	20%	20%	-
(b) Second Overshoot	8%	8%	-
NOISE			
(a) · Weighted Luminance (RMS)	-64dB	-58dB	-64dB
(b) Weighted Chrominance (RMS)	-58dB	-52dB	-58dB
(c) Total Low Frequency Random and Periodic (p-p)	-45dB	-45dB	-45dB
(d) Low Frequency Random (p-p)	-52dB	-52dB	-52dB
(e) Interchannel Crosstalk	-55dB	-45dB	-52dB

Table 1
The tolerances shown in this paper are those used within the United Kingdom IBA network for day-to-day operations. The direct path covers the station presentation equipment chain — from the input from the PTT to the output to the transmitter. The worst path covers a typical program compilation chain, including three vision mixers and their ancillary equipments; each of the three mixers and its ancillary equipment has to meet the studio path tolerances. VTR performance is specified separately.

TABLE 2

Parameter No.	Parameter	Studio Centre Output (A)	British Telecom Network (B)	Main Transmitter Output (C)	Rebroadcast Transmitter Output (D)	Transposer Output (E)	A + B + E (F)
1	Signal/Random Noise, Unweighted (dB)	39	48	46	45	42	37
2	Signal/Noise, Luminance Weighted (dB)	48	56	52	51	48	44
3	Signal/Noise, Chrominance Weighted (dB)	42	52	52	51	48	40
4	Chrominance-Luminance Gain Inequality (%)	±7	+6 −12	±7	±18	±25	±28
5	Chrominance-Luminance Delay Inequality (ns)	±53	±65	±30	±75	±110	±140
6	K Bar (%)	5	3	1	3	4	9
7	K 2T Pulse (%)	5	2	2	3	4	8
8	K 2T Pulse/Bar (%)	5	2	1	3	4	8
9	K 50Hz Square Wave (%)	5	4	1	1	1	8
10	Luminance Non-Linearity (%)	15	14	7	14	20	34
11	Differential Gain (%)	15	10	5	10	15	28
12	Differential Phase (degrees)	15	10	4	10	15	28
13	Chrominance/Luminance Crosstalk (%)		±6	±3	±8	±10	

Table 2
The tolerances shown in this table are estimates of those expected to be met over the designated parts of a typical United Kingdom broadcasting chain for some 90% of the broadcasting time. The results in Column F are derived by addition on a power law basis, according to CCIR Recommendation 451.

TABLE 3

BLACK SHADING	
(a) Inner Zone – luminance	3% Peak-to-peak
(b) Overall (whole field) – luminance	5% Peak-to-peak
(c) Overall – colour separation difference	2% Peak*
* A change of not more than half of the limit may occur in any 10% of the picture width or height	
WHITE SHADING	
(a) Inner zone – luminance	5% Peak-to-peak
(b) Overall (whole field) – luminance	10% Peak-to-peak
(c) Overall – colour separation difference	6% Peak*
* A change of not more than half of the limit may occur in any 10% of the picture width or height	
RESOLUTION	
(a) Centre (0.5–5.0MHz)	100 ± 20%
(b) Corners (5.0MHz)	40% to 110% (of Centre)
WAVEFORM RESPONSE	
(a) Negative pulse maximum overshoot or pre-shoot	25% of pulse height
(b) Pre-shoot minus overshoot	0 ± 10% of pulse height
GEOMETRY	
(a) Inner zone	1% of picture height
(b) Whole field	2% of picture height
REGISTRATION	
(a) Inner zone	0.15% of picture height
(b) Whole Field	0.4% of picture height

Cont'd

TABLE 3 Cont'd

LATENT AND SPURIOUS IMAGES	
(a) Line Scan Ringing	5%
(b) Blemishes, tube spots and other defects	Impairment level 4
STREAKING	
(a) Short-term luminance	1%
(b) Short-term colour separation difference	Less than 1%
(c) Long-term luminance	2%
(d) Long-term colour separation difference	1%
FLARE*	
(a) DC Flare	$\pm 2\%$
(b) AC Flare	$\pm 7\%$
GREYSCALE	
Differential error between any Y, R, G, or B signals in a single studio, OB vehicle or combination of sources used to contribute to single productions	2%
NOISE	
(a) Weighted Luminance (RMS)	−48dB
(b) Weighted Chrominance (RMS)	−43dB
(c) Total Low Frequency Random and Periodic (p-p)	−45dB
(d) Low Frequency Random (p-p)	−52dB
LAG*	
(a) Green channel	7%
(b) Colour separation difference signals	3%

*   Target figures not mandatory for the time being

Table 3

The tolerances shown in this table are those used within the United Kingdom IBA network for day-to-day operations. The cameras are set up for the tests in accordance wih the normal operating procedures and are made on the combined lens and camera.

Fig. 1. The picture illustrates the prototype arrangements of the IBA's computer-operated spectrophotometric analysis of cameras equipment.

The New Generation Television Recorder — A Broadcaster's Perspective

K. P. Davies and M. Auclair
Canadian Broadcasting Corporation
Montreal, Quebec, Canada

1. INTRODUCTION

For the television broadcaster, the recorder plays an essential role, as the majority of television programs that are transmitted today come from recordings. The recorder is used widely in the field and in the studio for production recording, in the studio for post-production editing and program assembly, at the presentation studio for the playback of program segments, commercials, promotional material, and in the network for program delay and regional rescheduling. By the time the sound and pictures reach the viewer, they will have been recorded and reproduced between three and six times on the average, and more recording generations would be useful, particularly in production and post-production, if the resulting quality could be made acceptable.

The broadcaster's equipment is used frequently in a wide variety of operational situations and hence a single recording format for all applications is desirable. The new tape format, which the Broadcaster is seeking, will be common to all applications and hence great care must be taken in its specification. It must meet the current and potential needs, it must be technically and economically realizable and must, where possible, avoid placing hard limits on future improvements.

Although the various configurations of the machine will share a common tape format, and share many common parts, there will doubtless be several versions of the machine, each optimized with features for a particular task-field production, studio post-production, multi-cassette distribution release. There may well be different quality levels. Clearly, this family of machines will be very different to those currently available and the design approach must be significantly different.

2. OPERATIONAL ENVIRONMENT

An exhaustive list of all operational applications is essentially impossible, as television production pushes further into new areas, but the following can be identified and categorized as important for the broadcaster.

2.1 Field Recording

Production recording in the field, or using similar single-camera techniques in a dry studio, demands a machine that is transportable, rugged, highly reliable, operator friendly and insensitive to temperature, vibration, shock and foreign material of all kinds. Scene lengths tend to be short, production "special effects" are of very limited utility and monitoring/maintenance needs are best automated wherever possible.

Playback performance must be adequate only to establish the quality of its own recording or to make a few "after-hours" work copies in the field. This environment suggests a compact, reliable, recording machine using small sealed cassettes.

2.2 Studio Post-Production

If we assume that post-production will remain on tape, then the need is for rapid and precise scene location and editing capability, with highest quality playback and recording quality over several generations and with a wide range of source tapes. While many of the features demanded can be obtained by the use of intelligent processors, the basic reliability, accuracy and tape handling must be designed in, as must audio and video quality and editing accuracy. Size and weight are not major concerns and the studio offers a benign combination of temperature, humidity and cleanliness. Maintainability must be emphasized as downtime may become very expensive.

2.3 Distribution Uses

The operation of a television station, network, cable system or broadcast satellite, consists of the threading together in real-time under the viewer's (and sponsor's) scrutiny of numerous recorded segments of various lengths, origins and quality levels. Distribution may also require extensive record/playback operations to maintain time-zone and regional network schedules. Generally, distribution operations are driven by a computer system that ties together the machine control, switching and logging functions with those of traffic and scheduling and hence the recorder operates principally as a computer peripheral in the playback mode. In this application, the tape format selected must be adaptable to cassette operation and cassettes must be capable of reliable and efficient automatic loading from the library, identification and playback, with segment lengths from a few seconds to over an hour. Due to the cost impacts of downtime, the machine must be very reliable, maintainable and self-testing in all areas of its operation. Production features are not a priority need and size/weight concerns are of secondary interest.

2.4 Summary

The broadcaster needs then a range of machines which will share a common tape format, many essential modules and will be optimized and economic for the specific tasks of his plant. One single machine design is unlike to meet the needs adequately as the operational constraints vary widely from one use to another.

3. SIGNAL FORMS

The new recorder must be far more versatile than its predecessors in the variety of signal forms that it will handle, as the broadcaster is rapidly moving away from simple monophonic audio and NTSC video in the directions of multi-track digital audio and component video in both analog and digital forms, to obtain better quality, more flexibility and to prepare for component broadcasting via DBS. The interfacing needs for analog audio and NTSC video are well known, but in need of the improvements noted in section 4.

The interfacing requirements for digital audio, and component video are currently under close scrutiny in SMPTE, EBU, AES and CCIR and final standards are likely very soon. There remain many questions, however, regarding such things as audio/video synchronization, time-code in video and audio forms, ancillary signal processing, test signals etc which will take some time to solve. Broadcasters are participating in these discussions and generally envisage a recorder with a high quality video track, four audio tracks and a utility data track that are usable through interchangeable interfaces with the various signal forms. The recorder format could be simplified by making a 2:1 track relationship between component signals and composite NTSC signals and simple integer (e.g. 10:12) ratios between the track layout for 525 and 625 signals.

4. TECHNICAL PERFORMANCE

At the present time, video and audio quality at the broadcaster's studio output is set largely by the accumulation of impairments over several generations of recording in production, distribution and presentation, as cameras and terminal equipment are already essentially transparent. In the future, as the plant moves towards higher quality levels in video components, there will be increasing pressure to improve the recorder. As a practical objective, some broadcasters suggest that the majority of the studio output should be CCIR Grade 4.5 or better (on a 5 point quality scale) which must be achieved, in many cases, after six generations of recording currently and potentially ten in the future. While this is a long way from "total transparency", it is still a formidable task for the recorder designer when translated into permissable impairments at each generation. For instance the video signal-to-noise ratio must be at least 55 dB and the luminance K-rating cannot exceed 0.25 percent at each generation. Similarly, the audio signal-to-noise ratio must be at least 75 dB with non-linear distortion below 0.1 percent and very tightly-controlled frequency response.

It seems unlikely that such large performance improvements can be achieved using analog recording techniques at reasonable tape consumptions and costs, while retaining current operational features and adding new ones. It is clear there must be an increasing focus on digital recording techniques which can provide these levels of technical performance and offer also improvements in productivity, reliability and maintainability.

The new recorder must also offer high quality recording of data for time-code, production use, editing control, synchronization etc. While the broadcaster has little direct experience to set the objectives here, it seems likely that a data rate between 38.4 Kb/sec and 57.6 Kb/sec will be required with a corrected error rate less than 1 in 10^8. This again represents a significant design task for the new recorder, and lends further evidence to the need for a digital recorder. SMPTE and EBU have made good progress in the definition of a standard control interface for the VTR and this should also be incorporated into any new machine for the broadcasters plant. The technical performance of the new generation of recorders must be extremely good.

5. RECORDING MEDIA

From the broadcaster's viewpoint the choice of the recording media is not of direct concern. However, he will be looking for small size, cassette mounting, low cost, interchangeability, multiple sourcing, long mechanical life, freedom from drop-outs, archival stability, fast shuttling, over-write editing etc, all of which are directly affected by the choice of a tape media, its size, the packing density and record/ playback head selection. The choice of a tape media and the recorded patterns are key decisions in progress towards this new recorder and must be made on the basis of the priorities: - interchangeability, adequate operational margins, operational ease and reliability and good tape life. The broadcaster needs a machine that will do his job without any gambles involved.

5.1 Coating Materials

There are three basic contenders for the recorder, which will use a thin tape with long, narrow tracks. A tape thickness near that of Beta/VHS cassettes is foreseen (about 16-20 micro-meter - 0.6-0.8 mil). Based on 25.4 mm (1 in) tape, tracks likely would be 170 mm (6.7 in) long with a pitch of 45 micro-meter (1.8 mil). Coating choices include:

- Cobalt-Doped Gamma-Ferric-Oxide. This is the normal formulation for analog video-tape and hence it is well understood, backed by a great deal of experience and widely distributed. It has good freedom from drop-outs and a coercivity of about 700 Oersteds with achievable packing densities of 4-6 Mb/cm^2 (30-40 Mb/in^2).

- Metal Particle Tape. This technology is now at the early production stage for video applications and there remain concerns regarding head-wear tape wear and drop-outs to overcome. The coercivity is approximately 1400 Oersted and potential packing densities near 16 Mb/cm^2 (100 Mb/in^2) are reported.

- Evaporated Metal Tape. This technology promises very high packing densities but is essentially at the laboratory level currently. Its long-term performance is not clear.

Taking account of the broadcaster's priorities of reliable interchange, adequate operational margins and good tape life, it is clear that a design based on ferric-oxide tape has advantages and that future developments or the use of new tape formulations could add better margins, longer cassette durations and the like. Strategically, the introduction of a new recorder, bringing together new technologies and new unproven tape formulations seems an unacceptable combination of risks.

5.3 Tape Width and Cassette

The broadcaster's needs are for a workable cassette with a length of at least one hour, which is reasonable in size, weight and form while being usable in both automatic and manually loaded machines. In addition, the cassette must have long life, allow high-speed shuttle with the tape threaded and offer good mechanical protection.

Tape widths between 12 mm (½ in) and 25.4 mm (1 in) are attractive but the region 19 - 25.4 mm (0.75 - 1 in) gives the best combination of packing density, mechanical complexity and operational convenience, with a small advantage in shuttle-time and tape utilization for the 25.4 mm (1 in) width.

5.3 Track Pattern

Selection of a track pattern is a complex issue but the broadcaster's concerns are not the pattern itself but its operational consequences. The designer must consider particularly:

- Worst-Case Interchange. Track-following servos will almost certainly be required for this reason and to perform "stunt" modes such as picture in shuttle and slow-motion. (Stop motion will be from a frame store).

- Editing. Video and audio tracks must be editable independently and under worst case conditions. Track-following servos cannot be used to correct errors in record without some considerable complication.

- Audio. Audio data must be independently editable and will likely be recorded as time-multiplexed blocks at the ends of the video tracks. To provide timed pre-reading (for overlapped splices) the playback head must deflect over a number of tracks.

- Data Dispersion. To minimize the effects of head and tape related errors, spatially adjacent data words from the picture should be scrambled to non-adjacent positions on the tape, while noting the limitations imposed by high-speed playback. Multiple, parallel tracks containing several video blocks offers advantages.

There is a need for the reproduction of video, reference audio and time-code data over the full range of machine speeds. Suitable longitudinal tracks and coding schemes will have to be chosen.

The broadcaster needs a track pattern that meets these current objectives, offers good production flexibility and provides a vehicle for future growth. The choices of media, cassette and track details must be made soon and many broadcasters believe that there now exists enough data on the needs and appropriate technologies that this can now be undertaken.

6. PRODUCTION FEATURES

The list of production features to be found on any machine will vary from one version to another, as dictated by application. The essential requirement is that the tape format chosen, in conjunction with appropriate electronic processing should offer the desired range of features while still permitting low-cost small-size machines with minimum features and not unduly limiting innovative developments in the future. The format must then support:

- Basic record and playback of one video channel, four audio channels and a data channel with confidence playback in record mode.

- Independent editing of any combination of channels and editing between channels without timing or performance compromises with overlapped audio edits.

- Usable video and audio reproduction in shuttle mode, perhaps with audio derived from a longitudinal reference track.

- Slow-motion, video-only playback with good picture quality at selected speeds between −1 and +2 times play speed. Some speeds may be economically unfeasible in unsophisticated processors.

- Time-code recoverable in all modes. Editor to be referenced to time-code, data (source time-code), audio time-code or tape frame count (footage).

- Closely related versions of the format for 525 and 625 line standards and at $\frac{1}{2}$ and twice the 4:2:2 component standard data rate.

Many extra features in processing, editing and control can be obtained by suitable electronics and this is to be encouraged, as it keeps the basic tape format simple, and retains the concepts of compatibility and expandability, which are essential to the development of the new generation of recorders.

7. OTHER CONSIDERATIONS

The previous sections of this paper have addressed, from the broadcaster's viewpoint, the major points of the technology, the production requirements and the desired technical performance of the new recorder. It is useful to review some other related concerns that may have a bearing on the design and introduction of the machine, though not of the highest priority.

7.1 Human Concerns

There is a continuing need to simplify the operation and maintenance of television equipment so that there can be a greater concentration on the creative use of the medium and as equipment performance becomes better less intrusion by the limitations of the medium into artistic decisions. The current widespread use of $\frac{1}{2}$ in and $\frac{3}{4}$ in portable equipment in ENG and in production well illustrates this point. This new generation of recorders must continue and expand this concept. The machines must be completely operable by people skilled in production. Tapes must be in cassette format to avoid handling, threading errors and contamination. The machine itself demands stability, reliability, self-checking, on-line monitoring and diagnostics and user-oriented controls, driven by friendly software. There will exist a need for user-defined controls, readouts etc to customize the controls for the work at hand. The checking system must report in meaningful messages and be programmed to call the operator only when the problem needs a decision, taking internal corrective action when needed. The machine must deliver full performance by design and not substitute operator skills to overcome circuit short-cuts.

7.2 Maintainability

There is no doubt that the recorder will be a complex device, though much of this complexity will lie in replicated digital logic elements, and in software. Due to the digital nature of the machine, failures will tend to be catastrophic rather than the gradual impairments in performance encountered in analog machines. It will also be working in an environment where downtime can be very expensive.

There is an obvious need then for inclusion of self-test features in all paths of the machine and for an internal monitoring/ diagnostic system to check performance continuously, perform any possible control functions (e.g. Bit-swapping in memory) and to isolate and report fatal faults. The digital nature of most of the recorder, while a bane in complexity, is a blessing in simplifying the inclusion of these features.

7.3 Production Methods

It is likely that the introduction of the new recorder will make large changes in production methods, due to its high multi-generation capability and also due to the concurrent conversion of TV studio operations to components, in many cases using digital interconnection. Some significant development in recorder usage will then take place within the short period after its introduction and the designer must set aside some areas into which he can introduce the new features that evolve, without necessitating major redesign of the machine.

8. CONCLUSION

The New Generation Television Recorder is needed by the broadcaster soon and is, in fact, not a single machine but a family of machines sharing common tape formats and many components. The machines must offer very high levels of performance in the studio, in post-production and in distribution and be capable of working with the common signal forms of NTSC composite video, 4:2:2 component video and possible 4:1:1 or 4:4:4 component video signals in the future. It is clear that the machine performance, in both technical and production terms, can best be met using digital techniques and that the interchangeability and reliability aspects demand a very conservative approach to tapes and heads where technology changes slowly.

The broadcaster is not seeking video utopia. His needs continue to be high quality, flexibility, reliable tape interchange and predictable, reliable performance over long periods of time. We believe that the conclusions that are suggested in this presentation will be found to be a practical and realizable basis by which to measure the acceptability of the new generation of recorders in broadcasting.

Kenneth P. Davies is Assistant Director of International Engineering at the Canadian Broadcasting Corporation in Montreal, Canada, where he is responsible for technology planning and engineering liaison with external organizations. He is also Chairman of the SMPTE Working Group on Digital Video and of the sub-group on digital audio of the Working Group on Digital Television Tape Recording. He is a Fellow of SMPTE.

Marcel Auclair is Assistant Director of the Studio Systems Department at the Engineering Headquarters of the Canadian Broadcasting Corporation in Montreal, Canada. He is responsible for equipment development, planning and installation for the radio and television studio throughout the Corporation. He is active in the Working Group on Digital Television Tape Recording.

Tape Selection and Mechanical Considerations for the 4:2:2 DVTR

Yoshio Fujiwara, Kazuo Ike and Takeo Eguchi
Sony Corporation, Atsugi Plant
Atsugi-shi Kanagawa-ken, Japan

1. Introduction

During the past five years a large number of experimental DVTRs have been constructed each adding considerably to the knowledge of how to record high density digital video signals on magnetic tape. However, few of the published or demonstrated experiments indicated any progress in the development of the mechanics or tape. There are a number of reasons for this which may be summarized as follows:

- The initial concern was with the required record/replay performance and the signal processing.

- To design the final mechanism the essential prior information includes tape width, recording format and the nature of the tape to be used.

- Since the design of a completely new mechanism requires a large investment in engineering resources the development takes rather a long time. It did not make sense to develop individual mechanisms for the past experiments without the knowledge described above.

- The desirable tape properties have to be a compromise between the mechanical constraints, production costs and the limitations of the physics of recording. Additionally progress in tape development is constrained by the fact that it is difficult to forecast the quality of mass produced tape from experimental samples.

For these reasons, at least in Sony, all of the experimental DVTR mechanisms were modified standard products or constructed from standard piece parts. The mechanical structures and accuracy were far from ideal, but they did provide valuable basic information as to the needs of the final mechanism. Similarly the cassette design received very little serious consideration except as an extrapolation of known technology.

Recent progress in standardization of the 4:2:2 DVTR both in MAGNUM and SMPTE has clarified the outline mechanism and it is now appropriate to apply all of the present knowledge to the design of the final mechanism and tape. Recent discussions on these subjects in the committees have tended to be subjective, which is inevitable given the round table nature of the debates, and it is felt appropriate to make the design criteria clear from the manufacturing side in order for everyone involved in the DVTR format standardization to better understand the mechanical problems and their rationalization.

Therefore in this paper the following important topics which influence the

---

* General Manager, Video Products Div., Communication Products Group
** Project Manager of the DVTR, Video Products Div.
*** Principal Mechanical Engineer, Video Products Div.

final decision on the DVTR mechanical format are described.

- Selection of the tape material and its effect on the mechanical
  design

- Practical limitations on the tracking ability

- Relationship between the tape width and the following issues:

  a) Recording time
  b) Minimum allowable tape thickness
  c) Cassette size and weight
  d) Size of the tape transport
  e) Time required for full speed rewind or fast forward
  f) Loading mechanism and tape damage

2. **Tape Material**

The decision of which tape material should be adopted for the DVTR at this
moment is a sensitive issue, since there are three distinct possibilities,
each requiring different approaches either in recording technology or tape
handling the latter being in effect the mechanical design. As is now well
known, these possibilities are Evaporated Metal Tape, Metal Particle Tape
and Improved Oxide Particle Tape.

2.1 Evaporated Metal Tape

In fact the possible application of evaporated metal tape was indicated some
16 years ago [1][2]. However the physical characteristics and the
manufacturing process of evaporated tapes are totally different from those
of particle tapes. These seemed to be the major reasons why the use of
evaporated metal tape was not actively pursued. In addition, of course it
has some technial difficulties, among which is the requirement for a far
smoother surface to the base film.

As the thickness of the magnetic layer of the evaporated metal tape lies
generally in the range of $0.1 - 0.2$ µm, the unevenness of the surface of the
base film directly affects the performance of the tape in relation to the
frequency of drop-outs, spacing loss, modulation noise, and so on. The
output characteristics of evaporated metal tape have excellent properties at
shorter wavelengths as was reported in a paper submitted almost two years
ago [3]. During the last two years a continuous effort has been made to
improve some of the drawbacks and as a result, stable and good results can
now be obtained reasonably consistently in experimental batches. However,
the technology for evaporated metal tape does not yet seem to be totally
mature and the establishment of the mass production process is still a few
years away. Under such circumstances, despite its attractive capabilities,
it does not seem appropriate to assume the use of evaporated metal tape in
the standardization process.

2.2 Metal Particle Tape

Metal particle tape, on the contrary, has many similarities to oxide tapes
and the principal difference lies in the nature of the magnetic particle.
The manufacturing process and the characteristics are almost identical to
those for oxide tapes. At this moment metal particle tape is almost
completely developed though it has not yet been manufactured as a product,
except for audio use.

The only drawback which metal particle tape seems to have is that high magnetic fields and hence high currents are required for recording as well as for erasure. This may not be a problem if the frequencies involved are low, but if the frequency is high (for example 50MHz is already high enough) this requirement is a burden not only for ferrite heads used in recording but also for the recording electronics. In fact, Manganese-Zinc single crystal ferrite, which is the most popular material for both recording and playback heads, is not capable of generating the necessary magnetic field in the recording gap, and the ferrite saturates before it reaches the necessary strength for metal particle tape because of its low saturation flux density.

Various approaches have been made to overcome this problem, yet so far, the overall performance has not been satisfactory. Therefore metal particle tape also may not be an appropriate material to be assumed as a standard.

2.3 Improved Oxide Particle Tapes

Oxide particle tapes have been used for almost three decades in magnetic recording, initially for audio recorders and subsequently for both audio and video recorders. The manufacturing process is already well established, new investment may not be required and the durability has been confirmed up to very high head to tape speeds in the region of some 40 - 50 meters per second. The major shortcoming of oxide tape is generally recognized to be the poor output characteristics at shorter wavelength, particularly below 1.0 μm. However, if a completely new design of tape is allowed this poor characteristic can be greatly improved. An example of an improved characteristic for such a tape is shown in Appendix A. These tapes improve the bit error rate induced by noise and confirm as feasible assumptions the areal packing densities currently considered by MAGNUM and SMPTE.

The selection of an improved oxide particle tape, therefore, looks the most practical in the present situation.

3. Practical Limitations on Tracking Accuracy

Tracking is one of the most important subjects in the design of a VTR. Mistracking causes an increase of error rate in the case of digital VTRs. The causes of mistracking can be classified as follows:

3.1 Static Mistracking

3.1.a Misalignment of the control head and/or servo circuitry results in mistracking though the amount is generally constant and can be easily minimized in the initial machine alignment.

3.1.b Tape Stretch caused by changes in environmental conditions can also produce mistracking. In this case, the amount of the peak to peak mistracking is proportional to the track length, and it cannot be removed in a simple manner.

3.1.c Expansion in the mechanism particularly that between the scanner and the control head caused by changes in machine temperature induces mistracking. This can however be minimized either by placing the control head beneath the center of the helical track or by introducing some thermal compensation.

3.1.d Track non-linearity results in mistracking. This problem is not observed when the same head is used both for recording and replay.

However, once a different head or mechanism is used to replay the tracks recorded by another recording head, the effect becomes noticeable.

3.2 Dynamic Mistracking

3.2.a Deviation from the nominal tape width, in other words, tape slitting inaccuracy or edge curvature, can cause mistracking. The degree of mistracking is not constant in this case and varies from position to position on the tape and from machine to machine as well.

3.2.b Residual irregularities in linear tape speed or in drum rotational speed contribute to mistracking. However, the latter has much less influence because the high inertia created by a massive drum rotating at high speed tends to smooth out the rotational irregularity. Further since its effect is approximately proportional to the track angle, its influence is almost negligible in the range of angles under consideration by MAGNUM and SMPTE.

3.2.c Head vibration induced by dynamic imbalance in the head disk can cause mistracking. This becomes more critical as the drum diameter becomes larger or as the drum rotational speed increases.

Although all of the mistracking problems described above can be solved or alleviated if automatic or dynamic tracking is introduced, each of the possible causes of mistracking needs careful study so that correct functioning can be ensured even for worst case situations.

In considering the practical limitation on tracking accuracy, bearing in mind the above factors, a useful criterion is given by the formula:

$$\text{Tracking Factor} = \frac{\text{Track Width}}{\text{Track Length} \times \text{Drum Diameter}}$$

The larger the value of the tracking factor the easier is the tracking, or in other words, the safer is the format. The situation for some formats is as indicated in Figure 1 though most of them were not designed for professional use.

For the type C format the tracking factor is given by:

$$TF = \frac{130 \times 10^{-3}}{410 \times 134.6} = 2.36 \times 10^{-6} \text{ (for 525/60 version)}$$

$$= \frac{160 \times 10^{-3}}{410 \times 134.6} = 2.9 \times 10^{-6} \text{ (for 625/50 version)}$$

Assuming that this represents good practice, the MAGNUM discussion format has a tracking factor of:

$$TF(DVTR) = \frac{45 \times 10^{-3}}{170 \times 77} = 3.44 \times 10^{-6}$$

which is larger than that of the Type C format. Of course, the validity of this formula has to be further investigated, but the result of this calculation on the proposed DVTR format is interesting and encouraging. Hence although practical tests and measurements have to be completed before the final format is settled, 35 - 50 μm of track pitch seems to be a practicable range of values.

4.   Considerations in the Selection of Tape Width

The selection of the tape width is a very important issue when product viability is considered. In the following section, some relevant technical aspects are described:

4.1 Recording Time

In an open reel VTR the maximum recording time is a relatively free choice defined by the reel size with an assumed thickness of the tape and the necessary servo arrangements. The situation is very different for the cassette VTRs, the major factor arising from operational considerations. As cassette operation is convenient for most purposes, for example program origination, post production, broadcast transmission, archive retrieval and so forth, the variation in recording times, and hence in cassette size, are therefore wide ranging. Practically, these requirements can be realized by only a few different cassettes, though unfortunately not in only one size. As the cassette size will be examined later from a different standpoint, the balance between the longest recording time per cassette and the associated problems are examined here.

In a recent survey on the use of cassettes in DVTRs for studio use [4], it was indicated that 72 percent of usage could be covered by a nominal one hour cassette. However, even so it is important to note that 28 percent of usage calls for cassettes of longer recording times.

To accommodate these demands, leaving aside the idea of using multiple cassettes, three possibilities exist:

4.1.a Design the mechanism so that it is based on the largest possible cassette, or on a one hour cassette with additional facilities to accept larger cassettes.

4.1.b Use tape of standard thickness for the post production type of activity where high durability but not necessarily long recording time is required, and use thinner tape for longer recording times if for example the purpose is program storage, or less demanding operations such as broadcast transmission are expected.

4.1.c Have two different tape patterns available, possibly different only in track pitch and track width, and design the DVTR to be compatible for both formats. In so doing the wider track format could be used wherever tight tracking accuracy is required, whereas the narrower track version could be used for extended recording times. The transparency of the DVTR and the adoption of azimuth recording may make this approach particularly interesting.

In practice, a combination of these three possibilities is conceivable and this will be studied further in depth.

4.2 Minimum Allowable Tape Thickness

As described in the preceding section, employing a thinner tape can be a powerful method either to extend the recording time or to reduce the cassette size.

Such an approach has been freely used in both audio and video cassettes for domestic products. The fundamental questions are what is the lower limit of the thickness and what are the criteria for deciding this limit.

In fact there are only a few basic criteria in determining tape thickness.

The first is the long term stability resulting from tape stretch. The base material, which is usually PET, polyethylene-terephthalate, has a very high value of Young's modulus (typically 400 - 600 Kg/mm^2) and generally has satisfactory yield and breaking strengths.

The real problem is the slight amount of tape stretch which occurs when the tape is wound with a certain amount of tape tension on the take up reel and is then kept for a long time under some critical conditions. In such cases, the tape stretch which occurred in the winding is not reversible and becomes permanent [5]. As described earlier, this permanent tape stretch results in mistracking.

The second criterion is the partial stretch at either or both edge(s) or the tape which can be caused by excessive stress exerted on the tape by wrongly adjusted or incorrectly designed tape guides. This risk is generally highest during the rewind or fast-forward mode. In addition, in the case of a cassette VTR; the loading and unloading processes can induce similar stresses. These problems can be expressed in terms of the buckling force [6].

Figure 2 shows an example of the buckling force situation. In theory, if the friction force along a guide, which is perpendicular to the tape movement is sufficiently low, the buckling force **P** can be expressed as:

$$P \propto \frac{t^3}{w^2}$$

where **w** is the width and **t** is the thickness of the tape. In Figure 2 curve A shows the practical situation for Betamax (domestic use), U-matic (industrial use) and Type C (professional use). In curve B, only Betamax is indicated and points X and Y on the curve are extrapolated for 3/4 inch and 1 inch tapes respectively taking the same proportions as for curve A. The physical meaning of the difference between curves A and B is that if the same machine is used the stresses in the tape are higher for B, but the strength of the base material is different. In fact the base material for curve A is what is known as a "balanced base" whereas that for curve B is described as a "tensilised base" (which has strength mainly along the length of the tape) and typical values of Young's modulus are 400 Kg/mm^2 and 600 Kg/mm^2 respectively. Assuming similar basic technology and materials for designing a DVTR mechanism, if the thickness of the tape is chosen along the curves shown, then the degree of partial stretch as well as long term stretch can be maintained within the range that we have already experienced with current products.

The tensilised base has the highest value of Young's modulus amongst the base materials currently available in quantity at low cost. If, therefore, this base material is used, the lower limit on thickness for 1 inch tape can be about 20 μm whereas for 3/4 inch it can be about 16 μm (points Y and X respectively). A similar but broader analysis in the consideration of tape stress in VTR design has also been made by W. Fell in 1979 [7]. Hence the perceived advantage that wider tape will lead to smaller projected areas for cassettes is largely offset by the ability of narrower tape to be also thinner for the same buckling effect.

4.3 Cassette Size and Weight

Two users' surveys have been made [4][8] regarding cassette size, weight and recording time, yet no detailed analysis has been made and hence no clear answer been given by manufacturers.

Figure 3 shows an example of cassette proportions for 1/2", 3/4", and 1" tape widths.

It is true that if the same tape area consumption is assumed then the cassette based on wider tape occupies a smaller projected area because the tape is shorter. However, the projected area of the cassette is not proportional to the width for the following two reasons.

- The necessary radius of the reel is approximately proportional to the square root of the tape length.

- As described earlier, the wider tape calls for increased thickness.

Appendix B gives a more detailed mathematical analysis of the projected area of the cassette.

The projected area can be minimized by having only one flange at each reel. However, practically either physical or mechanical problems do not always allow such an approach to be taken.

(The U-matic cassette, specifically the 60 minutes size, is now with hindsight seen to suffer some of these drawbacks. Although many improvements have been applied since its debut in the early '70s, it still has inherent deficiencies in its structure and is now becoming old fashioned. It should be noted therefore, when reference is made to 3/4 inch tape in this paper, it applies merely to the tape width and does not refer to the U-matic cassette.)

The thickness of the cassette is the sum of the tape width and some constant value which is unrelated to the tape width and is mainly made up of the flange and cassette shell thickness taking into account the necessary robustness and mechanical accuracy required [Appendix C].

The weight of the cassette is the sum of the weight of the tape which is the dominating factor and of the weight of the supporting parts which is virtually independent of the tape width. The calculated ratio of weights of 64 minutes worth of tape for 1/2, 3/4, and 1 inch tape widths respectively, is given in Table 1.

Figure 4 shows some calculated results for the thickness, volume, and weight of a cassette for 64 minutes assuming the following conditions:

1) From curve B in Figure 2, the tape thicknesses are 12.2 μm for 1/2 inch, 16 μm for 3/4 inch, and 19.4 μm for 1 inch respectively.

2) 3 mm of the tape width in total is reserved for 3 longitudinal tracks.

3) The ratio of the fully wound tape diameter, called outer diameter and

indicated as **OD** in Figure 4, to the hub diameter (**ID**), is taken as 3.5 : 1.

4) The same tape consumption is assumed for each tape width. A tape consumption of 287 mm/sec by 3/4 inch is tentatively employed which is the value derived from the MAGNUM discussion format.

5) The calculated volume of the actual cassettes is given by the following formula.

$$V = \text{length} \times \text{depth} \times \text{height (all in mm)}$$

$$= (2 \times \mathbf{OD} + 15)(\mathbf{OD} + 10)(\text{tape width} + 13)$$

6) Details for calculating the weight of each cassette are given in Appendix C.

Mathematically, for one hour recording, the cassette having the smallest volume is that having a tape width just below 3/4 inch. Both 1/2 inch and 1 inch cassettes have larger volumes for the following different reasons. For 1/2 inch, the utilization of the tape width is worse than that for 3/4 inch because of the 3 mm reserved for the longitudinal tracks. For 1 inch tape, the projected area is not very different from that of 3/4 inch because of the two reasons previously given, whereas the thickness of the cassette is directly increased by the difference of the tape width, 1/4 inch or 6 mm. The cassette weight as shown increases continuously with the width of the tape.

The tendency of the curves for size and weight shown in Figure 4 remains similar even when the ratio of **OD/ID** is varied. Thus when considering the balance of requirements in projected area, weight and volume of cassettes, that based on the use of 3/4 inch seems to be the most reasonable compromise.

4.4 Size and Weight of the Tape Transport

The size of the tape transport is particularly important when a portable machine is considered.

In a portable VTR, the combination of cassette size and the area required for tape loading (including the scanner) almost completely defines the machine size at least in analog VTRs. Since the cassette size has already been analyzed in the preceding section, only the tape loading area is studied here. The calculated results are shown in Figure 5, assuming the loading mechanism illustrated in the same figure, which although different to that shown in Figure 9, is still based on the same concept.

It can be seen that within a practical range of wrap angle, wider tape always requires more loading area. In addition, if the same mechanical accuracy is desired, a larger mechanism needs tighter tolerances. To make matters worse, wider tape requires greater tape tension both in theory and practice, and to comply with this higher tension the mechanism must be even more robustly designed to be free from bend or twist which would degrade the mechanical accuracy. In consequence the weight of the machine increases as the tape becomes wider.

4.5 Time required for Full Speed Rewind

Unlike domestic VTRs, professional machines usually require fast rewind and fast forward for program search or in order to change the tape. However the situation may be different in the cassette VTR for the following reasons:

1) In cassette systems, the tape can be changed at any point of the program within a few seconds. Therefore, unless the purpose of rewind or fast-forward is to get to a specific portion of the program within a given short time, rewind or fast-forward does not have to be so rapid.

2) It is desirable to keep the reel size as small as possible in order to make the cassette smaller for a given recording time. On the contrary, it is desirable to make the hub size as large as possible in order to reduce rotational speed of the reel as it becomes difficult to control tape tension when the speed is too high. Although there are not many professional cassette VTRs on which to base a judgement, except those used for very short program segments with very quick access, it is likely that the former issue is the overriding factor at the expense of rewind or fast forward speed.

The wider tape in this issue has an advantage because the total tape length is shorter than that of narrower tape. Table 2 shows the results of approximate calculations of the time required to rewind one hour cassettes assuming 50 times normal speed for rewinding and neglecting the periods of acceleration and deceleration which may be of the order of a few seconds.

It is obvious that some of the figures in Table 2 are not realistic because even in the type C format the maximum tape speed in rewind is of the order of 12 m/sec with a tape which is as thick as 27 - 30 μm while all of the tape thickness in Table 2 are less than 20 μm.

Table 3 gives more realistic figures here assuming the maximum rewind tape speed to be 12 m/sec. As is seen in this table, the shortest rewind time is obtaind with a 1 inch cassette though whether this is sufficient to justify its choice is debatable when the other important factors are considered.

4.6 Loading Mechanism and Tape Damage

The design of the loading mechanism is the most unique and critical problem associated with a cassette VTR. The major technological difference between cassette and open reel VTRs exists in the degree of freedom allowable in the design. For example, in an open reel machine the take up and supply reels can, within limits, take up any position within a three dimensional space, whereas for a coplanar cassette VTR the reels must lie in a two dimensional plane. The situation is slightly different for a coaxial type cassette but similarly the degree of freedom is reduced. In a helical scan VTR, it is essential to wrap the tape around the scanner so that the loci of the head path creates the helical scan and this requires three dimensional alignment between the tape, guides and scanner.

If the positions, angles and directions of the two reels are totally arbitrary as in open reel VTRs, this problem does not exist and the necessary alignment can be established without making the mechanical design too complex, though it still requires careful deliberation. In the cassette system, there are two basic concepts for accommodating the three dimensional problem just described together with a two dimensionally constrained cassette. In principle, the requirement is to provide the necessary distance in height between the entry and exit guides in front of the scanner so that the proper helix angle can be obtained. One method is to tilt the scanner with respect to the cassette plane and adopt folding guides (either V or Λ shaped) as shown in Figure 6. In this case, the total friction would be increased by these guides because the need for tilting allows only fixed guides to be used. As an example the domestic VHS video recorder employs this concept.

The other method is to introduce a twist, taking sufficient distance between the scanner and the cassette to reduce the degree of twist per unit length on the tape, and to provide the necessary alignment around the scanner. The friction problem could then be alleviated by introducing roller guides instead of fixed ones. The drawback of this method is that time required for loading and unloading is greater than for the former method as the total length of the tape path is inevitably longer. However from another viewpoint this is not a disadvantage since the increased tape length between scanner and cassette allows better damping of vibration or irregular rotation of the cassette reels through the visco-elastic nature of the tape material.

In the following section some of the details of both loading methods are considered.

Figures 6, 7 and 8 show transparent views of the tilted scanner for 3/4 inch and 1 inch tape in each case and for 180°, 240° and 270° wrap angle respectively. Comparing these illustrations clearly demonstrates:

1) The tilt angle of the drum increases as either the tape or width increases and/or when the wrap angle increases.

2) The larger the tilt angle the greater is the difference between the tape positions associated with the loaded and unloaded conditions respectively.

In any event for this type of loading system the tape must be shifted either upwards or downwards along the surface of the scanner until the loading is complete. During this process the tape has to accept some differential stress, which occurs mostly around both edges, hence causing partial stretch or possibly even damage if the loading process is repeated many times at the same position. This drawback may be reduced by more sophisticated or complex mechanisms. In the case of the VHS recorder, because the tape width is 1/2 inch and the nominal wrap angle is 180°, this effect can be small and may well be harmless. The difference in the design objectives, domestic versus professional, may also endorse this loading method.

Figure 9 illustrates an example of the alternative loading method. Here the tape is first twisted between the two tape guides (1 - 2 and 5 - 6) and wrapped by the drum guides (3 and 4) around the scanner. As the necessary difference of the tape heights at the two drum guides is provided between the guides 2 - 3 and 4 - 5, it is not necessary to tilt the scanner itself.

The distance between the guides 1 - 2 and 5 - 6 is decided by the need to maintain the tape stress caused by the twist at both edges of the tape below a certain limit. The measure for this limit of the tape twist is generally expressed in terms of the number of degrees per centimeter or per inch. Based on this loading method, if the comparison is made between 3/4 inch and 1 inch tape widths assuming the same cassette and scanner dimensions, then theoretically the ratio of the distances between the guides 1 - 2 (L1) and 5 - 6 (L2) becomes 1 to 1.8 as shown in Figure 9.

It is important to note that the ratio of L1 to L2 remains constant even if the loading mechanism is quite different to that indicated in Figure 9 and further remains so for different ratios of cassette to scanner dimensions.

The following advantages may be observed for this loading method:

- The path taken during the process of loading becomes very close to that used in recording or replay. That is to say there is no requirement for any special stress to be applied to the tape during the entire loading/record/replay/unloading sequence.

- In constrast to the earlier method since each of the tape guides can be orthogonal to the tape movement, some or possibly all can be roller guides, greatly assisting in the reduction of friction.

As was described earlier, the overall length of the tape path based on this loading method becomes longer than for the tilted scanner method and this can be a drawback if the time required for loading and unloading is seemed to be very important.

The compromise therefore, might be some combined form. However, from the preceding description it is now clear that for both types of loading and unloading mechanism, narrower tape has advantages in tape damage, access time, and the space required for the loading and unloading.

Conclusion

In the consideration of the final mechanism to be used for the 4:2:2 digital component VTR the widest view possible should be taken of all of the applications for the format and a balance obtained between solutions to the conflicting problems.

Having established that improved oxide tape is likely to be the preferred recording medium for the first generation of machines and the limitations on the tracking accuracy obtainable with good mechanical engineering practice, the possibilities for machine and cassette size and weight become fairly closely constrained. From a restricted view, one inch tape has a clear advantage in terms of fast forward and rewind characteristics. Narrower tape has advantages in terms of smaller, lighter and more tolerant mechanisms though for half inch tape or less the fast forward and rewind times become a dominating disadvantage.

Taking all the factors into consideration it has been demonstrated that a tape width in the region of 3/4 inch is reasonably optimum in terms of recording time, size, weight and simplicity of mechanism and cassette, and in fast forward and rewind time.

It seems sensible therefore to choose 3/4 inch as a known width within the industry rather than any other. This would allow the widest application of the format given the presently accepted technology.

The recommended use of 3/4 inch tape should not be inferred to mean the use of the present U-matic cassette which as described is not capable of being further developed, and it is therefore appropriate to consider an entirely new design of cassette more suitable for use in a digital VTR.

Acknowledgements

The authors are greatful to Mr. K. H. Barratt, Technical Director of Sony Broadcast Limited U.K. for his valuable advices in writing this paper, and to Mr. S. Koriyama, Deputy General Manager of Communication Products Group, for giving them an opportunity to write this paper. They are also indebted to the engineers who actually computed and prepared the charts for this paper.

REFERENCES

[1] C.B. Pear, "Magnetic Recording in Science and Industry", published in 1967 by Reinhold Publishing Corporation, pp 73.

[2] D.E. Speliotis, "Magnetic Recording Materials", Journal of Applied Physics 38, 1967, pp 1207 - 1214.

[3] K. Ozawa and T. Eguchi, "Recent Developments in Tape Technology for the Digital VTR", Reference Report submitted to MAGNUM and SMPTE, Jan. 1982.

[4] Appendix to circular letter, "The use of cassettes with DVTRs for the studio", G243/3 of the EBU distributed to the members of specialist group MAGNUM.

[5] H. Watanabe, T. Asai and I. Ouchi, "Reversible and Irreversible Dimension Changes in Polyethylene-Terephthalate Film", Proceedings of the 23rd Japan Congress of Materials Research. Published by the society of Materials Science Japan, Kyoto, Japan, pp 282-286, 1980.

[6] This reference can be found in most books on basic mechanical engineering, e.g. "Mechanical Engineer's Reference Book" 11th edition, 1973. Edited by A. Parrish, published by Butterworth & e.g. Co Ltd, pp 7 - 49.

[7] W. Fell, "Concerning the Influence of the Elasticity of Magnetic Tape on Some Parameters of Magnetic Recording", Paper for the international conference on Video and Data Recording, 24 - 27 July 1979 at the University of Southampton, Hampshire, England.

[8] DIGITAL VIDEO TAPE CASSETTE PREFERENCE SURVEY Prepared by Digital Video Recording Study Group Sponsored by the SMPTE. Circulated April 1983.

Tape Width (actual)	Tape Thickness	Tape Lengh	Tape Volume	Relative Volume/Weight
1/2 inch (12.65 mm)	12.2 µm	1827 m	282.0 cm^3	0.84
3/4 inch (19.00 mm)	16.0 µm	1102 m	335.0 cm^3	1
1 inch (25.35 mm)	19.4 µm	789 m	388.0 cm^3	1.16

Table 1. Total and relative volume/weight of tape for 64 minutes.

Tape Width	Tape Length	Linear Tape Speed	Tape Speed during Rewind	Time required
1/2 inch	1827 m	476 mm/sec	23.79 m/sec	
3/4 inch	1102 m	287 mm/sec	14.35 m/sec	77 sec
1 inch	789 m	205 mm/sec	10.25 m/sec	

Table 2. Rewind time for 64-minutes cassette (at 50× normal speed).

Tape Width	Tape Length	Tape Speed during Rewind	Time required
1/2 inch	1827 m		152 sec
3/4 inch	1102 m	12 m/sec	92 sec
1 inch	789 m		66 sec

Table 3. Rewind time for 64-minutes cassette (at constant speed).

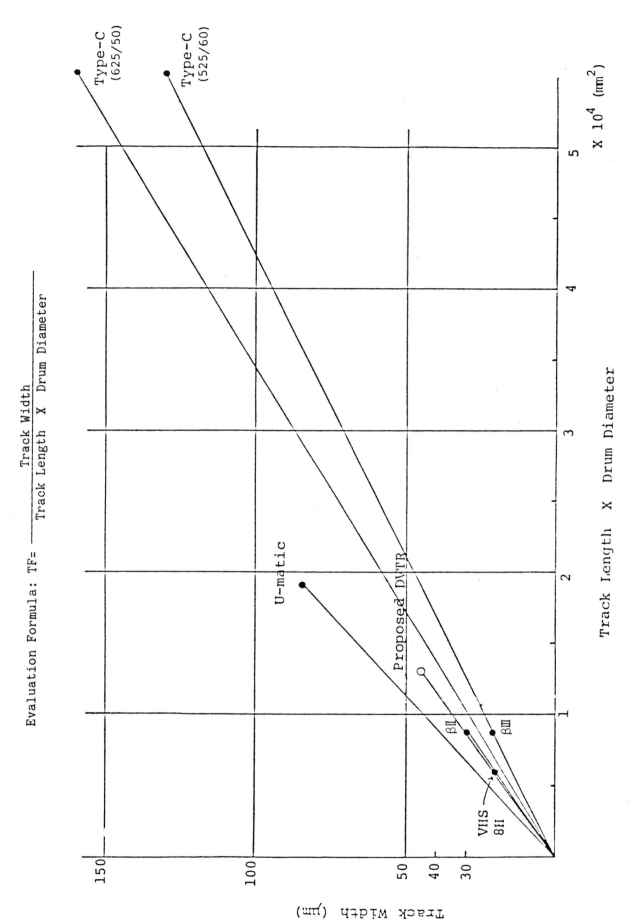

Fig. 1. Tracking Factors for Various Tape Formats.

Evaluation Formula: TF= $\dfrac{\text{Track Width}}{\text{Track Length} \times \text{Drum Diameter}}$

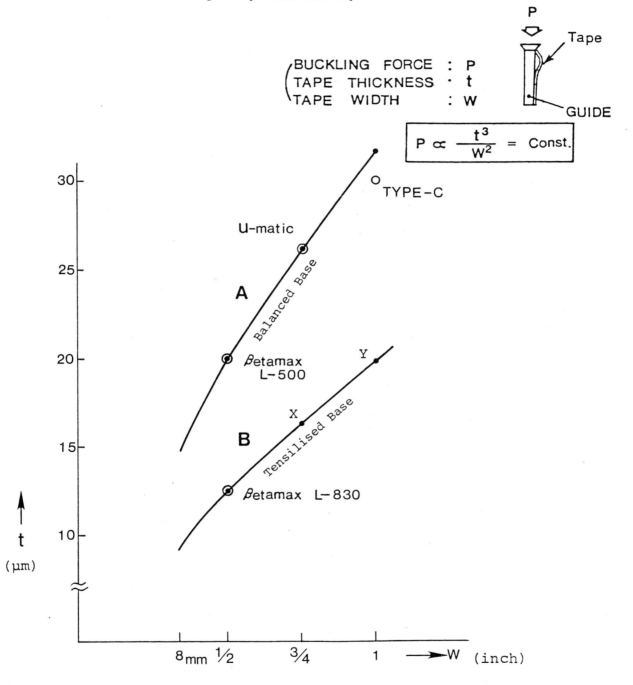

Fig. 2. Tape Width versus Tape Thickness.

BUCKLING FORCE : P
TAPE THICKNESS : t
TAPE WIDTH : W

$$P \propto \frac{t^3}{W^2} = \text{Const.}$$

Fig. 3. Cassette Proportions for Different Tape Width.

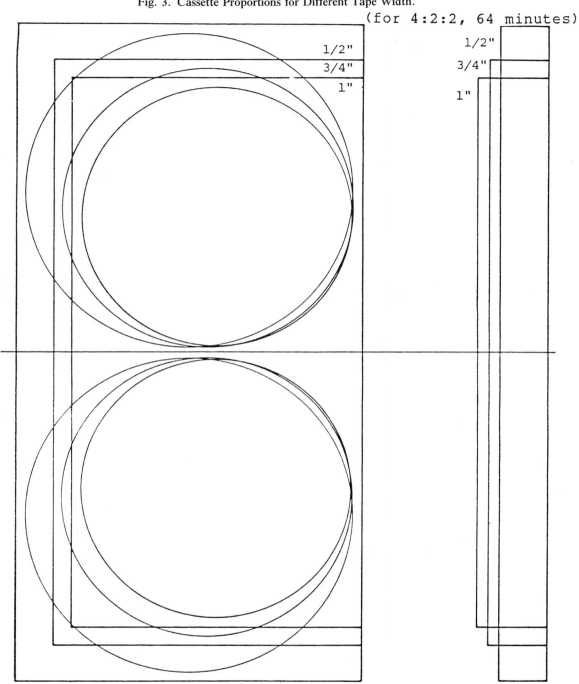

(for 4:2:2, 64 minutes)

Parameters assumed

Tape Width (actual)	Tape Thickness	Linear Tape Speed	Total Tape Length
1/2 inch (12.65 mm)	12.2 μm	476 mm/sec	1827 m
3/4 inch (19.00 mm)	16.0 μm	287 mm/sec	1102 m
1 inch (25.35 mm)	19.4 μm	205 mm/sec	789 m

Fig. 4. Weight and Volume of Cassette versus Tape Width.

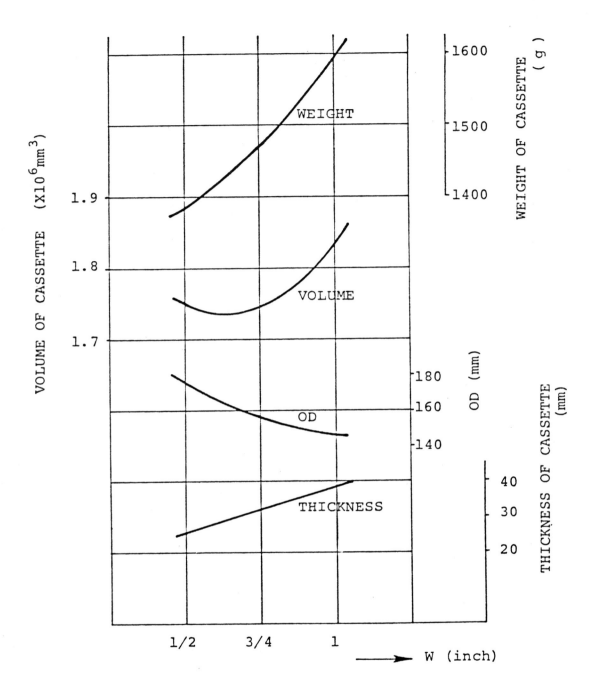

64 min CASSETTE

Tape thickness assumed:

1/2": 12.2μm, 3/4":16μm, 1":19.4μm

Fig. 5. Space Necessary for Tape Loading.

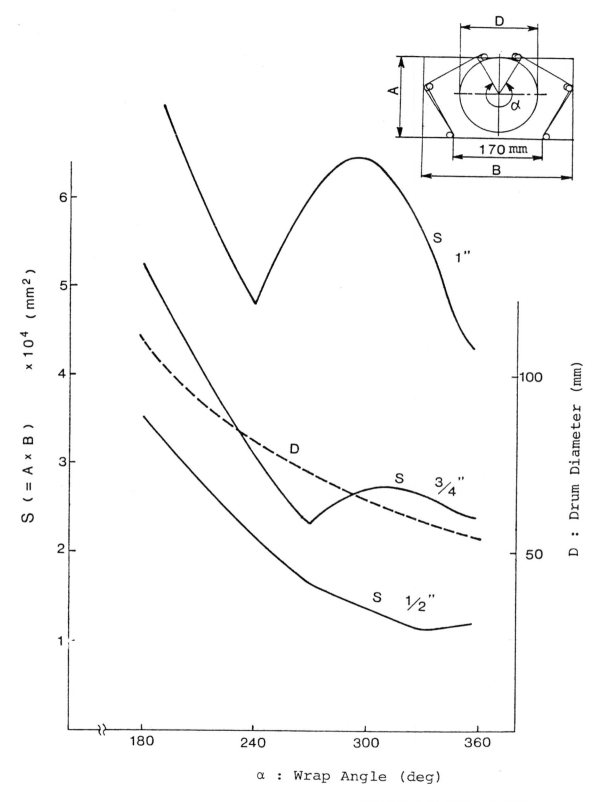

α : Wrap Angle (deg)

TRACK LENGTH : 170 mm

(As per MAGNUM discussion format)

Fig. 6. Aspect of Tape Loading and Tilted Scanner (180° Wrap).

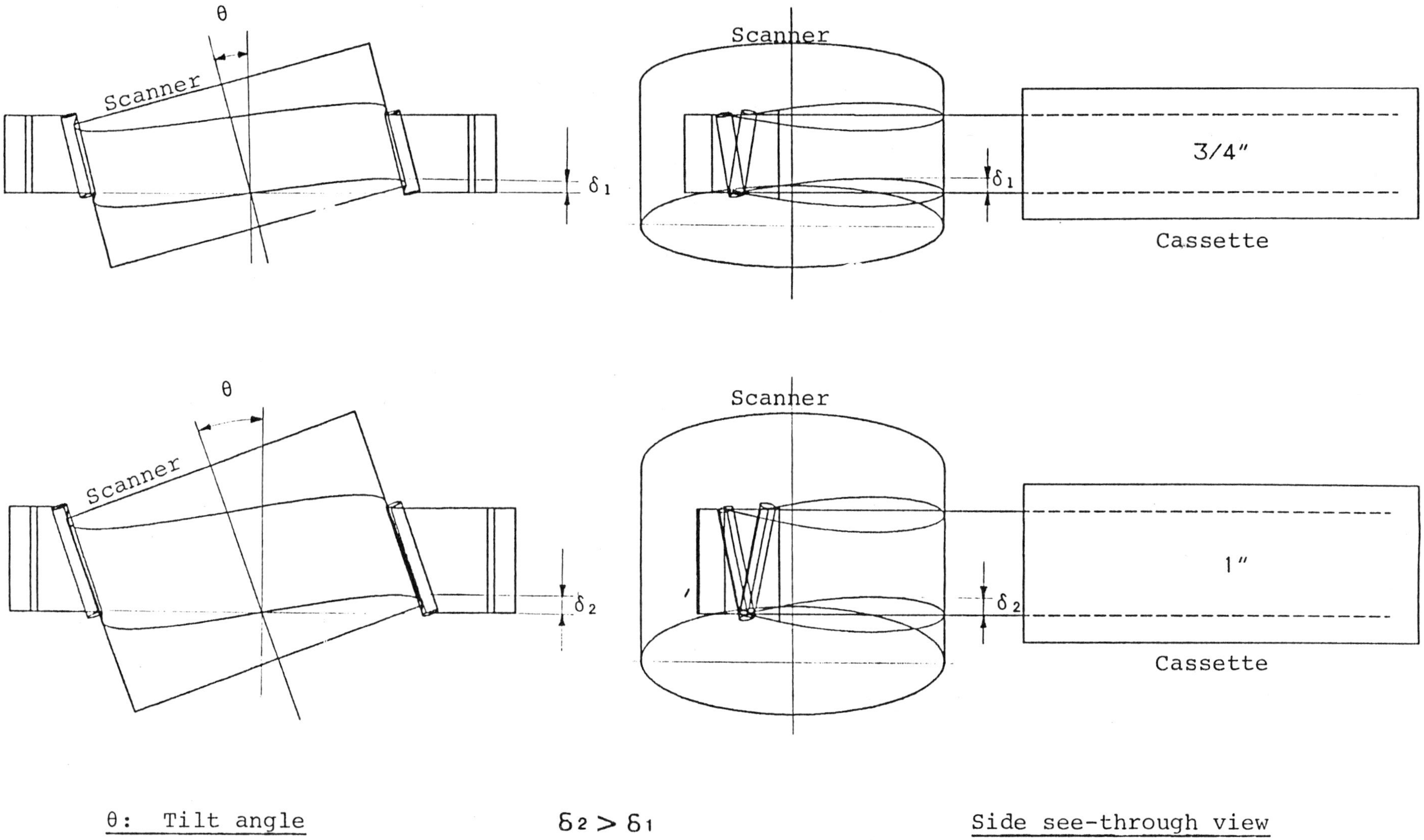

$\delta_2 > \delta_1$

Side see-through view

θ: Tilt angle

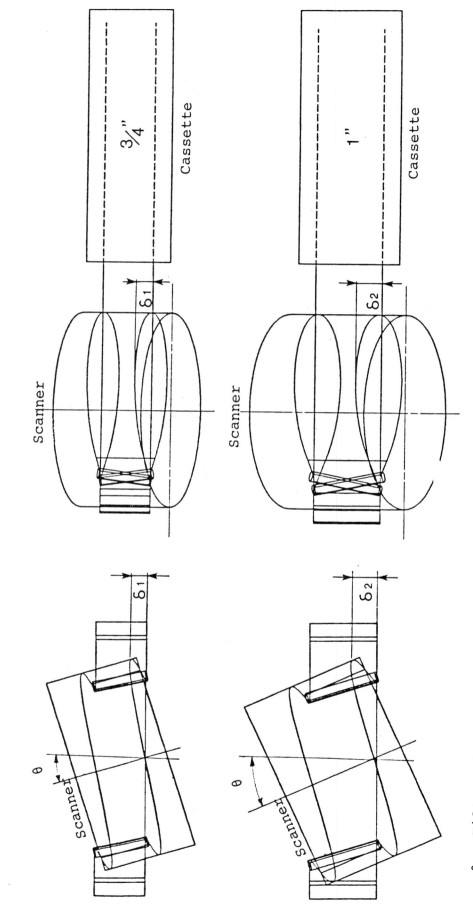

Fig. 7. Aspect of Tape Loading and Tilted Scanner (240° Wrap).

Side see-through view

$\delta_2 > \delta_1$

θ: Tilt angle

Fig. 8. Aspect of Tape Loading and Tilted Scanner (270° Wrap).

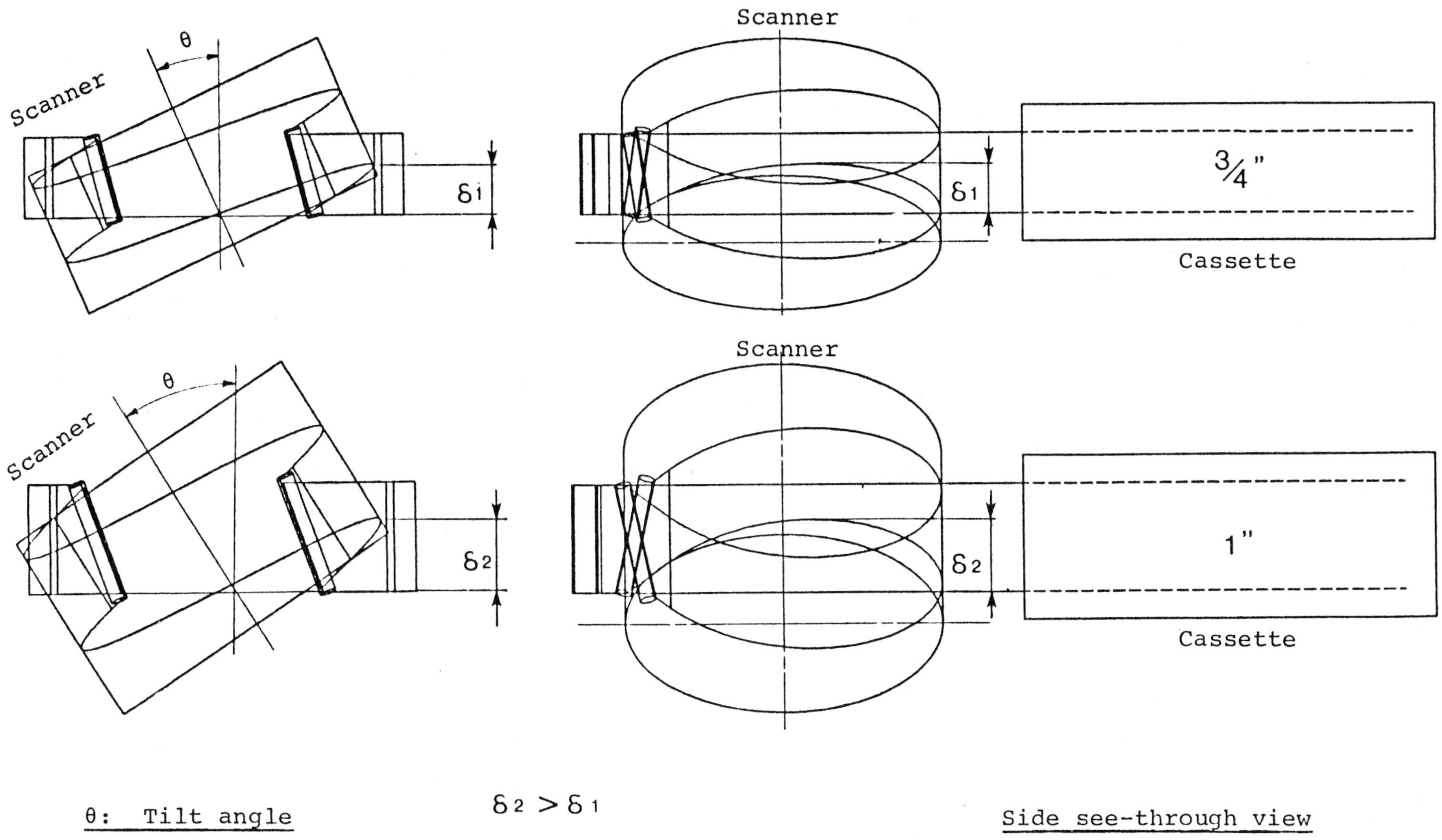

Side see-through view

$\delta_2 > \delta_1$

θ: Tilt angle

120

Fig. 9. Aspect of Tape Loading with Tape Twist.

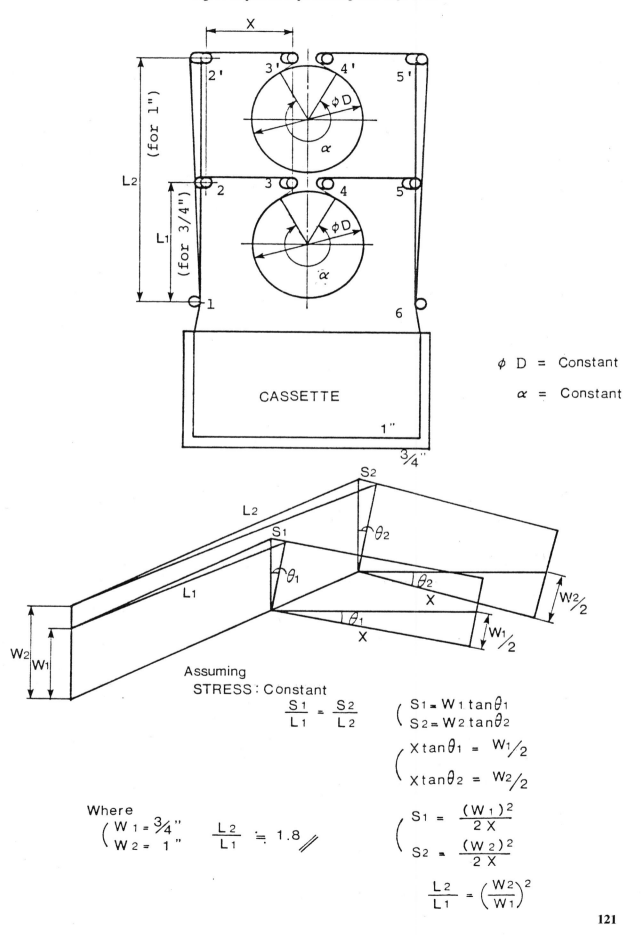

ϕ D = Constant

α = Constant

CASSETTE

Assuming
STRESS: Constant

$$\frac{S_1}{L_1} = \frac{S_2}{L_2}$$

$$\left(\begin{array}{l} S_1 = W_1 \tan\theta_1 \\ S_2 = W_2 \tan\theta_2 \end{array}\right.$$

$$\left(\begin{array}{l} X \tan\theta_1 = \dfrac{W_1}{2} \\ X \tan\theta_2 = \dfrac{W_2}{2} \end{array}\right.$$

Where

$$\left(\begin{array}{l} W_1 = \dfrac{3}{4}" \\ W_2 = 1" \end{array}\right. \qquad \frac{L_2}{L_1} \doteqdot 1.8 \,/\!/$$

$$\left(\begin{array}{l} S_1 = \dfrac{(W_1)^2}{2X} \\ S_2 = \dfrac{(W_2)^2}{2X} \end{array}\right.$$

$$\frac{L_2}{L_1} = \left(\frac{W_2}{W_1}\right)^2$$

Appendix A Aspect of Improvement on Oxide Tape

Appendix B   <u>Calculation on the radius of the reel</u>

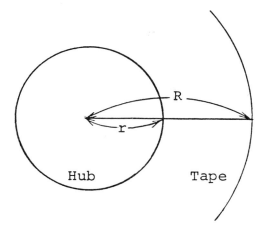

Hub   Tape

1) As the area occupied by the tape on the projected reel area is equal to the product of the tape thickness **t** and the total tape length **L**.

Therefore, $(R^2 - r^2) = t \times L$

$$R^2 = \frac{t \times L}{\pi} + r^2$$

2) Assuming **R = 3.5 r**,

$$R^2 - r^2 = R^2 \left(1^2 - \frac{1}{3.5^2}\right) = \frac{t \times L}{\pi}$$

hence, $R = 0.589 \sqrt{t \times L}$.

From Table 1 and by the formula obtained above, the value of the radius can be obtained as in the following table.

Radii of reels for 64 minutes cassette by different tape width

Tape Width	t	L	R	(Length of the Cassette)* (4 x R)
1/2 inch	12.2 µm	1827 m	87.9 mm	352 mm
3/4 inch	16.0 µm	1102 m	78.2 mm	313 mm
1 inch	19.4 µm	789 m	72.9 mm	291 mm

* The thickness of the shell, the space between two reels and the that required between the maximum tape diameter and the reel are all ignored. The actual cassette length, therefore, gets slightly longer.

Appendix C-1   <u>Calculation on the weight of a cassette</u>

Denoting   **Wc**: weight of a cassette

Wt: weight of the tape calculated by the formula given below,

Wr: weight of the reels calculated by the formula given below,

Ws: weight of the shells calculated by the formula given below,

Wc = Wt + Wr + Ws .

Each element of the mass can be further expressed as:

$$\textbf{Wt} = 2\pi[(OD/2)^2 - (ID/2)^2]W\rho_1$$

Where **OD**: outer diameter of the tape

ID: inner diameter of the tape

W: tape width

ρ_1: mass density of the tape

$= 1.55 \times 10^{-3}$ [g/mm^3]

$$\textbf{Wr} = 4t_1(OD/2)^2\pi\rho_2 + 2[(ID/2)^2-(ID/2 - t_2)^2]\pi W\rho_2$$

where t_1: thickness of the flange = 1.5 [mm]

t_2: thickness of the hub = 4 [mm]

ρ_2: mass density of the reel

$= 1.05 \times 10^{-3}$ [g/mm^3]

$$\textbf{Ws} = [ABC-(A-2t_3)(B-2t_3)(C-2t_3)]\rho_3$$

where   **A**: width of the cassette = 2**OD** + 15 [mm]

B: depth of the cassette = **OD** + 10 [mm]

C: height of the cassette = **W** + 13 [mm]

t_3: thickness of the shell = 2 [mm]

ρ_3: mass density of the shell

$= 1.05 \times 10^{-3}$ [g/mm^3] .

- continued to C-2 -

Appendix C-2 <u>Cassette structure assumed</u>

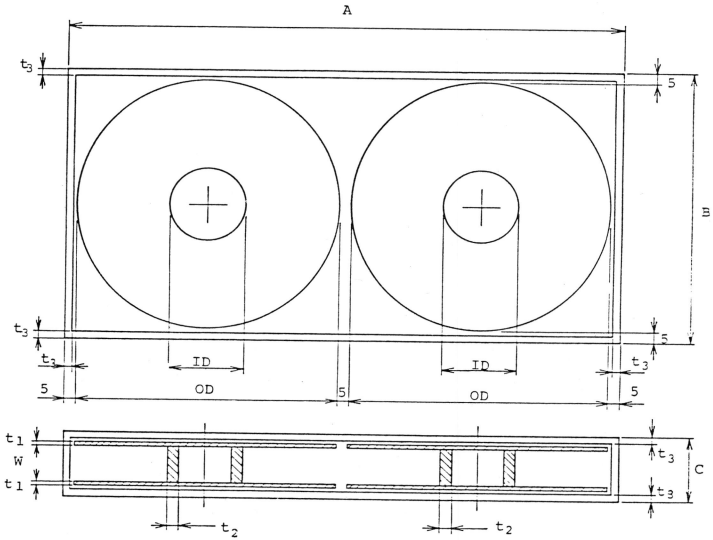

Yoshio Fujiwara received B.S. degree in Electrical Engineering from Tohoku University in 1961. Since the late 60's, he has been engaged in the development of a number of VTRs which include one-inch Type C VTRs and more recently the digital VTRs. Presently he is General Manager of Video Products Division of Communication Products Group. He is a member of the SMPTE and the Institute of Television Engineers of Japan.

Kazuo Ike received the B.S. degree in 1968 and the M.S. degree in 1970 in Mechanical Engineering from Keio University. He joined Sony in 1970 and was involved in the development of the process technology for magnetic tape manufacturing until 1972. Since 1973 he has been engaged in the development and design of the various VTRs which include BVH-500 and 1000, type C one-inch VTRs. He is presently Principal Mechanical Engineer in the Video Products Division.

Takeo Eguchi joined Sony after graduating from Tokyo University of Agriculture and Technology, where he received the B.S. degree in Electrical Engineering in 1967. Since 1978, he has been involved in Digital Video Recording Project in Sony and is presently the project Manager. He is a Fellow Member of the SMPTE and the Institute of Television Engineers of Japan.

Technical Choices for a Video Recorder

John P. Watney
Ampex Corporation
Redwood City, California

Introduction

Since the introduction of Video Tape Recorders there has been a steady improvement in technology which first went into improving picture quality as black and white gave way to color and low band to high band. When the 2" transverse recorder gave way to the 1" helical recorder the advance was not so much in picture quality, except for the elimination of segmented fields, but in economy and operational features. Variable speed reproduction and picture in shuttle are now so well established that users wonder how they ever managed without these features. The advent of affordable digital processing has added a bewildering array of capabilities to the producer's bag of tricks. It is also contributing to an awareness that the number of tape generations, which present VTR technology allows without significant degradation in picture quality, is not adequate for the effects being sought. In addition there is an awareness that a degradation in picture quality does not necessarily accompany storage and retrieval. The time is ripe for the definition of a new generation of Video Tape Recorders which offer more than just a marginal improvement in picture quality.

Digital technology promises a quality which is limited only by the data rate one is prepared to pay for, and computer systems have given digital recording a reputation of being free from errors and free from maintenance. It is natural, therefore, to look to digital recording for the new generation of video tape recorders. Digital recording has, however, had to wait for improvements in recording technology before it was able to offer a sufficiently high data rate at an economical cost. These improvements in technology have on the whole not been incorporated into analog VTR's. It is natural, then, to ask whether an analog VTR format could not be designed today which would offer the desired improvement in picture quality without incurring the cost and complexity commonly associated with an equivalent digital VTR. This paper will compare Composite and Component digital recording with a conceptual specification for improved analog recording. Comparisons will be based on picture quality, cost and utility.

The Digital Video Tape Recorder

Given appropriate error protection the picture quality in a digital system is fully determined by the initial digitization of the original analog signal. For a component system the standard has been set at 8 bit samples taken at a rate of 13.5 M samples per second for the luminance channel and 6.75 M samples per second for each of two chrominance channels. This standard allows virtually transparent coding and decoding except for the most critical picture material. DVTR standardization efforts on both sides of the Atlantic are converging on a strawman format, the essential details of which are compared with corresponding parameters from the "C" format in Table I. The product of head/tape speed and number of channels is 100m/sec. While not required by the format, practical considerations require 4 head channels. Both systems use 1" tape.

	DVTR STRAWMAN	"C" FORMAT
Track pitch (μm)	40	182
Shortest wavelength (μm)	0.9	2.5*
Number head channels	4	1
Head/tape speed (m/sec.)	25	25.4
Long. tape speed (m/sec.)	0.2	0.24

* WHITE LEVEL

Table 1. Comparison Between DVTR Strawman and C Format.

While no standard has been set for digitizing a composite video signal, it is generally recognized that 8 bit samples should be taken at either 3 or 4 times the color subcarrier frequency. As 3 times is marginally adequate for the video bandwidth requiring sharp cut off filters, and a sampling rate of 4 f_c is more convenient for processing, the rate chosen will be a compromise between tape cost and performance. If four f_c is chosen then the resultant sampling rate of 14.3 MHz for NTSC is only a little more than half the gross sampling rate for the component system. If the recorded wavelength is reduced to 0.85μm, the same basic recorder, but with half the number of heads, may be used for composite recording.

The Analog Video Tape Recorder

To be competitive with a DVTR the AVTR would have to be able to dub to 10 generations and maintain a quality at least as good as a first generation "C" format recording. This would require an improvement of at least 10dB in signal to noise ratio and a reduction by 20dB of any spurious components which add linearly. For the composite AVTR an improvement of greater than 10dB would be required of the chrominance signal.

In order to compare the advantages and disadvantages of analog recorders with the new standards being defined for digital recorders, we will first examine a format for component and composite analog recorders which attempts to significantly improve quality by making use of advances in recording technology which are implicit in the digital standards. These include the recording of shorter wavelengths on better tapes, better tracking which allows the use of narrower tracks, and processing which allows time expansion and contraction.

For the composite AVTR the signal to be recorded will be divided into two channels, one containing the odd TV lines and the other the even lines. Each line will be stretched by a factor of two to make a continuous signal of half the original bandwidth. An additional 7% of the bandwidth is saved by stretching the active part of each line into part of horizontal blanking. Using a grey level frequency of 16MHz and a deviation of ±3MHz, each channel is recorded into a separate 32μm track on the tape recorder. With a head to tape speed of 25 meters per second the tape consumption will be half that of a 'C' format recorder.

The component AVTR will record on four tracks in parallel. The luminance channel will be divided between two tracks as described above for the composite recorder and each chrominance channel will be recorded on its own track. The tape consumption will be approximately the same as that of a 'C' format recorder.

Table II list the factors which govern the signal to noise ratio of a tape recorder and compares the AVTR format as described above with the 'C' format and the format of the Ampex XVR-80, a special VTR, which is used for recording x-ray images. Each of the factors and its influence on signal to noise ratio is discussed briefly in what follows. The table assumes a 2½ MHz bandwidth for each channel. In order to achieve a 5½MHz luminance bandwidth and 2 3/4MHz chrominance bandwidths the tape speeds and FM frequencies for the component AVTR could all be scaled up by 10%.

	Reference Type 'C' System	XVR-80 Recorder	AVTR
Tape Channel Bandwidth (MHz)	15½	18 (−·6db)	29 (−2·7db)
Grey level carrier (MHz)	9	16	16
Grey level wavelength (μm)	2·8	1·6	1·6
Grey level spacing loss (db)	7·8	13·8 (−6db)	9·3 (−1·5db)
FM deviation (MHz)	±1	±2 (+6db)	±3 (+9·5db)
Base Bandwidth (MHz)	5·0	10 (−9db)	2·5 (+9db)
Line expand into blanking			7% (+0·9db)
Track width (μm)	128	128 (0db)	32 (−7db)
Improved tape			(+2db)
Total Relative Signal/Noise		(−9·6db)	(+10·2db)

Note: Number in parentheses are estimated S/N relative to 'C' format

Table 2. Factors in Signal-to-Noise Ratio.

Due to spacing and other losses the signal to noise ratio of a tape channel deteriorates rapidly as the recorded wavelength decreases. In a 'C' format recorder the optimum playback equalization results in a straight line response which goes through zero at between 16 and 17MHz. The resulting channel noise, before demodulation, has a nearly white spectrum. The integrated noise power is thus proportional to the channel bandwidth, which in this case is approximately 15½MHz, extending from 1 MHz to 16½MHz. It will be assumed that this proportionality holds true for the bandwidths chosen for the AVTR considered in this paper. The channel bandwidth required extends to include pre-emphasis overshoots for full black to white or white to black transients on the carrier plus sidebands for the base band frequencies. The amount of pre-emphasis used involves a trade off between several practical and theoretical considerations which will not be considered here. It will be assumed that the AVTR will use the same pre-emphasis of 8dB (2½x) as is specified for the 'C' format recorder and that the break point will be appropriately scaled. The component version could possibly benefit from a nonlinear pre-emphasis similar to that used on ½" component ENG recorders, but that will not be considered either. For a low frequency deviation from 13Mhz to 19MHz , a pre-emphasis of 8dB and an allowance of 2½MHz for baseband sidebands the AVTR will require a tape channel which extends from 1½Mhz to 30½MHz.

Within the 'C' format equalized bandwidth the carrier amplitude decreases linearly with frequency, but as the bandwidth is extended for the AVTR it will be assumed that the carrier amplitude falls off exponentially with the ratio of equivalent spacing loss to wavelength, in accordance with the Wallace model.

$$\text{Spacing loss} \sim \frac{\text{spacing}}{\text{Wavelength}} \times 55 \text{ dB}$$

For a 'C' format recorder the equivalent spacing is about 0.4μm. For the AVTR we will assume a tape, with the surface finish and high frequency response of that required for the digital recorders, which has an equivalent spacing loss of about 0.27μm. Another assumption implicit in the above is that the relative contribution of electronics and tape noise to the total noise remains the same as in present 'C' format recorders. This will require more careful design, the choice of devices with improved noise performance, and shorter gap lengths in reproduce heads, all of which are part of contemplated designs for digital recorders.

Other things being equal, the signal to noise ratio of an FM system is proportional to the deviation. Due to noise triangulation the noise power is proportional to the cube of the base bandwidth. Pre-emphasis can modify this to some extent, but as the pre-emphasis is appropriately scaled Table II assumes the cubic relationship. This relationship applies to the bandwidth reduction of 2x derived from multiplexing the signal between two tracks as well as the 7% reduction derived from expanding the active part of the line into part of the horizontal blanking.

The dependency of signal-to-noise ratio on track width is a function of the relative contribution of tape noise power, which is proportional to track width, and electronics noise power, which is independent of track width. With the improvements in electronics noise assumed earlier it will be assumed that tape noise is still the major contributor in a system with $\frac{1}{4}$ the track width of the 'C' format. Table II provides for a 7dB degradation in signal to noise ratio which allows 1dB for a greater contribution from electronics.

Not only do the tapes envisioned for the new generation of digital recorders have a better high frequency response, but they also have a higher absolute output due to a higher coercivity, and less modulation noise. An improvement of 2dB in signal to noise ratio has been assumed.

In Table II the column for the XVR-80 predicts loss of 9·6dB in signal-to-noise ratio, relative to a 'C' format recorder, which agrees reasonably well with the specifications for this recorder. Although it does not make use of narrower tracks or improved tape, this result does lend some credence to the prediction of approximately 10dB improvement for the AVTR. In addition to the simple improvement in signal-to-noise ratio the increase in modulation index by a factor of 3 is expected to reduce the chroma noise dependence on modulation noise by making the system less sensitive to dynamic equalization changes. The folded sideband corresponding to the significant 12th harmonic of the color sub-carrier is 55dB down in this AVTR format, so that moire' will not be a problem. Combining the above factors is expected to allow the 10th generation composite AVTR quality to be equivalent to the first generation 'C' format quality. As the chroma signal-to-noise ratio is still expected to be a limiting factor, the component version of this recorder might be expected to provide better quality over more generations, as well as providing all the processing advantages associated with a component signal.

A limiting factor for all analog recorders which does not exist for digital recorders is the requirement for the signal to pass through several low pass filters with each tape generation. The high carrier frequency and narrow base bandwidth relax the requirements for a very sharp cut off on the demod filter, and the sampling rate for the digital processing can be raised sufficiently to ease the design of anti aliasing filters. The cumulative effects of many filters in tandem is not expected to be a limiting factor.

Alternate Composite AVTR

For the composite AVTR an alternate, pseudo component multiplexing scheme can be considered which has the promise of offering better chroma quality at the expense of a higher tape consumption, better control of the base band transient response, and an additional tape channel. In this system the composite signal to be recorded is sampled at 3 times the color sub-carrier frequency and then distributed amongst 3 analog FM tape channels with each channel always receiving the same phase of samples. This has the advantage of converting the color sub-carrier into 3 DC components, the relative magnitudes of which define its phase and amplitude.

132

This removes problems associated with noise at the high end of the band, sensitivity to phase distortion, etc. In some sense this is equivalent to decoding the composite signal into chrominance components, but each component will contain many aliases, due to under sampling, which are only resolved (cancelled) when the components are resampled and recombined with the appropriate phase relationships after play back. In principle, each of the 3 components require a bandwidth of $\frac{1}{2}$ of the color sub-carrier frequency resulting in a gross bandwidth requirement of 5·4MHz. In practice real filters will require a greater bandwidth to avoid intersymbol interference between samples on each of the playback channels. Such interference will be inconsequential in picture areas with little detail, but will generate beat components and color shifts in areas with either luminance or chrominance detail. The same will hold true for time base errors but the absence of a color sub-carrier would make it feasible to use a pilot tone for time-base correction. The amplitude responses of the channels will have to be matched as in a component system. If an excess band width of 20% is allowed, for a gross bandwidth of 6.5MHz, and the three channel FM standards are appropriately scaled with a corresponding speed change, then the tape consumption for this pseudo component recorder will be 30% greater than for the composite recorder. The final recombined and bandlimited output signal will have a better signal-to-noise ratio.

Comparison between the DVTR and the AVTR

Table III compares estimates of the manufacturing cost of the AVTR and DVTR, both composite and component, with those for a current 'C' format recorder. It may be seen that approximately 50% of the cost of a studio VTR is independent of whether it is digital or analog, and also of the number of channels. The main reason for the rapid rise in cost of the analog recorders in the progression from one channel ('C' format) through two channels (composite AVTR) to four channels (component AVTR) is that each channel requires a digital time base corrector with codecs and velocity compensation. It should be noted that the composite DVTR does not include codecs which would be required if it were to be used in an analog environment. It is estimated that this would add approximately 4% to the cost.

ITEM	CURRENT 'C' FORMAT	AVTR		DVTR	
		COMPOSITE	COMPONENT	COMPOSITE	COMPONENT
(1) SCANNER	10	13	16	13	16
(2) TRANSPORT MECHANICS	9	9	9	7	7
(3) VIDEO ELECTRONICS	22	38	71	29	52
AUDIO ELECTRONICS	7	7	7	9	9
SERVO AND CONTROL	9	9	9	9	9
(4) FST	11	13	15	8	10
(5) PACKAGE, MDA, PWR SUPPLIES	29	24	24	24	24
CONTROL PANEL	3	3	3	3	3
TOTAL	100	116	154	109	130

Table 3. Percent of Costs Relative to Current C Format Total.
Notes:
(1) Scanner includes AST and heads.
(2) Digital transports have no longitudinal audio.
(3) Analog video electronics include TBC with A/D and D/A.
(4) FST of digital electronics, particularly audio, less than analog.
(5) VPR-2B higher because of separate TBC packaging.

A factor not taken into account in Table II is the effect of new manufacturing technology such as the use of VLSI. If the expected sales volume warrants the additional investment, then significant savings in production costs can be achieved, chiefly in digital electronics. It is estimated, for example, that the cost of the composite DVTR could be reduced by 23%, and the composite AVTR by 15%.

It may be seen that, contrary to a common misconception, the cost of a DVTR is not expected to be significantly different from that of present analog recorders. If a new format, higher quality analog recorder were to be designed along the lines presented in this paper, it would probably cost more to produce than the equivalent digital recorder.

The advantages that are associated with digital recorders are well known, so they will be only briefly mentioned here. Although the quality of the first few generations of analog pictures may be just perceptibly higher on critical material than that of a digital system, the AVTR could in no way claim to be transparent over many generations to the extent of a DVTR. Even in the first generation a DVTR will handle, virtually transparently, tape defects which would be noticeable on the AVTR. In addition, the proliferation of digital processing in other television equipment would benefit from the absence of codecs in an all-digital system. Within the recorder itself digital recording allows greater use of self diagnostics on the signal path. Monitoring of raw error rates can give warning of impending problems before they are serious enough to defeat error protection and become evident to the user.

There would seem to be very little to recommend a new generation of analog recorders. Even if all the interfaces, whether component or composite, were analog, the recorders themselves should still be digital.

Comparison between Component and Composite

The choice between component and composite recording is not nearly as simple. There is probably no single correct solution as a composite recorder would be correct in a composite environment and a component recorder would be correct in a component environment. Until fairly recently it was held by many that because final transmission to the user would remain composite for the forseeable future, and because of the substantial investment in composite production equipment, that the market for component recorders would never be significant. It was held that their use would be restricted to a very few specialist, top-of-the-line applications. The advent of component ENG recorders has however, seen growth at the opposite end of the picture quality spectrum with component switchers and other equipment being produced as the need arises. The same will no doubt occur at the top end as well, justifying the position of the SMPTE and the EBU. In large installations the change over to digital components will take place in one studio or in one editing suite at a time.

The facts of composite broadcasting and of investment in composite equipment in small installations will however not go away. The incentive to upgrade to the advantages of digital recording while maintaining compatibility with existing equipment will result in much pressure for a composite digital recorder. Compatibility is not the only issue. Composite recorders offer positive advantages to the broadcaster. Firstly, the cost of ownership is less in terms of purchase price, maintenance (head replacement) and tape cost. Secondly, a given size of cassette will run for twice as long on a composite recorder as it will on a component recorder. The longest cassette being considered, 7-1/2" X 13", will play for 3 hours using 1" tape or 2 hours using 3/4" tape on a composite DVTR. Many observers feel that the market for composite DVTR's will be larger, at least initially, than for component DVTR's.

The present trend in the DVTR standardization process will ensure the emergence of a component standard, but the interest in a mechanically compatible composite standard is not very strong. There are many, particularly in Europe, who feel that <u>if</u> there is to be a 1/2 rate subset of the standard it should be for a 2.1.1 component recorder, not a composite recorder. If the conclusions of the previous paragraph are correct, then those who would like to see a composite DVTR should make themselves heard.

John P. Watney was born in South Africa and received degrees in engineering and in physics from the University of Cape Town and an engineering degree from Stanford University. He worked at Marconi's Wireless Telegraph Co. in England and for the C.S.I.R. in South Africa before joining Ampex Corp., California, in 1964.

Perpendicular Magnetic Recording Technology

M. P. Sharrock and D. P. Stubbs
3M Company
St. Paul, MN 55144

Abstract

Perpendicular magnetic recording, in which the direction of
magnetization is predominantly perpendicular to the plane
of the tape or disk, is a relatively new technology that
promises information densities significantly higher than
those currently used. New recording media and heads are
being developed and impressive results can be demonstrated.
The head design and the proximity of the head to the
recording surface remain, however, factors of critical
importance to high-density information storage, just as in
conventional magnetic recording.

Introduction

The goal of research and development in magnetic recording
is to increase the information density stored on the
surface of tapes or disks. An increased density can be
used by the video system designer to achieve various
objectives; these include higher image resolution, a more
compact physical format, or the implementation of digital
technology.

Information density in magnetic recording is related to the
number of magnetic flux reversals, or transitions, per unit
area of the tape or disk and also to the detected
signal-to-noise ratio. This paper will deal only with the
goals of enhanced transition density and signal strength;
minimizing noise is an additional concern which involves
control of magnetic domain size and surface irregularities.

Conventional magnetic recording technology utilizes
magnetization directions that lie predominantly in the plane
of the medium, whether tape or disk, as shown in Figure 1.
Dramatic improvement in information density has come about
largely through improved head design together with the use
of media having higher coercivities and smoother surfaces.
The coercivity of a magnetic material is the field needed
to reverse the direction of its magnetization, and is
closely related to the stability of a high-density
recording pattern. Surface smoothness determines how
closely the recording or playback head can approach the
magnetic material. Figure 2 shows the progressive increase
in surface information density in various recording
systems. Figure 3 shows the advance of volume storage
density in video media over a period of 30 years.

An area of potential improvement in magnetic recording
media is the magnetization intensity of materials. Most
currently-used media are of particulate construction. That

is, they employ small discrete magnetic particles dispersed in a tough, flexible binder. The presence of the organic binder obviously dilutes the magnetization of the recording material, reducing the available signal strength. Advanced media, currently under development, use continuous thin films of magnetic metal alloys to achieve higher magnetization intensity and also exceptionally smooth surfaces.

With the increased attention to continuous films has come a strong interest in perpendicular recording (also called vertical recording) as a possible route to acceptable signal strength at higher densities than can be achieved by the longitudinal, or in-plane, method. Some thin metallic films, especially cobalt-chromium alloys, have ideal magnetic properties for perpendicular recording; moreover, the vertical mode is highly suitable for productively utilizing the high magnetization intensities afforded by the metallic films.

Figure 4 shows the differences between the two modes of recording and suggests the motivation for moving toward the perpendicular mode. In longitudinally recorded media, small magnetized regions are positioned with their like poles in close proximity and repelling each other; in perpendicular recording, the magnetized regions are arrayed with unlike poles together, an intuitively more stable situation.

The comparison can also be made from the point of view of the so-called "demagnetization" field, a self-generated internal field by which every magnet opposes its own magnetization (Figure 5). This field depends upon the magnet's shape, becoming stronger if the magnet is made shorter along its direction of polarization. The demagnetization field is proportional to the material's magnetization intensity, and so will become increasingly important if recording technology moves away from particulates and toward metallic films. In longitudinal recording, the self-demagnetization effect in each magnetized region is compounded by fields due to the nearest neighbors and, furthermore, becomes more intense as the recording density increases and the regions between transitions become shorter. Reduction of the magnetic coating or film thickness decreases demagnetization effects but also tends to weaken the signal. In perpendicular recording, however, the self-demagnetization effect in one magnetized region is opposed by fields due to its nearest neighbors and actually becomes weaker if the distance between transitions is made smaller compared to the coating thickness. Increasing the coating thickness thus tends to decrease demagnetization as well as to enhance signal strength.

Since the demagnetization phenomenon weakens with increased transition density in the perpendicular recording mode, one might expect that conversely it might become highly unfavorable at relatively low densities, where the distance

138

between transitions becomes large compared to the magnetic film thickness. This is true, but only at positions far from the transitions. The transitions themselves remain sharp and distinct and thus useful in systems of interest for video recording, where the information is contained in the timing or frequency of transitions. Thus a large useful bandwidth is available. If it is desired to record, using a direct analog format, a low-frequency signal such as the audio track that accompanies video, a pulse-width modulation scheme can be used [1].

Background

Perpendicular recording was first proposed and discussed decades ago [2, 3, 4], but the recent intense development began with the work of Iwasaki and co-workers [5-10] on cobalt-chromium films. This group also pioneered the use of a high-permeability metal film beneath the Co-Cr layer [7]; the composite structure provides magnetic flux linkage, which reduces demagnetization and enhances the effectiveness of the special head used [5, 7]. Numerous other laboratories have become active in developing Co-Cr media, both with and without the underlayer [11-15]. A variety of head designs have been used with these media. Figures 6A and 6B show the double-sided head and the dual-layer medium developed by Iwasaki and co-workers. Figure 6C shows a simpler perpendicular head; it is less efficient than the configuration shown in Figure 6A but requires access from only one side of the tape or disk. A conventional ring head can also be used with a perpendicular medium (Figure 6D); this combination has been found effective both by theoretical modeling [16] and by experiment [17] and has been incorporated into a practical flexible-disk system [18]. The ring head is a very sensitive device for reading signals, but questions have been raised concerning its effectiveness in recording truly perpendicular magnetization patterns [19, 20]. The use of two separate heads, a single perpendicular pole (Figure 6C) for recording and a ring head (Figure 6D) for reading, has been found to be advantageous in that it combines the perpendicular recording abilities of the single pole with the recording sensitivity of the ring. This arrangement gives a high output amplitude and requires access from only one side of the recording medium [19]. If one head is to be used for both recording and reading, then the ring head has a number of advantages. It apparently offers adequate recording performance, and when made with a very small gap has good reading sensitivity up to very high densities. Also, the technology of ring head design and manufacture is well established.

Current materials research for perpendicular recording involves continuous thin films other than Co-Cr [21-24] and also barium ferrite particles [25, 26]. The latter are dispersed in a binder and coated on a flexible backing as in conventional video tapes; they thus may have some economic advantages over continuous metal films, which are made by plating, sputtering, or vapor deposition. Efforts are also being made to produce recording tapes that have needle-shaped magnetic particles, similar to those used in conventional audio and video tapes, oriented perpendicular to the surface [27].

Proponents of perpendicular recording on Co-Cr claim not only a relative freedom from demagnetization effects [5] but also a magnetic microstructure that lends itself to sharp, well-defined magnetic transitions [6, 28]. Some longitudinally magnetized metal films, in contrast, have been observed to form jagged, "saw-tooth" transitions between regions of opposite magnetization [29-32]; this characteristic if applicable to longitudinal media generally would tend to limit transition sharpness and thus the achievable recording density. See Figure 7.

Despite the importance of demagnetization phenomena and magnetic microstructure, a major limitation on magnetic recording density is the inherent resolution with which the head can record or read. This resolution necessarily deteriorates with increased spacing between the head and the medium, although it also depends upon head design [33-36]. Head-to-medium spacing, which depends upon the smoothness of the recording surface, is a consideration that is common to perpendicular and longitudinal recording and may well prove to be the ultimate limiting factor in both.

While all methods of magnetic recording operate under limitations imposed by head-to-surface spacing, they need not be equally sensitive to this parameter. Experimental [37] and theoretical [38] studies have claimed that the use of a ring head with a perpendicular medium is subject to a stronger dependence upon spacing than that encountered with other head-medium combinations. The extra sensitivity to spacing appears to be involved in the recording, as opposed to reading, process. These findings do not imply that the ring head is undesirable for perpendicular recording, but they do emphasize the importance of spacing phenomena and the need for further research in head design.

Some Typical Results

Research and development work on Co-Cr films, as well as other advanced recording materials, was begun at 3M some years ago. Figure 8 shows a plot of output amplitude vs. transition density for a Co-Cr coated flexible disk, produced in a 3M laboratory. It was recorded and read with a conventional ferrite ring head of the type used in VHS video cassette recorders; performance is clearly superior to that of a disk coated with typical particulate material designed for VHS cassette tape, with respect to both the maximum output and the rate at which the output falls off with increasing density. Figure 9 shows results for the same media with an advanced video head of very small gap but still of conventional ring construction. The dependence of output amplitude upon density, at least out to 100,000 magnetic reversals per inch, is fit very well by a mathematical model based on that of Wallace [39]. This model takes account of head design and spacing from the medium, but not of self-demagnetization. Consequently, the performance of the Co-Cr medium appears to be largely limited by the head and by the quality of the head-to-medium contact. It must be stressed that the heads used are not optimized for the experimental Co-Cr film and in fact were designed to optimize the performance of the conventional video tape material with which the Co-Cr is compared. Much higher output amplitudes have been obtained from similar Co-Cr media through the use of special perpendicular recording heads [11, 19]. To put the densities shown in Figures 8 and 9 into perspective, a currently-used C-format professional video recorder operates at a maximum of about 26,000 magnetic reversals per inch and a VHS cassette recorder up to about 44,000.

An example of what could be accomplished using advanced recording materials may be drawn from the area of digital video. The data stream for broadcast-quality digital video is between 200 and 300 million bits per second. The linear density capability shown in Figure 9 could provide about 100,000 bits per inch, using an encoding scheme where each magnetic reversal transmits one digital bit of information. A track density of 2000 tracks per inch (which is entirely feasible) would then lead to an information density of about 200 million bits per square inch. The tape usage for digital broadcast video would thus be little more than one square inch per second, as compared with ten square inches per second for analog reproduction by today's C-format recorder. Advanced recording technology could bring the benefits of digital video and at the same time reduce tape usage, if densities already achieved in the laboratory are fully translated into practice.

Conclusion
The recording densities shown in Figures 8 and 9 for an experimental perpendicular recording material are significantly greater than those in current use, and are limited largely by the head's design and spacing from the surface. At the same time, however, thin film media designed for longitudinal magnetization are also being developed and tested at densities where the head and its spacing are significant limitations [40-41]. In yet another approach, advanced particulate media (made by conventional coating processes) are attaining recording densities that rival those of the thin film materials through the use of particles that effectively support magnetization in all directions [42]. These so-called "isotropic" media are designed to use a favorable combination of longitudinal and perpendicular magnetization. Advanced recording processes can thus exist on a continuum from pure longitudinal to pure perpendicular.

The perpendicular mode of magnetization appears to have some fundamental advantages, especially with regard to demagnetization effects, over the longitudinal mode at high densities. Fully realizing the potential benefits of these advantages, however, will require further attention to head design and spacing.

The competition beween the various modes of recording is to some extent a competition between the practical characteristics of the materials that make them possible. These characteristics include wear properties, chemical stability, and the economics of manufacturing. Also important are freedom from information "drop-outs", due to defects, and noise properties, which depend upon surface smoothness and magnetization structure. Almost certainly, no one material will be found best for all applications.

Advanced materials designed for perpendicular magnetization have achieved impressive recording densities in the laboratory and are now moving into practical applications. The first will apparently be in the area of disks for digital data [18]; only further development and extensive testing in the field will be able to determine the ultimate impact of materials such as Co-Cr upon video recording.

Acknowledgement
The authors wish to thank N. J. Kirchner, C. E. McCaskey, C. D. Moe, and L. D. Wald for assistance in preparation and testing of experimental media, as well as A. R. Moore for helpful discussions and information.

References
[1]   T. Fujiwara and K. Yamamori, "Perpendicular Recording of Analog Signals by Means of Pulse Width Modification," IEEE Trans. Magn., MAG-18: 1244-1246, Nov. 1982.

[2]   W. K. Westmijze, "Studies on Magnetic Recording," Philips Res. Rep., 8: 148-157, 161-183, 245-269, 343-366, Apr., June, Aug., Oct. 1953.

[3]   A. S. Hoagland, "High-Resolution Magnetic Recording Structures," IBM J. Res. Dev., 2: 90-104, Apr. 1958.

[4]   G. J. Y. Fan, "Analysis of a Practical Perpendicular Head for Digital Purposes," J. Appl. Phys., 31: 402S-403S, May 1960.

[5]   S. Iwasaki and Y. Nakamura, "An Analysis for the Magnetization Mode for High Density Magnetic Recording," IEEE Trans. Magn., MAG-13: 1272-1277, Sept. 1977.

[6]   S. Iwasaki and K. Ouchi, "Co-Cr Recording Films with Perpendicular Magnetic Anisotropy," IEEE Trans. Magn., MAG-14: 849-851, Sept. 1978.

[7]   S. Iwasaki, Y. Nakamura, and K. Ouchi, "Perpendicular Magnetic Recording with a Composite Anisotropy Film," IEEE Trans. Magn., MAG-15: 1456-1458, Nov. 1979.

[8] S. Iwasaki, "Perpendicular Magnetic Recording," IEEE Trans. Magn., MAG-16: 71-76, Jan. 1980.

[9] S. Iwasaki, K. Ouchi, and N. Honda, "Studies of the Perpendicular Magnetization Mode in Co-Cr Sputtered Films," IEEE Trans. Magn., MAG-16: 1111-1113, Sept. 1980.

[10] S. Iwasaki, Y. Nakamura, and H. Muraoka, "Wavelength Response of Perpendicular Magnetic Recording," IEEE Trans. Magn., MAG-17: 2535-2537, Nov. 1981.

[11] K. Yamamori, R. Nishikawa, T. Asano, and T. Fujiwara, "Perpendicular Magnetic Recording Performance of Double-Layer Media," IEEE Trans. Magn., MAG-17: 2538-2540, Nov. 1981.

[12] T. M. Coughlin, J. H. Judy, and E. R. Wuori, "Co-Cr Films with Perpendicular Magnetic Anisotropy," IEEE Trans. Magn., MAG-17: 3169-3171, Nov. 1981.

[13] R. Sugita, T. Kunieda, and F. Kobayashi, "Co-Cr Perpendicular Recording Medium by Vacuum Deposition," IEEE Trans. Magn., MAG-17, 3172-3174, Nov. 1981.

[14] S. Kadokura, T. Tomie, and M. Naoe, "Deposition of Co-Cr Films for Perpendicular Magnetic Recording by Improved Opposing Targets Sputtering," IEEE Trans. Magn., MAG-17: 3175-3177, Nov. 1981.

[15] T. Wielinga and J. C. Lodder, "Co-Cr Films for Perpendicular Recording," IEEE Trans. Magn., MAG-17: 3178-3180, Nov. 1981.

[16] R. I. Potter and I. A. Beardsley, "Self-Consistent Computer Calculations for Perpendicular Magnetic Recording," IEEE Trans. Magn., MAG-16: 967-972, Sept. 1980.

[17] B. J. Langland and P. A. Albert, "Recording on Perpendicular Anisotropy Media with Ring Heads," IEEE Trans. Magn., MAG-17: 2547-2549, Nov. 1981.

[18] K. Yamamori, R. Nishikawa, T. Muraoka, and T. Suzuki, "Perpendicular Magnetic Recording Floppy Disk Drive," IEEE Trans. Magn., MAG-19: 1701-1703, Sept. 1983.

[19] J. Toda, K. Kobayashi, and M. Hiyane, "A Thin Film Head for Perpendicular Magnetic Recording," IEEE Trans. Mag., MAG-18: 1164-1166, Nov. 1982.

[20] Y. Nakamura and S. Iwasaki, "Reproducing Characteristics of Perpendicular Magnetic Head," IEEE Trans. Magn., MAG-18: 1167-1169, Nov. 1982.

[21] K. Fukada, Y. Kitahara, F. Maruta, and J. Ezaki, "Co-V Films for Perpendicular Recording," IEEE Trans. Magn., MAG-18: 1116-1118, Nov. 1982.

[22] M. Matsuoka, Y. Hoshi, M. Naoe, and S. Yamanaka, "Formation of Ba-Ferrite Films with Perpendicular Magnetization by Targets-Facing Type of Sputtering," IEEE Trans. Magn., MAG-18, 1119-1121, Nov. 1982.

[23] M. Ali and P. J. Grundy, "The Domain Structure and Magnetic Properties of Co-Cr,Mo Films," IEEE Trans. Magn., MAG-19: 1641-1643, Sept. 1983.

[24] J. Desserre and D. Jeanniot, "Rare Earth-Transition Metal Alloys: Another Way for Perpendicular Recording," IEEE Trans. Magn., MAG-19: 1647-1649, Sept. 1983.

[25] O. Kubo, T. Ido, and H. Yokoyama, "Properties of Ba Ferrite Particles for Perpendicular Magnetic Recording Media," IEEE Trans. Magn., MAG-18: 1122-1124, Nov. 1982.

[26] T. Fujiwara, M. Isshiki, Y. Koike, and T. Oguchi, "Recording Performances of Ba-Ferrite Coated Perpendicular Magnetic Tapes," IEEE Trans. Magn., MAG-18: 1200-1202, Nov. 1982.

[27] D. E. Speliotis, "The Promise of New Particulate Media for High Density Recording," International Conference on Magnetic Recording Media, Ferrara, Italy, Sept. 1983.

[28] K. Ouchi and S. Iwasaki, "Perpendicular Magnetization Structure of Co-Cr Films," IEEE Trans. Magn., MAG-18: 1110-1112, Nov. 1982.

[29] N. Curland and D. E. Speliotis, "Transtion Region in Recorded Magnetization Patterns", J. Appl. Phys., 41: 1099-1101, Mar. 1970.

[30] D. D. Dressler and J. H. Judy, "A Study of Digitally Recorded Transitions in Thin Magnetic Films," IEEE Trans. Magn., MAG-10: 674-677, Sept., 1974.

[31] T. Chen, "The Micromagnetic Properties of High-Coercivity Metallic Thin Films and their Effects on the Limit of Packing Density in Digital Recording," IEEE Trans. Magn., MAG-17: 1181-1191, Mar. 1981.

[32] G. F. Hughes, "Magnetization Reversal in Cobalt-Phosphorus Films," J. Appl. Phys., 54: 5306-5313, Sept. 1983.

[33] T. J. Szczech and R. E. Fayling, "The Use of Perpendicular Head Field Equations for Calculating Isolated Pulse Output," IEEE Trans. Magn., MAG-18: 1176-1178, Nov. 1982.

[34] D. J. Bromley, "A Comparison of Vertical and Longitudinal Magnetic Recording Based on Analytic Models," IEEE Trans. Magn., MAG-19: 2239-2244, Sept. 1983.

[35] B. K. Middleton and C. D. Wright, "An Analytical Model of the Write Process in Perpendicular Magnetic Recording," IEEE Trans. Magn., MAG-19: 1486-1488, May 1983.

[36] I. A. Beardsley and C. Tsang, "Sharp Transitions in Perpendicular Recording," Magnetism and Magnetic Materials (MMM) Conference, Pittsburg, Nov. 1983.

[37] S. Iwasaki, D. E. Speliotis, and S. Yamamoto, "Head-to-Media Spacing Losses in Perpendicular Recording," IEEE Trans. Magn., MAG-19: 1626-1628, Sept. 1983.

[38] B. K. Middleton and C. D. Wright, "Perpendicular Recording," I.E.R.E. Conf. Proc., No. 54: 181-192, April 1982.

[39] R. L. Wallace, Jr., "The Reproduction of Magnetically Recorded Signals," Bell System Tech. Journal, 30: 1145-1173, Oct. 1951.

[40] Y. Suganama, H. Tanaka, M. Yanagisawa, F. Goto and S. Hatano, "Production Process and High Density Recording Characteristics of Plated Disks," IEEE Trans. Magn., MAG-18: 1215-1220, Nov. 1982.

[41] C. S. Chi, K. A. Frey, R. A. Johnson, and W. T. Maloney, "Experimental Studies of Longitudinal and Perpendicular High Density Recording," IEEE Trans. Magn., MAG-19: 1608-1610, Sept. 1983.

[42] J. U. Lemke, "An Isotropic Particulate Medium with Additive Hilbert and Fourier Field Components," J. Appl. Phys., 53: 2561-2566, Mar. 1982.

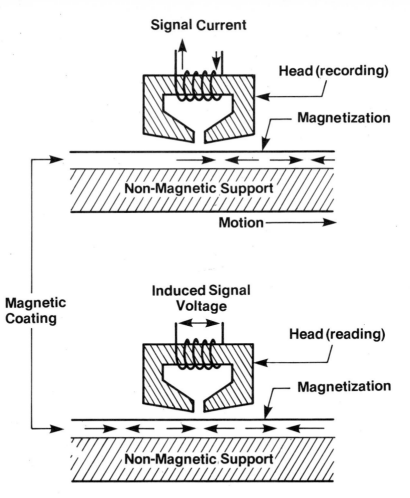

Fig. 1. The elements of conventional, longitudinal magnetic recording.

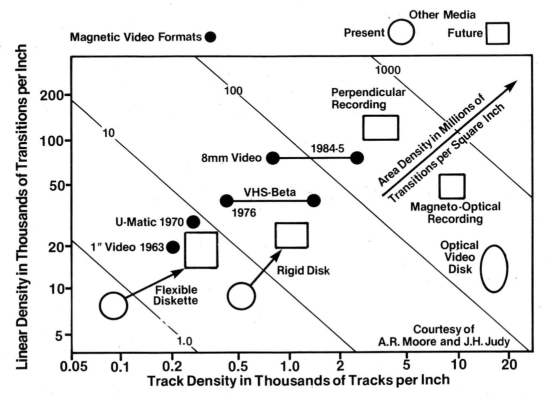

Fig. 2. Density of information on the surface of various recording media. Area density is the product of linear density and track density. A "transition" is either a magnetic reversal or the corresponding change in optical media.

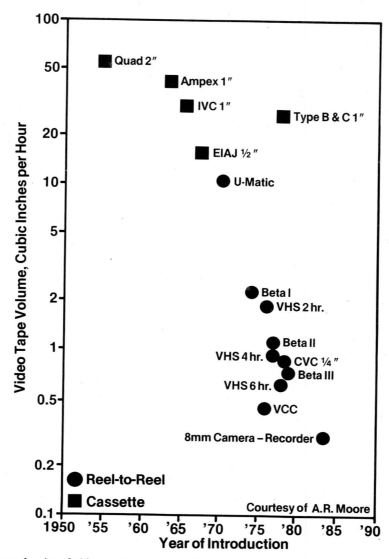

Fig. 3. Volume storage density of video media, expressed in terms of tape volume per hour of playback, plotted against year of introduction.

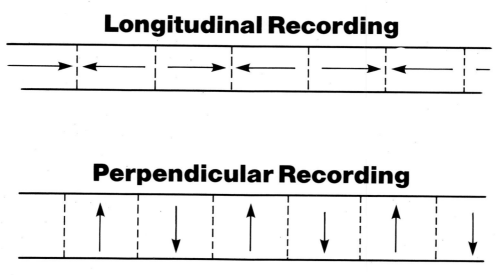

Longitudinal Recording

Perpendicular Recording

Arrows show direction of magnetization

Fig. 4. The geometries of longitudinal and perpendicular magnetic recording. For simplicity, only the magnetic coating is shown, without its support material.

A) Isolated Magnets

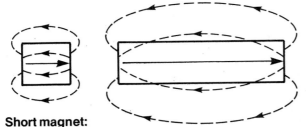

**Short magnet:
Strong internal field**

**Long magnet:
Weak internal field**

B) Very High Density Recording

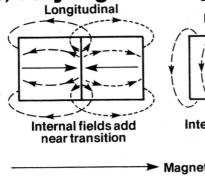

Longitudinal

Perpendicular

**Internal fields add
near transition**

**Internal fields cancel
near transition**

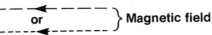

→ **Magnetization**

or } **Magnetic field**

Fig. 5.
A) The concept of the internal demagnetization field and its dependence on magnet shape.

B) The demagnetization fields in high-density longitudinal and perpendicular recording. Two adjacent, oppositely magnetized regions are shown for each method.

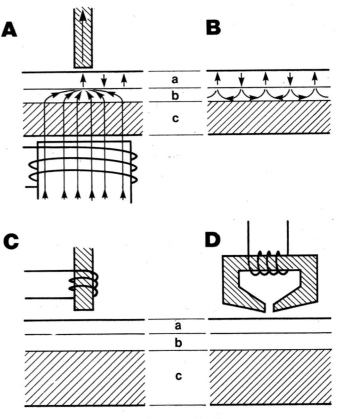

Fig. 6
A) Perpendicular recording head and dual-layer medium developed by Iwasaki and co-workers [5, 7], shown in the recording process. The recording field is driven by the auxiliary pole (shown below) and concentrated by the thin main pole via the high-permeability layer of the medium..

B) Dual-layer medium in the recorded state. The high-permeability underlayer adds additional stability to the magnetized regions by coupling the magnetization of oppositely polarized nearest neighbors.

C) Single-pole head used with dual-layer perpendicular medium.

D) Conventional ring head with dual-layer perpendicular medium. The high-permeability layer can be omitted for use with the ring head [18].

Arrows show direction of magnetization

a = Co-Cr
b = High-permeability alloy
c = Non-magnetic support

148

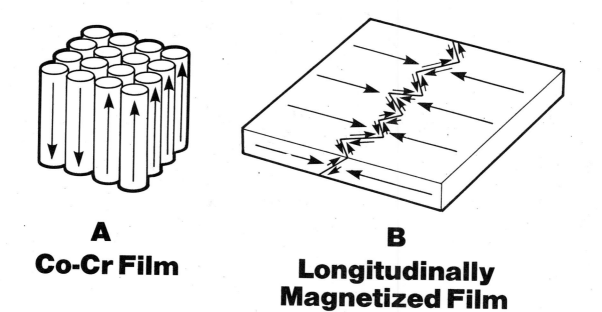

A
Co-Cr Film

B
Longitudinally Magnetized Film

Fig. 7.
A) Idealized diagram of magnetic domains in Co-Cr film, showing a sharp transition between upward and downward magnetization.
B) Simplified drawing of "saw-tooth" magnetic transition in longitudinally oriented film. Arrows show directions of magnetization.

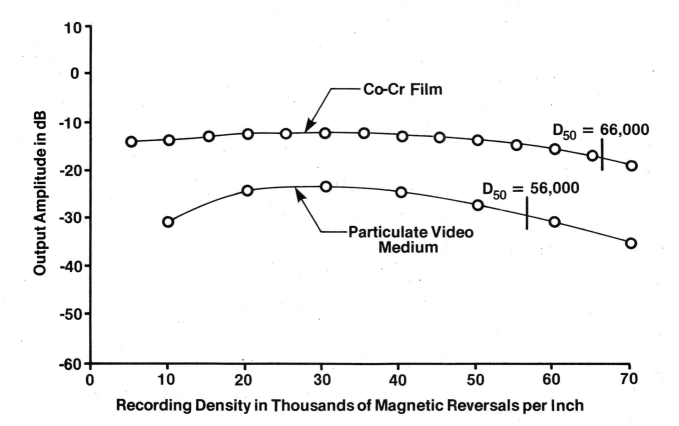

Fig. 8.
Plot of output amplitude vs. linear transition density for a dual-layer Co-Cr sputtered flexible disk (0.25 μm of Co-Cr over 0.50 μm of Ni-Fe on 2-mil thick polyimide film) and for a flexible disk using a conventional high-performance particulate material (particles and binder designed for VHS cassette tape). A conventional ferrite ring head (18 microinch gap) is used for recording and reading. The density marked D_{50} is that for which the output is a factor of two (6 dB) below the maximum; this is an approximate measure of the usable recording density. (For comparison in absolute terms with other results, the 0 dB level corresponds to 0.2 μV zero-to-peak output per m/sec per turn per μm of track width.)

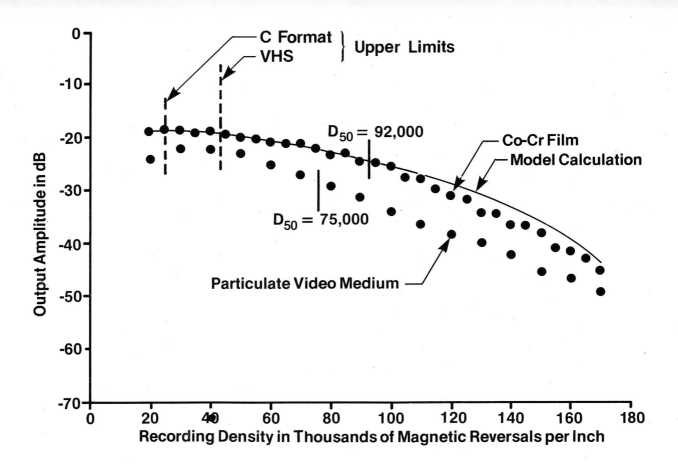

Fig. 9.
Plot of output amplitude vs. recording density, for the same media as in Figure 8, recorded and read with an advanced ferrite ring head having a 10.5 microinch gap. The smooth curve was calculated from a model based on that of Wallace [39] and reflects limitations due to the head's design and spacing from the medium, but none due to demagnetization in the medium. Approximate upper limits for the video recording densities used in the current professional C format and the VHS cassette format are shown for comparison.

Michael P. Sharrock was born in Columbus, MS, on January 25, 1945. He received the B.A. degree in physics from the College of St. Thomas, St. Paul, MN, in 1967 and the M.S. and Ph.D. degrees in physics from the University of Illinois, Urbana, in 1969 and 1973, respectively. His doctoral thesis was on Mössbauer spectroscopy of enzyme iron centers.

From 1973 to 1977 he was a Research Fellow in the Department of Biochemistry and Biophysics at the University of Pennsylvania, Philadelphia. From 1977 to 1979 he was an Assistant Professor in the Physics Department of Gustavus Adolphus College, St. Peter, MN. In 1979, he joined the Magnetic Audio/Video Products Laboratory of 3M Company, where he is presently working in the area of magnetic recording materials.

Daniel P. Stubbs was born in Minneapolis, MN in 1948. He received the A.B. in physics from Carleton College in 1970; the M.S. in 1971 and the Ph.D. in 1976 were received from Harvard University.

From 1976 to 1978 he was a Member of the Technical Staff in the Central Research Laboratory of Texas Instruments working on charge-coupled devices for imager applications. Since 1979 he has been at the 3M Company in St. Paul, where he is currently working on the testing of perpendicular recording materials.

Dr. Stubbs is a member of the IEEE Magnetics Society.

Developmental Trend for Future Consumer VCR's

Koichi Sadashige
Matsushita Electric Corp. of America
Secaucus, N.J.

INTRODUCTION

ENIAC, the first electronic computer developed by the University of Pennsylvania during World War II, is considered to be one of the ten most significant technical achievements of modern times. In fact, ENIAC has often been considered as significant a development as the harnessing of Nuclear Energy.

Today one can purchase an electronic calculator as powerful as ENIAC for approximately $30. They weight only a few ounces and fit in the palm of your hand. In comparison, ENIAC weighed approximately 30 tons and occupied an entire floor of a good size building.

In a shorter period of time, specifically since Ampex's demonstration of the first quadraplex video recorder in 1956, the technical art of video recording and the supporting electronic technology, has made equally astounding progress.

In 1983, 18 million video cassette recorders were produced world wide. The production rate of the VCR is approaching that of color television sets with both items essentially equal in cost.

Consumer VCR applications include, delayed viewing of on-air TV programs, home viewing of first run movies and amateur movie making.

What is the next stage of progress in video recording technology?

A color TV set is like an audio amplifier and a pair of loud speakers. It is the last link of the communications chain in the television medium. Audio amplifiers are fed by AM and FM radios, tape players and phonograph players. A color TV set, or more accurately a video monitor, must be fed by a variety of video sources. The VCR is just one of these sources. Conceivably, in time, every video monitor may have a VCR as a source input.

When the average household has upward of ten video monitors scattered around the house, as many VCR's may be in place. And such a time may arrive as early as the late 1980's.

The industry is preparing themselves for this next stage of VCR proliferation in households by developing a number of new product concepts. And, I would like to share with you some of the new development trends.

HIGH FIDELITY AUDIO SUPPLEMENT

Higher video recording density of modern VCR's are making the linear tape speed of VCR's even slower.

A slower tape speed, coupled with a relatively narrow track width allocated for longitudinal channels, makes high quality audio reproduction from a VCR a new technical problem.

Since the quality of video recording is being improved with the introduction of new video head materials and technology, the disparity between video and audio performance has become more apparent. To overcome these limitations, a totally new approach for audio recording was developed.

The approach utilizes FM audio recording by rotating heads. As shown in Figure 1 two FM carriers, 1.3 and 1.7 MHz for stereo recording were chosen. The two carriers are multiplexed to form audio FM channel which is recorded by two additional heads mounted on the rotating head wheel, as shown in Figure 2. Audio and video recorded tracks share the same area of the tape. The differences being that the audio head has a 30° azymuth angle in the opposite direction from the video head and its track width is narrower.

Since the audio FM carrier is approximately 1/3 of the video FM carrier frequency, the required head gap length is substantially longer. Narrower and longer wavelength audio tracks are recorded first and the wider and shorter wavelength video tracks are laid over the audio tracks. The longer gap length of the audio head enables recording to take place deeper in the magnetic layer than the short wavelength video FM recording. The video overlay recording, thus, does not erase the audio carrier to any significant extent.

The system block diagram in Figure 3 shows flow of video and stereo audio signals in both record and playback mode.

Full frequency range (20 to 20,000 Hz) reproduction and a dynamic range of 80dB are available from the system without any noise reduction scheme. Specifications are shown in Figure 4. The dbx noise reduction technique lowers the system noise floor by an additional 10dB, making the total available dynamic range to be 90dB.

SMALL DRUM VHS SYSTEM

The success of any video recording format in the marketplace depends greatly upon the high degree of interchangability among the recorders and recorded tapes. The VHS format for the consumer use, and its high quality deriviative, the M-Format for broadcast and teleproduction applications have been accepted widely throughout the industry because of their complete recorder/recroding interchangability.

Establishment of a single standard, either formal or defact in nature, sometimes impedes technological progress because a new entity must be compatible with current technology.

The overall external dimensions of a portable rotating head recorder depends greatly upon the size of the head scanner itself. Designing a new VHS recorder while trying to achieve a quantrum reduction in its size and weight represents an engineering challenge. A true technical innovation called the "extended wrapping technique" was developed by JVC engineers to overcome this problem.

Figure 5 shows this concept. In order to maintain the compatibility with the current VHS format, the track length, helical angle and all other format parameters must be identical. By wrapping the tape around a scanner to 270 degrees instead of 180 degrees, a smaller diameter scanner can be used while maintaining all format dimensions. The 41mm scanner has four heads instead of the two heads of a standard 62mm scanner. Recording sequences among the four heads are shown in Figure 6.

Lead angle, or the angle between the plane perpendicular to the head rotation and the tape guiding edge on the small diameter scanner, is adjusted so that the vertical displacement of the entire recorded track is exactly the same as the one made on a standard size scanner.

The physical arrangements of the tape transport system consisting of a 41mm scanner and VHS-C (VHS-Compact) cassette are shown in Figure 7.

8MM VIDEO RECORDING FORMAT - Background

In the late 1970's, Matsushita Electric and RCA jointly made the first serious attempt to develope an electronic equivalent of a motion picture camera. Their collaboration on this endeaver resulted with the introduction of the "RECAM" and "Hawkeye" video recording cameras in 1981 for broadcast applications.

The desire of the marketplace to have a consumer version of the video recording camera has led the industry to develop a new video recording format known as "8mm Video".

A relentless push to increase magnetic recording density in th 1970's has accellerated the developmental work on a new magnetic tape beyond what was known as the "high energy tape".

Chromium, or cobolt absorbed/absorbed, high energy Gamma Felex tape of 600 orstead variety has been the mainstay of video recording tape since the mid 1970's.

To increase the head output at a given wavelength, various attempts have been made to increase the coercivity of the tape. One approach has been to develop the metal partical coated tape. Figure 8 shows short-wavelength performance of various video types. The coordinate on 6MHz represents a recording wavelength of 0.6 micro meters at a writing speed of 3.75 meters per second.

At this wavelength, metal coated tape has an output 10dB higher than a conventional high energy tape.

Beyond this wavelength; the advantages of conventional metal coated tape diminish rather rapidly. This is due to the self-demagnetization effects caused by the relatively large thickness of the magnetic layer.

Properly manufactured metal evaporated tape, despite its lower coercivity, extends its short wavelength performance way beyond the metal coated tape because of a lack of self demagnetization.

The predicted reduction of tape usage per unit of time for the 8mm Video Recorder, as shown in Figure 9, depends on the application of the metal evaporated tape, or improved performance metal coated tape.

8MM VIDEO -- CONCEPT AND SPECIFICATIONS

Figure 10 shows the schematic view of the 8mm video tape format developed through cooperation of over 100 member companies of the special industrial committee. It is a worldwide standard applicable to both 525 line/60 field NTSC and 625 line/50 field CCIR television scanning rate.

Linear tape speeds are 14.345mm (.565") and 20.051mm (.789") per second for the respective two standards. 7.75 meter long tape held in the cassette provides 90 minute and 60 minute recording time respectively for the 525 and 625 line standards.

Video signals are recorded by using the time proven color under method.

As previously discussed, the problem of providing high quality audio reproduction at a linear tape speed of less than 1" per second from a tape with an ultra thin magnetic coating, is very difficult to overcome.

The problem has been solved by providing two alternate audio recording methods. Primary audio recording is done through FM and PCM technique by rotating heads. In addition, the format has provisions for two other longitudinal tracks for audio and cue channels. Rotating head FM carrier frequency allocations are shown in Figure 12.

Placement of the luminance FM carrier and the low frequency converted chrominance signal provides 2.2 MHz and 0.4HMz bandwidth capability for these two component signals. The audio FM carrier, located at 1.5 MHz, has an allocated deviation of plus minus 0.1 MHz.

An interesting technical feature of the 8mm video format is the automatic head tracking system with four pilot tones designated as f1 through f4, as shown in Figure 13.

The video head, with its track width slightly larger than the recorded track, picks up the pilot tone from both the right and left adjacent tracks. The capstan servo is driven to have the amplitude of the two hetrodyne tones generated by its own pilot tone and the adjasent track pilot tones sequal.

All pilot tone frequencies as well as the down converted chrominance carrier, are locked to the basic video scan rate in a relationship shown in Figure 14.

The pertinent components of the basic recorder/reproducer, and outline dimensions of a proposed cassette are shown in Figure 15 and 16.

SUMMARY

The 8mm Video Cassette Recorder, combined with a solid state or small diameter single tube color camera, is the first electronic image recorder system with the size and weight of an 8mm cartridge film motion picture camera. An alternate approach to further enhance the video quality of 8mm video, based on the time compression and expansion technique, is now being considered.

The introduction of digital color television receiver is expected in the near future. With this, the next logical development will be that of a digital consumer VCR to complement the transfer of TV receiver technology from the analog to digital domain.

Introduction of the 8mm VCR to the marketplace is not the end, but rather the beginning of a new era of consumer electronic technology.

Koichi Sadashige, a native of Japan, received his Bachelor of Science degree in 1947 from the University of Chiba. He attended the California Institute of Technology where he received his Master of Science degree in 1953. Until 1978, he worked for RCA Broadcast Systems, Camden, NJ in an engineering and engineering management capacity. While at RCA he was engaged in the development of color television cameras, video recording equipment, scientific instruments and optical systems.
In 1979 Koichi Sadashige joined Matsushita Electric Corp. of America as the Director of Engineering Development. At present, he is directing the overall activities of the New Technology Products Group, Panasonic Industrial Company, Secaucus, NJ. Mr. Sadashige has published 38 technical·papers in the United States, Germany, Great Britain and Japan. He is currently a member of the SMPTE Video Recording and Reproduction Technology Committee and on the Board of Editors for SMPTE. He was elected a Fellow of SMPTE in 1980.

VHS Hi-Fi Recording Spectrum

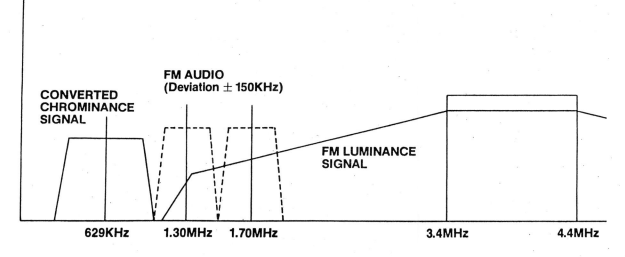

Fig. 1. VHS Hi-Fi Recording Spectrum.

VHS Hi-Fi Recording Format

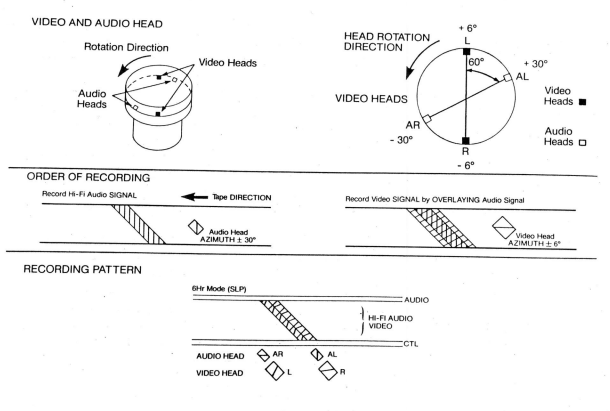

Fig. 2. VHS Hi-Fi Recording Format.

VHS Hi-Fi Recording System

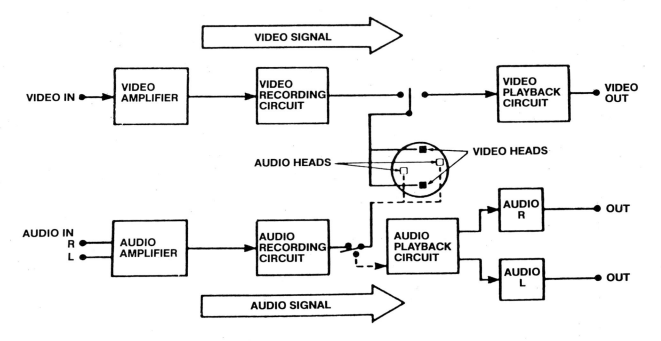

Fig. 3. VHS Hi-Fi Recording System.

Audio System Comparison Chart

	CONVENTIONAL VHS	**VHS HI-FI**
Audio Head	Stationary Head	Rotary Head
Recording System	AC Bias Recording	FM Azimuth Recording
Relative Head to Tape Speed	1 - ⁵⁄₁₆ I.P.S. (SP Mode)	228 I.P.S.
Noise Reduction	⫿⫿ DOLBY SYSTEM	HD dbx System
Frequency Response	50 - 12,000 Hz	20 - 20,000 Hz
Dynamic Range	50dB	More Than 80dB
Distortion	3%	Less Than 0.3%
Wow & Flutter	0.15%	Less Than 0.005%
Channel Separation	40dB	More Than 60dB

Fig. 4. Audio System Comparison Chart.

Standard and Small Drum VHS Scanning System

STANDARD VHS

SMALL DRUM VHS

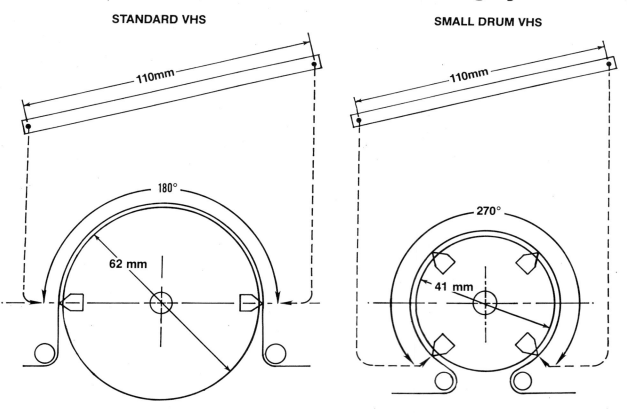

Fig. 5. Standard and Small Drum VHS Scanning System.

Small Drum VHS Head-Track Relationship

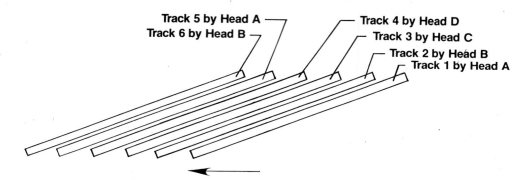

Track 5 by Head A
Track 6 by Head B
Track 4 by Head D
Track 3 by Head C
Track 2 by Head B
Track 1 by Head A

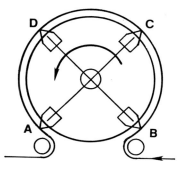

Fig. 6. Small Drum VHS Head-Track Relationship.

Small Drum VHS/VHS-C Cassette Tape Path Diagram

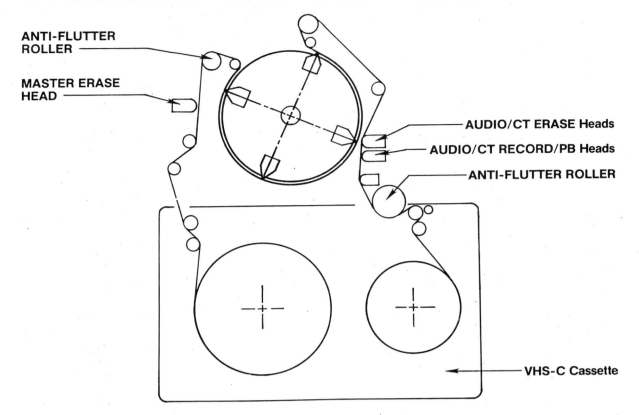

- ANTI-FLUTTER ROLLER
- MASTER ERASE HEAD
- AUDIO/CT ERASE Heads
- AUDIO/CT RECORD/PB Heads
- ANTI-FLUTTER ROLLER
- VHS-C Cassette

Fig. 7. Small Drum VHS/VHS-C Cassette Tape Path Diagram.

Tape and Recording Density
Metal Coated Tape and Metal Evaporated Tape

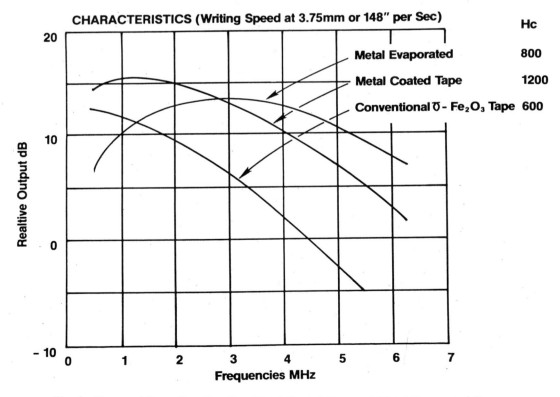

CHARACTERISTICS (Writing Speed at 3.75mm or 148″ per Sec)

	Hc
Metal Evaporated	800
Metal Coated Tape	1200
Conventional σ - Fe_2O_3 Tape	600

Realtive Output dB

Frequencies MHz

Fig. 8. Tape and Recording Density—Metal Coated Tape and Metal Evaporated Tape.

160

Trend of Magnetic Recording Density Improvement

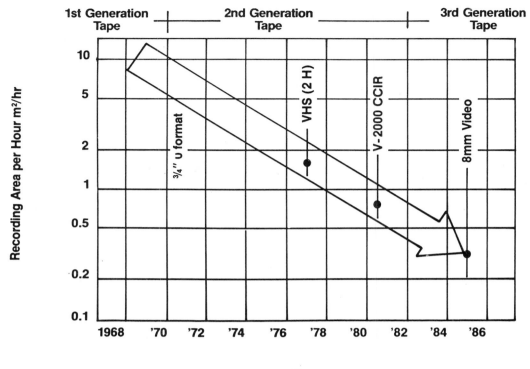

Fig. 9. Trend of Magnetic Recording Density Improvement.

Record Track Dimensions (1)

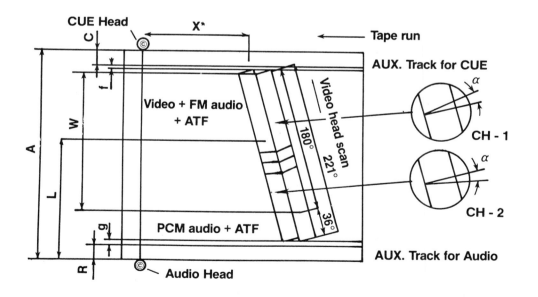

(Magnetic tape surface facing observer)
X*: Distance from CH - 2 video head 180° outlet point

Fig. 10. Record Track Dimensions (1).

Record Track Dimensions (2)

		Item
1.	(A)	Tape Width
2.	(V_t)	Tape Speed
3.	(Ø)	Drum Diameter
4.	(V_h)	Writing Speed
5.	(P)	Video Track Pitch
6.	(W)	Video Effective Width
7.	(L)	Video Track Center
8.	(T)	Video Track Width
9.	(C)	Auxiliary Track for CUE
10.	(R)	Auxiliary Track for Audio including optional Edge Guard (0.1)
11.	(f)	Video-to-AUX, Track Guard Width
12.	(g)	PCM Audio-to-AUX, Track Guard Width
13.	(Θ)	Video Track Angle (Tape stop)
14.	(Θ)	Video Track Angle (Tape runs)
15.	(α)	Video Head Gap Azimuth Angle
16.	(X)	Position of Audio and CUE Head
17.	(α_H)	H-Alignment

Fig. 11. Record Track Dimensions (2).

8 mm Video Cassette Recorder Format A Frequency Allocations

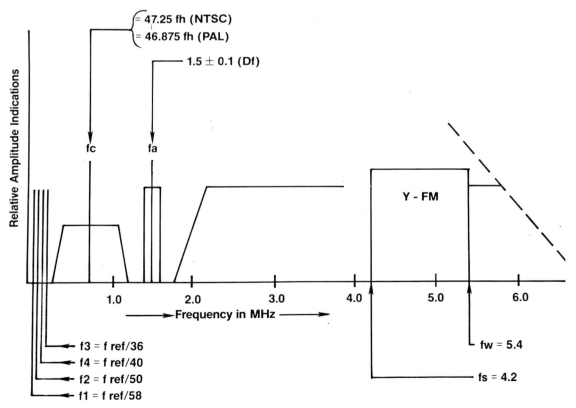

Fig. 12. 8-mm Video Cassette Recorder—Format A Frequency Allocations.

Head Auto-Tracking System

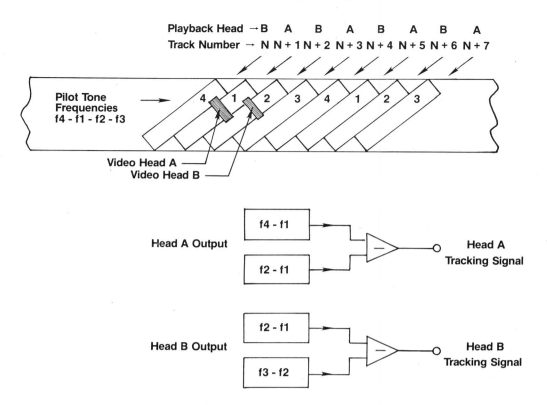

Fig. 13. Head Auto-Tracking System.

Record Reference Frequencies

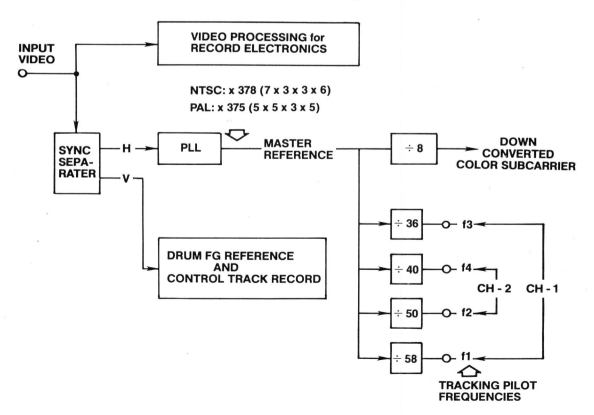

Fig. 14. Record Reference Frequencies.

Block diagram of recording NTSC or PAL color video signal

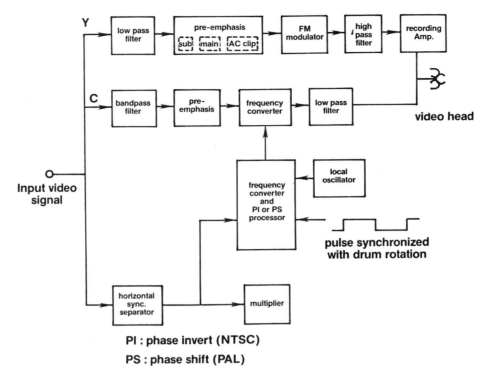

PI : phase invert (NTSC)

PS : phase shift (PAL)

Fig. 15. Block Diagram of Recording NTSC or PAL Color Video Signal.

Outline Dimensions / 8 mm Video Cassette

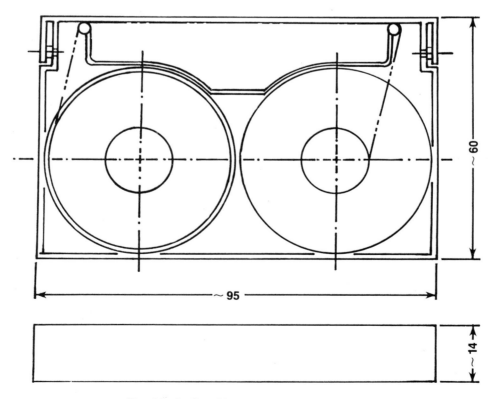

Fig. 16. Outline Dimensions/8-mm Video Cassette.

Optical Disc Technology for Permanent and Erasable Memory Applications

Koichi Sadashige
Matsushita Electric Corp. of America
Secaucus, N.J. 07094

and

M. Takenaga
Central Research Laboratory
Matsushita Electric Ind. Co., Ltd.
Kadoma, Osaka, Japan

INTRODUCTIONS

Use of a rotating disc as a means of storing analog or digital information offers one an indisputable advantage over a roll of tape. The advantage is, of course, the rapid accessibility to any part of the memory and the readily available means for indexing the information in storage.

One disadvantage of using a disc is the smaller amount of memory capacity in comparison to tape for a given physical volume. Unlike a roll of tape, the total memory surface of a disc must be protected by a jacket or a shroud, making it physically thick and thus less efficient as a vehicle for memory.

The recording density of magnetic memory has increased 1000 fold over the past two decades. In early 1960's the track pitch of a practical recording system was 20 mils. and the recording wavelength, or a flux reversal rate was about 2500 reversals per inch.

Today, the track pitch of 1 mil is not uncommon and flux reversal rate for a longitudinal recording is approaching 100,000 per inch. Experiments on vertical flux recording indicate that a flux reversal rate in excess of 200,000 per inch is now possible.

1 mil track pitch and 100,000 reversal per inch means a recording density of 100 mega bits per square inch. This very impressive density is a result of 20 years of relentless pursuit in the refinement of head material and fabrication technology, and magnetic media material.

Because of the head to media interface conditions, the best magnetic disc memory still operates at a recording density substantially lower than the tape memory.

During the course of pursuit for recording density improvements, alternative formats of recording, especially for disc recording applications, were examined extensively. Results of the search for an alternate medium for high density recordings, led to the development of the optical disc.

The area required for one bit of data on a optical disc, from the outset of optical recording development, was assumed to be only limited by the defraction limited laser beam spot size. A very high recording density in an order of 100 mega bits per square inch, thus, was believed to be achievable.

OPTICAL MEMORY DISC

Mass reproduced, read-only optical memory disc systems are currently operating at a recording density at or about 100 mega bits per square inch. Examples are "CD" Compact Audio Disc Players and Video Disc Players such as "VHD", "Laser Disc", and "Selectavision".

For broadcast and/or teleproduction applications, recording and playback capabilities are essential for the optical video storage system.

Early attempts for optical recorder/player systems were based upon a form of material transfer or removal.

Each recorded bit is a hole or a depression formed on a thin layer of inorganic or organic material coated on a glass or plexiglass platter.

Use of a high power laser for the formation of a hole or a depression on the platter makes this type of recording less energy efficient. Another basic limitation of this form of recording is that the process is irreversible.

DESIRED CHARACTERISTICS FOR AN OPTICAL MEMORY

The magnetic memory continues to be one of the most desirable forms of information storage devices. What we are looking for in an optical memory is, therefore, the characteristics of magnetic memory, combined with the inherent high density capability of optical storage means, as listed below:

1. In field record and playback.

2. Use of the same device or head for both recording and playback operations.

3. High energy efficiency

4. Environmental immunity of recorded and archieved material

5. In addition, the ability to re-record over a perviously recorded surface is highly desirable.

METAL-METAL OXIDE THIN FILM

To meet the aforementioned characteristics the form of recording must not entail physical alteration of the surface, but rather, alteration of its optical characteristics, i.e. the rate of optical transmission or reflection coefficients.

The laser beam should not evaporate and/or melt the material. It should be used as a means to heat the material and alter only optical characteristics.

For the best possible playback efficiency, the material should generate a high degree of optical property transfer before and after recording. The material should be a good infrared absorbant for high energy efficiency. For the long term integrity of the recorded information, the material should also be thermally stable and chemically inert. Of those organic and inorganic materials tested, metal-metal oxide of certain rare metals, i.e. Tellurium, Antimony, Germanium and Molybdenium are found to possess desirable properties. Figure 1 shows the change of light transmission property measured at a wavelength of 633 nanometers.

All test materials show an abrupt change in the transmission coefficient when heated to a certain temperature. Average level of oxygen content, shown by X, is always smaller than the stoichiometric value for the respective substance.

TELLURIUM-TELLURIUM OXIDE THIN FILM MEMORY

Because of a high degree of optical property transition with smaller amounts of infrared radiation, and overall superior thermal and chemical stability, Tellurium-Tellurium Oxide was determined to be the best material for both permanent and re-recordable optical memory.

Since the optical property of the material depends greatly upon the average level of oxygen content, X, selection of the proper level and accuract control during the manufacturing of the disc are both important.

The material has a greater depth of modulation (change of optical property) with a lower degree of infrared radiation when the X value is less than unity. Environmental stability of the material, however, is not optimum. At the X value of 1.1, modulation depth is somewhat decreased, but the stability of the recorded information is completely immune to environmental effects, a highly desirable characteristic. This is the selected value for both permanent and re-recordable memory material.

The memory layer is produced by a multi-source evaporation method as shown in Figure 2. By controlling the disc exposure time for pure tellurium and tellurium oxide, the desired value of X can be obtained.

IMPURITY ADDITIONS

Addition of small amounts of impurities such as Tin (Sn), and Germanium (Ge), further improve the properties of Tellurium-Tellurium Oxide as a re-recordable memory.

Effects of Germanium impurity additive are shown in Figure 3. While maintaining essentially the same depth of modulation, the transition temperatures were shifted upward with the addition of impurities. Upward shift of transition temperature improves the thermal stability of recording.

The effect of adding a small amount of tin to the basic material are shown in Figure 4. Unlike Germanium, addition of tin up shifts the transition temperature only by a moderate degree.

RECORDING, PLAYBACK AND ERASURE PROCESSES

The same solid state laser operating at a 830 nanometer wavelength is used for recording and readout (playback) operations with changes in power density.

The spot size for record/readout process is 0.8 micrometers in diameter and the applied power is 8mw and 1mw respectively for recording and readout.

A separate laser operating at a 780 nanometer wavelength is used for erasure with the erasing laser beam foot print optically elongated to cover an elliptical area of 1 X 10 micrometers. Power output of the erasing laser is 10mw. The reversible process of recording and erasing is shown in Figure 5.

A high power density laser beam is applied to the material for a short period of time, quickly raising the temperature of the area and shifting its light reflectivity from a high zone to a low zone.

To erase the spot and bring the reflectivity value to the former level, the material must be brought up to a temperature, which is substantially lower than in the record process, at a slower rate.

By elongating the erase beam foot print in the direction of disc rotation and reducing the power density of the laser spot, the beam foot print makes a larger exposure over the previously recorded spot and the power density to make the degree of temperature elevation smaller.

The change of light reflectivity from the unrecorded, blank condition to recorded condition and then to the erased, ready for rerecord state is shown in Figure 6.

The change of reflectivity is approximately 2:1 and the low reflectivity state is the recorded condition.

STRUCTURE OF THE DISC AND SYSTEM

The same basic structure apply for both non-erasable and erasable disc.

As shown in Figure 7 the recording material, Tellurium-Tellurium Oxide with a controlled amount of impurity for an erasable disc, is evaporated on the surface of the 1.1mm thick acrylic resin platter. The substrate has a pre-grooved laser guiding track of 700 angstroms deep and 0.8 micro meters wide with a track pitch of 1.65 micrometers. The recording material has a thickness of approximately 1200 angstroms, and it is over-coated by a transparent protective layer. Two discs are then glued together to form a double layer disc of 2.5mm thick.

The width of the guiding track is equal to the diameter of the recorded bit, and the depth is 1/8th of the laser wavelength.

Major components of a total recorder/reproducer system are shown in Figure 8.

Specifications for the standard 20cm non-erasable disc are shown in Figure 9. Total capacity of this 23,000 track disc is 700 kilo bytes.

The disc is also capable of analog FM signal recording for conventional video recording. At the recording wavelength of 1 micron, i.e. 5MHz FM carrier recorded on the inner most track at 5 meters per second writing speed, a C/N ratio of 55dB at 30KHz sampling bandwidth is obtainable.

SUMMARY

The first practical and popular application of an optical memory system, is for permanent document storage and retrieval purposes.

With 700 mega bytes of memory, 10,000 pages of 8" X 11" documents may be stored on a single 20cm disc.

A Single Disc Optical Memory System can now be complemented by a 50 disc capacity automatic disc handling system shown in Figure 10.

Light Transmission Characteristics

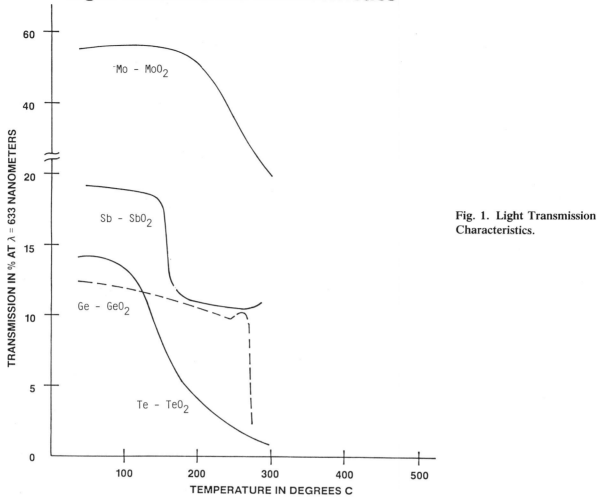

Fig. 1. Light Transmission Characteristics.

Multi Element Evaporation System

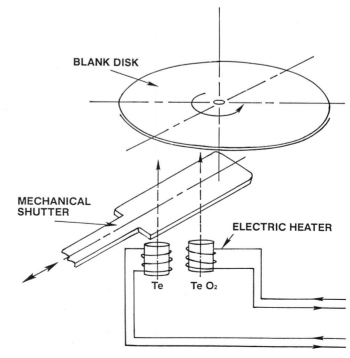

Fig. 2. Multi Element Evaporation System.

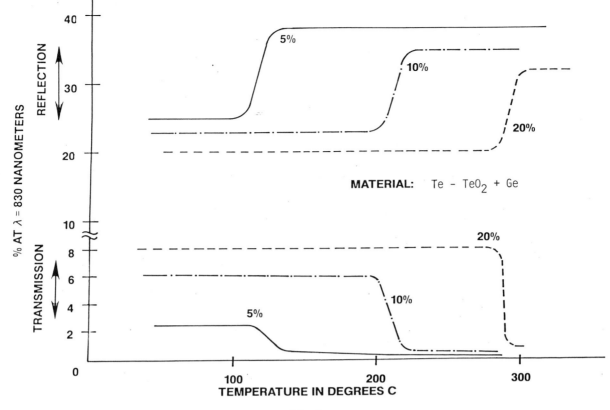

Fig. 3.

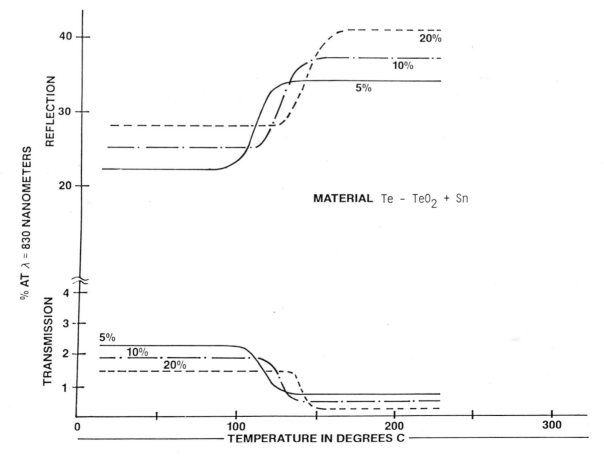

Fig. 4.

Record Layer Temperature

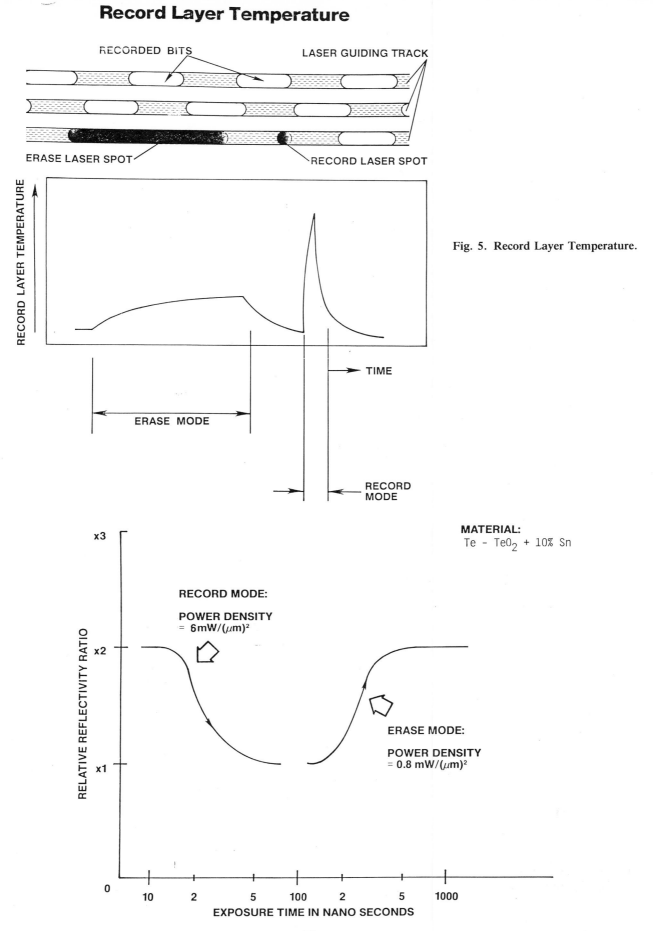

RECORDED BITS

LASER GUIDING TRACK

ERASE LASER SPOT

RECORD LASER SPOT

RECORD LAYER TEMPERATURE

TIME

ERASE MODE

RECORD MODE

Fig. 5. Record Layer Temperature.

x3

x2

x1

0

RELATIVE REFLECTIVITY RATIO

RECORD MODE:

POWER DENSITY
= 6mW/(μm)^2

ERASE MODE:

POWER DENSITY
= 0.8 mW/(μm)^2

MATERIAL:
Te – TeO$_2$ + 10% Sn

10   2   5   100   2   5   1000

EXPOSURE TIME IN NANO SECONDS

Fig. 6.

Optical Disc Structure

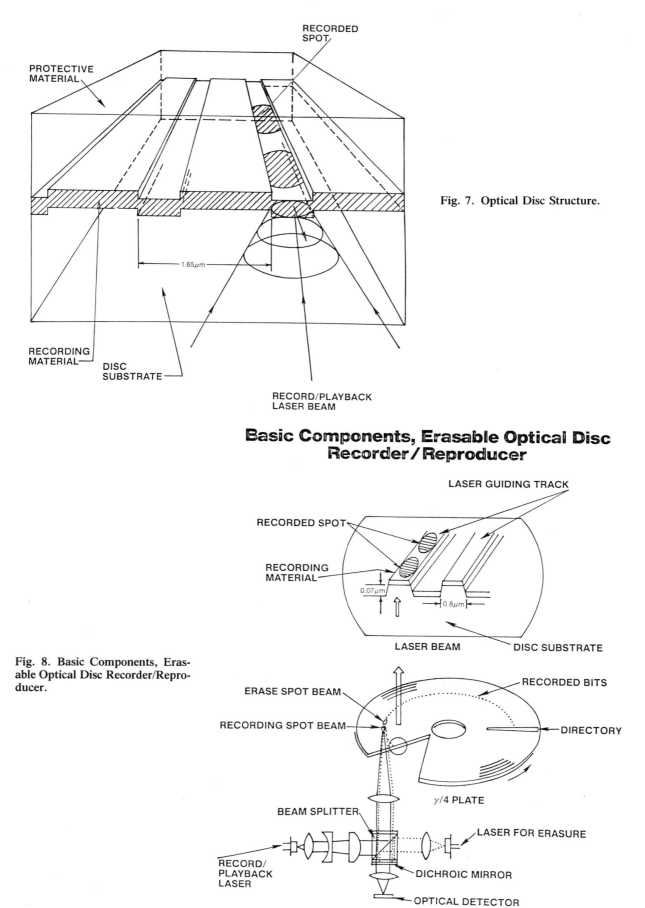

Fig. 7. Optical Disc Structure.

Basic Components, Erasable Optical Disc Recorder/Reproducer

Fig. 8. Basic Components, Erasable Optical Disc Recorder/Reproducer.

Specifications, Optical Memory Disc

DIAMETER	200 mm
THICKNESS	2.5 mm
RECORD LAYER MATERIAL	Te - TeO_2
DISC CONSTRUCTION	WITH PROTECTIVE COATING
TOTAL DATA CAPACITY	700 MB
TRACK STRUCTURE	SPIRAL TRACK WITH GUIDING GROOVE
NO. OF TRACKS	23.000
TRACK PITCH	1.65 mm
DATA CAPACITY PER TRACK	32 kB
RECORD/PLAYBACK LASER	DIODE λ = 830 nm
RECORD POWER	5 mμ
PLAYBACK POWER	1 mμ
DISC ROTATION	900 rpm
AVERAGE ACCESS TIME FOR A TRACK	0.3 sec
DATA TRANSFER RATE	5 MB/sec.

Fig. 9. Specifications, Optical Memory Disc.

Multiple Disc Automatic Handling System

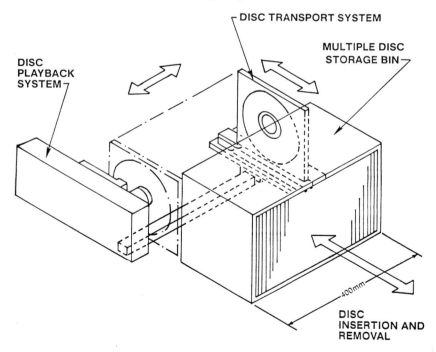

Fig. 10. Multiple Disc Automatic Handling System.

Multiplier-Adder LSI for Digital Video Processing

Seiichiro Iwase, Ichiro Kumata and Yoshitaka Hashimoto
Sony Corporation, Atsugi Plant
Kanagawa-ken, Japan

1. Introduction

Digital technology has been rapidly extended in its use to a wide variety of signal processing. Especially its use to video and broadcasting applications has opened up a "digital age". Various products, such as special effect generators, TV-standard converters, VTRs, noise reducers, etc., are beginning to employ digital signal processing and are expected to come into practical use in the near future.

Conventional digital video equipment, however, has a high power consumption and requires considerable space. The maximum operating speed of conventional arithmetic ICs is comparable to the video sampling rate, so time-sharing techniques cannot be applied and many high-speed arithmetic ICs must be used. In order to make the future digital studios practical, high-speed and low-power ICs for digital video processing must be developed.

Because multiplication-sum operation is a key operation in digital signal processing, a multi-purpose C-MOS multiplier-adder LSI, designated CX-7997, has been developed. It operates at 14.3MHz with a power consumption of less than 300mW. High-speed operation is obtained by employing a pipeline structure even though the C-MOS process is used. These new LSIs can be easily connected together. The basic operating structure of the new IC is shown in Fig.1. It has multiplier input ports A and B (10 bits each), adder input port C (16 bits), and output port D (16 bits). With sixteen operating modes such as multiplication-sum, multiplication, addition and various delay functions, The CX-7997 can be used for digital filtering, matrix operations, modulator/demodulators (encoder/decoders), and mixers.

This paper presents the design concept and possible applications of the new C-MOS multiplier-adder LSI (CX-7997), and reports the results of a series of tests.

2. Basic Structure of a Multi-Purpose Arithmetic Unit

A basic structure of multiplier-adder suitable for digital video processing as a multi-purpose arithmetic unit must be carefully studied in detail before the IC design. Therefore two application categories, digital filtering and inner product operations, are investigated.

174

2-1 Digital Filtering

In digital filter design there are two basic structures : Infinite Impulse Response (IIR) and Finite Impulse Response (FIR). The FIR structure is generally favored in video applications because it can easily provide linear phase characteristics, which are essential to avoid group delay distortion. The FIR structure is also well-suited for implementing adaptive filters because it is stable. When the clock rate is high, the IIR structure is not easy to implement because its feedback loops prohibit the pipeline structure discussed later from being easily applied. For this reason only FIR digital filters are discussed in this paper.

The convolution-sum behavior of an FIR digital filter can be described as

$$y(n) = \sum_{k=0}^{N-1} h_k(n) \cdot x(n-k) , \qquad (1)$$

where $h_k(n)$ $(k=0\cdots N-1)$ is the filter coefficient, N is the number of coefficients, and $x(n)$ and $y(n)$ are input and output sequences.

A representation of equation (1) is shown in Fig.2. The adders in Fig.2 are cascaded, so registers must be placed between the adders in order to obtain faster operation. Because of this the transposed-form in Fig.3 is preferable. In Fig.3 the adders are pipelined and the arithmetic units (surrounded by the broken line in the figure) can be cascaded to construct an FIR digital filter. The correlators can be built in the same manner.

2-2 Inner Product Operation

In video applications, the inner product operation is employed in, for example, matrix circuits, modulators in NTSC encoders and cross-fade circuits.

The inner product operation can be described as

$$y(n) = \sum_{k=0}^{N-1} A_k(n) \cdot B_k(n) , \qquad (2)$$

where $A_k(n)$ and $B_k(n)$ $(k=0\cdots N-1)$ are the input sequences, N is the number of additions and $y(n)$ is the output sequence.

A representation of equation (2) is shown in Fig.4. The adder-tree configuration in this figure is difficult to realize for the same reason as for the digital filter, so pipelined adders are used again. One solution is shown in Fig.5, however in this configuration each arithmetic unit requires a compensating delay. Since many stages of variable compensating delays in an arithmetic unit require a large number of registers and selectors, a reasonable compromise which will realize the inner product circuit using arithmetic units is shown in Fig.6. The arithmetic unit must of course also be used as an adder for the adder-tree.

3. Detailed Structure

3-1 Multiplier

The pipeline structure as shown in Fig.7 is used to obtain higher multiplication speed. Pipeline registers are placed after every adder array which provides partial-sums in the parallel multiplier configuration. This structure is different from the conventional high-speed parallel multiplier in that circuit elements are necessary for pipeline registers and also in that the product is determined from the LSB (S0) to the MSB (S7) in every clock period, so some delay time is required before all output bits are determined. The delay time caused by the pipeline register is well recognized in video and image processing, however, and does not cause any serious problems. The amount of circuit elements including pipeline registers is smaller than that of a conventional circuit in which a parallel arithmetic operation must be used when low-speed devices are used.

3-2 Adder

Figure 8 shows a block diagram of a conventional 6-bit ripple carry adder circuit. The circuit comprises of one bit flip-flops and one bit full adders. In each of the full adders, the two inputs from the left-hand side denote adding inputs, the output to the right-hand side represents the added output. The input from the bottom represents the carry input and the output to above represents the carry output to the more significant bits. Of course, if a circuit having a so-called carry look-ahead circuit is employed, all the bits can be calculated at high speed. In this case, however, even though a carry look-ahead circuit is provided, its operational speed is limited by the carry transmission speed. The flip-flops shown in Fig.9, therefore, are placed in the carry propagation path after every adder block of two bits in such a manner that more significant bits are given progressively larger delays. Although this circuit structure requires a compensating delay circuit which is formed of flip-flops and indicated by the broken line in Fig.9, the operational speed apparently is higher than that of the conventional adder circuit in Fig.8. When the adder circuit shown in Fig.9 is used in the pipelined adder as in Fig.3, 6 and 7, the delay is unnecessary except at the input of the first stage and at the output of the last stage. This delay facility in the new IC is selected by various modes, as is explained below.

4. Word Structure

The resolution of 8 bits per sample is generally required to obtain digital video signals of acceptable quality. It is

176

recognized, however, that round-off errors in 8-bit arithmetic result in significant degradation of overall system performance. To eliminate this problem, the word structure as shown in Fig.10 has been employed in the new IC. After some investigation, we decided that 10 bits by 10 bits multiplication would satisfy the majority of applications. The multiplier offers 14 bits by rounding-off the lower 5 bits of the product. In order to avoid an overflow problem, 2 bits of overhead is provided for, so the resulting product of 16 bits is added to the 16 bits of input C. This is enough to provide sufficient capacity for most digital video processing. Using this word structure the number of pins of the package is limited to 64, even though there are 4 input/output ports and 5 bits of mode control terminals.

5. Specifications

Table I shows the specifications of the new multi-purpose C-MOS multiplier-adder LSI. The circuit structure is shown in Fig.11. The parallelograms designated R show the registers for the data format in which the MSB is more delayed than the LSB. The triangles designated T show the compensating delay circuits indicated by the broken line in Fig.9. In order to obtain stable operation, registers are placed at input ports A, B and C, and output port D. A bypath from the input port BA to the adder is provided for adding its 16-bit input to the 16-bit input from port C. The input BA consists of 10 upper bits from port B and 6 lower bits from port A. Booth's algorithm is applied in the multiplier circuit in order to reduce the number of full-adders.

The functions of the mode control terminals M4,M3,M2,M1 and M0 are described in Table II. Sixteen operating modes can be provided as shown in Fig.12 by selecting the registers R and the delay circuits T by mode controls. These registers for variable delay selected by mode control M3 are used to compensate for the signal delay in various operating modes.

6. Applications

6-1 FIR Digital Filter

Since a register is placed at input port C in order to ensure stable operation, the FIR digital filter configuration shown in Fig.3 cannot be employed. Using the circuit shown in Fig.13, however, FIR digital filters with arbitrary coefficients can be easily obtained. In this configuration two pipeline branches of CX-7997s are used, one with odd-numbered coefficients and the other with even-numbered coefficients. The outputs of these two branches are added by another CX-7997 (mode 11001), providing the final output. Therefore, N+1 ICs are required to realize an N-tap FIR digital filter.

Input port C of the first ICs in both branches are set to zero. However, it can also be used to give an offset by putting a proper number or to give round-off capability by putting "1" at

the terminal one bit lower than the LSB of the output.
Using the circuit shown in Fig.13 in parallel, signals with a wide bandwidth such as high-definition television signals can be processed.

6-2 Inner Product Operations

An eighth-order inner product circuit, for example, can be built using the new ICs as shown in Fig.14. An Nth order inner product can be obtained using approximately 1.5 times N chips of CX-7997. Other circuits, such as an NTSC encoder, a cross-fade circuit in a chroma keyer and a matrix circuit for RGB-YIQ conversion can be realized as shown in Fig.15, 16 and 17.

7. Results of Experimental Evaluation

The CX-7997 was evaluated giving the ramp sequence and random sequence to the inputs, then observing the coincidence of the outputs with the pre-arranged correct output sequences. The correct operation for all input signal combinations and highly dynamic input signals were confirmed by the ramp and random sequences respectively. The design target of a maximum operational clock rate was at least 14.3MHz, however, the ICs have been found to operate up to 18MHz at the room temperature.

The experimental programmable FIR digital filter shown in Fig.18 was built to demonstrate the capability of the CX-7997. This filter has 31 taps with arbitrary coefficients. Using one 64K PROM for coefficient memory, more than one hundred filter characteristics can be obtained. Figure 19 shows a measured example of a low pass filter frequency response.

Other applications to low-power, small-size and low-cost digital video equipment are being considered. In the experimental digital NTSC decoder [1], for example, conventional bipolar multiplier ICs and adder ICs are used with ROMs and RAMs. Using this new IC, we expect to reduce the size 80% and power consumption 90%.

8. Conclusion

A new multi-purpose C-MOS multiplier-adder LSI (CX-7997) for digital video processing has been developed. Applying C-MOS technology and employing pipeline structure, the LSI has an operating clock rate of at least 14.3 MHz, sufficient for video processing with a low-power consumption of 300mW. A wordlength sufficient for video processing is carefully chosen to minimize the circuit elements.

The new IC was evaluated as a single device and also by constructing a programmable FIR digital filter, with satisfactory results. It is expected, using the idea of this new IC, that various digital video and image processing equipment can be realized with low-power consumption, small-size and consequently low-cost.

9. Acknowledgements

The authors would like to express their appreciation to Mr. M. Morizono, Deputy President of Sony Corporation, for giving them the opportunity to study this subject and permission to publish this paper. They wish to thank Mr. H. Yoshida, General Manager, Information Systems Research Center, for his advice and encouragement in this study. They also wish to thank their many colleagues in Sony Corporation who have contributed to the work described in this paper.

Reference

[1] Y. Hashimoto, "Digital Decoding and Encoding of the NTSC Signal at 912 Samples per Line", SMPTE Journal, Oct. '81, pp942-944.

Table 1. General Specifications of CX-7997.

```
Purpose                 : multiplication-sum operations for
                          digital video signal processing.
Functions               : (1) multiplication-sum operation
                              (10X10+16 bits)
                          (2) multiplication (10X10 bits)
                          (3) addition (16+16 bits)
                          (4) delay function
Operating modes         : 16 modes
Arithmetic operation    : 70 ns max. (14.3 MHz min)
cycle time
Power  dissipation      : 300 mW (when input is random sequence
                          at 14.3MHz)
Single power supply     : 5.0 V
Pipeline dely           : 18 cycle max.
I/O interface           : TTL compatible
Process                 : C-MOS technology, 2.3  m rule
Density                 : app. 15,000 Tr.
Package                 : 64 pin plug-in package  1.0"X1.0"
Temperaure range        : 0 to 70 C.
```

Table 2. Mode Selection Table.

	0	1
M4	multiplication-sum operation	addition
M3	without variable delay	with 2 clock delay after multiplier and 1 clock delay at BA input
M2	without triangular delay at BA input	with triangular delay at BA input
M1	without triangurar delay at C input	with triangular delay at C input
M0	without triangular delay at D output	with triangular delay at D output

The triangular delay stands for the two-bit sliced delay circuit
indicated by the broken line in Fig.9.

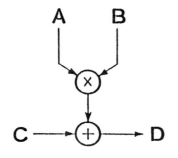

Fig. 1. Basic function of CX-7997.

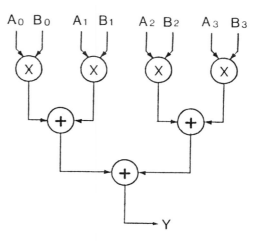

Fig. 4. Basic structure of inner product circuit.

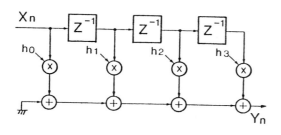

Fig. 2. Direct-form realization of an FIR digital filter.

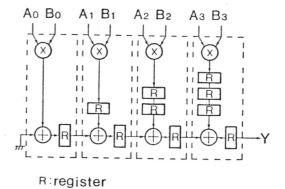

R:register

Fig. 5. An example of inner product circuit structure using the pipelined adder.

pipelined adder.

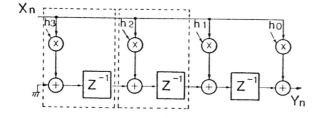

Fig. 3. Transposition of the network of Fig. 2.

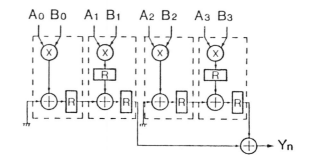

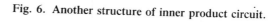

Fig. 6. Another structure of inner product circuit.

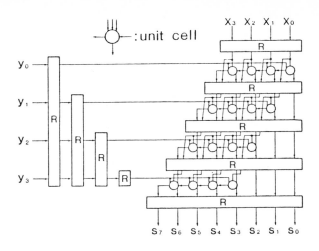

Fig. 7. Pipeline structure of parallel multiplier.

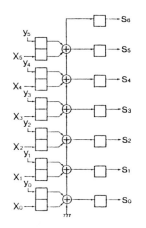

Fig. 8. Ripple carry adder circuit.

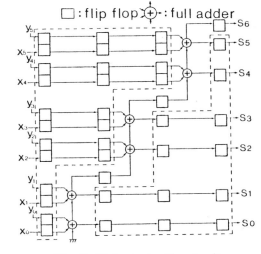

Fig. 9. High-speed adder circuit.

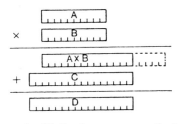

a. (multiplication-sum operation)

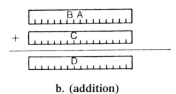

b. (addition)

Fig. 10. Word structure of CX-7997.

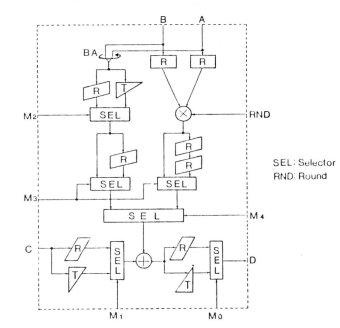

SEL: Selector
RND: Round

Fig. 11. Circuit structure of CX-7997.

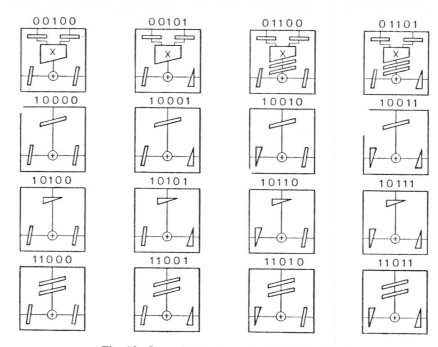

Fig. 12. Operating modes available for CX-7997.

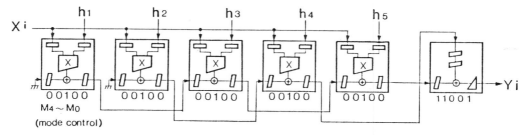

Fig. 13. FIR digital filter configuration using CX-7997.

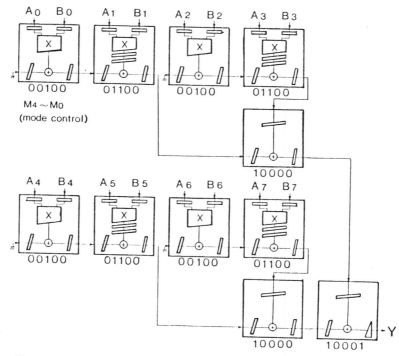

Fig. 14. Inner product circuit configuration using CX-7997.

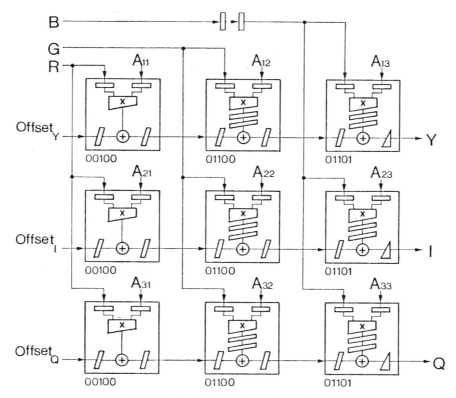

Fig. 15. Matrix circuit configuration using CX-7997.

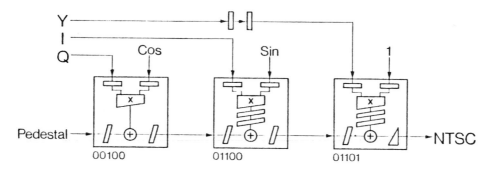

Fig. 16. NTSC encoder configuration using CX-7997.

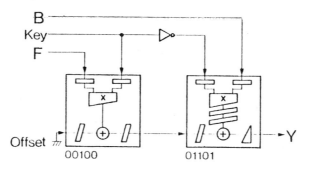

Fig. 17. Cross-fade circuit configuration using CX-7997.

CX-7997

Fig. 18. Experimental programmable FIR digital filter.

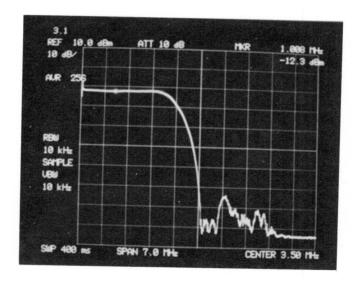

Fig. 19. A measured example of L.P.F. frequency response.

Seiichiro Iwase was born in 1951 in Tokyo, Japan. He received the B.S. degree in electrical engineering from Chiba University in 1974 and joined Oki Industry Co., Ltd. as an engineer of digital signal processing. In 1979 he joined Sony Corp. to work on digital video tape recording. At present he is working on digital video signal processing in Information Systems Research Center, Atsugi Plant.

Ichiro Kumata was born in Osaka, Japan, in 1955. He received the B.S. and M.S. degrees in Electrical Engineering from Keio University, Yokohama, Japan, in 1978 and 1980, respectively. He joined Sony Corp., Atsugi, Japan in 1980, where he has been working on the logic design of MOS LSIs for signal processors, microprocessors and microcontrollers.

Yoshitaka Hashimoto is Assistant General Manager of the Information Systems Research Center, Sony Corp. He was born in 1940 in Kyoto, Japan. He received the B.S. degree in Electronic Engineering from the University of Electro-Communications, Tokyo in 1964, and joined Sony Corp. Research Division in the same year. In 1968 he received the M.S. degree in Electrical Engineering from Stanford University, California after one year's study with the scholarship from Sony Corp. From 1972 to 1978 he was involved in the research work on digital signal processing of audio and video signals at the Sony Research Center. Since 1978 he has been involved in the development of digital video processing and record technology at Atsugi Plant.

From Studio to Home — How Good Is The Electronic Highway?

Alexander G. Day
Canadian Association of Broadcasters
Ottawa, Ontario, Canada

"A bird in the hand..": a picture in the home, "is worth two in the bush": is worth two in the studio. But this is only true if in transportation, the picture is not degraded appreciably. Present distribution techniques for NTSC television cannot reproduce studio quality. Improved pictures in the studio have little future application unless they can be delivered to the home while either retaining their intrinsic improvements or by being reconstructed by sophisticated receiver circuitry.

Our present electronic highway, then, is no six lane expressway, but more akin to a secondary road. Let us quickly review the degree of deterioration which does occur between studio and home.

Figure I lists typical quality factors such as signal-to-noise ratio (SNR), K-factor, and resolution to be found at various points in the system. Modern cameras can reproduce pictures with SNR around 55 dB, K-factor of 1%, and resolution of 500 to 600 lines. VTR's are capable of providing air-play dubs of 52 to 54 dB SNR, retaining a 1% K-factor, and resolution of 500 lines. Digital VTR's will do even better. At the studio output, typical values would be an SNR of 50 to 55 dB, K-factor of 2 or better, and resolution of 500 lines. And in future, the all-digital studio will improve these figures.

The studio signals may feed a transmitter directly, via terrestrial microwave, a network or at least an STL, or via a combination of microwave and satellite links. The overall quality would depend on a number of design or contractual decisions, -bandwidth, number and frequencies of aural sub-carriers, fade margins, diversity reception, and so forth. Typical at the transmitter input would be an SNR ranging from 48 to 52 dB, a K-factor between 2 and 3, and resolution of 450 to 500 lines. But now the real deterioration sets in.

The 6 MHz r.f. channel bandwidth used for NTSC is a serious constraint, and requires the video bandwidth to be reduced to a maximum 4.2 MHz, resulting in no better than 335 lines of resolution. The transmitter noise floor is only 48 to 50 dB below the video, and the best K-factor attainable is about 2 to 3 percent. The r.f. transmission is therefore between about 46 to 50 dB SNR, with a K-factor of 3-5% and 335 lines resolution, but even the professional quality transmitter demodulator can recover only some 320 lines after trapping out the aural carrier.

The typical receiver may recover the off-air signal directly, along with whatever deterioration due to noise, ghosting or interference the direct path provides. However, in Canada at least, the majority of receivers are connected to cable-TV systems, and very frequently with devices interposed between cable system subcriber terminal and the receiver itself.

As a consulting engineer, I had frequent opportunities to measure the performance of cable-TV systems. On average, in my opinion, the signal delivered to the typical subscriber would vary in SNR from 40 to 50 dB, with a K-factor of 4 to 6% and resolution of 300 to 320 lines. The receiver accessories, -converter, pay-TV descrambler or "address box" would have a wide range of effects, and frequently would reduce SNR by one or two dB, add about one % to K-factor, and lower resolution by perhaps 25 lines.

The receiver itself, in order to reduce colour crosstalk, usually rolls off 6 dB from maximum response at colour subcarrier, 3.58 MHz, and delivers a degraded picture of from 200 to 250 lines resolution, with a bad K-factor, and SNR in the 35 to 50 dB range. Video peaking, which adds overshoots to improve the detail subjectively, also adds noise to the picture. Colour saturation on the receiver is low because of the lowered response near colour subcarrier, and saturation must be increased, adding considerable noise to the colour display.

None of us can be very proud of the picture delivered at the end of the electronic highway. It is vastly inferior to the studio quality picture which started the journey.

And now we are promised substantially improved pictures at the source, enhanced definition, and high-definition TV. We are also being offered alternative methods of transporting our pictures to the home, and some of these can avoid the major constraint imposed by the 6 MHz r.f. channel bandwidth.

In some countries which have not yet exploited the UHF-TV band, it would be possible to increase channel bandwidths at UHF. This however, would call for a special breed of receivers, at increased cost, with dual-bandwidth I.F.'s for conventional and for wide-band TV, and probably requiring a split-sound design.

The direct-broadcasting satellite (DBS) offers a real opportunity for improvement, even on NTSC standards. The satellite links are nothing more than additional microwave hops, albiet long ones, and the Region 2 12 GHz plan provides for FM transmission in 24 MHz channels. The signal reaching the earth station receiver therefore can retain the quality typically delivered to our terestrial TV transmitters. Baseband video and audio can be provided directly into the video and audio circuitry of component-style receivers. No doubt, though, an r.f. modulator will also be needed so as to feed an r.f. signal into receivers not so equipped. We will be hearing later in the session, from Mr. Whitworth and Mr. Gressman, current information on plans for DBS, and from Mr. Chouinard on the picture quality attainable over DBS in the presence of interference.

Though there are some difficulties in incorporating wider-band HDTV channels into the existing Region 2 DBS Plan, these are not insurmountable, and co-operative action on the part of at least the countries of North America can be anticipated.

The 12.2-12.7 GHz band in the ITU table of allocations to be used here for DBS also provides for terrestrial broadcasting. However, only in fairly large countries which do not institute DBS is there any chance that terrestrial alternatives would be possible.

There are other satellite bands 22.5 to 23 GHz and 40.5 to 42.5 GHz allocated for Broadcasting Satellites, along with other services, and it is thought that the former band offers a good alternative for HDTV distribution including all-digital service, despite the problems associated with attenuation due to rainfall at these frequencies.

Considering cable alternatives for wider-band channels, FM is already used for cable transportaion of certain signals, and it would be possible to provide a subscriber service using FM. This could be compatible with the 12 GHz FM DBS signals. However, in most instances, a second cable would be necessary, with costs being very high. Present single cable systems have the capacity for some fifty 6 MHz channels, and could provide initially, a means to deliver improved signals using MAC technology. But in North America, at least, our off-air broadcasting spectrum is close to saturation. Broadcasters would need to retain their frequencies for compatible NTSC signals, and additional channels for a simultaneous, non-compatible MAC-type service are simply not available. Such signals would need to be provided directly to cable headends for distribution to the public, or alternatively, could use DBS or satellite-to-cable networks.

Regarding the capability of present cable system designs to transport better definition signals with minimum deterioration, we will be addressed by Israel (Sruki) Switzer during this session. Mr. Switzer has been involved at the cutting-edge of technology in cable system design for many years.

Fibre optics show great promise. Mr. Tsuboi will be describing advancements in this technology, particularly for the distribution of HDTV.

Up to the present, videocassettes and videodiscs for the home have not been designed to reproduce quality levels substantially different from those available through terrestrial off-air networks. Some do offer stereo sound, but little if any picture quality improvement. However, there is no major obstacle, particularly if an international standard emerges, to the provision of better quality magnetic or optical recordings for home use. Programs on these media could not replace broadcasting, but could supplement the choices available to viewers.

The all-digital studio provides the key for the generation of very high quality signals. Possibly ten years down the road, the electronic highway will provide for transportation of such signals to the home, using satellite or satellite to optical cable distribution, and the all-digital receiver will emerge as the eventual winner of the quality race. Mr. Lumbrink will be providing us information on digital development work at Bell Northern Research.

As the total revenues available for television expand, those based on advertising are being supplemented more and more by those based on subscription, and encryption methods become of greater interest. Mr. Keith Lucas will be describing techniques in this field.

To summarize, Figure II lists the presently-recognized distribution alternatives, together with their main attributes. It can be seen that we have little opportunity for major improvement in any of the schemes involving off-air terrestrial 6 MHz channels, and our crowded broadcasting spectrum offers little opportunity to reach the home using alternative terrestrial off-air transmissions. Satellites, either by direct broadcasting, or by satellite-to-cable networks show promise, and optical fibres may well surpass coaxial cable as the preferred local terrestrial distribution network.

However, given the smart receiver, and in particular the digital frame store in the receiver, our opportunities expand substantially, since some of the obstacles imposed by the 6 MHz channel can be avoided.

Figure III summarizes our future delivery options using enhanced quality techniques. It would appear that quality can be improved to any extent that the market will permit. The sophistication and the pocketbook of the home viewer will determine the level, and not the limitations of technology.

FIGURE I
SIGNAL QUALITY

AT OUTPUT OF	SIGNAL-TO-NOISE RATIO dB	K-FACTOR %	RESOLUTION - LINES
CAMERA	55	1	500 – 600
VTR	52 – 54	1	500
STUDIO	50 – 55	2	500
MICROWAVE/SAT	48 – 52	2 – 3	450 – 500
TRANSMITTER	46 – 50	3 – 5	335
CABLE SYSTEM	40 – 50	4 – 6	300 – 320
RX. ACCESSORIES	38 – 48	5 – 7	275 – 300
RECEIVER	35 – 50	5 – 20	200 – 250

FIGURE II
NTSC DELIVERY OPTIONS AVAILABLE TODAY

SYSTEM	BANDWIDTH	RESOLUTION	SNR
Off-air	6	poor	poor to fair
Off-air to cable	6	poor	poor to fair
Microwave or Satellite to cable	6	poor	fair
DBS - remodulated	6	fair	good
DBS-direct video	--	good	good
Cassette or Disc	--	poor	fair to good

FIGURE III
FUTURE DELIVERY OPTIONS

SYSTEM	STANDARD	RESOLUTION	S N R
Off-air	NTSC-MAC	fair	fair
Off-air to cable	NTSC-MAC	fair	fair
Microwave or Satellite to cable	NTSC-MAC	fair to good	good
	HDTV	excellent	good
DBS-direct video	NTSC-MAC	good	good
	HDTV	excellent	good
Fibre Optics	NTSC-MAC	good	excellent
	HDTV	excellent	excellent
Cassette or Disc	any	excellent	excellent
All Digital	any	excellent	excellent

Alexander G. Day, P. Eng., Vice-President, Engineering Services, CAB, graduated from the University of Toronto in 1943. He has a 41-year background in radio and television. He joined CAB January 1, 1980 as Director of Engineering and was promoted to Vice-President, Engineering Services, September 1, 1981. He is Past President, Canadian Association of Broadcast Consultants, former Vice-President of the CRTPB (now known as RABC) and past Chairman of its Television Broadcast Committee, as well as participating in various other committees of the RABC. He is the delegate from Canada to numerous international ITU conferences and a member of SMPTE.

On Picture Quality in Television Systems

Broder Wendland, Hartmut Schröder
Lehrstuhl für Nachrichtentechnik, Universität Dortmund
West Germany

Summary

Improving picture quality can be achieved with respect to VLSI techniques by signal processing within the given television standards, extending them or by complete new HDTV standards. In this paper some methods of improving picture quality published earlier are investigated. Subjective picture quality has been determined by subjective assessments.

A quality comparison is described between
- standard television system,
- progressive scan reproduction,
- vertical pre- and postfiltering,
- diagonal pre- and postfiltering,
- high line number (HDTV-) system.

The result of this comparison is, that the picture quality with diagonal pre- and postfiltering is superior to all other compatible improvements. Compared with the standard television system an improvement of at least 2 grades of the CCIR comparison scale is achievable. The real HDTV system is about 2.5 grades better than the standard system - at the price of a fourfold bandwidth for the transmission channel.

As a further result, it can be seen by these tests, that by progressive scan reproduction also a good improvement of picture quality can be achieved. The achieved subjective impression of resolution and sharpness is comparable to that of the vertical pre- and postfiltering method - therefore, there is no longer a justification for a general reduction of vertical resolution by Kell's factor.

1 Introduction

Improved picture quality is of course an essential goal for future television services. This can be achieved with respect to VLSI techniques and high sophisticated signal processing within the given television standards, extending them - or by complete new HDTV standards. Indeed, by signal processing it is possible to overcome completely all the deficiencies of present day television systems yielding a flicker-free television reproduction with higher resolution, higher sharpness and contrast and without artifacts. On the other hand, by a new television system with doubled line number and a doubled horizontal cutoff frequency a very good quality can be achieved also - at the price of a fourfold bandwidth for the transmission channels.

Therefore, to make possible a reasonable decision for future television systems, it has to be determined, which picure quality is attainable by a television system. So it is one of the essential questions, what is the amount of resolution and sharpness attainable for a given twodimensionally bandlimited channel. Furthermore, it has to be pointed out, what is the amount of e.g. aliasing, line structure distortion, flicker which just can be tolerated. More generally, it has to be determined, what is picture quality and what constitutes it.

On this background some methods of improving picture quality by signal processing published earlier, /1/-/5/, have been quantitatively investigated to their effects on subjective picture quality. These methods are listed and numbered in Figure 1:

(1) Standard television system
(2) Progressive scan reproduction /4/, /5/
(3) Vertical pre- and postfiltering approach /2/, /3/
(4) Diagonal pre- and postfiltering approach /2/, /3/
(5) High line number (HDTV) system, e. g. /6/

A comparison of the compatibly improved systems (2-4) to standard quality (1) as well as to the quality of a high line number system (5) will be described in this paper.

The achieved picture qualities have to be discussed in connection with their requirements on channel capacity and/or hardware, which also is shown roughly in Figure 1. So a compatible transmission over the standard channel is possible for the methods (2-4). High resolution monitors with at least doubled line frequencies are necessary for all improved systems. Cameras with doubled line numbers have to be used in the cases (3-5). A new transmission channel with a fourfold bandwidth is only essential for the HDTV system (5).

2 Resolution Bounds and Picture Qualities

For any television system the area in the twodimensional Fourier domain usable in the sense of resolution can be described very clearly by its resolution bounds. This resolution bound can reasonably be defined as the maximum resolution theoretically achievable just with a modulation depth equal to zero /4/. In horizontal direction this resolution bound is given by the spatial cutoff frequency f_c^x depending on the bandwidth and the line duration.

As it was shown in /3/ an optimum transfer function in the sense of maximum resolution and sharpness for all directions with negligible ringing as well can be achieved by proper pre- and postfiltering. By this the vertical resolution bound can be half the vertical scanning frequency, which is the spatial vertical cutoff frequency f_c^y. Without any pre- and postfiltering this resolution in the past usually has been reduced by Kell's factor (0.64) in the case of interlace free television systems. In this paper from the standpoint of picture quality it will be shown that there is no justification for Kell's factor in general. For interlaced systems there will be a reduction because of line flicker effects. Therefore, an (estimated) reduction factor of 0.6 as in /4/, is assumed.

For the various television systems shown in Figure 1 their resolution bounds are given in Figure 2. Therefore, for the standard interlaced television system (1) a vertical resolution bound of $\approx 0.6 \cdot f_c{}^Y$ is assumed. Applying progressive scan reproduction (2) by frame store techniques the resolution bound is described in the literature by Kell's factor: $0.64 \cdot f_c{}^Y$. By vertical pre- and postfiltering (3) the vertical resolution bound is increased up to $f_c{}^Y$. For all these systems (1-3) their horizontal resolution bounds are $f_c{}^X$.

An interlaced high line number system (5), e. g. described by Fujio /6/, has a vertical resolution bound twice as that one in the standard system: $\approx 0.6 \cdot 2f_c{}^Y$. Its horizontal resolution bound is also doubled to $2f_c{}^X$. The same vertical and horizontal resolution bounds in connection with a diagonal bandlimitation can be achieved within the given standards by means of diagonal pre- and postfiltering.

By scaling of resolution bounds a description of the maximum resolution achievable within a given television system is possible. It should be mentioned, however, that this scaling of resolution is not directly a scaling of picture quality. It is particularly the purpose of this paper to describe such a real quality scaling for the methods improving picture quality mentioned above. Furthermore, the results of the quality tests show that new resolution bounds should be defined for progressive scanning.

Besides real hardware implementation also by means of a computer simulation, the described 5 television systems have been implemented. Basing on this computer simulation subjective tests of picture quality have been performed under the following conditions:

- One quarter of a (4:3) television picture is simulated by a full conventional monitor. So the simulated standard system has 312 lines and an equivalent bandwidth of 1 MHz, whereas the simulated HDTV system and the high line number equipment has 625 lines and a bandwidth of 4 MHz.

- The described procedure has the opportunity to use standard equipment without quality restrictions (resolution, sharpness etc.), as it would be the case with present high line number equipment.

- Regardless of the fact that the described methods improving picture quality work properly for pictures with motion by motionadaptive techniques /4/, /5/, as a first step only still picures have been investigated for this paper.

- Quality assessments have been performed with 12 experts as comparison tests using the CCIR comparison scale. These assessments are published partly in more detail in /7/, respectively will be published in /8/.

The quality assessments have been performed by assessing the total impression of a picture as well as assessing some well chosen quality properties. These properties are "resolution", "sharpness" and "flicker reduction". Basing on this the single results can be arranged to a complete quality vector, which seems to be an adequate procedure to describe picture quality. Furthermore, defining and maybe standardizing such quality vectors with maybe some more components gives the opportunity of a quick quality comparison of different TV systems.

Therefore, in this paper results of the subjective tests are shown in terms of the described quality vectors and will be discussed in connection with the theory of picture pick-up and reconstruction taking into account some properties of the viewer's eye.

3 Interlaced Television Systems

Two of the five television systems mentioned above are interlaced systems, the standard system and the high line number system. The only difference between both are the line numbers and their bandwidths. So their properties are first discussed together.

Picture Pick-Up Process

The picture pick-up process can be described as a sampling process in at least two directions: the vertical direction and the temporal direction, in which the pictures are sampled linewise respectively picture by picture.

Figure 3a shows the video transmission system from the picture to be transmitted to the visual cortex of the viewer including processing of the viewer's eye. The picture with its threedimensional brightness function $s(x,y,t)$ corresponding to a Fourier spectrum $S(f^x,f^y,f^t)$ is filtered in the camera by a modulation transfer function $H_C(f^x,f^y,f^t)$ yielding a signal $B(f^x,f^y,f^t)$. By this filtering the influence of the optical system and the scanning spot of the camera pick-up tube is described.

Subsequently the resulting signal is sampled in the camera with line interlace scanning (Figure 3b). By this a serialized time depending signal is achieved which is transmitted on the video channel with a horizontal bandlimitation only.

At the receiver end the picture is reconstructed line by line by the monitor. A first spatial reconstruction filtering is realized by the monitor's transfer function $H_M(f^x,f^y)$. The complete spatio-temporal reconstruction filtering is performed by the monitor and the viewer's eye in connection. Hereby the monitor is processing only spatially whereas the processing of the eye is spatio-temporal. For simplicity the system is assumed to be linear including a linear eye model with a transfer function $H_A(f^x,f^y,f^t)$.

In the case of interlace scanning the line scanning pattern is shifted from field to field obtaining a twodimensional offset sampling grid in the y,t-plane as shown in Figure 4. This offset sampling grid corresponds to another offset sampling grid in the f^y,f^t-plane. We get for the spectrum of the sampled signal, as shown in more detail in /9/

$$B_\perp(f^x, f^y, f^t) =$$

$$= (1/4\tau d) \sum_{k=\infty}^{\infty} \sum_{\ell=\infty}^{\infty} B(f^x, f^y - k/2d, f^t - \ell/2\tau) \cdot [1 + (-1)^{k+\ell}] \quad (1)$$

which is nonzero only for $k + \ell = 2i$; $i = 0, \pm 1, \pm 2, \cdots$ yielding a diagonal repetition as shown in fig. 5 ($f_s^y = 1/d$).

Reconstruction Process

This sampled signal is then transmitted on the channel where only a horizontal bandlimitation is performed, which need not be considered here. So this signal is reconstructed by the monitor and the viewer's eye in connection with the complete spatio-temporal transfer function:

$$H_R(f^x, f^y, f^t) = H_M(f^x, f^y) \cdot H_A(f^x, f^y, f^t). \quad (2)$$

In conventional television systems the sampling theorem usually is violated in vertical and temporal direction: there is no sufficient bandlimitation before picture scanning, neither in vertical direction nor in temporal direction. This causes aliasing distortions such as stepping lines or waggon wheels turning backwards. These distortions principally could be overcome only by proper prefiltering at the transmitter end.

Furthermore, the reconstruction process by conventional television receivers is extremely defective: there is no sufficient bandlimitation in vertical direction and temporal direction as well. This causes irritating line structures, line flickering and large area flickering.

In addition this reconstruction is not performed independently in vertical and temporal direction. Consequently the interdependence between vertical and temporal processing should be described in the f^y, f^t-plane /10/, i. e. for $f^x = 0$. Figure 5 shows the twodimensional repeated spectra of a still picture scanned with interlace corresponding to equation (1). Depending on the resolution of the camera there is some aliasing in vertical direction producing overlapping (hatched areas). The infinitely extended vertical stripe at $f^t = 0$ is repeated diagonally. So there are repeated stripes at 25 Hz, 50 Hz etc. An equivalent representation can be given for 30/60 Hz repetition of frames/fields.

All of these spectra with an amplitude above the perception level e.g. lying within the thick line (estimated perception level) shown in Figure 5 may be perceived - weighted by the transfer function of the spatio-temporal reconstruction lowpass $H_R(f^x, f^y, f^t)$. Now the flicker distortions can be explained very clearly in the f^y, f^t-plane: 50 Hz flicker (C) is perceived mainly in connection with large areas corresponding to spectral contents at low vertical frequencies. 25 Hz components (B) appear mainly in connection with high vertical frequencies, e.g. at sharp horizontal contours. Simple vertical bandlimitation by the monitor or electronic circuits reduces both the 25 Hz components and the vertical resolution.

For a deeper insight into this concept Figure 6 shows vertical sections parallel to the axis of vertical frequencies. The first section (A) at f^t=0 shows the "perception" of the basic spectrum distorted by some aliasing and the nearest repeated spectra. Because of this the vertical resolution is degraded by the socalled Kell's factor ($\approx$ 0.64). The second section (B) at f^t = 25 Hz similarly shows the effective transfer function $H_R(0,f_Y,25)$ for 25 Hz components. There is a reduction of the perceived signal, but in connection with high vertical components (of the baseband) heavy line flicker will occur. This causes irritations subjectively reducing vertical resolution on account of which a second degradation factor, the interlace factor (0.6 ... 0.7) is used /6/.

It should be mentioned that this seems to be not adequate, because picture quality is degraded by line flicker. Vertical resolution is reduced, if the viewing distance is increased to reduce the effects of line flicker - but then also the horizontal resolution is reduced. Because of this understanding quality assessments as in /7/ have to be performed to show the interdependence of picture quality, line structure distortion and interlace scanning.

The third section (C) at f^t = 50 Hz shows the effects for 50 Hz components. They occur mainly in connection with low vertical frequencies, i. e. large areas. Because of the decreased amplitude of the reconstruction filter $H_R(0,f_Y,50)$ there is a further reduced perception, but large area flickering at 50 Hz is still a disagreeable distortion. May be, this is not true for 60 Hz.

Quality Comparison

The described deficiencies (aliasing, flicker etc.) of interlaced television are true for both, the standard system and the high line number system. Differences are given by the line numbers and the bandwidths. So there is of course a higher resolution for the HDTV system as it can be seen from Figure 2.

The quality comparison between both is shown - together with all other systems - in Figures 7 and 8. This comparison shows, that the total amount of improvement, which is possible by a complete new high line number system, is about 2.5 grades of the CCIR comparison scale for the total impression. The impression of higher resolution and sharpness is especially confirmed by this comparison. The flicker reduction of the high line number system is due to the fact that the monitors, the viewing distances and the picture material have been the same for all systems. So there is the same spot size but more lines per viewing angle for the high line number system. Also the picture signals have more spectral portions in the higher frequency ranges with respect to line frequency.

4 Compatible Improvements

Progressive Scan Reproduction

As shown in chapter 3 one of the most disturbing effects of TV systems are the flicker effects due to line interlace techniques in television. These well known effects are e.g. line flicker, line crawl, heavy 25 Hz flicker on horizontal contours of high contrast etc.

Moreover, the subjective improvement with respect to resolution of an interlaced television system with e.g. 625 lines compared to an interlace free system of 312 lines is very poor and does not exceed about 25...30%. This was already known by Prof. Schröter, who first introduced line interlace into electronic video systems /11/. Although the improvement is poor, line interlace technique is applied all over the world and causes the flicker effects mentioned above.

To get rid of these disturbing effects picture frame store techniques can be applied. For this matter there are some different approaches which are described in e.g. /12/, /13/, /14/. One of the early concepts to overcome 25 Hz flickering was developed at the University of Dortmund /4/, /5/ and is described with somewhat more detail in this issue /15/. Principally, the incoming signal of one field is delayed by a field store and is then mixed with the undelayed field. By this an output sequence is generated for progressive scan reproduction on a monitor with doubled line frequency. Obviously in a f^y, f^t-plane similar to Figure 5 there is no longer an offset sampling grid and no longer any 25 Hz component.

The achieved quality improvement (Figure 7) compared with the standard system is nearly 2 grades ("Lady with Hat") for the total impression and the flicker reduction and nearly one grade for resolution and sharpness. For the test chart "Water" the improvement is even somewhat more. On the other hand, compared with a high line number system progressive scan is over 2 grades ("Lady with hat") worse than the high line number system. The quality distance between standard and high line number system is about 2.8 grades. From Figure 7 can be computed, that the distance between progressive scan and the high line number system is about 1 grade, wheras the measured distance has been over 2 grades. This seems to be inconsistent and can only be understood realizing that the quality comparison of pictures enlarges the distance to the reference system, because the viewer is concentrated exactly to this difference. These problems are still under investigation, results will be published in /8/.

Above all, the quality assessments show, that progressive scan reproduction is a powerful method improving television picture quality.

Vertical Pre- and Postfiltering

As described with somewnat more detail in /2/, /3/ by proper vertical pre- and postfiltering (see Figure 1, No. 3) in connection with a high line number pick-up and reproduction, it is possible to get rid of aliasing and line structure distortion. By this an increased resolution can be achieved.

The improved receiver stores a conventional video signal in a frame-store. The frame-store delivers at its output a double-speed signal of 1 frame per field time. In the case of still picture areas this frame is composed of two fields belonging together. This signal is the same as for progressive scan reproduction. Subsequently the signal is interpolated vertically up to twice the line number, is divided into two fields and then reproduced on the monitor with interlace.

Because of this interpolation process there are gaps between the periodic spectra as shown in Figure 9. By this an offset sampling grid similar to equation (1) but with doubled line frequency is achieved. So it is possible to reproduce only the basic spectrum in vertical direction at $f^t = 0$. By this we get rid of the degradation of the reproduction expressed by Kell's factor. In any case we get a flat field reproduction without line structure. Large area flicker caused by 50 Hz components is not affected by this method (see Figure 9), but there is only a very small negligible amount of 25 Hz flicker. Obviously interlace flicker can be overcome by choosing a suitable vertical bandlimitation.

This concept has been implemented /3/, /5/. The transfer functions used for this implementation are shown in Figure 10. A camera modulation transfer function is assumed with about 35 % modulation depth at the vertical cutoff frequency $f_c{}^y$. Taking into account, that the prefilter at the transmitter end may be somewhat more expensive, the prefilter is realized with a steep slope to achieve compatibility as much as possible.

The postfilter transfer function, however, is implemented with respect to costs as shown in Figure 11 with no more than 5 different coefficients. By this postfiltering the interpolated signal is nearly optimum in the sense of maximum picture sharpness and resolution with negligible ringing as well. As can be seen from Figure 10, to reduce the expense of filtering implementation there is left some aliasing and also some distortion caused by adjacent spectra. But in connection with the reconstruction process of the monitor and the viewer's eye both residual distortions can be neglected.

By this vertical pre- and postfiltering picture quality is improved. Besides overcoming 25 Hz flicker the vertical resolution is increased: instead of ≈ 64 lines per 100 TV lines at least 80...90 lines can be resolved. Figure 11 shows a pattern with 80 lines per 100 TV lines. The conventional system (Figure 11a) fails, whereas the pre- and postfiltered system (Figure 11b) overcomes Kell's factor.

The picture quality comparison with the standard system (Figure 7) shows a subjective improvement of about 2 grades ("Lady with hat") respectively 2.5 grades ("Water"). The quality comparison with the high line number system shows a distance of about 2 grades ("Lady with hat") respectively 1.5 grades ("Water").

This improvement compared with progressive scan reproduction seems to be not so much, partly for some single quality properties as resolution and sharpness progressive scan reproduction is even superior or at least equivalent. The reasons for this seem to be as follows.

There is a line structure phenomena, that causes a viewer to assess a natural picture with higher resolution and higher sharpness, if the picture is structured by lines. This is true even if the picture shows artifacts, which obviously are false. So this subjective test shows clearly that the grade of flatfield honoured by the viewer has carefully to be chosen.

Furthermore, the vertical resolution of vertically pre- and postfiltered signals is equal to the horizontal resolution, if the resolution bounds are equal for both directions. From the subjective tests can be concluded that the subjective resolution (and sharpness) are nearly equal for the vertically pre- and postfiltered signal and for the progressive scan. For the latter Kell's factor has been used up to now, to specify the vertical resolution respectively to reduce horizontal resolution to get the same impression for horizontal and vertical resolution. This seems to be inadequate from the standpoint of picture quality, because resolution is not reduced in the subjective assessment of the viewer.

Therefore, it comes out, that there is no justification for a Kell's factor in general, neither for pre- and postfiltered signals nor for progressive scanned pictures - because of these subjective effects.

To conclude from these tests that vertical pre- and post-filtering compared with progressive scan reproduction is a poor method to improve picture quality seems to be wrong:

- A certain amount of additional line structure can be introduced by monitors with smaller spot size.

- The vertical interpolation generates gaps between the periodic spectra (see Figure 9). So there is the possibility to implement some nonlinear enhancement techniques /16/ in vertical direction without generating aliasing distortions. Maybe half a grade additional improvement on the CCIR comparison scale or even more in the case of noise distortion /16/ can be achieved.

- It depends on the application whether progressive scan or vertical pre- and postfiltering is superior. In the case of e.g. information retrieval or document transmission the improved resolution of progressive scan is not usable because of the danger of artifacts and errors. Vertical pre- and post-filtering yields an error free picture scanning and reproduction.

Diagonal Pre- and Postfiltering

One of the most powerful compatible improvements of picture quality can be achieved by introducing offset sampling in connection with diagonal pre- and postfiltering (Figure 1, No.4) and a high line number pick-up and reproduction. Again, it is possible to get rid of aliasing and line structure distortion. In addition an increased vertical and horizontal reolution can be achieved.

The final spectrum to be reproduced by the monitor is the same as in Figure 9. Again, the spectra are arranged on an offset sampling grid and there are gaps between the spectra. The corresponding spectra in the f^y, f^x-plane are shown in Figure 12 for $f^t = 0$ and $f^t = 25$ Hz (dotted areas). Again, we get an offset sampling grid with gaps between the spectra. The spectra lying within the area of the reconstruction filter (monitor and eye), which is assumed to be circular in the spatial f^y, f^x-plane, are the basic spectrum and small negligible parts of the 25 Hz components. So in total, we get rid of aliasing, line structure distortion and 25 Hz flickering components.

This concept has been implemented /3/, /5/, the transfer functions in diagonal direction used for this implementation are similar chosen to that of the vertical pre- and postfiltering, as in Figure 10. So, again, there is an optimization in the sense of video filtering with negligible residual distortions. Besides overcoming 25 Hz flicker vertical and horizontal resolution is increased. Figure 13 shows a zone plate pattern. The conventional system (Figure 13a) shows aliasing moiré and line structure distortion in vertical direction, whereas the system with diagonal pre- and postfiltering (Figure 13b) overcomes these distortions and shows a higher vertical and horizontal resolution.

The picture quality comparison (Figure 7) with the standard system now shows a considerable improvement of more than 2 grades ("Lady with hat") respectively 2,8 grades ("Water). Also the improvements for the single assessments (resolution, sharpness, flicker reduction) are very impressive.

The distance to the high line number system (Figure 8) is not more than about 1.3 grades. It should be mentioned, that this is not much because of the described enlarging effect of compared differences as mentioned above.

So it can be concluded from these comparison, that diagonal pre- and postfiltering is a very good method for compatibly improving picture quality. The achieved quality then is very near to that of a real high line number system. And again, there are further possibilities to improve picture quality, such as nonlinear enhancement, as for the vertical pre- and postfiltering approach.

Flicker Free Reproduction

As pointed out in detail e.g. in /15/ for all the described concepts compatibly improving picture quality pictures with motion can be processed by motionadaptive techniques. So it is possible for the progressive scan reproduction as well as for the vertical or diagonal pre- and postfiltering to implement 100 Hz converters for overcoming large area flicker without any motion blur.

Such a conversion can be realized e.g. by simple repetition yielding a 100 Hz field rate. The final spectrum of such a signal in the f^y, f^t-plane is shown in Figure 14. Obviously there is a total flicker free (25 Hz, 50 Hz) reproduction. As soon as monitors respectively projectors with 100 Hz field repetition i. e. a fourfold line frequency are available such a complete flicker free reproduction is available too.

5   Conclusions

In this paper some methods improving picture quality have been investigated with respect to their subjective picture qualities. These qualities have been determined by subjective assessments. A quality comparison has been described between

- standard television system
- progressive scan reproduction
- vertical pre- and postfiltering
- diagonal pre- and postfiltering
- high line number (HDTV) system.

One main result is, that there is no justification to reduce vertical resolution of progressively scanned pictures by Kell's factor in general. Such a reduction is only true for special patterns such as horizontal lines. It comes out that the subjective impression of resolution of natural pictures is nearly the same for progressive scan as for the vertical pre- and postfiltering. This is true even in the case of errors and artifacts by line structure distortion. If the subjective impression of resolution for both methods is the same, both systems can be characterized by the same resolution bounds and there is no sense for reduction by Kell's factor.

This is an important point, because if we apply the same modulation transfer function in horizontal and in vertical direction, we get the same resolution or sharpness in these directions. And in a twodimensionally bandlimited system with the same cutoff frequencies $f_c{}^y = f_c{}^x$ we should never reduce the horizontal bandwidth by Kell's factor if we apply progressive scanning (at the receiver).

Another main result is that progressive scan reproduction is a powerful method of improving picture quality. This method can be implemented by modifying only the receiver concept. The picture quality with diagonal pre- and postfiltering is superior to all other compatible improvements. Compared with the standard television system an improvement of at least 2 grades of the CCIR comparison scale is achievable. The real HDTV system is about 2.5 grades better than the standard system - at the price of a fourfold bandwidth for the transmission channel.

Acknowledgement

The authors like to thank very much

- the german ministry of research and technology (BMFT) for supporting these studies,

- Dipl.-Ing H. Elsler, Dipl.-Ing. E. Güttner and Dipl.-Ing. F. Stollenwerk for some results out of their works and helpful discussions.

References

/1/ Wendland, B.: Entwicklungsalternativen für zukünftige Fernsehysteme. Fernseh- und Kinotechnik 34 (1980), No. 2. pp. 41-48.

/2/ Wendland, B.: HDTV Studies on Compatible Basis with Present Standards. In "Television Technology in the 80's", published by the SMPTE, Scarsdale, New York, 1981, pp. 124-131.

/3/ Schröder, H.; Elsler, H.: Planare Vor- and Nachfilterung für Fernsehsignale. NTZ-Archiv, vol. 4 (1982), No. 10, pp. 303-312.

/4/ Wendland, B.: Entwicklungsalternativen für HDTV - Systeme. NTZ-Archiv, vol. 4 (1982), No. 10, pp. 285-291.

/5/ Uhlenkamp, D.; Güttner, E.: Verbesserte Wiedergabe von Normfernsehsignalen. NTZ-Archiv, vol. 4 (1982), No. 10, pp. 313-322.

/6/ Fujio, T.: High Definition Television of the future, IEEE Trans. on Broadcasting BC-26 (1980), No. 4, pp. 113-118.

/7/ Stollenwerk, F.: Qualitätsvergleich von Zeilensprung- und Vollbildwiedergabe. Frequenz, vol. 37 (1983), No. 11-12, pp. 334-344.

/8/ Stollenwerk, F.: to be published.

/9/ Schröder, H.: On Line-Free and Flicker-Free Television Reproduction. Circuits, Systems and Signal Processing, special issue on "Spatial-Temporal Filtering, just published.

/10/ Lucas, K.; Windram, M. D.: Direct Television Broadcasts by Satellite - Desirability of a New Transmission Standard. IBA E&D Report 116/81.

/11/ Schröter, F.: Fernsehtechnik I. Springer Verlag, Berlin, 1956.

/12/ Sandbank, Moffat: High Definition Television and Compatibility with Existing Standards. SMPTE-Journal, Vol. 9.2 (May 83) No. 5.

/13/ Jackson, R.N.; Annegarn, M.J.J.C.: Compatible Systems for High Quality Television. SMPTE Journal, Vol. 92, No. 7 (1983) pp. 719 - 723.

/14/ Clarke, C.K.P.: High Quality Decoding for PAL Inputs to Digital YUV Studios, BBC Research Department, Report BBC RD 1982/12

/15/ Wendland, B.; Schröder, H.: Signal Processing for New HQTV Systems. This issue.

/16/ Jacobsen, M.: Picture Enhancement for PAL-Coded TV Signals by Digital Processing in TV Receivers. SMPTE Journal 92 (1983), No. 2, pp. 164-169.

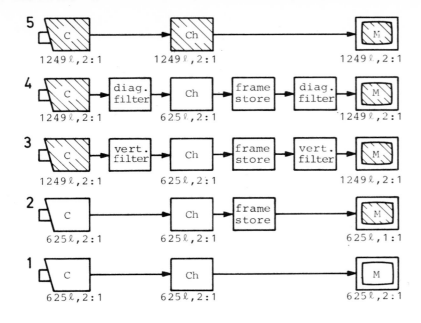

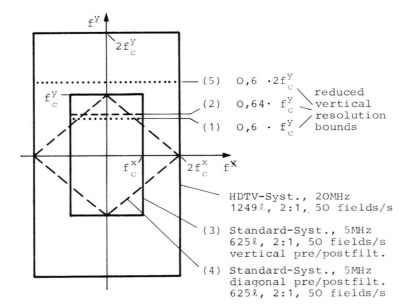

Fig. 1.
Transmission schemes for different TV systems.
(1) Standard system.
(2—4) Compatibly improved systems.
(5) High line number system.

Fig. 2.
Resolution bounds for different TV systems corresponding to Fig. 1.

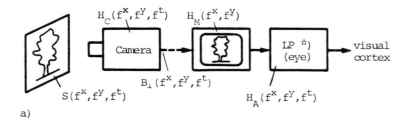

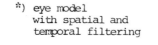

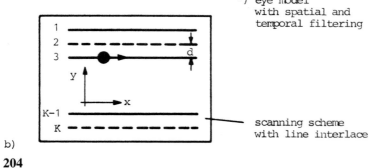

Fig. 3.
Video scanning and transmission.

204

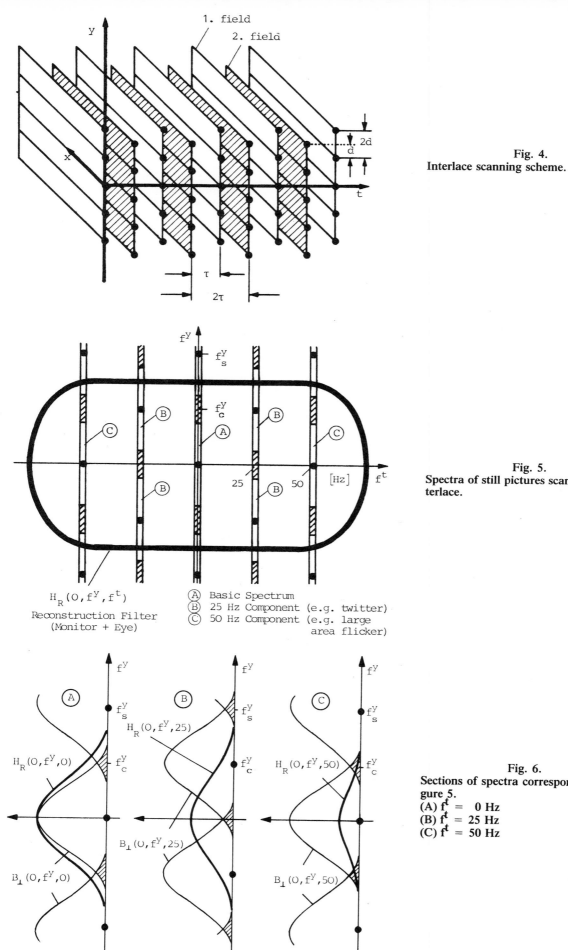

Fig. 4.
Interlace scanning scheme.

Fig. 5.
Spectra of still pictures scanned with interlace.

$H_R(0, f^y, f^t)$

Reconstruction Filter
(Monitor + Eye)

(A) Basic Spectrum
(B) 25 Hz Component (e.g. twitter)
(C) 50 Hz Component (e.g. large
    area flicker)

Fig. 6.
Sections of spectra corresponding to Figure 5.
(A) $f^t = 0$ Hz
(B) $f^t = 25$ Hz
(C) $f^t = 50$ Hz

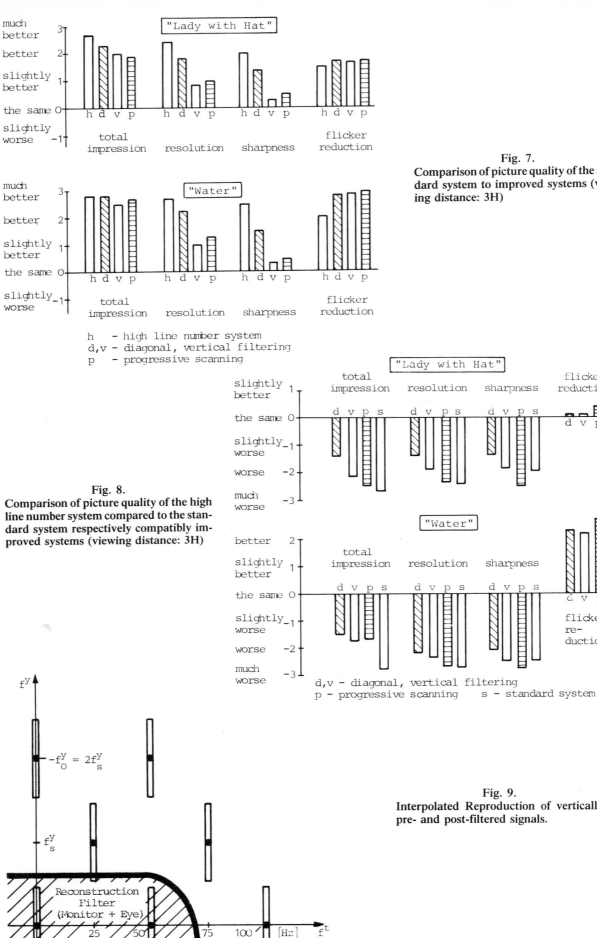

Fig. 7.
Comparison of picture quality of the standard system to improved systems (viewing distance: 3H)

h   - high line number system
d,v - diagonal, vertical filtering
p   - progressive scanning

Fig. 8.
Comparison of picture quality of the high line number system compared to the standard system respectively compatibly improved systems (viewing distance: 3H)

d,v - diagonal, vertical filtering
p - progressive scanning   s - standard system

Fig. 9.
Interpolated Reproduction of vertically pre- and post-filtered signals.

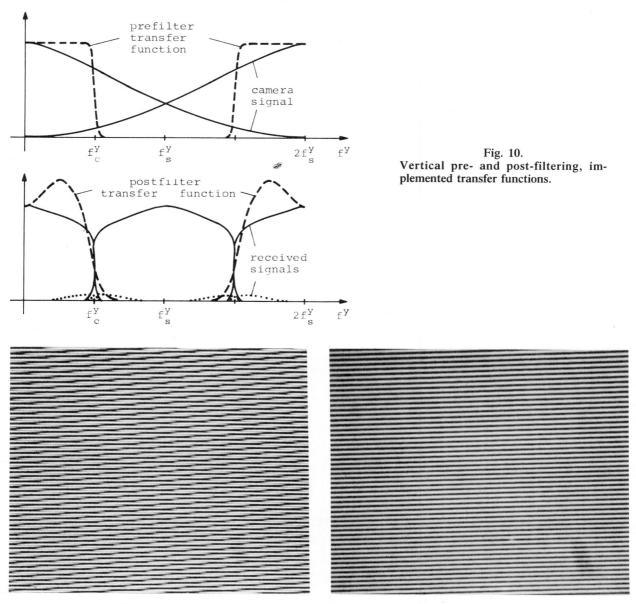

Fig. 10.
Vertical pre- and post-filtering, implemented transfer functions.

Fig. 11. Improved picture reproduction by vertical pre- and post-filtering.
(a) conventional   (b) flat field

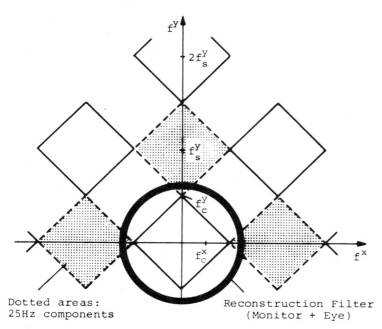

Fig. 12.
Diagonal pre- and post-filtering, interpolated reproduction.

207

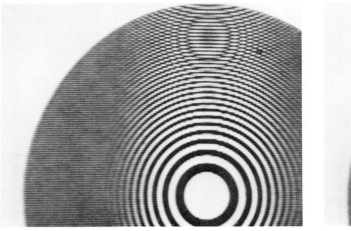
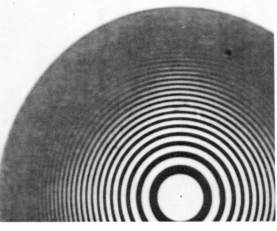

Fig. 13.
Improved picture reproduction by diagonal pre- and post-filtering
(a) conventional   °   (b) processed

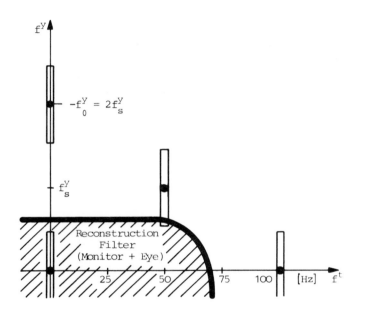

Fig. 14.
Total Flicker-Free Television Reproduction with 100 Hz Field Frequency.

Broder Wendland was born in Germany on May 16, 1934. He received the Ing. (grad) degree in electrical engineering from the Ingenieur School Berlin in 1957, and, the Diplom Ing. degree from the Technical University of Berlin in 1965. From 1965 to 1969 he was with the Heinrich Hertz Institute, Berlin, where he was concerned with data transmission techniques. In 1969 he received the Dr. Ing. degree. From 1969 to 1975 he worked at the research institute of AEG-Telefunken, Ulm, FRG where he was engaged in commercial picturephone techniques. In 1975 he became full professor at the University of Dortmund. Since 1979 he is working in the field of High Picture Quality Television Systems and High Definition Television. In 1980 he got the Eduard Rhein Prize '79 for his proposals for compatible improvement of TV-systems. In 1982 he became chairman of a HQTV study group which was founded by the Nachrichtentechnische Gesellschaft (NTG) and the Fernsehund Kinotechnische Gesellschaft (FKTG) to study all aspects of high quality television systems for the future.

Dr. Schröder received his Dipl.-Ing. degree in "Communication techniques" from the Technical University of Berlin in 1971 and his Dr.-Ing. degree in 1977 from the Technical University of Munich. From 1971—1977 he was with Siemens AG, Munich working in a research laboratory on video transmission and speech processing. In 1977 he joined the institute for communication techniques, University of Dortmund (Leader: Prof. Dr.-Ing. B. Wendland) as a chief engineer. There he works in the field of "High Quality Television" and gives lectures on signal theory and communications systems.

B-MAC, An Optimum Format for Satellite Television Transmission

John D. Lowry
Scientific-Atlanta Inc.
Toronto, Canada

A broad examination has been undertaken of the market requirements for distribution to the home via satellite of television programming and other services. While extensive discussion has taken place on the needs for Direct Broadcast Satellite (DBS), the format selected must be capable of distribution on Cable (CATV), through Satellite Master Antenna Television Systems (SMATV) for multiple family dwellings, and via UHF terrestrial broadcast. Commercial considerations require hard encryption of the audio and data, and hard scrambling of the video, combined with broad addressing and tiering capabilities, impulse pay-per-view, personal messages, teletext facilities, and potential expansion for extended definition television. These requirements are added to the basic essentials of picture and sound quality equal to, or better than, services presently provided.

During the past two years a transmission format meeting these market needs has been developed. The decoding hardware for both professional and consumer use is currently being reduced to a set of integrated circuits scheduled for completion in late 1984. The following is a discussion of some of the avenues that were examined, a brief description of the final system selected, and some of the rationale for this choice.

A NEW FORMAT

The initial impetus for the development of the system came from two directions: (1) the investigation of an improved format for DBS transmission and (2) a parallel effort investigating means to secure signals for pay television which is fast becoming a multi-billion dollar industry.

This requirement for scrambled signals which are by definition non-standard and the introduction of a completely new direct broadcast satellite service has presented the rare opportunity for the commercial success of a new signal format.

Both NTSC and PAL were designed for Amplitude Modulation (AM) transmission with the NTSC specification finalized in 1953, four years before the first Sputnik satellite was launched. FM transmission via satellite was not seriously contemplated at that time.

In a marketplace driven in part by the need to reduce dish size, noise in the signal is of great importance. With AM transmission noise is relatively flat in relation to frequency (Fig.1) whereas FM noise is triangular, increasing with frequency (Fig.2). The human eye perceives a noise characteristic that is basically the opposite and complementary to the triangular FM noise with visibility of noise maximized at lower frequencies (Fig.3). This optimal relationship of FM and human perception is not the case with the NTSC or PAL television systems, which frequency multiplex the colour information on a subcarrier at the relatively high frequencies of 3.58 MHz and 4.43 MHz respectively.

When the colour is demodulated down to baseband for display, the high amplitude noise which was present on the high frequency subcarrier is converted to low frequency noise and becomes much more visible (Fig.4).

DIGITAL SATELLITE TRANSMISSION

A number of methods have been explored to improve satellite transmission including the development of all-digital transmission systems. These have been seen to yield excellent quality at the receiving point, in some cases providing quality essentially equivalent to that transmitted. Due to the extremely high data rates required for video, all-digital transmission requires complex and expensive equipment at the receiver. Even with state-of-the-art large-scale integration, it is doubtful that all-digital transmission could be cost effective for use in the home in the 1980's or, possibly, well into the 1990's.

MULTIPLEXED ANALOG COMPONENTS

A hybrid system has therefore been selected which uses digital transmission techniques for the audio and data, combined with analog component video. This system known as Multiplexed Analog Components (MAC) was originally developed for satellite transmission by the Independent Broadcasting Authority (IBA) in the U.K. The chrominance and luminance are transmitted in a line by line, time multiplexed, rather than frequency multiplexed mode (Fig.5). Numerous technical papers have been published detailing the merits of sequential chroma/luminance transmission.

AUDIO/VIDEO FORMAT OPTIONS

For the past year and one-half there has been a great deal of discussion on the C-MAC format, but there are three other basic options open for the combining of data with video. These are described by the matrix of frequency multiplex or time multiplex at either baseband or RF (Fig.6).

A-MAC

A-MAC provides a baseband frequency multiplex of the audio and data on a subcarrier at approximately 7 Mhz (Fig. 7 and 8). This provides the advantage of an extremely rugged data channel, however, it has limitations on its potential for threshold extension, and bandwidth constraints on video for extended definition.

D-MAC

D-MAC employs frequency multiplexed data at RF. With video centred at 70 Mhz, for example, the data might be on a separate carrier at 85 Mhz. Audio and video can be uplinked from separate locations and exceptionally high data rates are possible, but two receivers are required and interference problems are raised.

C-MAC

C-MAC time multiplexes the data at RF (Fig.9) providing in excess of 20 megabits per second during the 9 microseconds that would otherwise be devoted to the horizontal blanking period. One advantage is the efficiency of direct demodulation from RF to digital data providing for high data rates for up to 8 audio channels. Separate demodulation of this data is costly and, in terms of baseband bandwidth (Fig.10), a transmission channel in excess of 10 Mhz is necessary for applications such as cable or SMATV.

B-MAC

B-MAC time multiplexes the audio and data at baseband using a multi-level code during the 9 microsecond "horizontal blanking" period (Fig.11). The video is essentially identical to C-MAC but the bandwidth of the system is held to just over 6 Mhz by utilizing the wide dynamic range of the transmitted "video" signal for multilevel data (Fig.12). This provides a satellite signal that can also be used for cable, SMATV, terrestrial microwave or UHF broadcast without the need for decoding at an intermediate distribution point.

In Satellite Master Antenna Television (SMATV) applications, for example, the B-MAC signal can be received from the satellite and passed directly through a cable system within the building for subscriber access control at each individual television set. This also provides the potential for high quality red, green and blue signals for the television display combined with digital stereo audio directly to each viewer.

Compared with C-MAC, B-MAC has the somewhat lower data rate of 1.8 megabits per second but it has many advantages over C-MAC including its compatability with conventional video tape recorders and demodulation with one conventional low cost satellite receiver. It also retains compatability with future extended definition systems using wider bandwidths (Fig.13).

DIGITAL SYNC

Sync is extremely rugged, yet it requires .2% of the total time as opposed to over 20% required for NTSC or PAL (Fig.14). Sync is carried on one line in the vertical interval as a highly redundant digital word and provides for receiver lockup at 0 dB carrier to noise. This will assist the amateur in dish set-up and satellite signal acquisition, and provide picture continuity under the most adverse reception conditions.

Through elimination of the traditional sync pulses and both the colour and audio subcarriers, FM deviation in the channel, IF filters, and the pre-emphasis/de-emphasis networks can all be optimized to yield excellent results. Smaller satellite receiving dishes or improved performance is achieved. B-MAC is also uneffected by most non-linearities in the transmission channel.

Further significant reductions in dish size can be achieved by reducing the video bandwidths and data rates for applications, for example, where "video cassette quality" pictures and 2-channel stereo sound are considered viable.

Standard NTSC or PAL satellite receiving equipment including dishes, low noise converters, receivers, and television sets can be used with the B-MAC system. Certain portions of this chain will be lower cost and have improved performance when their design is optimized for B-MAC. Of the systems studied, B-MAC yields the lowest cost satellite distribution system (Fig.15).

B-MAC ADVANTAGES

In summary, the principal advantages of the B-MAC system are:

a)   a component system eliminating cross luminance and cross colour effects;
b)   colour noise is reduced;
c)   colour bandwidth increased;
d)   red, green, blue signals are available for improved television display;
e)   rugged, truly digital sync;
f)   improved threshold extension techniques can be applied when all subcarriers are eliminated;
g)   dish size is reduced.

VIDEO SCRAMBLING

Scrambling of the analog video signal can be done in two basic ways. The amplitude of the signal can be varied or the video can be re-arranged in relation to time.

The most elementary scrambling system is sync suppression (or sync denial) which has been used for many years in the cable television industry in North America. Even in a controlled distribution cable environment, piracy of signals with many of the sync suppression systems runs high. With minor modification, some of the more sophisticated new television sets are capable of providing a locked picture in the absence of traditional sync pulses thereby automatically defeating such systems.

Sync suppression and sync denial are considered to be inadequate for satellite distribution if any level of controlled access is to be maintained even for the short term.

The more sophisticated scrambling methods include video inversion, line reversal, line segmentation or line rotation, line shuffling using a field store, and line translation.

Video Inversion

Video inversion is an amplitude system providing a relatively low order of security. It is particularly subject to non-linearities in the channel. Should there be black stretch and white compression in the channel when the transmitted video is inverted, this becomes black compression and white stretch yielding an amplitude flicker at the rate of the change from inverted to non-inverted video (Fig.16).

In general, all systems varying amplitude have provided relatively low security and, in some cases, low quality.

Line Shuffle

Use of a field store at both the transmit and receive points to re-organize the line sequence during transmission can provide highly obscured pictures. Effectively perfect reconstruction of the picture can be achieved in the descrambler through knowlege of the correct line sequence. This is potentially a high-quality scrambling system, but its cost will remain relatively high, particularly in light of the requirement for a random access memory in the decoder. Integrated circuits for field store use being developed today generally provide sequential access only.

Line Segmentation

Line segmentation or "line rotation" scrambling is essentially a technique where each line is divided into two segments which are interchanged in position for transmission (Fig.17). Portions of the line are repeated to mask the effects of the "splice". Using digital sampling, the lines are reconstructed in the descrambler with the repeated portion of the line around the splice discarded. This system, and variations of it, place excessive demands on specifications such as linearity, line tilt, and frequency response in the various equipment in the transmission chain.

Line tilt in the order of 3% to 5% is usually not visible to the human eye because of the gradual change across the picture (Fig.18). When even 1% tilt is added to a segmented line signal during transmission, the reconstructed pictures are visibly unacceptable (Fig. 19 and 20). When descrambled, the tilt becomes a dc level shift in the picture which changes from line to line as the scrambling patterns change, and manifests itself as highly visible low frequency noise (Fig.21). A total system line tilt specification of .3% is required to provide acceptable video. This defines a very basic rule about video: the clamp-to-video timing relationship must be held constant.

Should a segmented line picture be distributed via a vestigial sideband (VSB) cable system, another impairment problem is encountered. Any mistuning at the receiver causes a boost or attenuation of the low frequency component of the signal (Fig.22) thereby effecting the step response of the channel (Fig.23). A low frequency transition that is artificially created by line segmentation scrambling yields a long overshoot or undershoot recovery period which is visible in the descrambled video and has no relation to actual picture transitions (Fig.24).

Line Translation

Line translation scrambling uses a horizontal time-shift technique. The blanking time is varied on a line-to-line basis from a minimum of zero to a maximum of two times the normal blanking. The clamp period is tied to the video with that relationship held constant (Fig.25). This line translation, or "time base" scrambling system redistributes the picture information in time (Fig.26), yielding a scrambled picture that is totally obscure, yet can be reconstructed in the descrambler to a high-quality picture with no visible or measurable degradation or artifacts relating to the scrambling technique.

The scrambling is dynamic in that the patterns are changed every frame. A benefit, apart from controlling viewer access, is the decorrelation of transmission channel interference patterns when the pictures are descrambled. The only thing asked of the transmission channel is that it be relatively time invariant for approximately 100 microseconds, a specification easily met by every normal channel today.

B-MAC format decoding, line translation descrambling, or both together, require a maximum of three TV lines of storage. While providing both high security and high quality, the cost is low and it is compatible with CCD technology (Fig.27). The video descramble key is encrypted using the data encryption standard (DES) algorithm and is interleaved with other information in the digital data channel.

Data Channel

The digital data channel includes audio, addresses, the data decryption key, video descramble key, personal message data, and full field data as an option. The system supplies hi-fidelity digital stereo sound which can be connected to the viewers' standard hi-fi sound system.

Four-Channel Digital Audio

B-MAC has been designed with a four-channel digital audio system with 31.4 Khz or 31.2 KHz (two times the TV line frequency) digital sampling. A new enhanced delta modulation technique yields a dynamic range at the descrambler greater than 84 dB and very gentle failure under low carrier to noise ratio reception conditions. The audio is encrypted to the data encryption standard (DES). This encryption algorithm is applied on a bit-by-bit basis with the decryption keys and codes changing at irregular intervals. This provides dynamic DES encryption for the highest security commercially available.

A data channel with 94 K bits per second is standard. Any audio channel can be assigned to data transmission and reception, each channel providing 320K bits per second. Full field data is also available by replacing the picture with digital information. This yields an additional 10.8 million bits per second.

Addressing

The addressing technique provides for up to four billion addresses with redundancy for reliable reception. This high number of addresses provides for effectively infinite tiering. Addressing is at the rate of one million per hour. Effectively instant (1/4 second) access is provided to all authorized programs when the subscriber switches channels. The decoders are generic, and are capable of being addressed by any one or all program distributors using the system, depending on their desire to reach each individual viewer.

Text Services

Teletext is an integral part of the B-MAC system with 200 pages of encrypted or clear text available to all or any specific user with 20 seconds access. Uses include film sub-titles as a user option, sub-titles for the deaf, general and personal messages, program guides, current tiering and parental lock information and individual account status for monthly and pay-per-view billing including presentation of the bill itself.

Summary

The B-MAC transmission, scrambling and encryption system employs a satellite optimized format; highly secure yet low-cost scrambling; a high data channel capacity; virtually unlimited addressing; facilities for pay-per-view programming and infinite tiering; multi-channel digital audio; and hard encryption. Personal messages can be sent to any individial, group, or to all receiving points. Red, green, blue video is available along with baseband NTSC or PAL and RF channel outputs. B-MAC provides excellent potential for use of two channels on one transponder and leaves the door open for extended definition techniques in the future.

The current implementation of the system is designed for professional use at cable headends, tele-conferencing, and other professional applications to the 525 line standard. The technology is also being implemented as a set of custom integrated circuits for both 525 and 625 line standards (Fig.28). These custom ICs and other components will be carried on a printed circuit board approximately 6 inches by 9 inches and will be inserted into certain satellite receivers and become integral to the design of others (Fig.29). Sample quantities of this decoding equipment will be available late this year, with production quantities available in the first half of 1985.

216

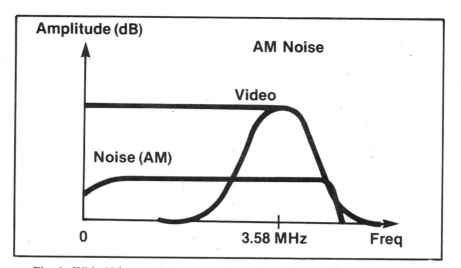

Fig. 1. With AM transmission, noise is relatively flat in relation to frequency.

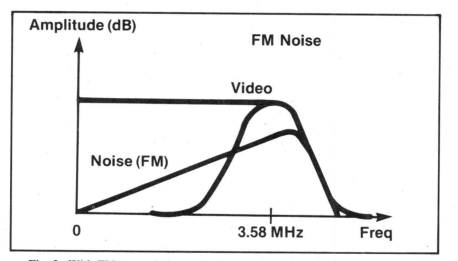

Fig. 2. With FM transmission, noise is triangular, rising with the frequency.

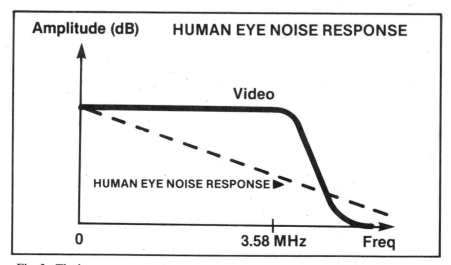

Fig. 3. The human eye perceives a noise characteristic which is essentially triangular decreasing with the frequency.

217

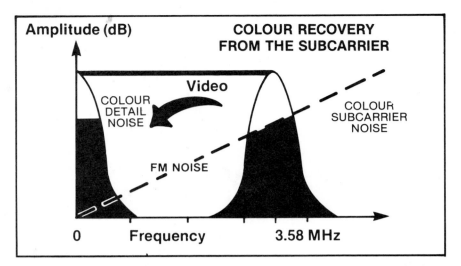

Fig. 4. Chroma demodulation converts high-frequency, high-amplitude noise into more visible low-frequency, high-amplitude noise.

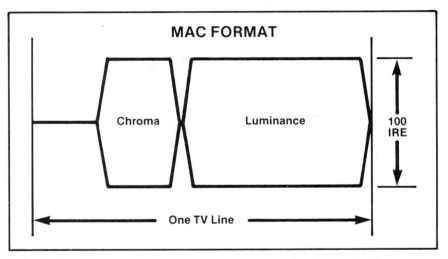

Fig. 5. Chrominance and luminance are time compressed and transmitted in a sequential format on each TV line.

FORMAT OPTIONS FOR DATA
COMBINED WITH VIDEO

	Frequency Multiplex	Time Multiplex
Baseband	A	B
RF	D	C

Fig. 6. Matrix of four possible format options.

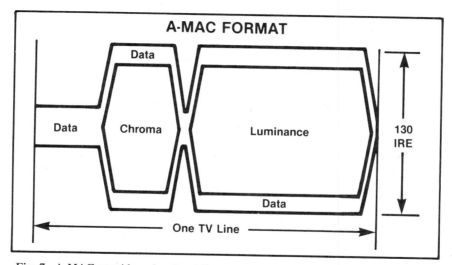

Fig. 7. A-MAC provides a baseband frequency multiplex of the audio and data on a subcarrier.

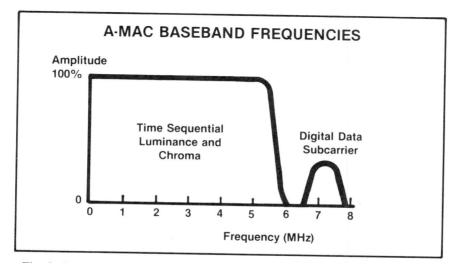

Fig. 8. Luminance and chroma occupy approximately 6 MHz with a digital data subcarrier at 7.16 MHz.

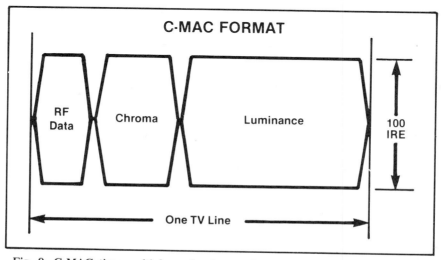

Fig. 9. C-MAC time multiplexes the data at RF with the baseband chroma and luminance on each TV line.

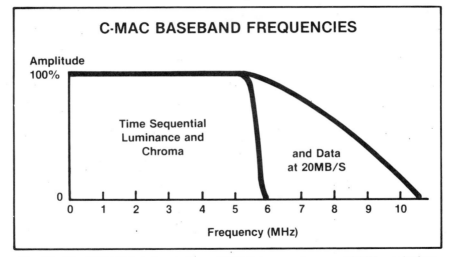

Fig. 10. The C-MAC data burst of over 20 Mbits/sec requires over 10 MHz equivalent baseband bandwidth.

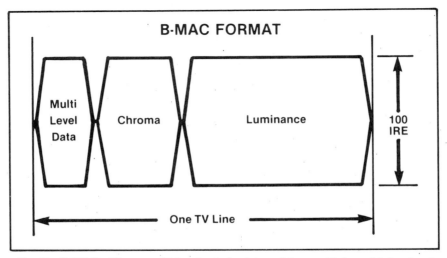

Fig. 11. B-MAC utilizes a multi-level code for data and time multiplexes this baseband signal with chroma and luminance.

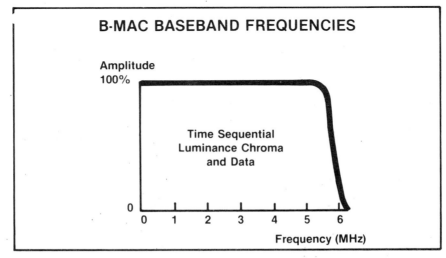

Fig. 12. The baseband bandwidth of B-MAC is held to just over 6 MHz for data, chrominance and luminance yet provides 1.8 Mbits/sec.

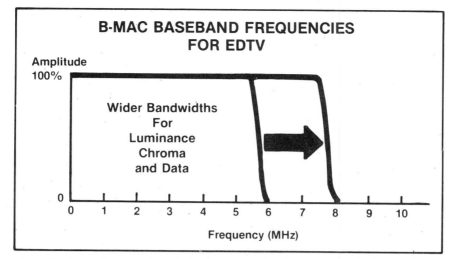

Fig. 13. A broad range of market requirements for the complete television delivery system are met by B-MAC.

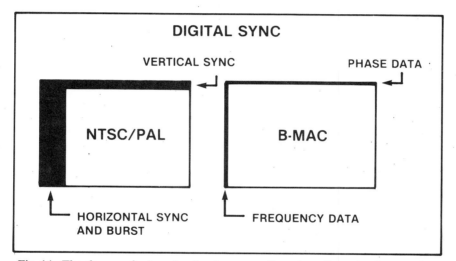

Fig. 14. The absence of subcarriers for chroma, audio or data allows simple expansion of bandwidths for extended definition television systems in the future.

MAC FORMAT OPTIONS

	A-MAC	B-MAC	C-MAC	D-MAC
Data Capacity (approx.)	2 Mb/s	1.8 Mb/s	2.5 Mb/s	3 Mb/s +
Cable Compatible	no	yes	no	no
STV/MDS Compatible	no	yes	no	no
Conventional Satellite Receiver Compatible	yes	yes	no	no
VTR Compatible	no	yes	no	no
Compatible with EDTV Bandwidths	no	yes	yes	yes
Cost	medium	low	medium	high

Fig. 15. Sync is replaced by a digital code on one line in the vertical interval (defining the top left-hand corner of the picture), combined with a burst on each line for phase and frequency to generate all timing requirements.

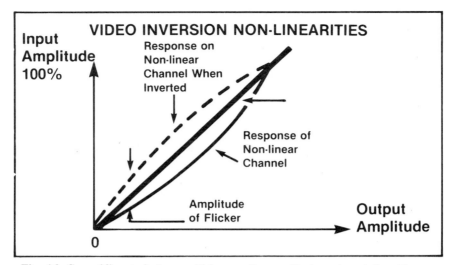

Fig. 16. Scrambling techniques which vary the amplitude or invert the video are subject to picture degradation due to transmission non-linearities.

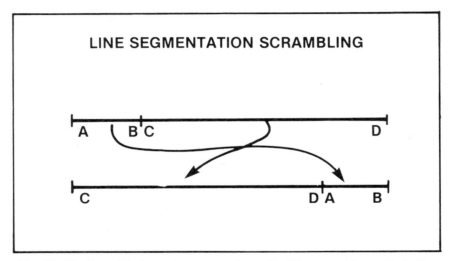

Fig. 17. The line might be cut in any one of, say, 32 different positions with the line AB, CD transmitted as CD, AB.

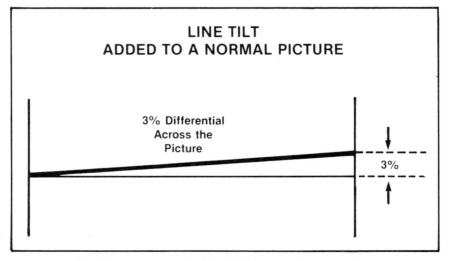

Fig. 18. A constant line tilt of 3% is normally not visible.

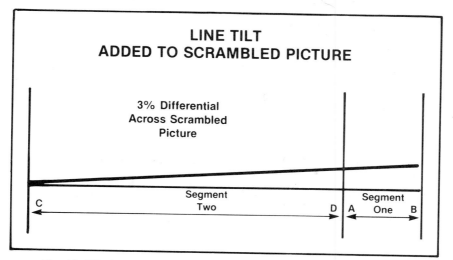

Fig. 19. Tilt is added during transmission to the scrambled line CD, AB.

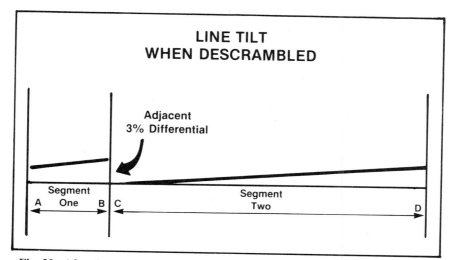

Fig. 20. After descrambling tilt is no longer a picture edge-to-edge gradual function.

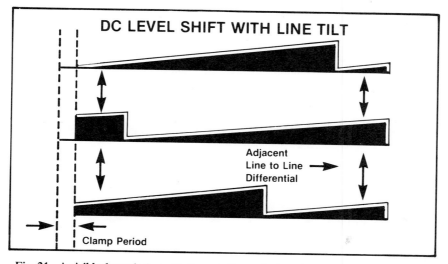

Fig. 21. A visible degradation with line rotation techniques is the DC level shift created by moving the video in relation to the clamp.

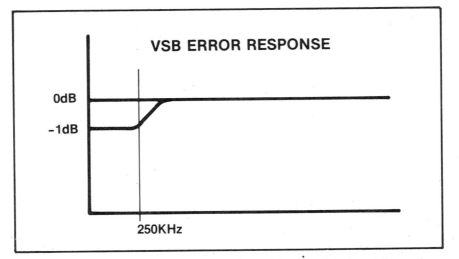

Fig. 22. In a vestigial sideband system such as cable, any mistuning at the receiver causes a boost or attenuation of low-frequency components.

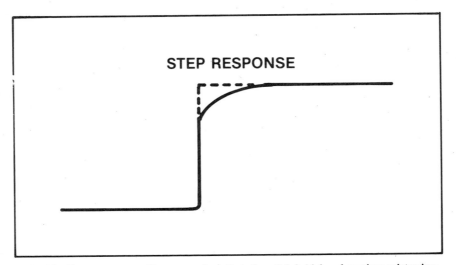

Fig. 23. Step response will vary as a function of vestigial sideband receiver mistuning.

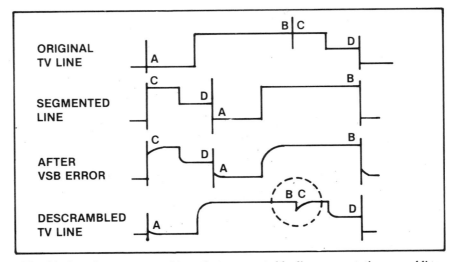

Fig. 24. Low-frequency transitions that are created by line segmentation scrambling yield a long overshoot or undershoot recovery period that has no relation to actual picture transitions.

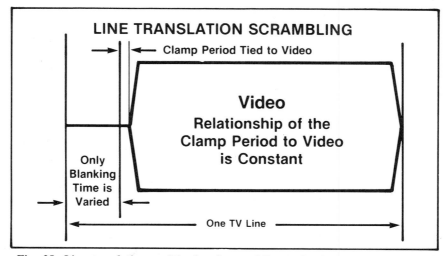

Fig. 25. Line translation or "timebase" scrambling maintains the video line and clamping period intact. Blanking time is varied from a minimum from 0 to a maximum of 2× normal.

LINE TRANSLATION SCRAMBLING

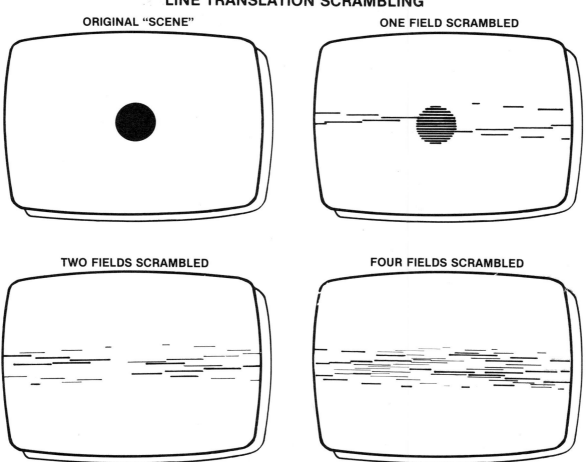

Fig. 26. Picture information is re-distributed in relation to time by the cumulative effect of reducing or expanding the horizontal blanking (data) period. The blanking (data) period is normal when averaged over each field.

VIDEO SCRAMBLING OPTIONS

	Sync Denial	Amplitude Reversal	Line Segmentation	Line Shuffle	Line Translation
Quality	high	low	low?	high	high
Security	low	low	high	high	high
Cost	low	low	high	very high	low
Compatibility with CCD	N/A	N/A	no	no	yes

Fig. 27. Line translation scrambling presents the most viable opportunity for a high quality secure consumer product.

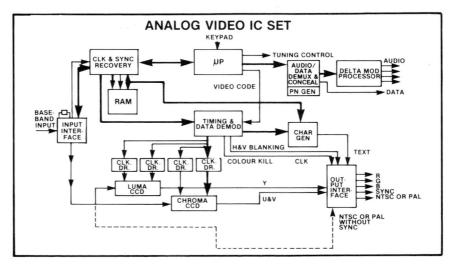

Fig. 28. A block diagram of the CCD implementation of the B-MAC descrambling and decryption receiver. It is compatible with both 525- and 625-line systems.

PROPOSED P.C. BOARD LAYOUT

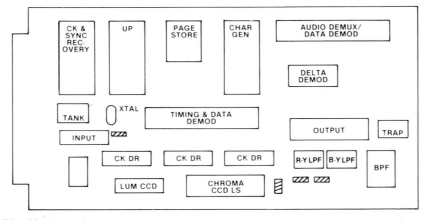

Fig. 29. Printed circuit board layout for the initial consumer implementation of the B-MAC system.

John Lowry started his career in television at the CBC in Toronto in 1952. In 1961, he worked on the development of the first electronic editing system for videotape in cooperation with Ampex Corporation and Advertel Productions. Mr. Lowry spent 6 years in film production and was co-developer of the Wesscam stabilizer for helicopter photography. In 1971, he developed the Image Transform signal processing and videotape-to-film conversion system. In 1976 Mr. Lowry founded Digital Video Systems, where he has pioneered numerous aspects of digital television. Today he is a member of the corporate staff of Scientific-Atlanta and Chairman of Digtal Video Systems.

Mr. Lowry is a Fellow of the SMPTE and has six patents on video noise reduction, image enhancement and film recording systems, with others pending.

Fiber Optic HD-TV Transmission Technologies

Toshinori Tsuboi, Koichi Asatani and Tetsuya Miki
Yokosuka Electrical Communication Laboratory, NTT
Yokosuka, Kanagawa, Japan

1 Introduction
High-definition Television (HD-TV) offers more realism than
the NTSC 4MHz Television System. Thus, HD-TV is expected to
be the next generation TV system and most of the HD-TV
equipment, such as HD-TV cameras, CRT monitors, projecting
monitors, VTRs and signal processors have already been
developed. Therefore a development of HD-TV signal
transmission systems is one of the most important items to
be studied at this time.

The HD-TV system proposed in Japan has 1125 horizontal
scanning lines, and a luminance signal bandwidth of 20MHz.
The bandwidth of the composite HD-TV signal is 20MHz to
30MHz, posing a broadband signal transmission requirement
for which fiber optic technology is suitable. Yokosuka
Electrical Communication Laboratory (YECL) of Nippon
Telegraph and Telephone Public Corporation (NTT) has been
carrying out feasibility experiments for fiber optic HD-TV
transmission systems(1)~(4). YECL is now planning
laboratory tests and field trials of HD-TV transmission
systems.

This paper reviews the main HD-TV transmission experiments
in Japan, and describes the configuration of the field trial
system and its experimental results. This paper also
discusses design concepts of HD-TV distribution networks.

2 HD-TV system experiments in Japan
Japan Broadcasting Corporation (NHK) has proposed an HD-TV
system, as shown in Table I (5).

Direct broadcast satellite and fiber optic transmission
technologies are candidate media for HD-TV transmission
services. Major HD-TV transmission experiments in Japan are
shown in Table II. Based on our feasiblity experiments, we
developed a field trial system for HD-TV transmission.

3 Transmission system configuration
A long distance point-to-point HD-TV transmission system
consists of subscriber loops and a trunk line, as shown in
Fig.1. An analog baseband transmission has an advantage of
low cost, although SNR degradation occurs due to the
increased number of repeaters needed. Digital transmission
is necessary for long-haul transmission and SNR is
independent of transmission distance. Thus, analog fiber
optic transmission is used for the subscriber loops and
digital transmission is used for the trunk line.

In the PCM coding for HD-TV signals, at least 8-bit coding is required. Analog composite signal bandwidth is 20MHz to 30MHz. Thus, the transmission bit rate of digitalized analog composite signals is 400Mb/s to 800Mb/s. HD-TV signals and bit rates are shown in Fig.2. In Japan, fiber optic digital transmission systems suitable for HD-TV are shown in Table III. Besides these, F-6M which bit rate is 6.312Mb/s has been developed. Digitalized Time Compression Multiplexing (TCM) signal can be transmitted over the 5th order fiber optic transmission system (F-400M)(6).
A branching and routing switch for digital signals or TCM signals is needed to distribute HD-TV programs to many stations and to provide for selecting a single program source. Configuration of the field trial system is shown in Fig.3.

4 Design of TCM signal
4.1 Analog composite signals
The design of a composite signal format should take subscriber loops and trunk lines into consideration. There are two types of analog composite signals. One is based on an FDM scheme, and the other is the TDM scheme.

A half-line offset PAL (HLO-PAL) is an FDM format(5). The sub-carrier frequency of the chrominance signal is 24.3MHz and the composite signal bandwidth is 30MHz. The bit rate for the digital transmission of HLO-PAL is about 800Mb/s assuming that the sampling frequency is 4X(sub-carrier frequency) and that the quantizing is 8 bits.

YECL of NTT has proposed a Time Compression Multiplexing (TCM) format for HD-TV signal(3) that is based on the TDM scheme. The TCM signal bandwidth proposed is 20MHz. The bit rate for digital transmission of the TCM signal is about 400Mb/s. There is no cross-color due to transmission distortion on the line because the luminance signal and the chrominance signal are multiplexed in the TDM scheme.
The TCM signal is superior to the HLO-PAL signal from the point of view of the bandwidth, the bit rate, and the transmission characteristics. Thus the TCM signal has been adopted.

4.2 TCM signal format
The TCM signal used in feasibility experiment in YECL provides 0.73H as the scanning time(3),(4), where H is the total horizontal scanning time. In this paper, an improved TCM format is proposed to extend the scanning time.

(a) Luminance signal
The luminance signal bandwidth of HD-TV system is 20MHz. So, the luminance signal bandwidth in the TCM signal is set to 20MHz. The allocated period for the luminance signal can be extended to 0.776H. However, a standard scanning time is 0.8H and a monitor has an overscanning time of 5%. This

means that the effective scanning time is 0.76H. Thus,
0.776H scanning time practically covers the requirement.

(b) Chrominance signal
The luminance signal and the chrominance signal should be
multiplexed within the horizontal scanning time. The
wideband chrominance(Cw) signal and the narrowband
chrominance (C_N) signal are transmitted line-sequentially.
One-fourth of the period of the luminance signal can be
allocated for the chrominance signal. Thus, the chrominance
signal bandwidth is 5MHz and the time axis of the
chrominance signal is compressed by a factor of four in
order that the TCM signal bandwidth can be 20MHz. The
allocated period for the chrominance signal is 0.194H.

(c) Synchronizing signal
The synchronizing (sync) signal is used not only for
horizontal and vertical synchronizing but also for a timing
clock source and a phase alignment clock source between the
luminance signal and the chrominance signal. A burst
sine-wave sync and a conventional negative pulse sync are
available. Timing clock jitter from the burst sine-wave, is
more severe than from the pulse sync. The video amplitude
cannot occupy the full dynamic range for the pulse sync
signal, while it can occupy the full dynamic range for the
burst sine-wave sync signal. Also, the SNR of the video
signal for the burst sine-wave sync signal is better than
that for the pulse sync signal.
The sync error decreases to invert the phase of the
sine-wave in each line and good synchronizing performance is
achieved. Accordingly, the burst sine-wave has been adopted
as the sync signal. The sine-wane frequency is 12.947MHz.

(d) Audio signal
In the HD-TV system, there is a requirement to transmit a
high quality stereo audio signal. Pulse code modulated
(PCM) audio signals has been adopted to attain high quality.
There is not enough time in the horizontal scanning time to
allocate the audio signal. So, the PCM audio signal is
multiplexed into the vertical blanking period. The
allocated period is set to 50H in consideration of the
transmission bit rate. Enough time remains in the vertical
blanking period to also give additional services, for
example, 3ch audio program application in future.

Guard intervals prevent interference between the luminance
signal, the chrominance signal and the burst sync signal.
Total guard time is 0.009H. The TCM signal format and an
example of the TCM signal spectrum are shown in Figures 4
and 5.

4.3 TCM signal modulator and demodulator
In the modulator, the chrominance signal is digitalized by
an 8-bit A/D converter and stored in the random access

memory (RAM). Then, it is read out at a clockrate four times as fast as the writing clockrate, and converted back to an analog signal. Finally, the TCM signal is achieved by the multiplexing the time compressed Cw and C_N into the luminance signal.

In the demodulator, the TCM signal is digitalized by an 8-bit A/D converter and the chrominance signals Cw and C_N, are expanded. After the phase of each signal is aligned, each signal is converted back into an analog signal.

The PCM coding of the stereo audio signal is instantaneous companding from 13 to 11 bits with 7 segments. This coding rule is used to transmit FM broadcast programs in Japan. The sampling frequency is set to the horizontal scanning frequency 33.716KHz to enable easy multiplexing. An error correction bit is added, and the allocated period is 50H. Thus, the transmission bit rate is 20.715Mb/s. A block diagram of the TCM modulator and demodulator is shown in Fig.6. The main parameters of TCM signal are shown in Table IV.

5. Fiber optic HD-TV transmission system
Design objectives for main parameters between input of the TCM modulator and output of the TCM demodulator are shown in Table V.

5.1 Analog fiber optic transmission for subscriber loops
An optical fiber cable with graded-index multimode fibers was adopted for the subscriber loops. Loss is less than 4dB/Km for 0.85μm and less than 2.5dB/Km for 1.3μm, and 6dB down bandwidths are larger than 150MHz·Km for both 0.85μm and 1.3μm wavelengths(8).

Both LED's and LD's are optical source candidates for subscriber loops. The fiber-coupled power of the LD is greater than that of the LED. Thus, the maximum transmission length of an LD system is greater than that of an LED system. However, speckle noise (model noise) seriously affects transmission performance in LD and multimode fiber systems(9). Such techniques as superimposed pulse modulation and optical feedback to reduce speckle noise have been developed for 4MHz TV transmission(9). However, for HD-TV transmission, such techniques do not provide sufficient speckle noise reduction, since the bandwidth of the HD-TV signal is five times as wide as that of the conventional NTSC TV signal. The LED system is low cost and stable. Thus, the LED system has been adopted.

GaAlAs/GaAs-LED's in the 0.8μm region and InGaAsP/InP-LED's in the 1.3μm region are available. Optical fiber losses at the 1.3μm wavelength (~1dB/km) are lower than at the 0.8μm wavelength (~3~4dB/km). However, for fiber-coupled power, the temperature dependence of GaAlAs/GaAs-LED's is better than that of InGaAlP/InP-LED's as shown in Table VI. The maximum reach of GaAlAs/GaAs-LED's is longer than that of InGaAlP/InP-LED's, also, the nonlinear distortion of GaAlAs/GaAs-LED's is lower than that of InGaAlP/InP-LED's. Thus, the 0.89μm LED system has been adopted.

The configuration of an analog fiber optic transmission system is shown in Fig.7. Main parameters of the system are shown in Table VII.

5.2 Fiber optic digital transmission for trunk lines

The digitalized TCM signal can be transmitted over the 5th order fiber optic digital transmission system (F-400M). The F-400M system is being installed in the main trunk route in Japan, from Sapporo to Fukuoka by 1985. The route length is 2900Km. Thus, HD-TV service will be available in the main cities in Japan.

A high-speed PCM CODEC which converts TCM signals into 400Mb/s digital signals was developed. The coding method is 8-bit linear coding. The sampling clock is synchronous with the transmission line's clock so that no pulse stuffing is necessary.

Though the line section of the F-400M insures bit sequence independence (BSI), BSI is not maintained between coder/decoders and line terminals of the F-400M. An 8B1C code rule is adopted for excess zero code sequence suppression. The 8B1C code is one of the 8B9B codes. It consists of 8 coded bits and an associated complementary bit, which restricts the zero sequence to 9 bits and also helps to maintain the DC balance.

The frame format is shown in Fig.8. A frame length is 9 bits. Frame synchronization is accomplished by utilizing the complementary bit of the 8B1C code. The line bit rate is 397.2Mb/s, and the sampling frequency is 44.1MHz(=397.2MHz/9). A self-synchronizing scrambler is also tested to suppress static pattern jitter. The main parameters of the digital transmission system are shown in Table VIII.

5. Experimental results

Measured performance for the analog transmission system is shown in Table IX. The SNR of the CODEC is shown in Fig.9 and other measured performance for the digital transmission system is shown in Table X. Overall performance from the TCM modulator to the TCM demodulator (analog 2 links + digital 1 link + analog branching switch + digital branching switch) is shown in Table XI.
All performances meet the design objectives.

232

6. Distribution networks

Fiber optic technology is a key to the introduction of a wide variety of new information services, which will be provided via Information Network System (INS).
In the early stage, HD-TV will be utilized for leased line applications, teleconferences and video transmission services. Branching and routing equipments for analog and digital signals is necessary to distribute the HD-TV signal for these services.

Subscriber loops in the fully grown Information Network System will make full use of the potential capabilities of fiber optics. Wavelength-division-multiplexing (WDM) technology makes it possible to offer many kinds of services, such as telephone, high-speed data and video services through one fiber, creating economic advantage for the subscriber loops,as shown in Fig.10. In advanced cable HD-TV systems, which provide specific HD-TV programs according to subscribers' requests, the down stream path transmits HD-TV signals and the upstream path transmits requests from the subscribers.
Bit rate reduction technology will reduce the cost of the trunk line. These technologies will make HD-TV and other complex services feasible for "home-use" in the future.

7. Conclusion

The field trial system for HD-TV transmission over optical fiber was presented. Before the field trial, laboratory tests have been performed since January 1984. The feasibility of long distance HD-TV transmission has been confirmed through the laboratory test circuit between Musashino ECL and Asugi ECL which covers over 300Km by F-400M systems. The system will also be used in field trials in the Mitaka INS system in the suburbs of Tokyo and the International Science and Engineering Exposition in Tsukuba in March 1985.

Acknowledgment

The authors would like to express their gratitude to Dr. E. Iwahashi, Mr. S.Shinohara and Mr. S.Mano, YECL of NTT, for their encouragement. The authors are also grateful to Dr. J.Yamada and Mr. K.Maki for their discussions and Mr. H.Obara and Mr. N.Sakurai for their assistance in laboratory tests.

References

(1) K.Asatani, K.Sato, K.Maki and T.Miki :"Fiber Optic Analo Transmission Experiment for High-definition Television Signals Using Semiconductor Laser Diode" Electronics Letters, P.536, vol 16, no 14, July 1980.
(2) K.Sato and K.Asatani :"Fiber Optic Analog Video Transmission Using Laser Diodes" Rev. of ECL, NTT, (to

be published).

(3) J.Yamada, K.Maki and K.Asatani :"A Study on Digital
Transmission System for High-definition Television
Signals" Paper of Tech. Group Commun. Sys., IECE Japan,
CS-82-97, Dec. 1982 (in Japanese).

(4) K.Maki, J.Yamada and N.Sakurai :"A Feasibility
Experiment of Fiber Optic High-Definition Television
Transmission Using TCM and 400Mb/s Digital Signals"
Tech. Digest IOOC '83, June 1983.

(5) T.Fujio, J.Ishida, T.Komoto and T.Nishizawa
:"High-Definition Television System - Signal Standard
and Transmission" SMPTE J, P.579, vol 89, Aug. 1980.

(6) T.Ito, K.Nakagawa and Y.Hakamada :"Design and
Performances of the F-400M Trunk Transmission System
Using a Single-mode Fiber Cable" ICC'82, 6D.1.1, June
1982.

(7) K.Nakagawa, N.Ohta and T.Kanada :"Overview of Very High
Capacity Optical Transmission Systems" GLOBECOM'83,
P.121, Dec. 1983.

(8) K.Asatani, R.Watanabe, K.Nosu, T.Matsumoto and F.Nihei
:"A Field Trial of Fiber Optic Subscriber Loop Systems
Utilizing Wavelength-Division Multiplexers" IEEE
Trans.,Commun., vol COM-30, no 9, P.2127, Sept. 1982.

(9) K.Sato and K.Asatani :"Speckle Noise Reduction in Fiber
Optic Analog Video Transmission Using Semiconductor
Laser Diodes" IEEE Trans., Commun., vol COM-29, no 7,
P.1017, July 1981.

Table 1. Provisional standard for a high-definition TV[5]

Number of scanning lines	1125
Aspect ratio	5:3
Line interlace ratio	2:1
Field repetition frequency	60Hz
Video frequency bandwidth luminance(Y)signal	20MHz
chrominance(C)signal wideband(Cw)	7.0MHz
narrowband(C_N)	5.5MHz

$$\begin{pmatrix} Y \\ Cw \\ C_N \end{pmatrix} = \begin{pmatrix} 0.30 & 0.59 & 0.11 \\ 0.63 & -0.47 & -0.16 \\ -0.03 & -0.38 & 0.41 \end{pmatrix} \begin{pmatrix} R \\ G \\ B \end{pmatrix}$$

Table 2. Main features of HD-TV transmission experiments in Japan.

	Technical Research Lab. of NHK		Yokosuka Electrical Communication Lab., NTT			
Transmission technology	Broadcast satellite analog transmission	LED analog transmission	LD analog transmission	LD analog transmission	LD analog transmission	LD digital transmission
HD-TV signal format	Y-C separate	HLO-PAL	HLO-PAL	HLO-PAL	TCM	TCM-PCM
Modulation scheme	FM	Direct IM	Direct IM	Direct IM	Direct IM	PCM-IM
Bandwidth/ Bit rate	Y:75MHz C:25MHz	30MHz	30MHz	30MHz	20MHz	400Mb/s
Transmission distance	---	---	17Km	5.6Km	5Km	525Km *
Cable **	---	SI	SM	GI	GI	SM
Wavelength	(22GHz)	0.82µm	1.3µm	0.8µm	0.85µm	1.3µm
Phase ***	FR	TL	TL	FR	TL	TL
Test period	1978-1979	1978	1979	1980-1981	1982	1982

*   number of repeaters is 20, which is equivalent to 525Km.
**   SI : Step-index multimode, GI : Graded-index multimode
      SM : Single-mode
*** TL : Laboratory Test, FR : Field Trial

Table 3. Main parameters of fiber optic digital transmission systems suitable for HD-TV in Japan.

System	F-32M	F-100M	F-400M
Bit rate	32.064 Mb/s	97.728 Mb/s	397.2 Mb/s
Transmission code	Coded mark inversion(CMI)	8B1C	10B1C
Optical fiber cable	GI	GI (SM)	SM
Optical source	GaAlAsP-LD(S) InGaAsP-LD(L)	GaAlAsP-LD(S) InGaAsP-LD(L)	InGaAsP-LD
Optical detecter	Si-APD(S) Ge-APD(L)	Si-APD(S) Ge-APD(L)	Ge-APD
Repeater spacing	10 km(S) 20 km(L)	10 km(GI,S) 15 km(GI,L) 20 km(SI)	20 km
Transmission distance	-------	-------	2500 km
Error ratio	less than 10^{-11}/ repeater	less than 10^{-11}/ repeater	less than 10^{-11}/ repeater

(S) : Short wavelength
(L) : Long wavelength

Table 4. Main parameters of TCM signal.

TCM signal bandwidth	20MHz
Video frequency bandwidth	
luminance(Y)signal	20MHz
chrominance(C)signal*	
wideband (Cw)	5MHz
narrowband(C_N)	5MHz
Time compression ratio for chrominance signal	4:1
Audio signal	
bandwidth	15KHzx2channels
coding method	Instantaneous companding from 13 to 11 bits(7 segment)
sampling frequency	33.716KHz
line bit rate	20.715 Mb/s
Synchronizing signal	Burst sine-wave (12.947MHz)

*   Cw and C_N signals are transmitted line-sequentially

Table 5. Design objectives for HD-TV transmission system.

SNR (Unweighted)	41 dB
Attenuation frequency distortion	$\pm$ 1.5 dB
Line slope	$\pm$ 2 %
Field slope	$\pm$ 40 %

Table 6. Examples of LED's typical characteristics.

	GaAlAs/GaAs-LED	InGaAsP/InP-LED
Wavelength	0.89μm	1.3μm
Fiber-coupled power *	-13dBm	-19dBm
Cutoff frequency	55MHz	40MHz
Δλ	50nm	140nm
Nonlinear distortion **	48dB	36dB
Temperature dependence of fiber-coupled power (0°C ～ 50°C)	-0.1dB	-1.2dB

*   50/125 μm Graded-index
** Modulation index is 60% with predistortion compensation

Table 7. Main parameters of analog transmission.

Transmission signal	20MHz TCM signal
Transmission distance	2km
Optical fiber cable	Graded-index multimode
Modulation scheme	Analog Direct IM
Optical source	GaAlAs/GaAs-LED
Wavelength	0.89μm
Optical detector	Si-APD

Table 8. Main parameters of digital transmission.

Transmission system	F-400M
Coding method	8 bits linear PCM
Sampling frequency	44.1MHz
Transmission bit rate	397.2Mb/s
Transmission code	8B1C
Scrambler	Self-synchronizing scrambler

Table 9. Measured performances for analog transmission.

Items	Design objectives	Experiments
SNR (Unweighted)	45 dB	49.9 dB
Attenuation frequency distortion	± 0.6 dB	+0.32 dB −0.12 dB
Line slope	± 1 %	0.5 %
Field slope	± 8 %	5 %

Table 10. Measured performances for digital transmission.

Items	Design objectives	Experiments
SNR (Unweighted)	49 dB	52.8 dB
Attenuation frequency distortion	± 0.5 dB	+0.02 dB −0.38 dB
Line slope	± 0.8 %	0.6 %
Field slope	± 7 %	3 %

Table 11. Overall measured performances.

Items	Design objectives	Experiments
SNR (Unweighted)	41 dB	47.6 dB (Y) 41.8 dB (Cw) 42.0 dB (C_N)
Attenuation frequency distortion	± 1.5 dB	+0 dB, −0.7 dB (Y) +0 dB, −1.4 dB (Cw) +0 dB, −1.3 dB (C_N)
Line slope	± 2 %	2 %
Field slope	± 40 %	17%

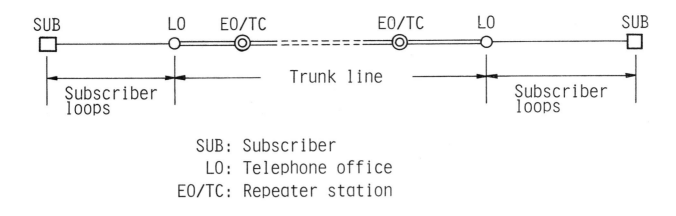

SUB: Subscriber
LO: Telephone office
EO/TC: Repeater station

Fig. 1. HD-TV transmission system

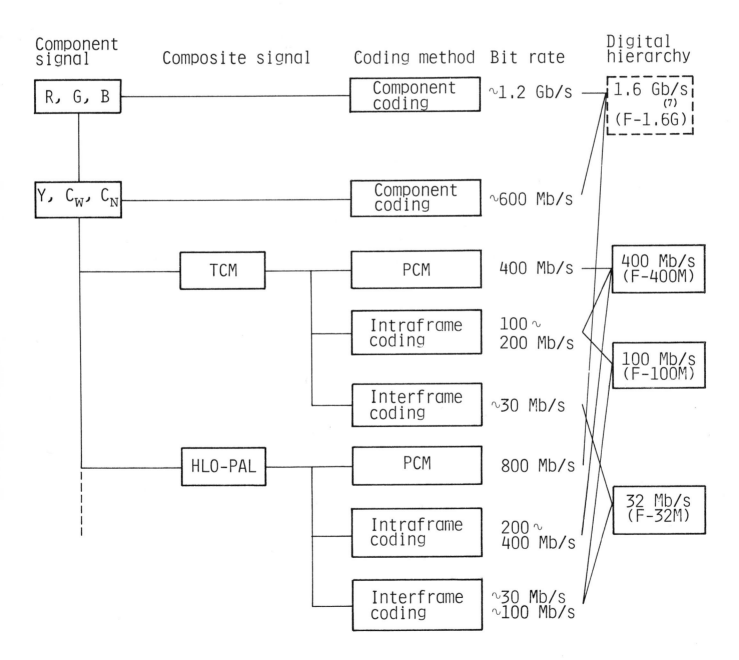

Fig. 2. Analog composite signals and coding methods.

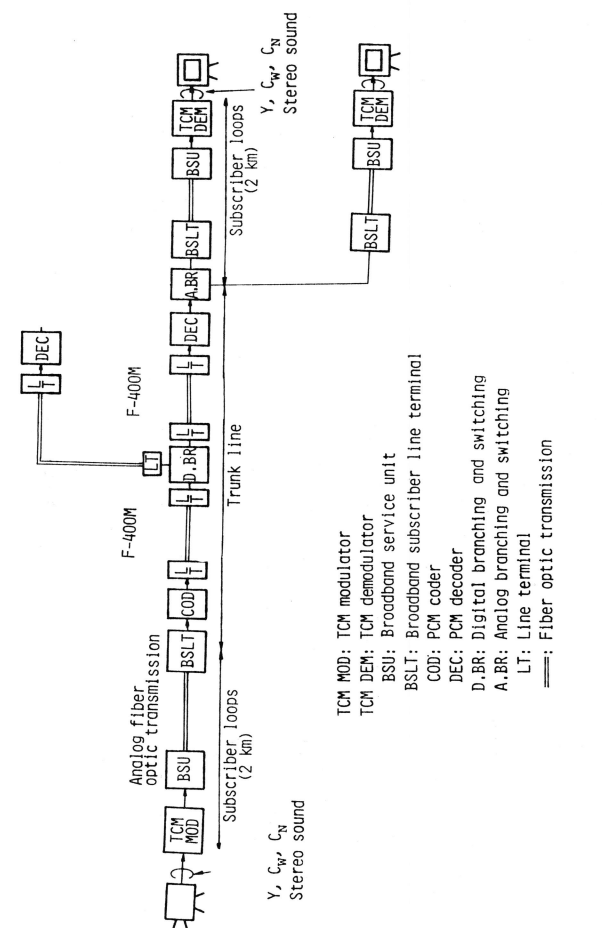

Analog fiber optic transmission

Subscriber loops (2 km)

Y, C_W, C_N
Stereo sound

Trunk line

F-400M

F-400M

Subscriber loops (2 km)

Y, C_W, C_N
Stereo sound

TCM MOD: TCM modulator
TCM DEM: TCM demodulator
BSU: Broadband service unit
BSLT: Broadband subscriber line terminal
COD: PCM coder
DEC: PCM decoder
D.BR: Digital branching and switching
A.BR: Analog branching and switching
LT: Line terminal
═══ : Fiber optic transmission

Fig. 3. Configuration of field trial system.

241

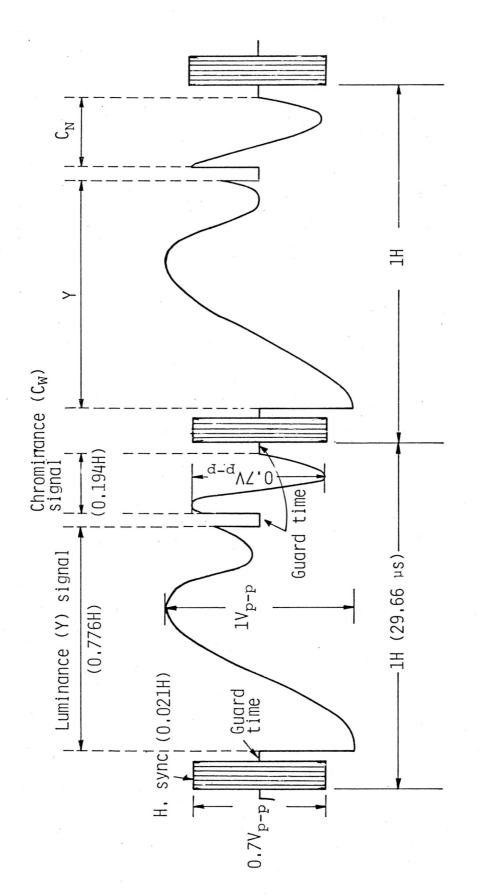

Fig. 4. TCM signal format.

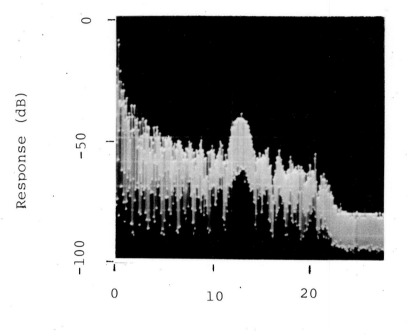

Fig. 5. TCM signal spectrum (Color bar).

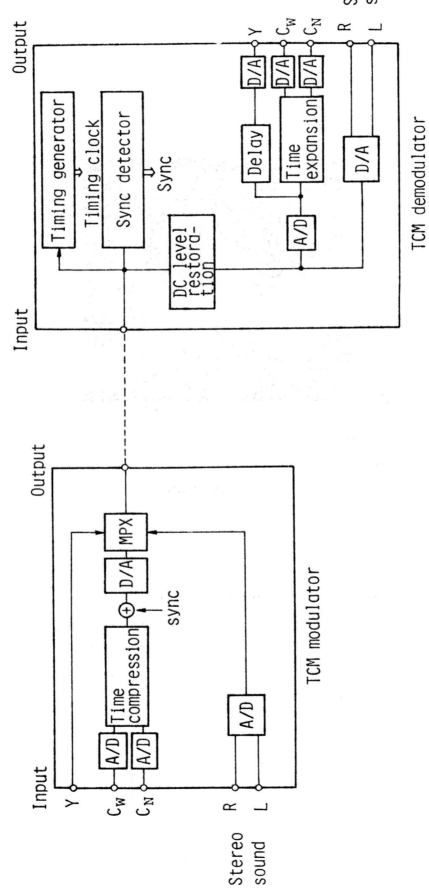

Fig. 6. Block diagram of TCM signal modulator and demodulator.

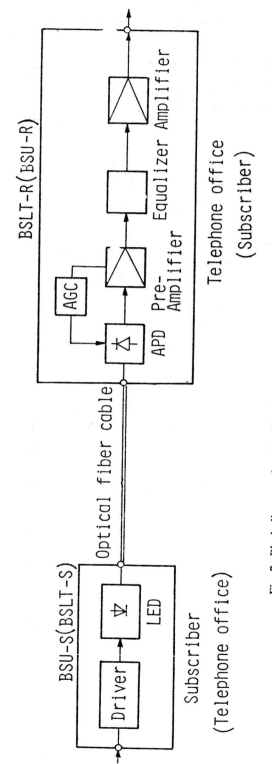

Fig. 7. Block diagram of analog fiber optic transmission system for subscriber loops.

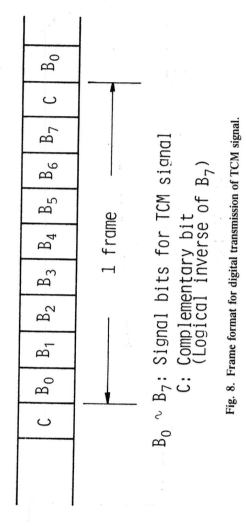

$B_0 \sim B_7$: Signal bits for TCM signal
C: Complementary bit
   (Logical inverse of B_7)

Fig. 8. Frame format for digital transmission of TCM signal.

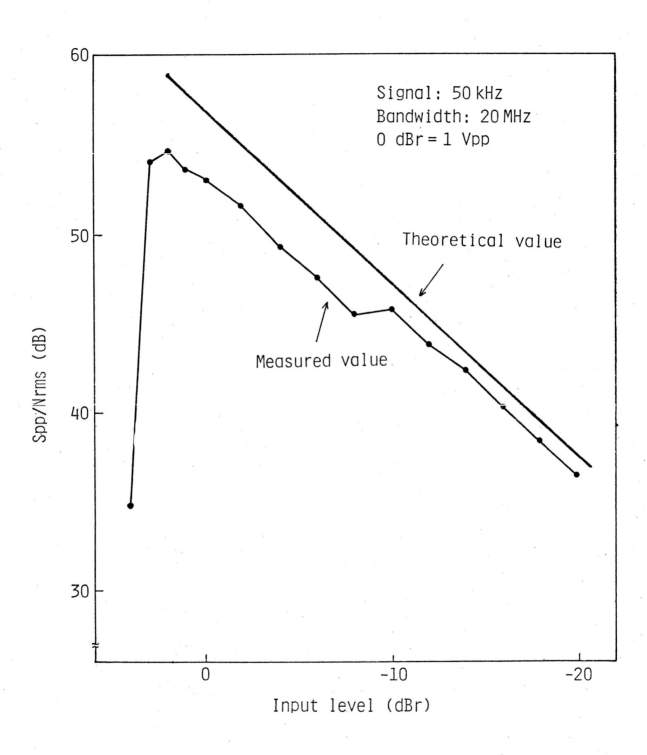

Fig. 9. Measured SNR of CODEC.

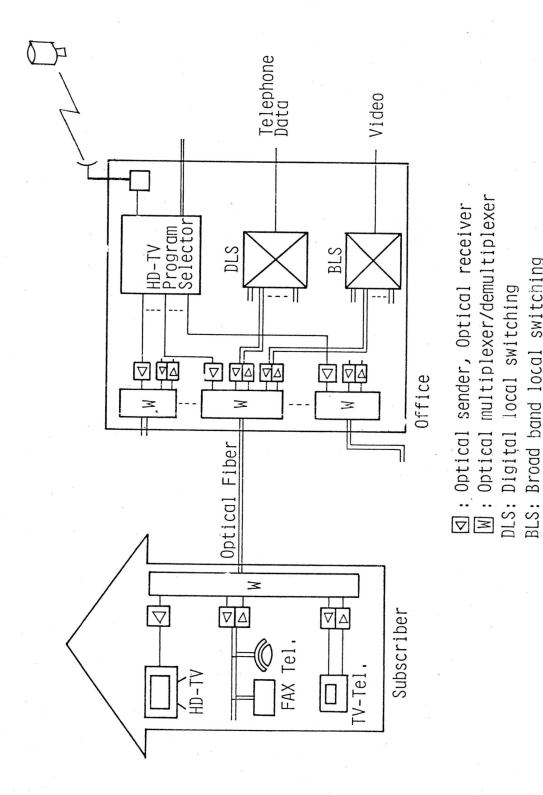

Fig. 10. A concept of subscriber distribution networks.

▽ : Optical sender, Optical receiver
W : Optical multiplexer/demultiplexer
DLS: Digital local switching
BLS: Broad band local switching

Toshinori Tsuboi was born in Aichi, Japan, on May 3, 1949. He received the B.E. and M.E. degrees from Waseda University, Tokyo, Japan, in 1973 and 1975, respectively. In 1975, he joined the Electrical Communication Laboratory, Nippon Telegraph and Telephone Public Corporation, Yokosuka, Japan, where he is a Staff Engineer. He has been engaged in research and development on voice coding systems, digital local switching systems, high-definition TV transmission systems and broadband communication networks. Mr. Tsuboi is a member of the Institute of Electronics and Communication Engineers in Japan. In 1983, he received the IECE's Young Engineer Award.

Koichi Asatani was born in Hiroshima, Japan, on November 4, 1946. He received the B.S.E.E., M.S.E.E., and D.E. degrees from Kyoto University, Kyoto, Japan, in 1969, 1971, and 1974, respectively. In 1974, he joined the Electrical Communication Laboratory, Nippon Telegraph and Telephone Public Corporation, Yokosuka, Japan, where he is a Senior Staff Engineer. He has been engaged in research and development on optical fiber transmission systems, high-speed digital data transmission systems, high-definition TV transmission systems, and broadband communication networks. Dr. Asatani is a member of the Institute of Electronics and Communication Engineers of Japan and the Office Automation Society of Japan.

Tetsuya Miki was born in Fukuoka, Japan, on January 31, 1943. He received the B.S. degree from Electro Communication University in 1965 and the M.S. and Ph.D. degrees from Tohoku University in 1967 and 1970, respectively.
In 1970, he joined the Electrical Communication Laboratory, Nippon Telegraph and Telephone Public Corporation, Japan, where he is Chief, Transmission System Section, Trunk Transmission System Development Division. He has been engaged in research and development on high speed digital and broadband analog transmission systems over a coaxial cable and a fiber optic cable for trunk line and subscriber loops.
Dr. Miki is a member of the Institute of Electronics and Communication Engineers of Japan and IEEE. He received the Achievement Award from IECE of Japan for his work on the fundamental development of fiber optic transmission digital system.

High Quality on Cable TV Including MDS

Israel Switzer
Cablecasting Limited
Toronto, Canada

'IMAGE QUALITY' CONSIDERATIONS IN CABLE SYSTEMS

Background

'QUALITY' considerations in cable systems have concerned themselves almost exclusively with noise and distortion. In common with other frequency division multiplexed (FDM) transmission systems, cable systems tread a narrow path between noise and distortion. Signal levels which are too low result in excessively low C/N and S/N, while signal levels which are too high produce excessive distortion Inadequate C/N results in 'snowy' pictures. The limiting distortion in multi-channel cable systems is now third order intermodulation. This results in 'waterfall' effects in non-coherent carrier systems and 'cross-talk' in coherent carrier systems. All of these effects are, of course, objectionable.

The cable systems business has evolved in a market environment in which variety, i.e. the number of signals, is more important than image quality. Systems operate with adjacent channels to cram the most signals into the least system bandwidth. Coherent carrier techniques are used to reduce distortion both by reducing peak composite signal levels and by reducing the subjective impairment effects of intermodulation. Video signal synchronization is being used by some systems to further reduce subjective effects of transmission distortions. Manufacturers of the thin film hybrid gain modules which are almost universally used in cable television repeater amplifiers are producing gain modules with remarkably good specifications for noise, distortion and flatness of frequency response.

Notwithstanding the remarkable sophistication of the equipment and the transmission technology, cable television image transmission must be considered mediocre by the standards employed by the television production industry. The cable television industry understandably tends to stretch the capabilities of the available equipment to the utmost. The FCC rules allow C/N as low as 36 dB. C/N in cable systems is measured in a 4 MHz bandwidth. It turns out that C/N in 4 MHz bandwidth translates almost directly to video weighted S/N with only minor numerical correction. Most recently designed cable systems aim for C/N of 43 dB. Although many cable subscribers, particularly those close to the distribution 'head-end', enjoy higher C/N ratio, many accept what video professionals would consider mediocre S/N. There is a similar pressure on intermodulation distortion, cable systems pushing for maximum economic efficiency and accepting image quality compromises.

This situation has arisen because cable television systems, by and large, do not serve professional viewers. Most subscribers served by mediocre cable systems have mediocre receivers - by professional standards - and would not know a really good picture if it popped out of the screen and offered to make coffee. The present cable television market judges the value of the service by the number and variety of television program services, provided practical standards of 'barely perceptible' impairment are achieved.

Cable transmission engineers have generally overlooked one major parameter which, in my view, also affects transmission quality. The effect of multiple, closely spaced reflections is not fully understood. I believe that these reflections, arising from the small impedance mismatches caused by the myriad of connectors and devices in the transmission path, and the small imperfections of the coaxial cable itself, cause a slight 'smearing' of picture detail - a loss of 'crispness'. The visual effect is that of a reduction of transmission bandwidth, even though we know that the broadband transmission system has not itself directly reduced the transmission bandwidth. Our operations engineers get complaints from subscribers who have a chance to compare good quality local television signals as received direct from a local broadcaster and as received through the cable system. There is a small but noticeable impairment in this circumstance which does not have to do with C/N, intermodulation or signal processing considerations. I attribute the impairment, as I have said, to multiple, low level reflections in the cable system.

High Quality Transmission of NTSC Signals

I consider this a topic of major importance. I am concerned that the new DBS services will point out picture quality 'disabilities' in cable service. I am told that COMSAT is designing an 'all-digital' origination center (Las Vegas) with the objective of providing absolute state-of-the art program origination for their DBS service. I believe that DBS service will be capable of providing higher quality image transmission than the present terrestrial television broadcasting system and certainly better than present cable systems. Cable television systems must anticipate this competitive pressure and respond with significant improvements in the cable distributed image quality.

HIGH DEFINITION TELEVISION (HDTV - 1125 line) has excited a great deal of interest in the professional television community and is starting to get some attention from the popular press. The present HDTV concept originated with NHK and has been implemented to the present demonstration level by several Japanese equipment manufacturers - SONY, MATSUSHITA, NEC. The May, 1983 International television symposium in Montreux, Switzerland had a large scale HDTV demonstration with demonstration programs taped by CBS and several European (including USSR) broadcast authorities. SONY staged an impressive HDTV demonstration at the 1983 NCTA convention in Houston.

HDTV is 'spectacular', particularly when projected onto a large screen by a good quality projector. Images closely approximate 35mm movie quality. The HDTV screen, as proposed by NHK, has a 5:3 aspect ratio compared to the 4:3 aspect ratio of conventional 525 line systems. The 5:3 aspect ratio approximates current 'wide-screen' motion picture presentation. Frame/field rate remains 30/60. The improvement in definition results in a significant increase in video bandwidth - about

20 MHz compared to the 4.2 MHz used by present broadcast systems. The system has, of course, high-fidelity stereo sound.

All of these attributes -

- 1125 scan lines
- increased video bandwidth
- high fidelity stereo sound
- 5:3 aspect ratio
- non-NTSC color encoding

result in a serious incompatibility with present broadcast television receivers. There is general acknowledgment that it will take many years to introduce HDTV as a broadcast service.

Just before going to Montreux I read an account of Joe Flaherty's presentation on HDTV at the NAB convention earlier this year. I am sure you know Joe Flaherty as chief engineering executive at CBS. Flaherty was complaining that there hadn't been any major improvement in television program origination quality in the last few years. HDTV was a new breakthrough in this area. This report moved me to write to Flaherty. I pointed out that 99.9% of the television audience in this country has yet to see a 'good' 525 line picture.

I believe that we will experience a 'generation' (10 years) of improved 525 line television before HDTV (1125 line) becomes a major factor in television broadcasting. It might turn out that improved 525 services actually delay introduction of 1125 line HDTV services because of the renewed investment in high quality 525 line receiving equipment. HDTV can follow as a cable service in due course. We will have to invent a new 'superlative' to market it.

Americans have a long standing reputation for not caring much about television picture quality. I believe that there is a 'quality' market in America which can be 'sold' on quality video, and that they will pay a reasonable price to get it. I believe that this 'quality' market segment subscribes to cable and that cable is the best way to reach them.

There was a similar situation in phonographs thirty years ago. CBS developed the LP microgroove record. Recording engineers were able to produce records with much better audio quality than had ever been produced before. The existing phonographs just could not reproduce the sound quality that the recording artists and engineers were putting into the new records. People had LP players but the pick-ups, the amplifiers and the loud speakers just weren't good enough. Improved phonograph components were developed and found a ready market as 'high fidelity' audio. There has been a continuing market for improvements in audio equipment over the last thirty years. We may finally have achieved the end of the technology chain in audio as PCM techniques provide 'ultimate' recordings, and amplifier and loudspeaker engineers find it increasingly difficult to wring out the last minor imperfections in audio reproducing equipment.

'High-Fidelity' 525 Line Video

There are two aspects of providing high quality 525 line service -

improvement of color encoding technique,

improvement of transmission.

Enhanced Video

Cable television represents a unique opportunity to introduce new color encoding techniques. Most cable systems firmly control subscriber terminal equipment - the addressable programmable converter/descramblers which are provided to control access to cable television services. The equipment is owned by the cable system and provided to the subscriber as part of the overall cable service. Much of this equipment operates in a baseband mode, i.e. they consist of complete demodulators which presently provide a composite video output. These baseband subscriber terminal units could just as easily provide improved color decoding with RGB output to the subscribers video monitor. This improved decoding could be improved decoding of NTSC encoded color or it could be optimum decoding of a new, more sophisticated color encoding system, such as the C-MAC component system which has been proposed.

Program originators, such as national Pay-TV networks, could originate in both conventional NTSC video and an improved 525 line mode. Cable systems could similarly distribute in both modes - most have spare channel capacity during a changeover period. When a cable system has completed a changeover of all of its subscriber terminal equipment it would distribute in the improved mode only, although program originators would have to distribute in dual mode to allow for a longer period of changeover in all of their affiliates. Alternately a cable network operator could provide head-end decoding and transcoding equipment for those affiliates who were not immediately prepared to change from NTSC distribution. Cost and complexity would be comparable to the video encyphering that some of these network operators will be providing soon.

Television broadcasters would have a more difficult conversion since they do not have the dual service transmission capability that many cable systems have. The market created by cable systems would, however, speed the introduction and acceptance of new-standard receiving equipment. Local broadcasters would, however, be under competitive pressure since the cable distributed networks would be taking advantage of the improved transmission technologies. Local broadcasters could meet this competition by setting up local area direct feeds of enhanced video to cable systems in their service area.

I am not an expert in the detail of various enhanced 525 line video systems which are being proposed, but I do perceive that they offer a significant enhancement potential and that cable systems can speed the introduction of a worthy enhanced video proposal.

Improved Cable Transmission - PERFECT PICTURE

The cable television industry is substantially committed to its present plant. It would be a very expensive and difficult task to replace amplifiers or other major components in existing or 'under-construction' cable systems. Feed-forward amplifiers, with significantly reduced distortion (at least 16 dB reduction in third order intermodulation) are on the brink of widespread acceptance and availability. Widespread retrofit of existing systems will, however, be quite expensive. Use of feed-forward amplifiers in cable system trunks would improve system C/N but would still leave the system with the problem of multiple, low level reflections.

252

Most new cable systems have 'spare' bandwidth available. I am proposing to several of my client systems that this bandwidth be traded for 'quality' in the traditional way, by use of frequency modulation (FM) transmission. In the first phase of an image quality improvement program the cable system would use FM transmission of ordinary NTSC video. FM transmission in a cable system would require 18 MHz of spectrum. Most new urban cable systems have enough spare spectrum to provide conventional VSB-AM transmission (6 MHz per channel) and high quality FM transmission (18 MHz per channel) at the same time. I call the service 'PERFECT PICTURE'. The FM video service would also have high quality stereo sound, probably in the form of discreet L and R subcarriers, but possibly in PCM digital format.

FM transmission would remove S/N as a quality compromise in cable system transmission. Other quality degradations in cable systems, such as intermodulation and 'reflections', have different, less visible, less objectionable manifestations in FM video transmission (intermodulation in the baseband and as small degradations in differential phase and gain).

Subscribers who opt for the 'PERFECT PICTURE' service would be provided with a special FM video receiver which would tune the desired FM video channel, demodulate and descramble it, and provide both composite and RGB outputs (as well as baseband stereo L and R sound outputs). 'PERFECT PICTURE' subscribers would be expected to have a high quality video monitor or projector in order to enjoy the benefits. It wouldn't make much sense to remodulate 'PERFECT PICTURE' to NTSC VSB/AM for an ordinary receiver. The special FM video receivers would be adapted from the DBS receivers which will now be manufactured in fair volume. The principal difference will be the tuner. The DBS receivers tune 12 GHz. The cable version will, of course, tune cable FM video channels in the 50 - 550 MHz range.

Major cable television services are now distributed by satellite. Most broadcasting networks now (or will soon) distribute their servce by satellite as well. Another way to look at my proposal is that it 'splits' the satellite receiver. These satellite-based video transmission systems are designed to provide 'professional' grade transmission. PERFECT PICTURE places the satellite downconverter at the cable system head-end and places the rest of the receiver in the subscriber's home in order to maximize transmission quality. It puts the TVRO right in the living room!

The second phase of a transmission improvement program would introduce enhanced color encoding with compatible optimum decoding in the subscriber terminal box.

HIGH DEFINITION SERVICES

HDTV creates special problems for cable transmission. 'Raw' HDTV has significantly increased video bandwidth. Transmission, even by spectrum conservative VSB-AM, will require substantially increased bandwidth compared to 525 line video. For purposes of discussion I will assume 20 MHz of bandwidth for noise calculation purposes.

It has become customary to calculate cable system noise (for NTSC transmission) in a 4 MHz bandwidth. The random 'KTB' noise in a 75 ohm system in a 4 MHz bandwidth is 1.1 microvolt or -59 dBmV. Overall transmission noise is calculated by taking into account amplifier noise figures and system operating levels. As I have said, the FCC minimum standard is 36 dB C/N. A C/N of 43 dB would be considered more usual for a 'good' cable system. This 43 dB C/N degrades by 7 dB to 36 dB C/N in the 20 MHz bandwidth of a HDTV transmission. HDTV service subscribers will probably have increased service quality expectations and the 43 dB S/N that we consider good for NTSC images might very well not be acceptable for HDTV images. I have not seen any published figures for S/N corresponding to various grades of HDTV transmission.

Frequency modulation might not be an available noise reduction option for HDTV transmission. We can realistically talk about 18 MHz transmission channels for enhanced 525 line PERFECT PICTURE service. FM for 20 MHz HDTV video would probably require at least 60 MHz per channel. This would cut our newest 500 MHz systems down to eight channels per cable. This kind of channel capacity reduction might be acceptable in Europe but is not acceptable here.

Some kind of bandwidth reduction technology would be very desirable. Feedforward amplifier technology might produce the 7 dB improvement in cable system C/N that conventional transmission would require. Some reduction in amplifier loading because of a reduction in the number of channels would also help somewhat. All in all, I fear that large scale, multi-channel HDTV service on cable will not be feasible without significant bandwidth reduction technology. I am sure that HDTV proponents are aware of this problem and that practical HDTV proposals will come forward with accompanying practical bandwidth reduction technologies.

CONCLUSION

I believe that image transmission improvement in cable will come about through a new interest in high quality video. It will first take the form of enhanced 525 line video, which will be followed some considerable time later by HDTV services. Cable systems will lead in the introduction of enhanced 525 line transmission by providing FM trnamssion along with improved color encoding techniques.

Israel Switzer is a graduate of the University of Alberta (Physics, 1949). He has been active in cable television engineering since 1954 with concurrent and prior experience in petroleum geophysics, television broadcast transmission engineering and electronic computer systems. Mr. Switzer is a resident of Palm Springs, California and Toronto, Ontario, and is a frequent contributor to cable television trade magazines, journals and technical programs. He is a member of SMPTE and IEEE, and is a registered Professional Engineer and designated Consulting Engineer in Ontario. He has significant engineering responsibility for the recent expansion of cable system channel capacity from 36 channels to the present 60 channel level. He has current engineering consulting responsibility for very large cable systems under development in the Virginia suburbs of Washington, D.C. and the north-west suburbs of Chicago.

NTSC and MAC* Television Signals in Noise and Interference Environments

Gérald Chouinard
Department of Communications
Communications Research Centre
P.O. Box 11490, Station H
Ottawa, Ontario K2H 8S2

and

John N. Barry
Philip A. Lapp Limited
904-280 Albert Street
Ottawa, Ontario
K1P 5G8

ABSTRACT

The quality of video signals delivered by future DBS systems will be governed by two main limiting factors: noise and interference. The results of a measurement program giving the susceptibility of the FM-NTSC television signal to noise and interference are reported. These results were obtained from the subjective assessment of the picture quality by a large number of viewers. Different types of viewers were used and the results were analyzed accordingly. A modelling of these results was performed using the logistic function. The noise results were compared to the previous TASO results to find the evolution in required television picture quality. The results of the interference tests were used to set the technical characteristics used for planning of DBS at the RARC-83.

A second phase in the measurement program was the comparative evaluation of the conventional NTSC coding and the MAC (Multiplexed Analogue Components) video coding system. This new coding system is gaining importance worldwide: it is proposed by the EBU as the standard format for DBS in Europe for 625-line television standards, and in North America work is being carried out to devise a 525-line MAC coding system to be used for DBS. This paper presents the preliminary results of a comparison study on the susceptibility of the MAC signal as compared to the susceptibility of the conventional NTSC signal to system noise as a function of over-deviation, co-channel interference and adjacent channel interference. This study was done using the baseline system parameters used at the RARC-83.

1. Introduction

Direct-to-home broadcast by satellite on a large scale will be realized within the next few years. Popularly known as Direct Broadcast Satellites (DBS), and identified officially in the CCIR as satellites in the Broadcast Satellite Service (BSS), these new satellites will rely on frequency re-use, polarization discrimination, and partial overlap of adjacent channels to maximize the number of channels available in the BSS.

This increased crowding in the orbit spectrum resource will likely lead to new forms of impairment in the end product delivered to the public. Accordingly, in establishing new services such as the Broadcast Satellite Service, major test programs to subjectively assess the effects of these various causes of picture impairment are required. New standards and system parameters for the BSS must be set, in the same way as they were set by TASO in the 1950's for terrestrial television broadcasting.[1]

A CCIR Regional Administrative Radio Conference, known officially as RARC-SAT-R2-1983 was held in June and July, 1983 [2]. The main purposes of this conference were to coordinate the interests of the various Administrations and to establish a plan for orderly development of the BSS

---

* Multiplexed Analog Components

in the American Continents. The planning was based on the technical parameters of a reference baseline system. One of the key parameters was the Protection Ratio (PR) which is taken to mean the relative strength of a wanted to an unwanted signal that will support a predetermined level of viewer acceptance. A critical input to establishing satisfactory standards for PRs is the determination of the subjective picture degradation caused by different types of interference. In particular, the threshold of perception of a particular type of impairment and the rate at which viewer acceptance tolerance changes with increasing interference are very important factors to be considered in the system design. In the BSS, these PRs have a first-order effect on satellite spacing, earth terminal antenna pattern (from the co-channel operation in adjacent satellites) and on channel spacing and polarization discrimination (from the partial overlap of the cross-polarized adjacent channels on the same satellite).

As part of the preparation for the RARC-83, a concerted effort was initiated by the Canadian Federal Department of Communications at CRC to conduct an extensive measurement program to evaluate the effect of noise and interference on quality of television pictures in the NTSC format[3]. The main goal of this exercise was to gather enough information on picture impairment caused by interference so that a sound decision could be taken at the RARC-83 as to the level of protection required between satellite systems. This work led to the specification of a co-channel protection ratio of 28 dB, and this figure was used for the planning of the Broadcasting Satellite Service at the RARC-83[2]. The results of a further measurement program conducted by P.A. Lapp Ltd.[4] under contract to the CRC became available following the RARC-83 and will also be considered here.

Also part of this measurement program was the gathering of information about adjacent channel interference. This work resulted in the definition of the protection ratio template adopted at the Conference. Consequently, adjacent channel protection ratios of 13.6 dB and −9.9 dB were adopted for planning purposes for the first adjacent and second adjacent channels respectively for an intercarrier spacing of 14.58 MHz (i.e. 32 channels of 24 MHz bandwidth in the 500 MHz band).

More recently, a new series of tests with MAC-formatted television signals was conducted. Systematic comparisons of the performances of MAC and NTSC coded video signals submitted to the same noise and interference degradations typical of satellite circuits, were conducted. The first part of this series covered the relative susceptibility of the frequency modulated MAC and NTSC signals to the presence of thermal noise in the transmission channel. These tests entailed the evaluation of the threshold of perception of the FM triangular noise, threshold noise and truncation noise for different levels of over-deviation. The second part covered the relative susceptibility of the frequency modulated MAC and NTSC signals to co-channel and adjacent channel interferences. The interfering signals were both MAC and NTSC encoded signals.

The results obtained in these comparative tests relate to the "just-perceptible" level of picture degradation and do not cover, as in the case of the NTSC tests, the progressive decrease in picture quality for the MAC coded signal as the noise and interference effects become more and more objectionable. Nevertheless, valuable conclusions can be drawn from these comparative tests as to the most effective way of using the satellite channel with MAC-encoded television signal as compared to NTSC. The results obtained from the interference tests will also be considered in the context of compatibility with the RARC-83 plan.

2. NTSC Test Program

The equipment set-up used to perform the NTSC test program was basically constructed around a wanted RF signal path to which RF noise and up to 4 interfering signals could be added. The frequency of each interfering signal could be adjusted to simulate co-channel or adjacent channel interference. The levels of insertion of noise and interference were adjusted with calibrated attenuators. The tests were made with frequency modulated NTSC signals. The video signal of the wanted path was obtained from a telecine chain. The video signals on interfering paths were off-air signals obtained from 4 professional AM-VSB demodulators. There was no synchronization relationship with the wanted signal.

The receiver filter was a non-equalized 4-pole Chebychev type filter at 70 MHz having an equivalent noise bandwidth of 22.7 MHz. A peak-to-peak carrier deviation of 9.52 MHz for a 1 volt video signal was used to obtain a 30 dB FM-improvement including weighting* and pre-emphasis such that S/N_w = 42 dB was available for a carrier-to-noise ratio of 12 dB. The standard pre-emphasis as specified in CCIR Recommendation 405[5] for System M/NTSC was used.

Two unmodulated sound sub-carriers at 5.41 MHz and 5.79 MHz were added to the video signal in the wanted and interfering paths. The deviation of the main carrier by each sound sub-carrier was 2 MHz peak-to-peak. Considering 5.79 MHz as the top baseband frequency, the Carson's rule bandwidth is 21.1 MHz, resulting in 7.25% extra bandwidth in the receive filter for these sound sub-carriers. A well-equalized video filter was inserted after demodulation to reject these two sound sub-carriers. No artificial energy dispersal was used.

Viewers in the CRC test were listed either as expert viewers, because they were familiar with TV picture evaluation, or concerned viewers, because they worked in a technical environment and were inclined to be more critical than average viewers. Three groups of concerned viewers and one group of experts numbering respectively 24, 23, 21 and 12 were used at CRC. In the Lapp series 103 non-expert or average viewers were tested. The first CRC group, Group "A", and the third group, Group "C", were presented with the same range of impairments caused by noise and interference. Group "B" and the expert Group "D" were exposed to lower levels of interference.

Group "C" evaluated these impairments on 2 moving scenes rather than 3 still slides. The results were found to be equivalent and tended to prove that the picture content is a more important cause of trends in results than the amount of movement in such pictures. It re-affirms the fact that still scenes are suffcient for this kind of picture impairment evaluation. This conclusion can be explained by the fact that the viewers become accustomed to the same moving scenes presented over and over again and begin to analyse impairments at specific locations and times, much like they would do with still scenes. Accordingly, the results of Group "C" will not be considered any further.

Viewing conditions for the CRC and the Lapp tests were as prescribed by CCIR Recommendation 500-2[6]. The picture material used was 35 mm colour

---

* Unified Weighting, see CCIR Recommendation 567-1[8]

slides chosen from standard sets as suggested by CCIR Recommendation 600[7]: "Girl in Green Dress" and "Beach Scene" from the SMPTE series and "Basket of Fruit" and "Make-up Scene" from the Philips series. Only the three first slides were used in the CRC tests except in the case of the "just-perceptible" tests on adjacent channel interference where the four slides were used. The Lapp tests used the four slides.

In the series at CRC, the test material was taken "live" from the telecine chain through the RF path of the set-up with different noise and interference settings and it was presented on a high quality studio monitor. For the Lapp test series, the same test set-up was used to pre-record on 1" C-Format video tapes a series of impaired and unimpaired scenes. The recorded sequences were then presented on P.A. Lapp Ltd. premices for picture quality assessment using the same reference viewing conditions.

Both direct and indirect anchorings were used. First, during the introduction, the viewers were shown the best and the worst pictures to be encountered during the test (direct anchoring). Indirect anchoring was used by presenting unimpaired and severely impaired pictures at random during the tests, without telling the observers.

Viewers rated scenes according to the CCIR 5-grade impairment scale shown in Table 1. The viewers were asked to score under the different opinion ratings without using the numerical scale.

Grade	Opinion Rating
5	Imperceptible
4	Perceptible but not annoying
3	Slightly annoying
2	Annoying
1	Very annoying

Table 1. CCIR five-grade impairment scale.

Impairments due to noise, co-channel interference, adjacent channel interference, multiple co-channel interference, and co-channel plus noise were assessed in both the CRC and the Lapp test series.

Each test session consisted typically of three to seven viewers in two 25-minute viewing periods separated by a 10-minute rest break, and preceded by a 10-minute introduction to the tests, which introduction included the showing of impaired and unimpaired scenes.

The scores given by viewers were translated into numerical ratings using the 5-grade numerical scale. From the numerical ratings, rating histograms were constructed for each particular test case and for each viewer group. Means, medians and standard deviations were then calculated in the usual manner. The results obtained for the 4 test slides were also grouped to find the results for average picture content. A more complex statistical analysis, described in section 3, was also carried out during the Lapp series of tests.

Further tests were conducted using trained observers to characterize more accurately the threshold of perceptibility of the adjacent channel interference as a function of inter-carrier spacing. The test conditions were the same as for the preceding tests except that, in the procedure, the observers were asked to set an attenuator at a level where they just began to perceive the interference.

Means, standard deviations and 95% confidence ranges of the means were calculated for all test conditions and were used to define the adjacent channel interference template proposed at the RARC-83.

3. Results of the NTSC Test Program

Figure 1 shows the results of the noise assessment obtained by the different groups. In order to compare with previous measurement programs, the results of the TASO Study reported by Dean [1] are also included in Figure 1. The RF (AM-VSB) signal-to-noise ratio used in the TASO study was converted for purposes of comparison to equivalent weighted S/N (unified weighting). The two curves reported here are for Miss TASO and seven other scenes used in the TASO experiments, in both cases impaired with broad-band RF noise. These results can be found in Figure 8 and 9 of Reference 1.

Figure 1 illustrates quite clearly a significant difference between the early TASO results, the CRC results and the LAPP results. The higher tolerance of the TASO group tends to indicate that the viewer expectation for higher picture quality has increased by 5 dB to 9 dB during the last 25 years. This would tend to indicate that the quality standards used in planning television services may need to be reviewed, having in mind the present viewer expectation for higher picture quality.

It can also be found from Figure 1 that the Lapp group scored the noise impaired pictures to a higher quality level than the CRC groups. The difference in required S/N is between 2 dB to 4 dB depending whether "concerned" or "expert" viewers are considered. Two reasons can be given for the difference between the Lapp group and the three CRC groups:

(i) Type of Viewer

The subjective measurements conducted by P.A. Lapp Limited used a group of viewers selected to represent a reasonably good cross-section of the population. These viewers, unlike the expert viewers and so-called "concerned viewers" who participated in Group A, B and D at CRC, did not have any experience in assessing television picture quality, nor did they have any knowledge of telecommunication satellite systems. This group represented the layman assessment of picture degradation.

CRC Group D used expert viewers from the broadcast industry, whereas groups A and B used technically minded viewers. The difference betwen expert and technically minded viewers seems to be about 2 dB. Group B is slightly more critical than Group A since the former was exposed to smaller levels of interference during the same tests. This produced a higher overall picture quality during the test presentation and made Group B slightly more critical.

(ii) Viewing Conditions

All groups assessed the picture quality from a distance equivalent to 4 to 6 times picture height. However, the Lapp group was shown a full range of impairment levels, whereas the three CRC groups were shown scenes of relatively high overall picture quality and fewer severely impaired scenes. In addition, the Lapp group was shown as unimpaired benchmark, scenes with residual noise from the video tape recorder. Although the effect of these differences in measurement procedure cannot be quantified, the qualitative reasons suggested seem to explain the relative positions of the mean assessment curves.

Results for the picture degradation caused by a single co-channel interferer are shown in Figure 2. Even though the results were obtained for a carrier deviation of 9.52 MHz, a normalization was done to 12 MHz peak to peak deviation which is a more common value for presenting interference results. This was done by decreasing the C/I values by 2 dB which is the difference in FM-improvement between 9.52 MHz and 12 MHz carrier deviations. The RARC-83 co-channel protection ratio (28 dB) is also shown for comparison purposes. CRC Group A and the Lapp Group were found to be some 2 dB more tolerant to co-channel interference than in the case of CRC Groups B and D. The responses of Group A and Lapp are very close except for the level at which the quality saturates (recall that Group A was presented with live material, whereas the Lapp group was presented with sessions recorded on tape). This is in contrast to the case of noise impairment, where the two groups gave different responses, and it tends to indicate that a trained viewer can become more critical than an untrained viewer for noise degradation whereas the training barely improves the criticalness in the case of co-channel interference.

A closer relationship than what was found in the case of triangular noise impairment tests is also to be expected because the ranges of impairments assessed by each group are closely matched in the co-channel tests for Groups B and D and for Groups A and Lapp (Groups B and D were presented with a range of interference 10 dB smaller than Groups A and Lapp). The viewers in Groups B and D became more critical, being presented with overall better pictures. The difference between Groups B and D is due to the difference in viewers' expertise and this difference was found to be smaller for interference assessment than noise assessment. This may be due to the fact that expert viewers from the broadcast industry are still not familiar with assessing co-channel interference on frequency modulated television systems.

Impairment caused by interference from three co-channel interferers was assessed by all groups. The general shape and relative position of the curves was found to be similar to the single entry case except that these new curves are shifted towards higher C/I by 3 dB to 5 dB. This shift means that three equal interferers produce the same impairment level as one single interferer 3 dB to 5 dB stronger than the power of each individual interferer. From the law of power addition one would expect this difference to be 4.8 dB. The experimental results tend to support the applicability of power addition for multiple co-channel interferers.

Interference from adjacent channels was assessed by all groups. The results for 15 MHz separation between FM carriers is shown in Figure 3. The RARC-83 adjacent channel protection ratio (13.6 dB) is also shown for comparison purposes. Groups A, B and D were tested with simultaneous upper and lower channel interference, whereas the Lapp group was tested with a lower channel interferer only. Note the rapid change of mean ratings as the C/I ratio changes by only a few dB. The steepness of this curve stands out compared to the co-channel interference curve shown in Figure 2. For ease of comparison, the same scales have been used on the two graphs. This drastic change in impairment level indicates a specific phenomenon: impairment due to adjacent channel interference is best viewed not as a smoothly changing variable but rather as a trigger point beyond which picture quality collapses quickly.

For this reason, adjacent-channel interference was studied in a special set of tests using a "just-perceptible" criterion. A scan of different inter-carrier spacings was done with 7 trained observers and the results are shown in Figure 4 where the threshold of perceptibility is given, averaged for all viewers and for the four test slides. Means and 95% confidence range of the means are shown. As was to be expected, the interference from the lower adjacent channel dominates and this is due to the fact that, since the direction of modulation of the FM carrier is such that the video synchronization pulse produces a decrease in carrier frequency, the interference from the lower adjacent channel is from the high frequency transients of the moving picture content which is more objectionable that the upper adjacent channel interference which shows as a slowly drifting vertical bar produced by the video synchronization pulse. For this reason, the lower adjacent channel interference was used in the Lapp test. Any DBS system should be designed to operate comfortably above these values of C/I, otherwise the reception quality could become unreliable and marginal because of the rapid increase in perceived impairment with low adjacent channel C/I values. Such an approach was used in setting the adjacent channel protection ratio at the RARC-83.

4. Logistic Fitting of the Measurement Results

As can be seen from Figures 1 and 2, the raw measurement results are somewhat difficult to use in the evaluation of the design objectives for a DBS system if the picture quality objective is to be around Q = 4.5. Firstly, the raw results contain variations of a random nature that need to be eliminated. Secondly, in most of the cases, there is a saturation effect at high quality levels which makes the analysis of the results meaningless in this region. The interpretation and comparison of the measurement results for the different groups requires a smoothing of the data and a representation by an appropriate analytical model.

The model proposed is a logistic fit to the mean of an idealized Gaussian population which would generate the same histogram of votes for each test condition as found experimentally. The details of such a fitting were described by Lessman [9]. The data on noise impairment shown in Figure 1 were fitted using this process. The fitted models, shown in Figure 5, are straight lines, relating the logarithm of the impairment unit (IMP) to the objective impairment (S/N), also on a logarithmic scale. This representation of subjective results is used by the CCIR and is explained in CCIR Report 405-4[10]. The system design objective suggested in CCIR Report 960[11] is also shown for comparison purposes. It happens to be very close to the Lapp results.

The same fitting process was applied to the data in Figure 2. Figure 6 shows the fitted models. The RARC-83 value (PR=28 dB) is also shown. It indicates that the BSS plan ensures a potential for high picture quality. The values noted above in the analysis of the results are drawn from these fitted models and could hardly be found reliably from the raw data representation in Figures 1 and 2.

As can be seen, these new figures can be used to draw much more accurate conclusions regarding the assessments of the different groups, especially for results at high levels of picture quality. The common limit in picture quality is normally considered to be the "just-perceptible" level. However, this level varies with viewers and there is still a statistical nature to it. Extrapolation using an analytical model based on impairment assessment using the 5-grade scale removes this artificial barrier.

4. MAC Test Program

A new video encoding format was developed in United Kingdom [12] for 625-line systems and is now proposed as the standard for DBS transmission in Europe [13]. Development work has also taken place in Canada on a similar encoding format for 525-line systems. This new encoding format is considered by its proponents as a potential replacement for the conventional NTSC system for DBS transmissions in North America. This new encoding format is characterized by time compression and time multiplexing of the luminance and chrominance components as opposed to frequency multiplexing as used in the more conventional systems. It is claimed that such encoding is more appropriate to FM transmission, ensuring a better balance of the noise degradation in the luminance and chrominance channels. The triangular nature of the post-detection noise spectrum tends to unbalance the noise degradation in the conventional coding systems by contributing more noise to the chrominance channels modulated on a subcarrier located in the high end of the video spectrum. As a result of time multiplexing, the cross-luminance and cross-color defects observed with the more conventional coding systems disappear completely. On the other hand, the alternate line chroma transmission used in the proposed MAC system tends to create vertical chroma aliasing, absent in NTSC transmission, if no appropriate vertical filtering is used.

Another advantage claimed by the proponents of MAC is that scrambling of the video signal by horizontal shift of the TV line is an inherent feature of the MAC encoding and decoding and that the picture quality is inherently preserved. A multiplex of sound and data signals can be carried on a sub-carrier above the highest video frequency (type A) or fitted in the line horizontal blanking interval and coded at baseband (type B) or at RF (type C) for greater capacity. Type C seems to be preferred in Europe, whereas North America seems to lean toward the lower capacity and lower complexity of the type B sound multiplex.

A new test program was initiated to assess and characterize the video portion of a B-type MAC format for 525-line systems in the presence of noise and interference. The noise tests consisted of the assessment of performance in a given channel bandwidth as a function of carrier deviation and carrier-to-noise ratio (C/N). The tests involved the evaluation of the "just-perceptible" level of background noise, FM threshold noise and truncation noise for different states of over-deviation. Parallel tests were conducted with NTSC for purposes of comparison. This approach was taken in order to determine the optimum level of over-deviation in a given channel bandwidth for both NTSC and MAC.

The interference tests involved a comparison of the susceptiblity of the MAC signal to MAC and NTSC interfering signals and the susceptibility of the NTSC signal to the same types of interfering signals. The intent was to determine whether the newly proposed coding system will produce more interference and/or require more protection than the baseline system used in the planning of the Broadcasting Satellite Service at the RARC-83. The compatibility of this new coding system with the RARC-83 plan which was developed on the basis of NTSC transmission is a very important factor in the establishment of actual system parameters.

262

4.1 MAC Test Set-up

In order to perform the proposed measurements, a test set-up was assembled in which the coding of the wanted and interfering signal paths could be switched easily between NTSC and MAC, leaving the conditions of the transmission path unchanged. The wanted signal was generated by a camera in a telecine chain with NTSC and RGB outputs. The NTSC signal was combined with 3 audio sub-carriers (5.14 MHz, 5.41 MHz, 5.79 MHz) and pre-emphasized according to CCIR Recommendation 405[5]. The levels were adjusted such that the 1 volt (pp) composite signal would produce 12 MHz peak-to-peak (pp) deviation of the carrier and each audio sub-carrier would deviate the carrier by 2 MHzpp at the normal deviation setting.

The wanted MAC signal was generated from the RGB outputs of the camera, using a prototype B-MAC encoder. A 6 μsec burst of a 7.16 MHz sine wave was present in the line horizontal interval to synchronize the MAC decoder. This unmodulated burst was set at the same amplitude as the video signal and was used to simulate the digital sound multiplex signal. The signal was pre-emphasized following a new frequency characteristic especially designed for the MAC coding. The level was adjusted so that the 700 mV pp MAC signal produced a 12 MHzpp deviation of the FM carrier.

These two pre-emphasized wanted signals were alternatively fed to the input of an FM modulator through a calibrated attenuator by which the deviation could be varied over a range of $\pm$ 10 dB about the nominal deviation of 12 MHzpp. No energy dispersal waveform was added and the FM modulator was AC coupled. Although DC coupling of the modulators is preferable for satellite transmission of frequency modulated television signals to stabilize the onset of truncation noise and adjacent channel interference with respect to the average picture level (APL), video clamping devices could not be added to the modulator at the time of these tests.

RF Gaussian noise and interference could be injected through calibrated attenuators in the RF signal path. The RF channel was linear, i.e. no allowance was made for non-linearity caused by a satellite transponder. The pre-detection channel filter was a 4-pole Chebychev type filter with an equivalent noise bandwidth of 22.7 MHz with no group-delay equalization (as used in the NTSC tests reported earlier). The FM demodulator was a conventional limiter discriminator. The output of the demodulator was fed to both MAC and NTSC de-emphasis networks and decoders respectively. The RGB outputs of these decoders were selected in accordance with the input signal selection and sent to a high resolution RGB monitor. Synchronization of the monitor was provided by external signals with built-in vertical and horizontal delays to compensate for the difference in delay between NTSC and MAC signal paths.

The interfering signals were full-field color-bars and multiburst test signals in both MAC and NTSC formats. These four interfering signals were pre-emphasized according to their respective formats. Three unmodulated sound sub-carriers were combined with the NTSC test signals and the levels were adjusted such that they would produce the same carrier deviation as in the case of the wanted NTSC signal. These interfering signals were frequency modulated and could be injected at RF on a co-frequency basis or as adjacent channel interference in the wanted signal path.

4.2 Test Conditions

The viewing conditions were in accordance with CCIR Rec. 500-2[6]. The viewing distance was 5 times the picture height. The wanted pictures were, for the noise test, one test slide from the SMPTE reference series "Girl in Green Dress" and one test slide from the Philips reference series "Toys and Blackboard", and the Multiburst and 75% color-bars test signals, both MAC and NTSC coded. In the case of interference tests, 4 test slides were chosen, 2 from the SMPTE series: "Girl in Green Dress" and "Close shot of a Couple", and 2 from the Philips series: "Toys and Blackboard" and "Blonde Girl with Flowers". The interfering signals were the Multiburst and 75% color-bars test signals in both MAC and NTSC standards. These interfering test signals were locked to the wanted signal and offset so that the vertical and horizontal intervals were visible on the picture monitor.

4.3 Test Procedure

All of the tests conducted to compare the performances of MAC and NTSC were made on the basis of threshold of perceptibility of the given impairment. All viewers were trained viewers who knew what kind of impairment they could expect.

In the case of the noise tests, the viewers were presented with the wanted picture and were asked to bring the carrier-to-noise ratio using a calibrated attenuator from a high value down to the level of perceptibility of background triangular noise; to keep decreasing the C/N to the level of perceptibility of threshold noise; and finally to the threshold of perceptibility of truncation noise. This was done for 6 different carrier deviation settings. The viewers noted the C/N at which these three different impairments began to appear. They were aware that, in some cases, some types of impairment would not occur and, in other cases, the impairment would be present whatever the C/N setting. The viewers were provided with a switch to remove the noise completely in order to make sure that the impairment perceived was really caused by noise.

In the case of the interference tests, the viewers were asked to adjust a calibrated attenuator to a level where they would just begin to perceive interference. A switch was provided to remove interference in order to make sure that the impairment perceived was really caused by interference. They were given full flexibility as to the way the just-perceptible level was to be reached, whether by decreasing the C/I or increasing it or by using the switch or a combination thereof. It seems that the preferred way was by slowly increasing the C/I from a point where the interference was obvious up to the point where, by using the switch, barely perceptible difference could be detected between the presence and absence of interference.

5. MAC-vs-NTSC Test Results

The results of the tests conducted to compare the performance of the MAC coding to the NTSC coding characterize a specific point on the psychometric curve relating the objective level of picture impairment (like S/N and C/I) to the level of quality as assessed by viewers (Q). This point is very often used since it is more easily defined and can normally be assessed with a higher degree of confidence than any other subjective quality level. This point is the "just-perceptible" level of degradation beyond which any improvement can not be detected.

5.1 Noise Test Results

A total of 10 trained viewers were asked to note the level of C/N at which the background triangular noise, the threshold noise and the truncation noise started to appear for 6 different carrier deviations and two test slides. These results are shown in Figure 7. Furthermore, in order to establish a range for the allowable over-deviation as a function of picture material for MAC as well as NTSC, tests were conducted by one expert viewer with, as wanted signal, a 75% color-bar (most likely the worst test signal for NTSC) and Multiburst (most likely the worst test signal for MAC) test signals. The results of these tests are shown in Figures 8 and 9.

In each of these three figures, the abscissa is expressed in dB relative to 12 MHz peak-to-peak carrier deviation. Each increase of one dB in deviation corresponds to 1 dB increase in FM improvement factor. The Carson's rule deviations for MAC and NTSC are also indicated in Figures 7, 8 and 9. The RMS sum of the peak-to-peak carrier deviation produced by the video signal and any sound subcarrier added to twice the top baseband frequency defines the Carson's rule bandwidth. It was found that 12 MHzpp in a filter bandwidth of 22.7 MHz represents 1 dB overdeviation for NTSC and 1.5 dB for MAC.

With respect to the threshold of perceptibility of FM background noise, it was found that for a color-bar test signal (Figure 8), MAC required a C/N of 1 dB lower than NTSC. The situation seems to be reversed in the case of Multiburst (Figure 9). Averaging over 2 test slides and 10 viewers (Figure 7), MAC seems to require a C/N that is 0.2 dB higher than in the case of NTSC. This tends to indicate that, for the same carrier deviation, MAC offers a better noise FM improvement for highly saturated colored scenes whereas NTSC offers better noise FM improvement for scenes where the luminance information is predominant. For average pictures, both coding systems seem to offer approximately the same improvement in terms of FM background noise.

In absolute terms, it is interesting to note that the variation in S/N at the threshold of noise perceptibility in the case of NTSC is rather large between the different wanted signals going from 46 dB (unified weighting) for the Multiburst, to 50 dB for the average scene, and 55 dB for the color-bars. These S/N values were computed in the case of NTSC, knowing the C/N and the FM improvement factor which depends on carrier deviation. This is found to be consistent with results found in the NTSC tests described earlier in this paper. It was found that, for both coding systems, the most demanding situation in terms of large S/N required to avoid impairment caused by FM background noise occurs for pictures containing saturated colors. This is the case where MAC shows the greatest improvement over NTSC as shown in Figure 8.

Such results were to be expected since, due to its triangular nature, the FM noise spectrum affects less the chrominance information in the case of MAC. In a comparison between noise performance of MAC versus PAL reported by Windram et al [12], the color noise improvement was claimed to be 3.6 dB. In the case of MAC versus NTSC, this improvement is likely to be slightly smaller since the noise imbalance created by the triangular noise spectrum will be less for NTSC, the color sub-carrier being at a lower frequency (3.58 MHz) than in the case of PAL (4.43 MHz). The same Report [6] indicates a decrease in S/N for the luminance signal of 2.9 dB for MAC over PAL. Three main factors affect the S/N performance of the MAC encoded luminance signal as compared to NTSC: the increase in noise power due to the wider baseband bandwidth of the time-compressed video signal, the actual increase in carrier deviation due to the removal of the synchronization pulse and the use of a different pre-emphasis network.

Using the cubic relationship of the time compression ratio and the square relationship of the increase in signal amplitude due to the removal of the set-up level and the synchronization pulse, the signal-to-noise ratio would be decreased as follows:

$$\Delta S/N = 30 \log (2/3) + 20 \log (140/92.5)$$
$$= -1.7 \text{ dB}$$

This, however, does not take into account the different pre-emphasis networks which, in relation with the noise weighting characteristic, would lead to a slightly different value.

The threshold of perceptibility of FM threshold noise seems to stay almost constant in the case of MAC for different levels of over-deviation (Figures 7 and 8) except in the case of Multiburst where it starts to increase at a very high level of over-deviation (Figure 9). Such is not the case for NTSC where the FM threshold seems to increase progressively with over-deviation. In the case of an average test slide (Figure 7), this gradual increase only begins beyond 3 dB over-deviation relative to 12 MHzpp. This rise in FM threshold for NTSC seems to be the factor limiting the possible amount of over-deviation in the case of the two test signals (Figure 7). It should be noted that the FM threshold noise in the case of NTSC appears as streaks on the screen whereas in the case of MAC coding, it appears as tiny dots. The nature of these impairments may lead to a different perceived impairment level between the NTSC threshold noise and the MAC threshold noise.

Truncation noise is characterized by the appearance of noise during high amplitude transitions. This type of impairment should not be under-estimated in establishing the acceptable level of over-deviation and the performances of threshold extension demodulators. It is caused by the lowering of the instantaneous C/N, during large transitions where an important part of the power spectrum falls outside the receive filter bandwidth. For the color-bar test signal (Figure 8), over-deviation of a NTSC signal hits a hard limit at around 3.5 dB relative to 12 MHzpp. This is due to truncation noise which looks like edge tearing (black to white transitions become unstable and noisy). This rather low limit is due to the presence of the 3 sound sub-carriers. In the case of the Multiburst test signal, it seems that truncation noise is the limiting factor for MAC. This is due to the fact that for MAC, steep luminance transitions have their spectrum even more spread outside the filter bandwidth due to the 3/2 time compression. In all cases, for the MAC coding, the truncation noise is more constraining in terms of limiting the amount of over-deviation than the increase in the FM threshold.

Assuming a C/N of 10 dB, above which no impairment caused by FM threshold noise or truncation noise should be perceivable, the allowable amount of over-deviation beyond the 12 MHzpp as found from Figures 7, 8 and 9 is listed in columns 2 and 3 of Table 2 for the three types of picture material tested. The fourth column in the table indicates the difference in permissible over-deviation as referenced to 12 MHzpp between MAC and NTSC. The fifth column indicates the absolute weighted S/N required for NTSC at the level of perceptibility of FM background noise. The sixth column indicates the difference between the equivalent S/N achievable by MAC and NTSC for the same C/N and same deviation. The seventh column indicates the difference in S/N achievable if the maximum allowed over-deviation was used to improve the S/N.

Picture Material	MAC DEV.	NTSC DEV.	Δ DEV.	S/N NTSC	Δ S/N meas.	Δ S/N max.	ΔC/N
Slides	3.3	1.8	1.5	50	− 0.2	1.3	0.37
75% Color Bars	5.2	0.6	4.6	55	+ 1.0	5.6	1.56
Multiburst	0.7	0.2	0.5	47	− 1.0	− 0.5	− 0.13

Table 2. Allowable over-deviation (dB) before perceptibility of picture impairment at C/N = 10 dB. (Reference deviation: 12 MHzpp for NTSC and MAC).

Column 6 shows that, when the spectrum usage in the channel filter is maximized, the MAC encoding can improve the background S/N over what is achievable with NTSC by 1.3 dB in the case of the two test slides and by 5.6 dB in the case of color-bars. In the case of the Multiburst, NTSC can give a background S/N of 0.5 dB better than the MAC coding.

Assuming that the goal is to achieve the same RMS noise performance, the larger over-deviation achievable with MAC can be used to decrease the receiver filter bandwidth and thus increase the received C/N and therefore decrease the onset of threshold effects. Such a computation was made assuming a linear relationship between the Carson's rule bandwidth and the bandwidth used at the given state of over-deviation, for any given deviation. The results are indicated in the last column of Table 2. It shows that MAC gives 0.37 dB and 1.56 dB improvement over FM threshold in the cases of the two test slides and the color-bars test signal respectively whereas it would increase the FM threshold by 0.13 dB over NTSC in the case of the Multiburst test signal. These results tend to show that the potential improvement of MAC over NTSC is very dependent on picture content, being larger in the case of saturated color scenes. Although relatively small, this improvement seems to show up when it is the most needed, i.e. where very high S/N are required. This indicates the improved balance in noise degradation between chrominance and luminance channels achieved by MAC.

5.2 Co-channel Interference Test Results

Tests on the just-perceptible level of impairment were also conducted with two interfering signals. Color-bars and Multiburst test signals, MAC and NTSC encoded, were frequency modulated with the same deviation (12 MHzpp) and injected, one at a time, at the same carrier frequency in the RF signalpath. The level at which this interference becomes perceptible was assessed by 17 viewers using 4 test slides. All combinations of coding for the wanted and interfering signals were assessed. The results averaged over all test slides and all viewers are given in Table 3 for the Multiburst (MB) and color-bars (CB) interfering signals as well as the average (AV) for these two interfering signals. These results are expressed in terms of carrier-to-interference ratio (C/I), that is the number of dB's at which the wanted carrier needs to be kept above the interfering carrier power.

| | Interfering Signal | |
	NTSC	MAC
NTSC	MB = 24.3 CB = 26.1 AV = 25.2	MB = 24.4 CB = 26.2 AV = 24.4
MAC	MB = 24.3 CB = 25.1 AV = 24.7	MB = 23.6 CB = 25.1 AV = 24.4

Wanted Signal

Table 3. Co-channel interference results (C/I in dB).

It can be seen from the table that the susceptibility of the four combinations of codings is almost equivalent in the case of co-channel interference. MAC into MAC seems to be slightly better (by 0.8 dB) than NTSC into NTSC tending to indicate that the MAC coding would be slightly more robust to co-channel interference than NTSC coding. Also, the fact that MAC interfering into NTSC and NTSC interfering into MAC are no worse than NTSC into NTSC allows for full flexibility in the use of these two coding systems in terms of co-channel interference. The results also show that for both types of coding, the color-bar test signal tends to produce more co-channel interference than the Multiburst test signal. The fourth slide used, containing saturated red areas, was found to be especially critical to interference when it was coded in NTSC giving C/I of 28 dB for all interfering signals. For this same fourth slide, NTSC encoded, interference from a MAC color-bar test signal required a C/I = 29 dB averaged over the 17 viewers. In this specific case, the RARC-83 protection ratio was exceeded by 1 dB.

The type of impairment produced by co-channel interference is relatively non-coherent for both MAC and NTSC codings, producing wormy effects rather than distinguishable background shapes as is the case for AM-VSB type interference. Hence, it is expected that scrambling will have limited influence on co-channel interference. However, before any definite conclusion can be reached, subjective measurements are needed to evaluate the effect of scrambling the picture information on co-channel interference performances. Limited observations tend to indicate that the increase in carrier deviation will increase the robustness of the FM-MAC signal to co-channel interference much the same way as in the case of FM-NTSC. Over-deviation can thus improve the noise performance as well as the co-channel interference performance.

5.3 Adjacent Channel Interference Test Results

Adjacent channel interference tests were conducted in a manner similar to those for the co-channel case, using the same 17 viewers and same 4 test slides. The viewers were asked to adjust the attenuation on the interfering signal path so that the impairment was just perceptible. The intercarrier spacing was set at the RARC-83 value: 14.58 MHz (giving 32 channels, 24 MHz wide, in the 500 MHz DBS band). The channel filter used was a simple 4-pole Chebychev type filter with an equivalent noise bandwidth of 22.7 MHz.

Both upper and lower adjacent channels interference was assessed for all combinations of wanted and interfering signal codings and the carrier to interference ratios (C/I) required at the just perceptible level of interference were averaged over all viewers and all test slides to give the results shown in Tables 4 and 5.

| | Interfering Signal | |
	NTSC	MAC
Wanted Signal NTSC	MB = 4.3 CB = 4.4 AV = 4.3	MB = 7.4 CB = 7.2 AV = 7.3
Wanted Signal MAC	MB = 4.2 CB = 2.4 AV = 3.3	MB = 6.1 CB = 6.8 AV = 6.5

Table 4. Upper adjacent channel interference results (C/I in dB).

| | Interfering Signal | |
	NTSC	MAC
Wanted Signal NTSC	MB = 5.5 CB = 2.9 AV = 4.2	MB = 7.2 CB = 5.1 AV = 6.2
Wanted Signal MAC	MB = 5.7 CB = 3.9 AV = 4.8	MB = 9.1 CB = 9.2 AV = 9.2

Table 5. Lower adjacent channel interference results (C/I in dB).

Very specific trends can be found through analysis of these results. For the conditions of the test, the MAC encoded signal produces more interference in the adjacent channel than the same signal with NTSC encoding. The MAC signal is slightly more robust when it is interfered by the upper adjacent channel but seems to be more susceptible to lower adjacent channel interference than NTSC coding. This can be explained by the fact that due to the non-linear nature of the transmitted signal (gamma pre-correction in the camera), disturbance in the black levels is made more noticeable than the same disturbance in the white levels. Because of the sense of modulation, black levels are more affected by lower adjacent channel interference. This is also the case for NTSC but to a lesser extent due to the presence of the synchronization pulse. No systematic difference in the results was observed between the use of color-bars or Multiburst test signals as interferers.

In both cases of adjacent channel interference, the tests indicated that the use of MAC encoded signals for both wanted and interfering signals will require a higher level of protection than in the case of NTSC. This additional protection seems to be in a range between 2.2 dB and 5 dB. These results were constrained only in very few cases by the presence of the 7.16 MHz data-burst. However, it should be noted that these results were obtained using channel filters with relatively slow roll-off characteristics. It is likely that these values of required protection will decrease if filters with sharper roll-off characteristics are used.

The NTSC coding is susceptible to disturbances caused by amplitude and phase responses of the IF filter because of the presence of the color sub-carrier. The MAC coding is more robust to such non-linear distortions since it is basically a black and white transmission. Use of sharper filters may be easier with MAC thereby possibly offsetting the disadvantage in adjacent channel interference. This advantage is not clear however since sharper filter roll-off and phase inequality is likely to affect the performance of the data-burst.

More specific assessments can be drawn in the case of adjacent channel interference as to the effect of scrambling. Since the adjacent channel interference is actually the instantaneous adjacent carrier excursion within the wanted channel bandwidth, this interference looks like highly coherent interference displaying the sharp transitions of the interfering pictures. In this case, scrambling will be helpful in randomizing these transitions and making them appear more like random noise. An improvement in adjacent channel interference protection can therefore be expected if scrambling is used. The additional power falling in the wanted channel will however lead to an apparent decrease in the total C/N and contribute to the onset of threshold noise and truncation noise.

Even though higher values of protection were found to be needed for certain combinations of wanted and interfering signals, all values averaged over each test slide were found to be at least 3 dB below the protection ratio set at the RARC-83 for adjacent channel interference (13.6 dB). MAC encoding would still be compatible with the plan developed at that Conference. Serious thought should be given to the fact that the use of over-deviation in order to improve noise performance and co-channel interference performance could increase the adjacent channel interference. These three factors should be considered along with the onset of threshold and truncation noises to seek an optimum operational point. Nevertheless, if this adjacent channel protection ratio was to be exceeded, this would be a domestic problem in the context of DBS in North America since all channels from the same orbital location were assigned to the same country in the plan.

6. Conclusion

The first phase of this measurement program consisted of evaluation of the performance of the FM-NTSC television signal in a noise and interference environment representing the likely situation in the 12 GHz DBS band. The results of these tests were used at the RARC-83 to set baseline system parameters for the planning of the service in much the same way as TASO results in the 1950's were used to establish guidelines for the planning of terrestrial broadcasting.

Comparing the results on noise impairment obtained during this measurement program with the TASO results, it was found that the viewer's expectation for television picture quality has increased by 5 dB to 9 dB. Comparing the values set by the RARC-83 for the co-channel and adjacent channel protection ratios and the results obtained for interference degradation, it can be seen that the Conference has set system parameters that will allow for potential high quality DBS services. It was also found, from the test results, that a decrease in S/N or co-channel C/I would gradually decrease the picture quality whereas in the case of adjacent channel interference, the picture quality seems to collapse below a certain threshold in C/I. This conclusion tends to indicate that the adjacent channel interference should be kept beyond the level of perception to make sure that an operating margin is provided for in normal system design.

The second phase of the measurement program consisted of a systematic comparison of the performance of the NTSC and MAC television encoded signals. Both codings were exposed to the same noise and interference degradations, typical of the DBS environment. The noise tests determined the level of over-deviation allowed in a given channel bandwidth. The criterion was based on the increase in the onset of FM threshold noise and truncation noise. The level of perceptibility of the FM triangular noise was also assessed for different picture content and it was found that, with the consideration of the allowable over-deviation, the MAC encoding can provide slightly better performance than NTSC (1.3 dB). Although small, this improvement is greatest for pictures where the highest S/N is required (saturated colors) indicating a better balance in noise degradation as a function of picture content.

The co-channel interference results indicated that MAC encoded signals are slightly more robust (0.8 dB) to interference than NTSC. It also indicated that the mixed use of MAC and NTSC produces less interference than NTSC into NTSC thus showing that the use of MAC is compatible with a plan developed on the basis of NTSC. Due to the non-coherent nature of the co-channel interference for both types of coding, the authors conjecture that signal scrambling is not likely to improve significantly the co-channel interference situation.

In the adjacent channel case where the interference is of highly coherent nature, scrambling of the television signals will likely decrease the effect of interference. Both methods of coding were found to be within the RARC-83 protection limit without the use of scrambling. MAC was however found to produce more perceivable adjacent channel interference than NTSC by 2 dB to 5 dB. It is likely that steeper channel filter roll-off characteristics will improve the situation for both codings. In the case of MAC, since it is basically a black and white video transmission, it is likely that the data-burst performance rather than the video performance will constrain the channel filter amplitude and delay characteristics.

The comparison of MAC and NTSC methods of coding was only done at the level of perceptibility of noise and interference. Even though the results of these tests permitted some valuable conclusions to be drawn, more complete evaluation will be required to establish the virtues and draw-backs of MAC coding versus NTSC coding as assessed from the subjective picture quality. Such additional tests could describe the progressive transition from perfect picture quality to system outage for noise impairment (FM truncation and threshold noises) and co-channel interference. As part of these tests, the ultimate (unimpaired) quality achievable with MAC and NTSC would need to be assessed.

In a broader scope, a comparative evaluation of MAC and NTSC should include the scrambling performance, the audio and data performance and most importantly the upward compatibility with enhanced-definition-television (EDTV) and high-definition-television (HDTV).

Acknowledgements

The authors would like to thank the Director General Space Technology and Applications for permission to publish this paper. The valuable contribution of the late Dr. M. Bouchard in the early phases of this program is also acknowledged.

Mr. M. Zanichkowsky developed and implemented the system of computer programs and data files required to analyse the results of all of the tests; Ms. Charlene Balko organized and supervised the tests with 100 non-expert viewers at Philip A. Lapp Limited. Their contribution to the success of the program is sincerely acknowledged.

The participation of Digital Video Systems Inc., Toronto, Canada was very much appreciated. They made the last part of this test program possible by providing the MAC encoder and decoder units.

REFERENCES

1. Dean, C.E., "Measurement of the Subjective Effects of Interference in Television Reception", Proc. IRE, Vol. 48, No. 6, Part I, pp. 1035-1047, June 1960.

2. Final Acts of the Regional Administration Conference for the Planning of the Broadcasting-Satellite Service in Region 2 (SAT-83), Geneva 1983.

3. Bouchard M., Chouinard G. and Trenholm, R., "Subjective Evaluation of the Noise and Interference Protection Ratio for Frequency Modulated NTSC Television Signals", CRC Report No. 1367, Communication Research Centre, Ottawa, Canada, December 1983.

4. Lapp, P.A., "Final Report on the Subjective Evaluation of Impaired Television Pictures and Statistical Analysis of the Results", Department of Communications, Contract Report no. DOC-CR-SP-83-043, Canada, 1983.

5. CCIR Recommendation 405, Volume XI, XVth Plenary Assembly, GENEVA, 1982.

6. CCIR Recommendation 500-2, Volume XI, XVth Plenary Assembly, GENEVA, 1982.

7. CCIR Recommendation 600, Volume X & XI Part 2, XVth Plenary Assembly, GENEVA, 1982.

8. CCIR Recommendation 567-1, Volume XII, XVth Plenary Assembly, GENEVA, 1982.

9. Lessman A.M., "The Subjective Effects of Echoes in 525-line Monochrome and NTSC Color Television and the Resulting Echo Time Weighting". Journal of the SMPTE Vol. 81, December, 1972.

10. CCIR Report 405-4, Volume XI, XVth Plenary Assembly, GENEVA, 1982.

11. CCIR Report 960, Volume XI, XVth Plenary Assembly, GENEVA, 1982.

12. Windram W.D. et al., "MAC-A Television System for High-Quality Satellite Broadcasting", Experimental & Development Report 118/82, Independant Broadcasting Authority, Winchester, U.K.

13. Mertens H. and Wood D., "The C-MAC/packet System for Direct Satellite Television", EBU Technical Review, No. 200 (August 1983).

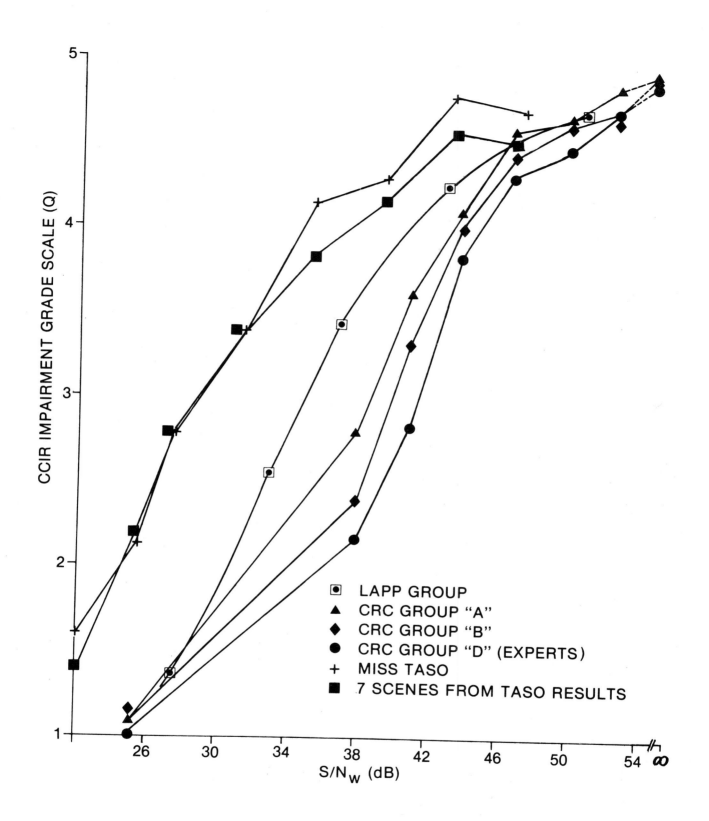

Fig. 1. Picture quality degradation caused by noise (unified weighting + de-emphasis = 13.8 dB).

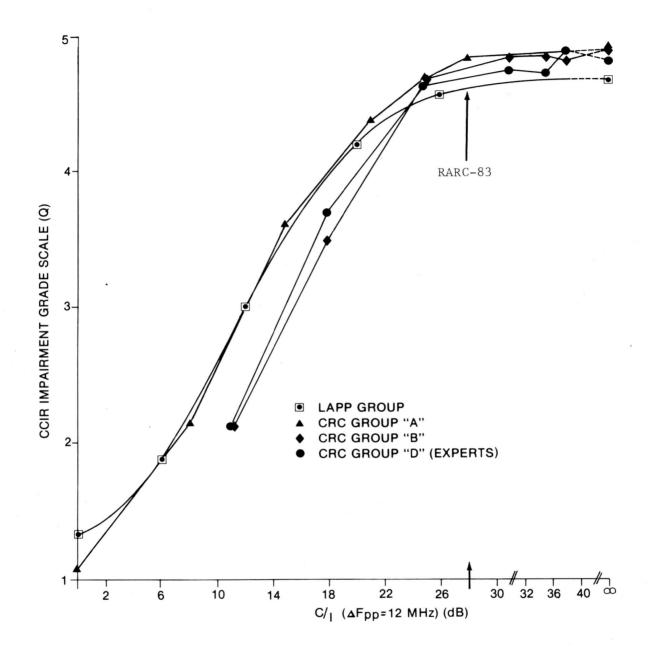

Fig. 2. Picture quality degradation caused by co-channel interference.

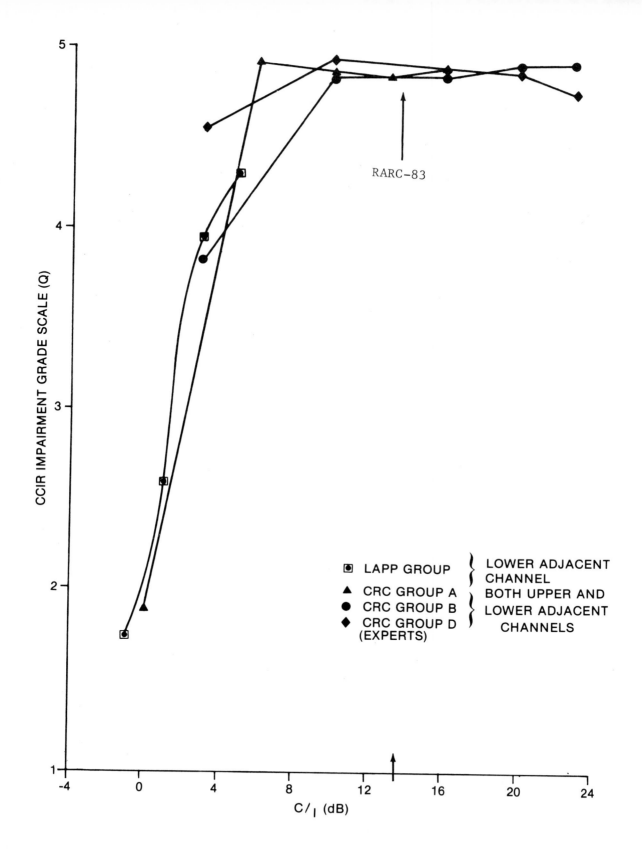

Fig. 3. Picture quality degradation caused by adjacent channel interference (carrier separation = 15 MHz, Dev. = 9.52 MHzpp).

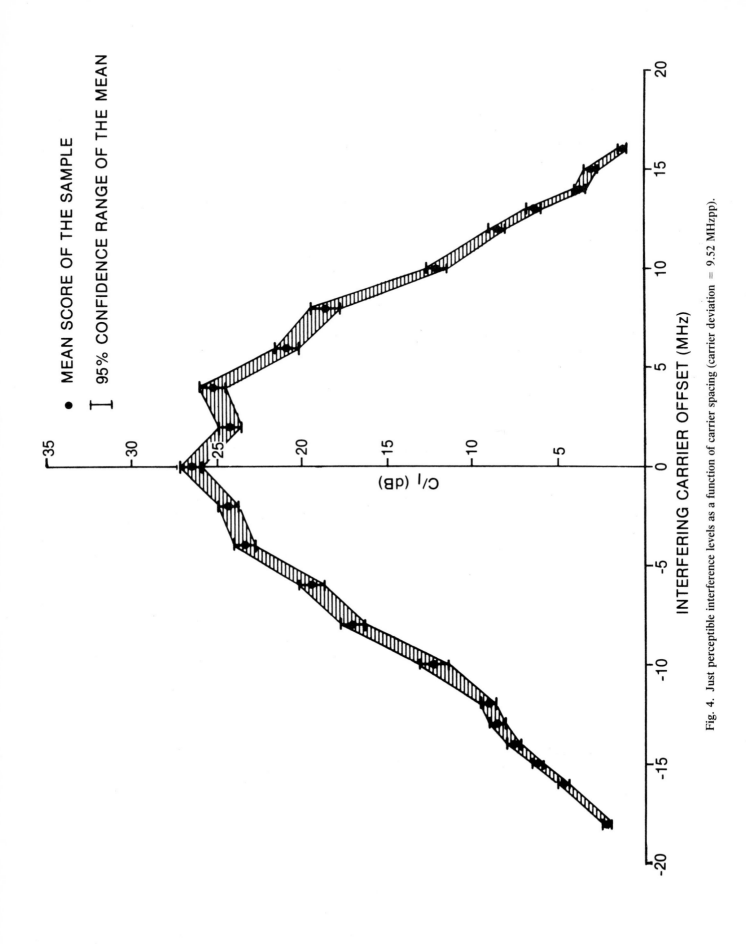

Fig. 4. Just perceptible interference levels as a function of carrier spacing (carrier deviation = 9.52 MHzpp).

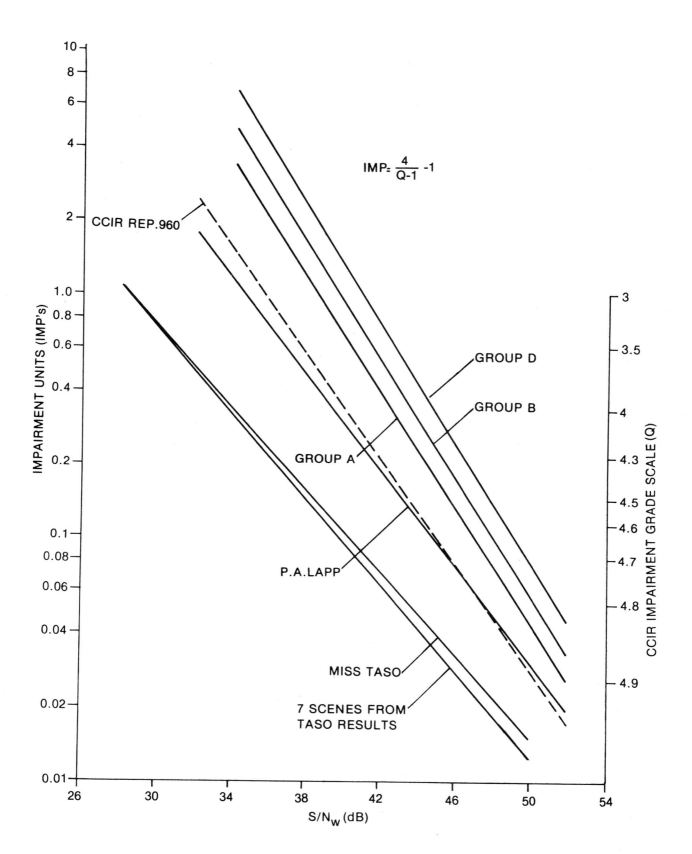

Fig. 5. Logistic fits to experimental results (noise impairment).

277

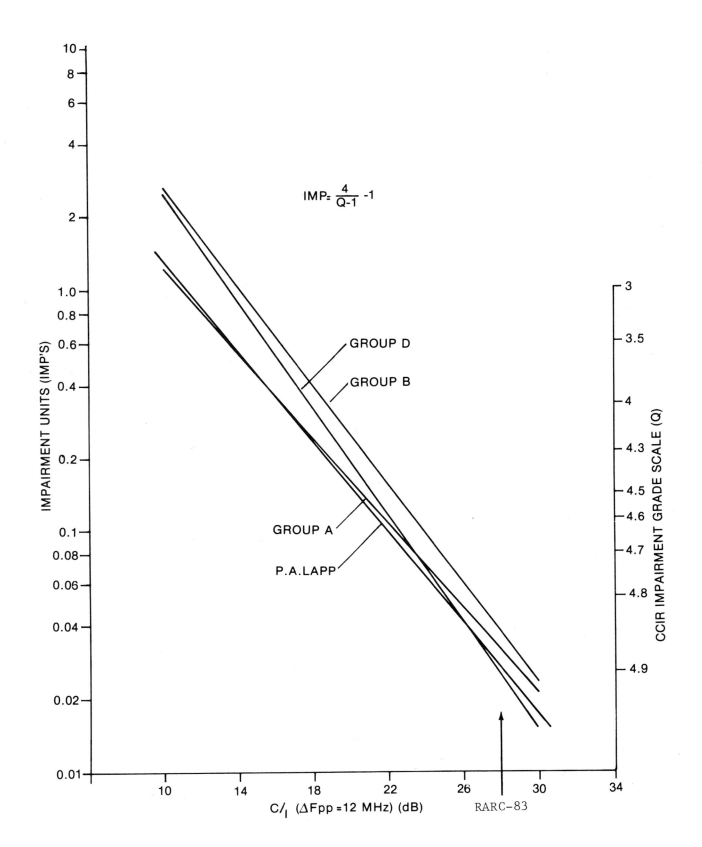

Fig. 6. Logistic fits to experimental results (co-channel interference).

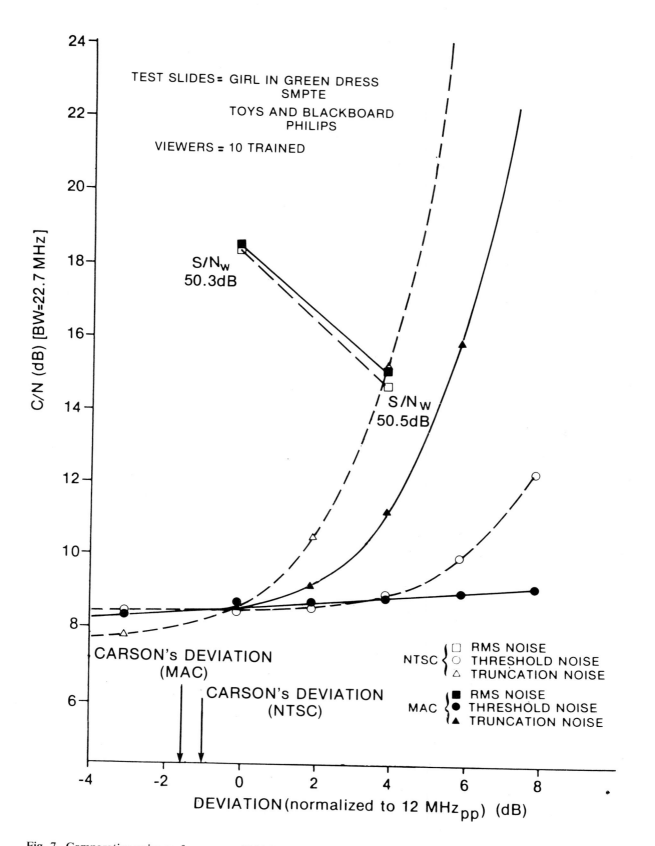

Fig. 7. Comparative noise performances of MAC and NTSC as a function of carrier over-deviation (two test slides).

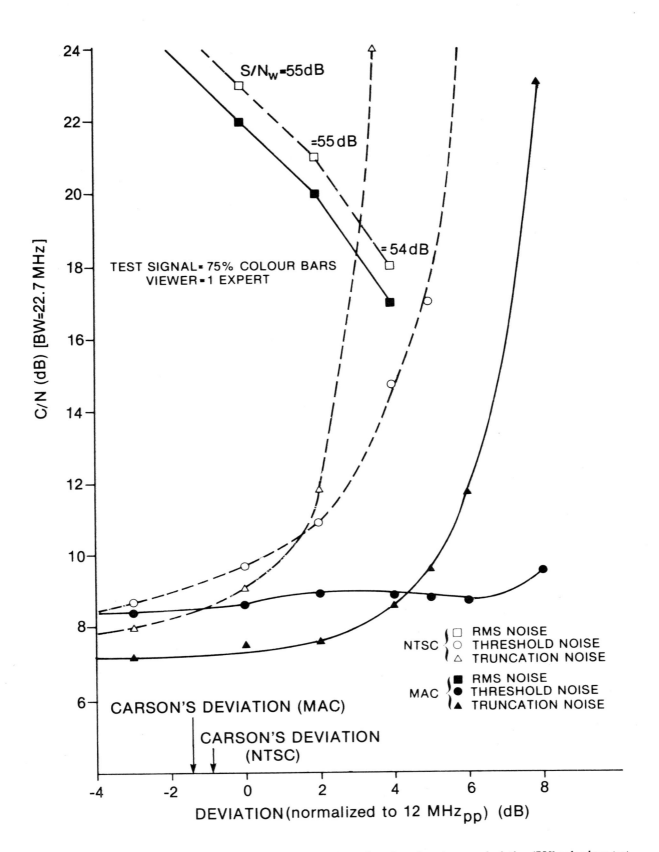

Fig. 8. Comparative noise performances of MAC and NTSC as a function of carrier over-deviation (75% color-bars test signal).

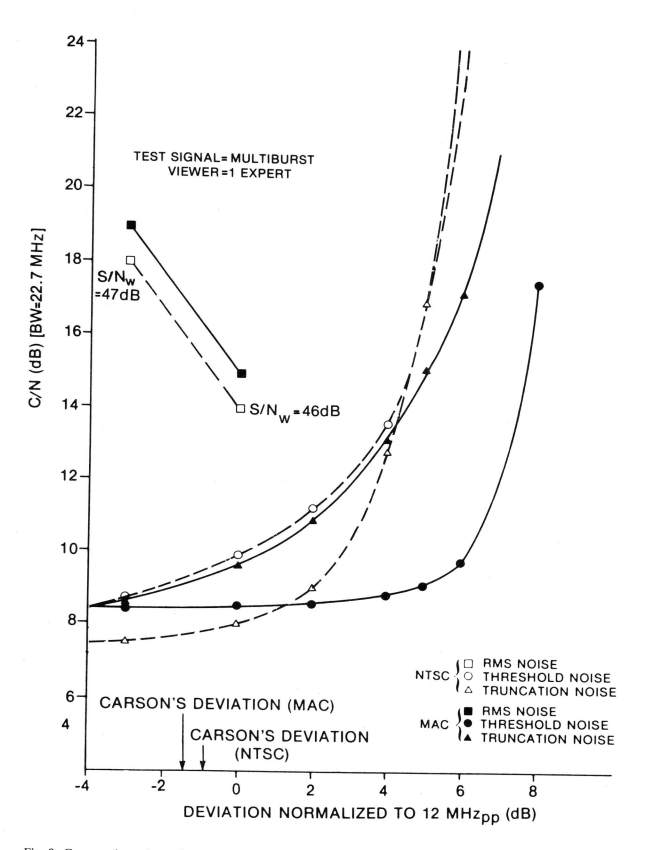

Fig. 9. Comparative noise performances of MAC and NTSC as a function of carrier over-deviation (multiburst test signal).

Gérald Chouinard worked 5 years for the Canadian Broadcasting Corp. in the field of International Relations (technical). His main involvement was the preparation of the RARC-83 for DBS planning. After joining the Federal Department of Communications in 1981, he carried out technical studies for the preparation of the RARC-83 under the Space Technologies Directorate. He is presently involved in DBS technical studies and spectrum-orbit utilization studies.

John N. Barry, Ph.D., P.Eng., Senior Consultant, was born in Loretto, Ontario in 1927. He received his post-secondary education at the University of Toronto between 1945—1950 and 1956—1959, receiving the Ph.D. degree in 1960. He joined Philip A. Lapp Ltd. as a senior consultant in 1981. Since joining the company, he has become involved in engineering studies of cable systems performance, television impairment, microwave transmission, satellite communications and remote sensing. Before coming to Lapp, Barry held senior research management and policy positions in the Space Branch at DOC. His earlier career work spans over twenty years in electronics research in such fields as radar, lasers, optical communications and satellite engineering. From 1975 to 1976 John was project manager for the final assembly, test, launch and post-launch checkout of the Joint DOC/NASA HERMES satellite mission.

Distribution and Broadcasting Satellites: European Projects and Problems

Rudolf Gressmann
Director
EBU Technical Centre
Brussels, Belgium

It is becoming almost a common place to say that Europe has, in all fields of technology, more problems than projects : it is a continent divided into two parts politically and within that frame-work, the western part consists of a number of independent countries of different sizes, languages, cultures, political systems, degrees of industrialisation, etc.

In broadcasting technology these differences from the North American situation in particular, together with the still fundamentally different approach to the basic philosophy of broadcasting as a mass medium, lead to rather formidable problems in technical standardisation. Common broadcasting standards are increasingly important; because, more and more, the critical size of the market for the production of consumer products, is greater than any of the individual European countries.

1. Direct broadcasting satellites

The need for one single transmission standard for DBS is recognised by all parties involved in the process of standardisation in Europe: broadcasters, industry, telecommunications administration and governments.

So far, only one proposal for such a standard has been made: the C-MAC/packet system developed and agreed by the European Broadcasting Union.

The specification for this system was sent to the CCIR in 1983 and it has been described in detail via a number of publications; therefore I will only recall, in very general form, its objectives, its principal characteristics and its performance.

The aim was to devise a transmission system

- which used the capacity of the 27-MHz channels for DBS in the 12 GHz band in an optimal fashion without any infringement of the interference rules laid down in the WARC-BS-1977 for ITU Regions 1 and 3;

- which was to be the transmission standard adapted to the quality of the agreed digital 4:2:2 production standard;

- which, by fulfilling the different DBS requirements of all European countries, could be acceptable by each of them, and,

- which enabled receiver manufacturers to construct a single type of receiver which could be used all over the continent.

The main characteristics of this system can be described as follows:

- the structure of the complete signal continues to be based on the principles of a 625-line television signal with 2:1 interlacing

- the picture continues to be transmitted in analogue form

- the sound and all data services are transmitted in a digital form

- the analogue and digital components are arranged together, in variable proportions, in a time-division multiplex

- the time multiplexing of both the analogue and the digital components is effected at radio-frequency (C-type modulation)

- the luminance and colour-difference signals are themselves transmitted in TDM technique (MAC); they are frequency modulated as indicated in the Final Acts of the WARC-BS-1977

- the digital elements are modulated according to a four-state phase-shift keying modulation system (2-4 PSK) and arranged in packets of fixed lengths.

Having set out the reasons for using the name C-MAC/packet we can now quickly glance at some of its parameters and applications.

Fig. 1 shows the structure of one 64-µs scanning line.

This structure is based on a clock frequency of 20.25 MHz, this being chosen mainly for two reasons :

First, the inherent quality of the broadcast transmission standard is matched to that of the world-wide digital studio production standard, recommended by the CCIR.

If we compress, by the factors 3:2 and 3:1, the luminance and colour-difference signals with their respective sampling frequencies of 13.5 and 6.75 MHz we arrive at the figure of 20.25 MHz.

Secondly, for the digital components, a bit-rate of 20.25 Mbit/s is close to the capacity limit of the 27-MHz satellite channel when four-state phase-shift keying is used.

Given these conditions, each line contains a total of 1296 clock periods which, leaving aside those periods reserved for transitions between service components and for auxiliary purposes, are used in normal operations for the transmission of :

- a digital burst of 203 bits; 195 of these carry useful information, this corresponding to a mean bit-rate of about 3 Mbit/s;

- in turn, the analogue colour-difference components (350 clock periods) and the luminance component (699 clock periods).

Now let us have a look at the way in which the 625 line periods are organised in a full frame period of 40 ms. <u>Fig. 2</u> shows the structure for the case under consideration. I should stress that the intervals allocated to each element have the values shown here and in the preceding diagram <u>only</u> in the case of so called "normal video conditions"; the intervals can be modified in both the horizontal sense (length of a component on the line) and in the vertical sense (number of lines used for that component within each frame). These intervals are governed by time-multiplex control data which are transmitted in the special data burst which occupies the whole of line 625. In particular, it is possible to lengthen the digital burst to the point where full-channel data are transmitted or, alternatively, to shorten it with a view, for example, to altering the aspect ratio of the picture.

In this configuration the data area contains 162 packets, starting in line 1 and ending in line 624. I shall come back later to this feature.

Synchronisation for the system is entirely digital. It is achieved by recognition, either separately or together, of a line synchronisation word of 7 bits and a frame synchronisation word of 64 bits inserted in line 625.

The principles of the MAC video coding system have been described in various publications; it has been developed largely in the UK's IBA at Crawley Court (UK). The EBU specification adheres to the original general principles, but it does incorporate several refinements.

As we have already seen, the MAC system is designed to transmit a quality corresponding to the future digital studio standard, i.e maximum bandwidths of about 6 MHz for the luminance signal and 3 MHz for the U and V colour difference signals.

The luminance signal is time-compressed on a line-by-line basis, in the ratio 3:2, and the bandwidth it occupies in the transmission channel is therefore increased in the same proportion. The compression is achieved by digitally sampling the signal which then loads a line store: this is read out at a higher frequency than the input and the signal is then restored to analogue form.

The colour-difference signals are subjected to time-compression of similar form, but this time the compression ratio is 3:1; the colour-difference bandwidth therefore remains equal to one-half of that of the luminance, as in the 4:2:2 digital standard.

The luminance and colour-difference signals are then arranged side-by-side in a single television line and are thus transmitted as a time-multiplex. The result is that the cross-colour and cross-luminance effects inherent to the PAL, SECAM and NTSC systems are eliminated. The final bandwidth of the MAC signals is 1.5 times that of the luminance signal at the picture source.

The colour-difference signals are transmitted alternately on successive lines; in other words, it is a line-sequential system. In this way the horizontal and vertical resolutions are approximately matched for the luminance and colour-difference information, but vertical pre-filtering is used to reduce the visibility of vertical aliasing to an acceptable level for the colour-difference signals.

Summarising, it may be said that the MAC system is a time-multiplex of time-compressed luminance and line-sequential colour-difference signals. Its principal advantages are an improvement in quality, resulting from the elimination of cross-colour and cross-luminance and the increase in component bandwidths, together with improved RF performance, largely because of the noise characteristics of FM, and its great flexibility as regards future enhancements.

Packet multiplexing of the digital signals for sound and data has been developed very largely by the CCETT laboratories at Rennes (France). The bit-stream of such a signal is made up of packets of fixed length.

Fig.3 shows the packet structure.

We recognise first, in the header: the address, a continuity index and a protection suffix and thereafter, the useful data area consisting of one packet-type (PT) byte which is used for sound services only and then 90 bytes for the sound services.

As we have seen already, in normal operation a total of 162 packets are transmitted in each 625-line digital frame.

The corresponding capacity of just over 3 Mbit/s can be used in any required manner, as and when appropriate. In particular, the television picture can be accompanied by the following sound components, each based on a 32 kHz sampling frequency (which permits an audio bandwidth of 15 kHz):

- either 4 sound signals with uniform coding and second-level error protection

- or 6 sound signals either with uniform coding and first-level error protection or with 14-10 near-instantaneous companded coding and second-level error protection

- or 8 sound signals with 14-10 near-instantaneous companded coding and first level error protection.

In each case a number of packets is left open for other uses. One of these is the identification of services. In fact, the multiplicity of services or service components which can be broadcast simultaneously in a single channel, either in the form of components of the time-division multiplex, or within the packet multiplex, requires the provision of an identification system to help users gain rapid access to the wanted service. This service-identification system must therefore offer:

- a readily-obtained list of available services;
- a means for automatically configuring the receiver and its decoders to suit the choice made by the user;
- a rapid indication of which service is being received.

These requirements have resulted in the development of a very elaborate system which I cannot describe in detail here. Let me just mention the data which are broadcast as a function of the selected transmission mode.

First of all we have seen that the whole of line 625 is reserved for a special data burst which, in addition to providing frame synchronisation, contains mainly information concerning :

- date and time
- satellite channel
- TDM configuration and details of the TDM multiplex itself.

Secondly, there is one dedicated digital channel, made up of all the packets bearing the address "0". It is reserved for the identification of the services carried in the packet multiplex. The coding structure is that recommended in CCITT Recommendation S.62 for teletex control. The transmitted information includes coded indications and also clear-language text, of variable length, which may be displayed on the television receiver screen or on a special display device. These include all the information needed by the public concerning the services and the programmes provided at a given moment in time by the operators of the system.

For a typical example in which the channel carries a television programme with original sound, three commentary sound signals and subtitles in three different languages, together with two radio services and four different teletext services, the bit-rate needed in the dedicated channel is of the order of 12kbit/s or 16 packets/s.

Thirdly, the information transmitted at the level of one digital service channel is concerned only with a service or service component and it is carried in the same digital channel as the service itself i.e., it uses packets bearing the same address as the service. These interpretation blocks (BI in the Fig.) normally have a length of one packet and the main information coded in them enables, amongst other things, the receiver to recognize the type of sound signal transmitted e.g. mono or stereo, type of coding and error correction, etc.

The system so far described is much better suited than NTSC, PAL or SECAM for television services where conditional access is required such as "Pay-TV" or "Subscription-TV". EBU studies in this field are in hand. They foresee the use of PRBS (pseudo-random binary sequence) generators for component rotation of the vision signal and digital scrambling of the sound and data signals. The optimum means of distribution of the key information for the PRBS generators is still under discussion, but one possibility is the transmission, over-air, of encrypted keys. The system must, of course, have some means of discriminating individual users, and a number of possibilities are being discussed for user access systems, such as the smart card, card and PIN system and over-air addressing. These systems essentially decrypt the encrypted key information. The question of whether all services should be scrambled, with some having a freely available key, is still to be decided.

Finally, some remarks about the performance of the system. We have already seen its great flexibility and the amount of headroom it leaves for future developments. The system indeed makes optimal use of the frequency spectrum attributed to satellite broadcasting in Europe. In a more specific sense, technical performance, which has been verified experimentally, is evidently one of the principal factors determining the choice of a new system.

For the picture, the MAC system eliminates cross-colour and cross-luminance effects, leads to appreciable increases in component bandwidths and improves the RF performance. Subjective evaluations have shown that the final quality is barely 0.1 grade (in the 5-grade quality scale) below that of the 4:2:2 digital studio standard where screens of conventional size are used.

As far as the basic sound quality under normal reception conditions is concerned, listening tests have shown that all of the forms of coding mentioned gives high quality within the dynamic range suitable for domestic listening conditions. No noise is audible on normal programme material originated from high-quality sources, although programme-modulated noise is perceptible with companded coding on very critical passages such as pure sine-waves.

The failure characteristic takes on a different form for the analogue components, for which the quality falls off gradually, and for the digital components, for which the service remains excellent down to a certain limit beyond which the degradation rapidly becomes severe.

In the MAC system, the colour-difference signals are not carried on a sub-carrier, and hence the noise power per unit bandwidth is less than in the case of composite PAL or SECAM signals; it is therefore to be expected that the failure characteristic will fall off more gradually. This has indeed been confirmed in many subjective tests conducted by the EBU. The first threshold effects (luminance spikes on the picture) were observed at C/N ratios of between 8 and 10 dB. The first audible clicks on the sound appeared at a C/N ratio of about 8 dB.

It must be stressed that, although these figures correspond to a perceptible impairment, the quality would still not be unwatchable or unlistenable. If we define the service failure point as lying halfway between quality grades "poor" and "bad", failure for a television service occurs between about 2 and 3 dB for the picture, i.e about 2 dB below the figure for a PAL or SECAM picture, and between about 3 and 4.5 dB for the sound depending on the type of coding and error correction.

In other words, the use of the C-MAC/packet system could mean considerably larger coverage areas than those obtainable with the reference system used at the WARC-BS in 1977.

As regards interference, subjective tests have also shown that the C-MAC/packet system satisfies the conditions imposed by the WARC-BS 1977 relating to protection ratios.

We can conclude that the C-MAC/packets system is more than just another television broadcasting system such as NTSC, PAL or SECAM. Its introduction may well open up a new era in broadcasting. In the past each broadcast channel, used in any of the frequency bands allocated to the broadcasting service, has generally been used for a single service, e.g. for a radio programme or a television programme.

The C-MAC/packet system brings with it the complete abandonment of this one-to-one relationship between channels and services. It is designed to provide for the variable and evolutionary broadcast transmission of a group of services within the limits of a channel which is that defined for satellite broadcasting by the WARC-BS-1977.

The composition of that group of services may vary from country to country or, more precisely, from transmitter to transmitter and, for each transmission, from one period of time to another.

One may be forgiven for wondering whether this flexibility is disquieting to those who are responsible for the media policy in some European countries. However, the broadcasters in the EBU have concluded that this system, devised collectively by a team of engineers and scientists from many countries, constitutes an optimal broadcasting system. It is ideally adapted for 12 GHz satellite broadcasting and, incidently, we believe its signals can be distributed over many kinds of cable networks without loss of quality. Its performance is excellent as far as reliability, quality and ruggedness are concerned. It lends itself to user-friendly hardware and it is future-oriented in that it can be tailored to all foreseeable applications and stands us in good stead for whatever the imagination of future engineers may bring. Although it may be ranged amongst the most sophisticated consumer products offered to the public, we are convinced that hardware cost will be reasonable. With this last point in mind, and considering the fact that the first DBS services may well start in Europe not later than two years from now, we feel that it should become a recognized European standard without further delay.

The question arises, why this is not yet the case. As part of their analysis of the question the governments of France, the United Kingdom and the Federal Republic of Germany have formed a number of working groups in order to investigate what has been termed "questions which need further examination" with a view to convening a European governmental conference which is to take a decision in the matter.

We are not aware of any official statement as far as composition, mandate, time-scale, or any results of work of these groups are concerned.

The United Kingdom government has recently stated in Parliament, that they are committed to the C-MAC/packet system, but the official attitude of the two other governments was still unknown at the time of writing this text.

The two main obstacles to the final adoption of this proposal by governmental authorities seem to be:

a) receiver cost predictions
b) the compatibility of the system with existing and planned cable systems.

Both questions have been studied extensively within the framework of the EBU activities and both questions have found - in our opinion - satisfactory answers. We are left therefore to conclude, that any remaining objections to standardise the system are more of a political nature than of a technical nature.

To understand this better, I shall briefly refer to the European situation with regard to cable distribution of television and sound broadcasting programmes.

2. Cable distribution

The development of cable distribution systems in Europe has followed a
very different pattern from that in the USA. In the beginning its main
purpose was to improve the reception quality of the national television
programme or programmes in shadow areas, and then also to provide signals
for programmes from neighbouring countries in border regions where the
field-strength was too weak to provide a satisfactory picture by means of
an antenna of reasonable size. The latter type of cable system can be
found mainly in the smaller countries of Europe which have many
neighbours: Belgium, the Netherlands, Switzerland, Austria. Thus, for
example, about 85% of the Belgian households are now connected to
extensive cable networks providing them with up to 16 programmes, 12 of
which are originated in other countries.

However, until recently, there was no question of authorising the cable
operators to produce their own programmes; they remained simply
distributors of existing programmes that could be picked up somewhere
within the limits of the national territory.

With the advent of distribution satellites, a radical change in media
policy took place in the larger countries. In particular in France,
Germany and the United Kingdom plans began to emerge to gradually cover
these countries with a national cable distribution system, by using either
traditional coaxial cable techniques or glass-fibre networks, or a
combination of them. Satellites, either those developed by the European
Space Agency and exploited by the Eutelsat organisation (the ECS-system),
or national satellites, or even Intelsat-controlled satellites could then
link, at least for a rather long initial period, the "islands" of cabled
towns together. These cable systems can thus be fed, from the beginning,
not only by local or national programme providers, but also by commercial
programme originators in any European country, or indeed - why not -
extra-European country.

It is understandable that governments who have developed plans of this
sort, may find it difficult to see a place for DBS in this scenario. If,
by one future means or another, the population has already, via cable and
distribution satellites, the choice between, say, 30 television and a
similar number of radio programmes, why then undertake the additional
effort of developing and financing a DBS system which can, after all, do
nothing more than add a maximum of five further television programmes ?

Of course, this view is not shared by everybody, and indeed the argument
that the future rather lies in DBS, and that therefore cable systems
should help to develop DBS and not the other way round, has its
proponents.

According to this perspective, DBS and cable distribution are seen to be
complementary, not as an alternative, and thus the EBU has engaged in
studies to use the proposed DBS standard for cable networks.

Such studies are being carried out primarily in France and Germany; they would enable a complete C-MAC/packet signal to be carried without loss of capacity or quality in a cable system (i.e in a CATV system as well as in a master antenna configuration). Fig. 4 shows the basic philosophy of these possibilities. Experiments show that the bandwidth requirement of 27 MHz for DBS can be reduced to suit any type of cable system, for example :

- to 7 MHz by using a B-MAC/packet system with a quaternary (4-level) digital signal (where, however a certain loss of resolution must be accepted), or

- to between 10 and 14 MHz with vestigial-sideband amplitude modulation for vision and duobinary modulation for sound and data.

3. Satellite projects

In the field of satellites belonging to the fixed-satellite services and foreseen for, or capable of, transmitting broadcasting programmes, the first operational system will be the ECS-system of Eutelsat. Figs. 5 and 6 and 7 show the attribution of TV/downlinks to various European countries and to the EBU within the three spot-beams and the Eurobeam of that system. Together with similar national satellite projects in France, Germany, the United Kingdom and the Scandinavian countries, there will be, towards the end of the 1980s, a large number of facilities capable of feeding cable-systems all over Europe. But it seems doubtful, whether these channels will all be used by then, or indeed later.

As far as broadcasting-satellite services (DBS) are concerned, most of the projects so far known have been developed primarily in order to promote the European space and telecommunications industry. In chronological order, these projects, all of which, with one exception, are based on the characteristics of the WARC-BS-1977 Plan, are:

- TDF-1 and TV-SAT, a common project financed by the French and German governments respectively, to be launched at the end of 1985. Both have three WARC-channels. One of the TV-SAT channels will use purely a digital sound broadcasting system developed in Germany (16 stereophonic programmes), and which is not related to the C-MAC/packet proposal. It may be mentioned however that the latter could provide an almost identical facility. The remaining five channels will probably transmit television programmes and it is to be feared that they will use SECAM and PAL, possibly with analogue sound (two monophonic channels or one stereophonic channel). These transmissions have, however, been qualified as experimental or pre-operational.

- UNISAT of the United Kingdom, to be launched 1986/87, with two television channels, possibly one of which will be in a conditional-access mode. This may well be the first operational DBS-system in Europe, and, as already stated, it is likely to use the C-MAC/packet system.

- L-SAT (Olympus) a large multi-purpose platform to be launched by
  the European Space Agency (ESA) in 1986/87. It will use an
  orientable downlink antenna which will enable any part of Europe and
  parts of North Africa and the Middle East to be covered, and
  requires therefore authorisation from the relevant signatories of
  WARC-BS-1977. One of the two television channels will be used for
  Italian coverage and the other, most probably, by Members of the EBU
  who wish to carry on, for three years initially, with programme
  experiments for a pan-European service. Because of the need for a
  large number of sound channels (and, possibly, sub-titling
  facilities) for such a programme, the PAL or SECAM transmission
  systems (with analogue sound) are totally unsuitable for this
  experiment.

- TELE-X, a Swedish multiple-purpose experimental project, with the
  participation of certain other Nordic countries, to be launched
  1987/88. There are to be three TV transponders, two of which can be
  used to cover, in accordance with the WARC-BS-1977 Plan, the
  Scandinavian area.

There are certainly more plans at a less advanced stage of planning or
construction.

We can however, already conclude, that the absence of a Europe-wide
agreement amongst governments, if continued, on a common transmission
standard, will be a serious obstacle to the development of DBS in Europe
and that thereby European industry is in the process of losing a unique
opportunity to regain leadership in the field of modern consumer product
technology.

Thus at the end of my talk, I can only emphasize, with some regret, what I
said at the beginning:

Europe has more problems than projects, and whilst some of the
projects may look promising, their realisation is often hampered by
problems generated by the Europeans themselves.

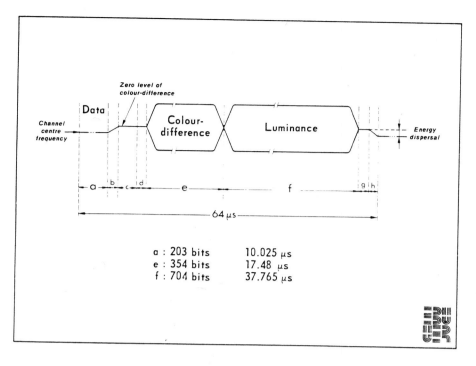

Fig. 1.

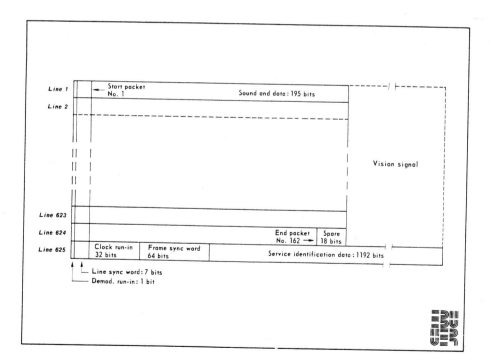

Fig. 2.

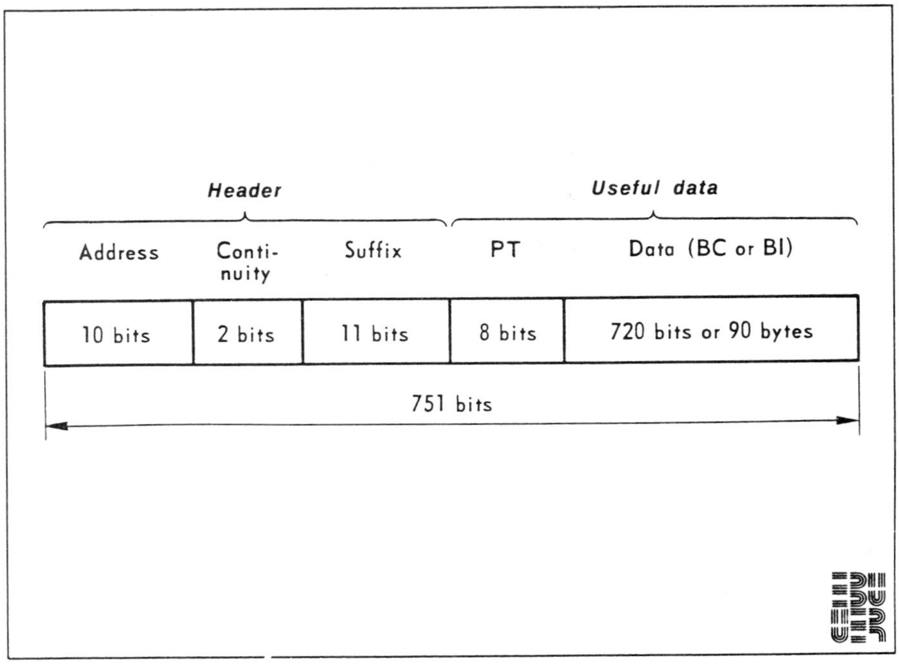

Header
Useful data
Address
Conti-
nuity
Suffix
PT
Data (BC or BI)
10 bits
2 bits
11 bits
8 bits
720 bits or 90 bytes
751 bits

Fig. 3.

12 GHz
Reception from satellite
Conversion(s) and channel selection
FM and 2-4 PSK demodulators
B = 27 MHz
B = 14 MHz
Processing of components of time-division multiplex
Television receiver
Audio chain
Teletext and other decoders
Conversion(s) and channel selection
AM - VSB demodulator
VHF/UHF
Reception from cable network

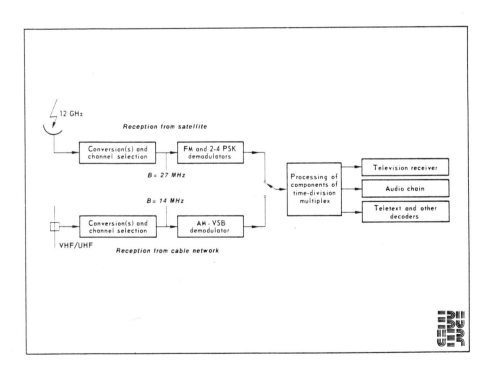

Fig. 4.

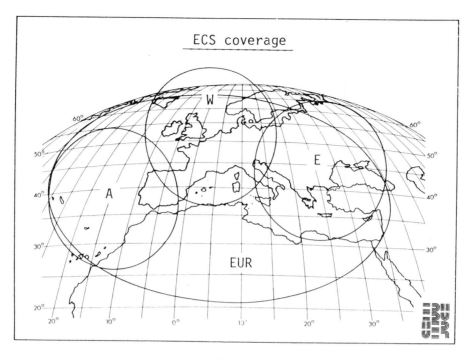

Fig. 5.

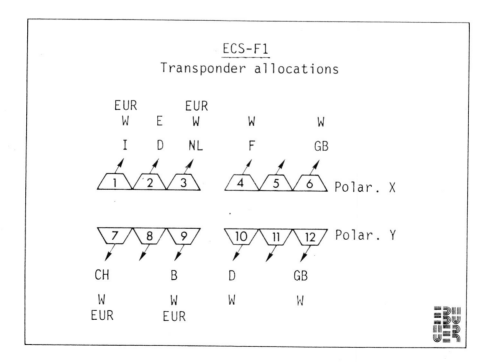

Fig. 6.

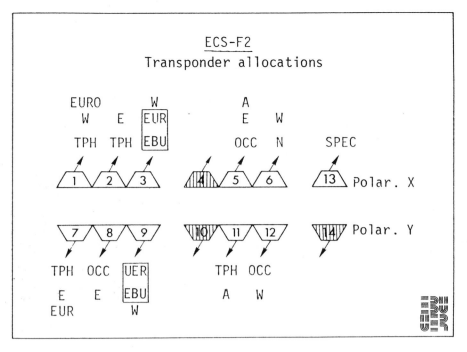

Fig. 7.

Rudolf Gressmann was born in 1920 in Hamburg, Germany, where he attended the University and received the degree of "Diplom-Physiker" in 1951. He began his professional career by joining the central technical services of the Nordwestdeutscher Rundfunk in Hamburg the following year. In 1955, he became a member of the staff of the Technical Centre of the European Broadcasting Union (EBU) in Brussels, Belgium, where he initially specialized in the preparation of international frequency-assignment plans. He was appointed Deputy Director of the EBU Technical Centre in 1972 and became its Director two years later. He is a Fellow of the Society of Motion Picture and Television Engineers (SMPTE) and a Member of the Fernseh- und Kinotechnische Gesellschaft (FKTG) and of the Nachrichtentechnische Gesellschaft (NTG). He is also a Corresponding Member of the International Broadcasting Convention (IBC) and has published numerous articles in the technical press.

Direct Broadcast Home Terminals — Status Report

R. Dennis Fraser, President
ALCOA-NEC Communications Corporation
Elk Grove Village, IL

The evolution of technical considerations for Direct Broadcast Satellite Service (DBS) has or certainly promises to place the home TVRO terminal directly in the arena of new television display technologies. There are few broadcast services which have incorporated the embodiment of more varied and sophisticated technologies ... from gallium arsenide monolythic integrated circuits to DES encryption algorhythm standards and antennae efficient at frequencies not many years ago considered to be unfit for transmissions of any variety. This paper will briefly summarize the status, developments and technology which are to be embodied in this new broadcast service.

Those of us involved in the DBS concept are perhaps most limited by existing display technology. The current norms of consumer equipment capabilities are proving to be a relative high cost burden on the finalization of new display techniques as new techniques must be limited or modified to accommodate standards developed decades before satellite transmission was feasible. DBS has given rise to practical, yet difficult questions of how to introduce for instance, an additional 40dB of dynamic range in an audio signal to conventional receivers as digital audio transmission techniques hurdle headlong into the low-cost analogue environment of the home receiver. The issue of incorporating high or extended definition television capability into transmission standards that for now must exist in an NTSC world present problems of economy of spectrum in which transmission costs per Hertz exceed any previous economic norms; namely high power satellites. A quipster recently equated the reinvention of existing technology by saying that had Thomas Edison been of limited mind set we would, today, be enjoying the use of larger candles. The DBS industry is attempting on the whole to provide a service in which existing display technology is satisfied without sacrifice of future capability. This goal is repleat with difficulties in setting hard standards, and costs in downgrading temporarily signal capabilities that represent tomorrow's services. The progress that is being made is perhaps best reviewed by a look at the basic elements of the DBS TVRO equipment that will appear in the home.

The most obvious element of the home reception equipment is the parabolic reflector. The reality of DBS has rested in no small measure on the ability for ease of installation of the antenna, the performance of that antenna and the long term stability and survivability of the antenna in a wide variety of environments. It is safe to say that the offset parabolic reflector has become the norm for DBS in that two major problems are overcome by its application: (1) a 60cm reflector cannot tolerate the shadow loss created by the presence of the LNC directly in the middle of the signal path and (2) the offset dish attains a more vertical attitude of the reflector in those climates where ice and snow accumulation would most seriously impair link perfomance. The efficiency of the DBS antenna becomes far more critical when manufacturing than does, for instance, the considerations for C-Band (4GHz) antennae. Precision stamping of metal must be held to within a ten-thousandth of an inch over the entire surface of the reflector that is designed for 12GHz application. Paint type and application cannot destroy the surface tolerance and must in fact act like Teflon in repelling surface build-up of foreign matter. A properly designed offset parabolic antenna for 12Ghz application must attain better than 70% efficiency to allow for link budget variations introduced by weather, settling of structures (particularly in Northern climates) and less than accurate installations as regards pointing errors. The present plans for deployment of high-power DBS services will see the 0.6 Meter antenna as the most common size used throughout the United States.

The Low Noise Converter (LNC) represents an integral part of the antenna system that through its associated feed horn and polarization control has forced existing LSI technology to a new frontier. The goal of providing DBS technology at reasonable consumer pricing prohibits the use of discrete circuit FET technology which has been so popular in C-Band LNA or LNC construction. The need for superior carrier to noise performance, environmental stability and broadband performance has dictated that MIC or MMIC technology be applied to DBS equipment. Such LSI technology is rare, difficult to attain in integration but holds promise for future applications well beyond DBS. When one considers local oscillators operating at switching speeds measured in GigaHertz, it is not difficult to imagine CPU switching speeds limited only by memory access time; this is one of the underlying driving forces for this new display technology that is not immediately apparent. The LNC in the final analysis is a super low noise element of the DBS System that provides a broadband 1GHz I.F. to the heart of DBS's new display technology ... the Indoor Electronics Unit.

The DBS Indoor Electronics Unit (IDU) is where the business of new display technology and, in fact, the business of DBS will occur. Originating with a broadband FM I.F. the IDU has the responsibility for coherent conversion of visual, aural and data signals to the consumer environment. One of the most commonly overlooked basic facts of satellite television transmission is that it is an FM transmission standard which is not quickly correlated to our existing AM visual conventions. Setting aside the cpabilities of new technologies, the final order of business for the IDU is to convert the FM transmission standard to the AM/FM requirements of today's television receiver; dependent upon the philosophy employed by the DBS programmer, the outputting of baseband video and audio signals are also a requirement of the IDU. Channel selection via the use of Frequency Locked Loops or similar techniques appropriate for the 1GHz I.F. and channel spacing is yet another basic function of the indoor unit. Whether this selection of channels is five channels, thirty-two channels or one hundred channels is the basis of standardization efforts best addressed by a separate paper reviewing that work in progress as it is also related to colocation of spacecraft as of yet undecided by the Federal Communications Commission. The basics of the IDU having been defined, let's look toward those signal features and functions that have been revealed or proposed that would define DBS as a new display technology.

AUDIO TRANSMISSION

At least one and perhaps more of the existing DBS license holders have incorporated the transmission of digital audio in multiple channelization with their signal parameters. The application of this technique promises at least three system features: (1) the attaining of quality in reception only now emerging in the discrete Compact Digital Disc technology of the audiophile world, (2) the ability to dynamically assign and reassign multiplexed data as audio coherent signals (stereo, mono or bilingual) or as data formatted for auxillary services such as program downloading to computers and (3) a form of encryption for the television signal which simultaneously provides superior services while protecting economic investments in the programming. Some digital audio services proposed for DBS would provide for signal to noise and dynamic range capabilities perhaps exceeding those of the Compact Disc format standard. Such capability would require that television audio be taken seriously by the consumer and the broadcaster and that the home reproduction equipment from amplifier to speaker be evaluated in the same light as a state-of-the-art component audio system. As previously indicated, should the full range of such an audio system be utilized, some limiting or compression will be required when this capability is delivered to conventional reception equipment. Various concepts present the digital audio capacity as either a discrete transmitted signal or more than likely a basic function of the video waveform residing in sync.

VIDEO TRANSMISSION

The issue of video transmission, as reflected in the preceeding comments on digital audio, is at best complex. One service already on the air is utilizing conventional NTSC video with separate aural subcarrier in a standard associated with today's C-Band reception characteristics. The more likely transmission method being considered is the use of multiplexed analogue components including the digital audio as a single carrier. This method has been proven to deliver better link performance through (1) the inherent technique and (2) the absence of the aural subcarrier which causes less concentration of energy in the visual carrier of a transponder. In retrospect, the use of an enhanced video transmission standard will provide better link performance, a greater ease (if not inherent ease) of encrypting the video signal and an apparent improvement of video quality when the signal is viewed on receivers capable of RGB video inputs. It is well to footnote that the majority of potential DBS customers will, if for no other reason, denote a distinct signal difference by virtue of being free of terrestial signal abborations caused by multiple path diversities and other ground transmitted signal abnormalities. There is no question that the video portion of the DBS signal will represent to the most severe critic an upgrade of display quality.

DATA TRANSMISSION

Perhaps one of the most exciting and promising aspects of the DBS business is the data capacity that is being envisioned as integral to the transmission standard. While this capability is optional to the DBS programmer and the subject of recommended standardization proceedings, the capabilities are functionally unlimited as pertains to teletext-like services, discrete downloading of data such as computer programs, video games and even data-based additional television signals such as freeze frames. The DBS receiver will contain the capability for interface to other microprocessor based devices. The practical ability to deliver auxillary services as part of the video entertainment business will be realized yet this year in far greater capacity than will be possible through today's alternative means.

TRANSACTIONAL FUNCTIONS

The DBS Indoor Electronics Unit will be a "smart" terminal for those programmers using enhanced transmission standards. The basis of pay programming will be functionally implemented to permit pay-per-view which is accounted and even directly billed to the consumer through the IDU allowing a keen competitive edge over preauthorized or continuously billed systems. The ability for parents to code-set the ratings of programming that younger family members may view is yet another function of the smart receiver associated with sophisticated DBS services. The logical (and planned) interface of the DBS Receiver to the telephone will permit interactive functions for the consumer and the ability for a programmer to poll and receive instantaneous ratings of viewership for programs in progress. The planned technology of systems (such as Comsat's STC, for instance) will permit discretely addressing millions of viewers in a matter of hours for any number of purposes which are just baselined at transactional functions. In the early 1960's Bell Labs produced a film which showed the "home of the future" being controlled via touchtone control from central computers. DBS represents an enhancement of this as of yet unrealized promise in concentrating switching and addressing functions where they might well best reside ... on a non-terrestial basis. These last few statements may well sound as optimistic as Bell's early 1960's film and before new enhanced display capabilities give way to science fiction, let's conclude by reviewing the status of this DBS industry.

DBS, which by FCC action has become a generic term, is presently alive and in service at 12GHz. USCI, a venture of General Instruments, Prudential Insurance and others is presently delivering five channels of service to a broad area of the Northeastern United States via leased transponders on Canada's Anik satellite. The USCI service is a low power service and as such requires dish sizes which are in excess of those DBS services committed to higher power satellites. The minimum dish size, on average, for reception of USCI is 1.2 Meters. Satellite Television Corporation, a subsidiary of COMSAT, will inaugurate service to the Eastern Seaboard of the United States in the Fall of this year utilizing focused beams from SBS-4 and permitting the installation of .6 Meter (2 foot) antennae for reception of multiple channels incorporating digital audio, extended data capacity and enhanced transmission techniques. During 1985 and 1986 satellites will be launched from which a single bird will permit the steerable transmission of up to eight 230 watt transponders on a nationwide basis. Further action of the FCC, world regulatory bodies and the industry itself will finally determine the complexion and indeed success of this new delivery medium, but the long awaited promise of a new and enhanced compliment to today's entertainment services is present and being well accounted for in planning that which will see new display technologies entering our homes yet this year.

R. Dennis Fraser has spent his entire career in the broadcast industry in positions ranging from Director of Engineering, writer-producer-director to his current position as President of ALCOA-NEC Communications Corporation. Mr. Fraser has been associated with NEC Corporation for the past ten years, primarily as Vice President and General Manager of NEC America's Broadcast Equipment Division. Mr. Fraser attended Michigan State University.

Signal Processing for Wide Screen Television: The Smart Receiver

Joseph S. Nadan, Philips Laboratories, Briarcliff Manor, N.Y. and
Richard N. Jackson, Philips Research Laboratories, Redhill, UK

The television receiver is growing in complexity and sophistication. It will accept input from tape, disc and home computers as well as broadcast and cable TV material. Shortly, Direct Broadcasts from Satellites (DBS) will be added to the list. The major question next to be tackled is how to achieve extended definition and widescreen presentation. Previous papers from our laboratories (1, 2) have identified a range of possible approaches to this challenge, ranging from optimization of the performance achieved within the traditional NTSC and PAL coding formats to altogether new systems based on scanning and transmission standards in excess of 1000 lines. It is now our opinion that the latter approach is not the optimum. Direct use of such high line numbers calls for unacceptably large transmission bandwidths. Signal processing may solve that problem. However, practical factors, such as the availability and social acceptability of very large screen display systems for the home, mean that the overall resolution implied by 1000 plus line systems may not in fact be needed.

In this paper we therefore concentrate on the definition of some practical goals for future television systems and on outlining how these may be achieved by using v.l.s.i. techniques in home receivers. Three factors figure largely in our consideration of these goals:

- It is desirable that the picture area be enlarged, but only if this implies expanding the effective view of the world. We thus reiterate our belief in the need for an "Enhanced Viewing Experience".

- A corollary to the above is that New Television must be noticeably and saleably different from existing television. The industry must be able to derive 'bottom line benefit' if it is to make the investment necessary to deliver this new concept to the viewer. There is, in effect, a "Just Valuable Difference" which must be exceeded by a successful product.

- We also continue to believe in an evolutionary approach to extended definition: an orderly progression from an up-grading of existing systems such as NTSC to new extended definition concepts. The key to this approach rests in the v.l.s.i. frame store. This will be economically viable for home receivers in the future and will make possible the design of 'smart' receivers which can adapt to a variety of signals and display a number of formats.

THE DISPLAY GOAL

In choosing a target for future television displays, it is important that we take into account both sociological and technical factors. While it is desirable to widen the "window on the world", there are several limits to be considered. These include the environmental impact of the display in the home, the cost, the brightness and resolution performance, the bandwidth of the signal-carrying medium and so on. A doubling of the viewing angle would produce a highly noticeable increase in 'impact' and perhaps exceed the "Just Valuable Difference". However, if this were achieved by straightforward extrapolation of present systems, it would result both in a fourfold increase in transmission bandwidth and in large and expensive displays. Two strategies may be used to overcome these problems. One is to change the aspect ratio of the display and the other is to improve the coding method so that some information to be displayed will not be transmitted over the channel but will be locally interpolated (see below).

WIDE ASPECT RATIO

Widening the aspect ratio of the display beyond the present 4:3 has many advantages. The most obvious one is that it presents the viewer with a more pleasing format for live television by matching the shape of the display more nearly to the human visual field. Since wide aspect ratios have already been in use in film for many years, the compatibility of television with film source material would be greatly improved. It should also be remembered that, for a given picture repetition rate, the signal bandwidth rises as the square of the line number. For a given picture area, the wider the aspect ratio the fewer the scanning lines. Thus wider aspect ratio is triply desirable.

Greebe et al. (3) have pointed out that several factors limit the area of display that may reasonably be expected to be practical in the foreseeable future to about 0.5 square meter. Our suggested goal is thus for a picture having an aspect ratio of 5.33:3 with a width of 37" and a height of 21", compared with the existing upper limit picture which is approximately 21" wide by 16" high. Fig. 1 shows the increase in "window" given by this format. We believe that such displays will become commercially available before the end of the decade and that by proper design, particularly in preserving screen black level, rear projection displays of this format will attain the desired subjective performance at reasonable cost.

FEATURES BENEFITS OF A 5.33:3 ASPECT RATIO

Can a 5.33:3 aspect ratio display be successfully introduced into a television environment dominated (initially) by 4:3 aspect ratio source material? In fact we think such a format may well provide consumer value with presently available N.T.S.C. signals. The format allows twelve small 4:3 aspect ratio pictures to be presented for selection of channels when the receiver is first powered-on. This multiple picture in a picture format

(MPIP) is illustrated in Figure 2a. It also allows simultaneous viewing of one large 4:3 picture and three smaller pictures on one display as illustrated in Figure 2b. There is, of course, a vital component needed to achieve this, as well as to enable signal processing for future picture enhancement: the television frame store.

TELEVISION PICTURE STORAGE

Until the advent of v.l.s.i. technology, the idea of storing a complete television picture - or even one field of a picture - was just a dream. Recently, however, Pelgrom et al. (4) presented a paper describing a digital field memory specifically designed for television applications. The essential point about the store is its serial nature. Since television signals constitute a serial information stream and since many applications for TV stores do not require random access, a serial store is well suited to the television need. As a result the experimental field store chips developed by Philips use a digital CCD technology in which each chip represents one bit of a complete television field: a total capacity of 308 Kbit. (This number derives from the European 625-line system but the stores operate on NTSC standards as well.)

In operation, the input television signals are demodulated to component form and digitized at the accepted SMPTE 13.5 MHz luminance sampling rate but with a 4:1:1 Y,U,V format. The samples are then organized as a serial data stream with a clock rate of 20.25 MHz. Internally, each chip has a Serial Parallel Serial (SPS) structure. This is used to reorganize the data into parallel data streams, which are subsequently recombined to form a serial data output. The organization allows high bit capacity and low power consumption. The chips have an area of 34.8 square millimeters, a power dissipation of 350 mW and are capable of being clocked at speeds of up to 40 MHz. The way to enhanced television is now open.

THE FIRST STEP TO ENHANCED TELEVISION

The first evolutionary step on the road to widescreen television
should be to make the best possible use of existing NTSC transmissions. Using picture memories we can:

- Eliminate unwanted artifacts, such as cross-color and
  noise.

- Improve horizontal resolution to the full system
  capability.

- Overcome the "display factor" to improve vertical reso
  lution, and

- Add features such as multiple picture-in-picture (MPIP)
  presentation.

Methods of achieving the first two improvements have been described and demonstrated elsewhere and will not be detailed here
except to note that the horizontal resolution improvement which
may be obtained by using field store comb decoding techniques on
NTSC signals is from about 3 MHz to 4.2 MHz. This implies an
increase from 312 to 437 elements per picture width - a factor
of 1.4 improvement. If a similar improvement in vertical
resolution were obtained, then the overall resolution of the
picture would be double that obtained in conventional NTSC
receivers, although the aspect ratio would, of course, remain at
4:3.

SEQUENTIAL SCAN CONVERSION

We have obtained good results in the removal of vertical aliasing
and interline flicker effects and the improvement of perceived vertical resolution by transcoding the incoming interlaced signal, at
the receiver, to sequential scan display format. That is: all
525 lines are displayed in sequence during one 60th of a second.
Figure 3 illustrates the nature of this task. The sloping lines
represent fields of the incoming signals with transmitted
picture elements at the points indicated by the crosses. If we

are to display a complete picture of 525 lines in 1/60th of a second, we must somehow derive extra lines, as indicated by the circles. In a still picture, samples in the adjacent field may be time-shifted using a field store to fill the gap. We may construct a new pixel in E for example, either from an adjacent pixel in line A or from an interpolation between adjacent pixels in lines A and B.

Figure 4a illustrates what happens on movement. Whereas the still picture is correct, a horizontal moving bar is represented in the wrong time sequence and breaks up. The situation actually illustrated is for an A-B interpolation. The blur effect is different using direct time-shift but is still annoying. An alternative way of deriving E is from adjacent spatial samples C and D. In this case there are no motion problems but the vertical resolution is impaired (Fig. 4b). The approach we adopt to solve this dilemma is to detect motion in the picture and to switch adaptively between the two types of interpolation. The final performance is not yet perfect but results are encouraging.

To give an impression of the overall improvement to be expected from signal processing, Fig. 5 compares part of a composite coded/decoded picture on a conventional resolution shadowmask display, with a full bandwidth (component) signal displayed by sequential scanning on a high resolution shadowmask. For accuracy it must be stated that photograph 5a was taken using a single field exposure and 5b, using a two field exposure. Although this is not strictly a fair comparison, we think that the subjective impression given is close to that observed in a live picture.

NON-SHARED BANDWIDTH SYSTEMS: THE NEXT STEP

The vertical resolution improvement derived from sequential scanning has not yet been fully determined but it does appear to be greater than the factor of 1.3x by which the height of the picture must be increased to meet the proposed target and it carries the additional benefit of greatly reducing line flicker effects. Thus it may be possible to meet the display goal without actually increasing line number at all. This has yet to be verified. However, there remain the problems of achieving a horizontal resolution increase of at least 1.8x and of changing the aspect ratio.

This next step forward could be achieved by the adoption of non-shared-bandwidth transmission, such as Multiplexed Analogue Component (MAC) coding, which could be introduced either on Direct Broadcast Satellite (DBS) systems, or on pre-recorded media, or via cable distribution systems.

Historically, color television signals have all been encoded by a technique in which the luminance and chrominance signals share the same bandwidth. For European Satellite television distribution, however, a new coding system known as MAC-C is proposed which uses temporal multiplexing of these components. This system makes a welcome break-away from the constrictions of band-shared coding methods since it avoids the cross-effects that characterize conventional systems and opens the door to extended picture display in the future. Although the initial marketing effort for MAC-C in Europe has focused on suiting the DBS picture delivery medium, examination of the coding method shows that an important change has taken place in the transmission format which may eventually be used to advantage for future widescreen systems.

FORMAT CODING IN MAC

In the proposed EBU MAC-C system, the transmitted raster (Fig. 6) no longer forms a direct representation of the picture material. Instead it has become a time-controlled "map" of picture information which has been time-compressed and redistributed at the source as shown. At the receiver, the signal must be stored, processed and rearranged for the display. S. L. Tan pointed out (private communication) that with this method, the picture need no longer conform to the conventional 4:3 aspect ratio. Indeed, the parameters of the signal could be flexible such that a large but finite number of alternative formats might be transmitted, providing a control signal was sent from the source to the receiver indicating which format was currently in use.

Provision for just such a control signal has been built into the MAC-C specification and a number of ways of using this for future television systems are already being explored. In addition to enabling aspect ratio changes, these experiments also make use of (e.g.) the signal blanking period to carry additional information for extended definition. Windram et al. (5) have described a system in which the blanking intervals carry the extra information required to extend pictures from 4:3 to wider aspect ratios. In our laboratories we have tested an experimental system in which the chrominance information is carried in the field blanking interval, while the whole of the normal line time is devoted to a wideband luminance signal having a wide aspect ratio. Another possible format allocates part of the transmission to the fine detail of the scene which may be updated more slowly than other picture components, as suggested by Glenn (6). We are doing research to determine the range of validity of this approach and will report results when these become available.

TWO CHANNEL SYSTEMS

Using DBS channels in association with MAC coding, allows a wider-than-normal baseband modulation to be used so that extended definition signals can become possible. This is not necessarily the case for other media, such as cable for example. Our thinking for these cases is that the use of two channels for a single extended definition picture may possibly represent an acceptable compromise between value to the consumer and bandwidth cost. It is certainly still feasible to consider MAC coding these other media and to indicate to the receiver when a two-channel format is being used. Thus still further prospects for extension are feasible.

TOWARDS THE 'SMART' RECEIVER

Recapitulating what we have said, let us consider the television receiver of the future. When switched on, this clever device will present the viewer with a "preview" of available channel options. When an option is selected, the receiver will adapt itself to conform to the required aspect ratio and presentation format. Standard NTSC transmissions will readily be recognized because of the absence of a format 'word'. Nevertheless by storing and processing the signal an improved reception will be obtained. Signals from new media, using analogue component coding, will be examined to determine the format in use and the receiver will make full use of its signal storage and processing capability to provide an Enhanced Viewing Experience. At any time the viewer may preview other sources or store and hold a given picture for close examination. It's a smart receiver!

One year ago, in a scintillating speech given at the Conference Luncheon of the 17th SMPTE Annual Television Conference (7), Dr. Boris Townsend foreshadowed the advent of the smart receiver which "could adapt a number of performance parameters to suit the incoming signal". With the advent of v.l.s.i storage, that receiver is a large step nearer reality.

ACKNOWLEDGEMENTS

We wish to acknowledge the contribution of many members of our research team to this paper. In particular, the contributions made by Dr. R. S. Prodan, Mr. M. G. Hulyer, Mr. D. W. Parker, and Mr. M.J.J.C. Annegarn in the field of sequential scanning conversion and motion detection, should be mentioned.

References:

1.   Jackson, R.N., Tan, S.L., "HiFi TV: Toward the Enhanced Viewing Experience", International Broadcasters Conference Record, September 1982 (published IEE).

2.   Annegarn, M.J.J.C. and Jackson, R.N., "Compatible Systems for High Quality TV", JSMPTE, Vol. 92 #7, July 1983.

3.   Greebe, C.A.A.J., vanderPolder, L.J., Tan, S.L., "HiFi TV: Its Limitation and Possibilities", 13th Int. TV Symposium Record, Montreux, May 1983.

4.   Pelgrom, M.J.M. et al., "A Digital Field Memory for Television Receivers", IEEE Transaction on Consumer Electronics, Vol. CE-29, #3, August 1983.

5.   Windram, M.D., Marcom, R., Hurley, T., "Extended Definition MAC", IBA E&D Report #120/83.

6.   Glenn, Dr. W.E., IGC Conference, High Definition Television, Monterey, CA, July 10-12, 1983.

7.   Townsend, Dr. Boris, IBA, 17th Annual SMPTE TV Conference, SMPTE Journal, Apr 1983, Vol. 92, No. 4.

Fig. 1. Extended TV Window compared with normal format.

(a)

Power — On

M — PIP

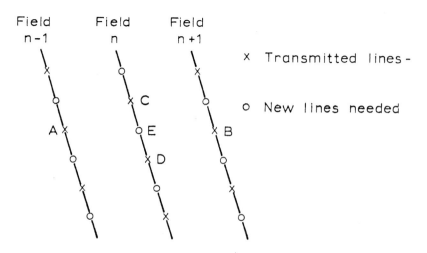

(b)

4 × 3 + 3 PIP

Fig. 2a. Multiple Picture-In-Picture (M-PIP).

Field n-1   Field n   Field n+1

× Transmitted lines

o New lines needed

Fig. 3. Interlace-to-Sequential Scan Conversion.

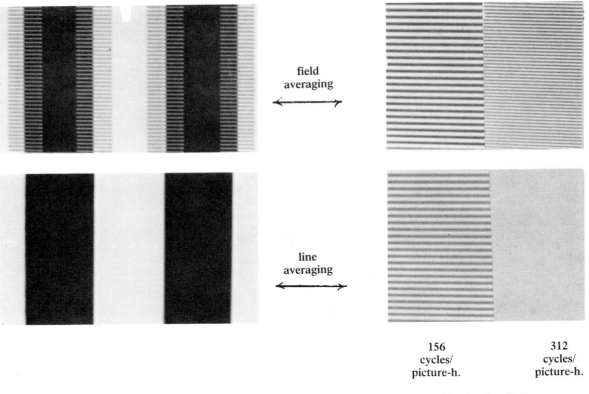

field averaging

line averaging

156 cycles/ picture-h.

312 cycles/ picture-h.

a). Horizontally Moving Bars

b). Grating Patterns

Fig. 4. Interlace to Sequential Scan Conversion Effects.

Fig. 5a. Conventional Bandshared picture displayed on normal CRT.

Fig. 5b. Component Video Signal picture displayed on high resolution CRT.

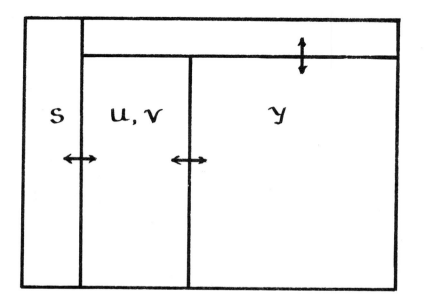

Fig. 6. C-MAC Transmission Raster Format.

Joseph S. Nadan is Director of Electronic and Optical Systems at Philips Laboratories in Briarcliff Manor, New York. He joined Philips in 1976 and has worked on digital optical recording and television systems. Before joining Philips, Dr. Nadan taught Electrical Engineering at the City College of New York where he was Assistant Dean of the School of Engineering. Dr. Nadan is a senior member of the IEEE, and a member of Sigma Xi, Tau Beta Pi, Eta Kappa Nu, and Beta Gamma Sigma.

Richard N. Jackson is Head of the Video Systems Group at Philips Research Laboratories at Redhill in the United Kingdom. He joined Philips in 1956 to work on color television systems and displays and has subsequently published many papers on television topics. He is currently responsible for a number of video projects including picture processing and display. Mr. Jackson is a Fellow of the Institution of Electrical Engineers, a member of the I.E.E. Professional Group on Television and Sound, and an invited member of the SMPTE Study Group on HDTV.

Recent Development in Large Screen Video Display Equipment Technology

Koichi Sadashige   and   S. Ando
Matsushita Corporation of America   Matsushita Communications Industrial Co., Ltd.
Secaucus, N.J. 07094   Yokohama, Japan

INTRODUCTION

Video display systems and equipment are rapidly becoming the primary source of information, communication and entertainment in today's ever sophisticated society.

The expanding use of this equipment demands increasingly comples capabilities and performance standards.. Video display equipment must now satisfy the needs of one viewer in the darkened living room, or ten-thousand viewers in brightest outdoor stadium.

Matsushita Electric Industrial Company and its communications equipment subsidary -- Matsushita Communications Industrial Company -- recognizes these needs, and have developed and manufactured an array of sophisticated color video display equipment to encompass all possible applications and conditions.

Viewing Conditions And Environment

Current television scanning standards are based on a vertical scan of 525 or 625 lines. Through the loss of resolution by the kell effect, the maximum vertical resolution of commercial television scanning standards is degraded to approximately 300 pixcels. Optimum area resolution capability requires each pixcel to have a unity aspect ratio. If the vertical-horizontal image aspect ratio is 3 to 4, the number of horizontal pixels should be 400.

Looking at Figure 1, in terms of normal 20/20 vision. This means that the human eye is capable of resolving 1 minute arc of solid angle provided that the contrast ratio is at its full excursion. In terms of television viewing, the eye is capable of resolving pixels at a 100 percent contrast ratio if the viewing distance is 6 times picture height.

If we also take into account the fact that the viewer should resolve picture detail of reducing contrast ratio with increasing pixel size, the optimum distance for television viewing should be approximately 4-to-6 times picture height as shown in Figure 2.

In Figures 3-to-5, we've diagrammed typical television viewing conditions in a variety of different situations normally encountered at home and in a small auditorium. The seating density of our auditorium is much like it is in this room-- the standard 24-inch column spacing and 32-inch row pitch which is used in most theaters, auditoriums, and airliner cabins.

Additionally, the diagonal image dimensions of a video
display can vary by upwards of a thousand timex when it is
used to satisfy viewing populations as diverse as 2 or 20,000.
This relationship is illustrated by Figure 6. An equipment
manufacturer must satisfy these needs while trying to maintain
the aforementioned optimum viewing conditions.

As shown, the current generation of single CRT direct
viewing display and three CRT projector units can essentially
meet these requirements up to a population size of approximately
200. For larger needs, we have developed two types of large-
scale display systems -- the color liquid crystal display
and the tricolor incandescent lamp mosaic display trademarked
Astrovision.

These two systems not only provide large images but they
improve quality by overcoming the fundamental weakness of a
CRT based display--the lower brightness that comes with increasing image size. In fact, as Figure 7 shown, new systems are
bright enough to be suitable for outdoor daylight applications.

COLOR LIQUID CRYSTAL DISPLAY SYSTEM

This system was specifically developed to fill the gap
between large projection CRT displays and the tricolor
incandescent lamp mosaic display. The inherent nature of the
system makes it suitable for applications requiring a vertical
image dimension of between 50 and 300 inches.

The color liquid crystal display system is a back illuminated image transmission system meaning that image brightness
is solely dependent on the level of back illumination. The
system is suitable for both indoor and outdoor applications.

Figure 8 details the display panel, which consists of:
(A) and illuminator; (B) a liquid crystal panel; (C) light
dispersant color filters; and (D) LCD driver circuitry.

Liquid Crystal Light Valve

The liquid crystal panel (B) acts as a valve controlling
the amount of light travelling from the illuminator to the
color filters. As shown in Figure 9, at an applied potential
of 12-volts, the gate host panel has a maximum transmission
efficiency of 20-percent. The light transmission level drops
virtually to zero with zero applied potential, thus giving the
system an inherent contrast ratio of approximately 70 to 1.

LCD light output is coupled to the light dispersion
capability of the color transmission filters. The band pass
characteristics of the filters are designed to match the NTSC
chromaticity diagram. The light output capability of the
three color sources are shown in Figure 10.

A high image contrast ratio is maintained by treating the
front surface of each color filter to reduce the effect of
incidental light.

Illuminator

The back illuminator for this system required the development of a special high-quality flourescent lamp with a panchromatic light output. As Figure 11 shows, the spectrum energy distribution of these lamps consists of three high output lines located at 450, 540 and 620 nanometers.

Overall, the system is also energy efficient. Both the illuminator and the light valve are extremely well designed to give the display an overall power efficiency of one kilowatt power input for every square meter of image size (55-inch diagonal).

And color quality is uncompromised by high efficiency. The system's color reproduction capability, as shown in Figure 12, is essentially equal to an NTSC CRT display.

Wide Viewing Angle

The light dispersion characteristics of the color filter, the final stage of the display system, are responsible for the wide viewing angle capability as characterized in Figure 13.

The diagram shows the deviation angle from the true center axis of the display panel for 50-percent brightness reduction. As shown, the viewing zone extends plus and minus 60-degrees horizontally, 55-percent below the axis, and 20-percent above.

Color Matrix And Scan Progression

Individual primary color sources, red green and blue, are all vertically oriented, and those vertical elements are staggered in columns that are displaced by half an element size as shown in Figure 14. Each complete pixel consists of a green cell from one column and the red and blue cells from the adjacent column. Because of this displacement, the timing of incoming primary color video signals must be pre-adjusted, on both the horizontal and vertical scan directions in order to properly synchronize the images so they will correspond to the original.

Video To Light Transfer Characteristics

The LCD illuminator's transfer of an electrical input into a light output is different from a cathode ray tube transfer. As Figure 15 shows, the gamma of an LCD display is less than unity, as compared to 2.2 or more for a CRT display. In addition, the time constant, especially rise time, is highly dependent on applied voltage, which affects the system's aperture response. Rise and fall time characteristics of LCD system are shown in Figure 16.

Because of these special input-output characteristics, conventional video sources must be modified with special signal processing circuitry -- including both gamma and aperture correction -- in order to properly interface with LCD equipment.

Summary

In summary, the salient features of the color liquid
display system include:

○ Brightness that is greater than is found on conventional,
single CRT direct view equipment.

○ A diagonal image of up to 500-inches.

○ A contrast ratio exceeding 70-to-1.

○ A 120-degree viewing angle.

In addition to all these features, the system's high
fidelity color reproduction makes this advanced technology video
display equipment perfect for any number of indoor or outdoor
applications.

ASTROVISION LARGE SCREEN INCADESCENT LAMP MOSAIC DESIGN

The growing needs for large, primarily outd-or, television
and information display systems has prompted Matsushita to
develop a system known as "Astrovision." The trademarked
system is a mosaic display based on incandescent lamps.

Display Screen

The heart of the system is the display screen, whcih
consists of numerous groups of incandescent lamps. Each lamp
group has one lamp from each of the primary colors -- red,
green and blue. The lamps are arranged along the points of an
equilateral triangle. Each triangle represents one pixel.
The pixels are densely packed together to provide for the
highest po-sible resolution, which is limited only by the area
of each pixel and the overall size of the screen.

Because of varying screen size requirements, three
different bulb sizes, and thus, pixel sizes are available.
Figure 17 illustrates different bulb sizes and pixel configurations. By using three different pixel sizes, as Figure 18
shows, it's possible to tailor make a screen as small as
10-feet or as large as 60-feet in height.

Light Source

The use of incandescant lamps as the light sources for a
color television or video display system presents special
technical problems. Such systems demand fast reaction time
and accurate color and gray scale renditions.

Incandescent lamps vary its color temperature and react
slowly to varying electrical inputs. However, the use of
alternate light sources, such as small cathode ray tubes or
light-emitting diodes, will severely limit the total amount
of light emmission, and thereby restrict the range of potential
system applications.

Several characteristics are desirable for any video display light source:

(1) An extended operating life with little or no change in light output, hue, or color saturation purity.

(2) The availability of three primary colors whose chromaticity coordinates closely match NTSC color primary points.

(3) A gray scale whose range extends to at least 37dB without a shift in color temperature.

(4) A short time constant for real time display of television images.

(5) A low reflectivity to ambient light to increase contrast reproduction.

We've developed special light bulbs and driving techniques to meet the abovementioned requirements.

(1) Extended Life

Because the rate of tungsten filament evaporation is directly related to its absolute temperature by a power of 5.5, a special filament configuration and support structure was developed to lower filament temperature. The result is a bulb with a design life of 2,000 hours under maximum operating conditions. However, because the lamps are normally only driven to an average picture level (APL), the actual operating life is longer, in the neighborhood of several thousand hours.

(2) Three Primary Colors

The system's bulbs reproduce the three primary colors clearly because of a special exterior coating which filters out all unwanted ranges of the visual spectrum.

To maintain the purity of the red, blue and green colors over an extended period of time, the transmission characteristics of the coating must maintain a stable spectral or transmissional response. Special high-temperature, heat-resistant materials have been developed to keep the characteristics constant. Furthermore, Figure 19 shows that both the bulb's inner and outer surface, beyond the color filter, have been treated with a low reflectivity coating to reduce unwanted internal and external reflection. The spectral characteristics of the blue, red and green light sources are shown in Figure 20.

(3) Gray Scale

The bulb's light intensity is controlled by modulating the width of a constant amplitude 60 Hz pulse which is fed into the bulb. Based on the 6-bit word that's used to drive the pulse width modulator, the gray scale's reproduction resolution is one part in 64. Application of a constant amplitude pulse assures a constant color temperature from a light source, regardless of its intensity.

(4) Time Constant

Because ohmic filament resistance increases with rising temperature, an incandescent lamp has a longer rise than fall time, resulting in a reproduced image that's slightly integrated, or with a substantial loss of apeture response.

To compensate for this phenomenon, the variable width pulse applied to the bulb has been modified to have a differentiated leading edge.

(5) High Contrast Image Reproduction

In addition to the non-reflective coating on the inner and outer bulb surfaces, a further precaution has been taken to eliminate unwanted ambient light. As Figure 21 shows, a special shroud has been installed to direct unwanted radiation towards the rear of the display board.

Electronic System

The overall electronic system is shown in the block diagram labelled as Figure 22.

Input video is converted into a digital signal through an A-toD converter whose sampling frequency is determined by the number of pixels in the display screen. Normally, the number of pixels in the horizontal image line is tied to the sampling frequency by an integer relationship. Generally, the number of horizontal display image lines is smaller than the active number of horizontal lines per TV field. Scanning line interpolation is necessary to compensate for this non-integer relationship.

A unity relationship between the vertical scan rate and the bulb driver circuitry is maintained, or the display is reproduced at the television field rate.

In addition to time constant compensation, the driving circuitry for incandescent bulbs requires special gamma correctors, as shown in Figure 22. The driver input to light output characteristics are different for each primary color, because each color bulb must be driven to a different level of color temperature in order to achieve an optimum light output that's consistant with a desired bulb life expectancy. Gamma characteristics are shown in Figure 23.

The duration of the least significant bit of the 6-bit word for the pulse width modulators is 1/64th of the field period, resulting in a modulator output than can vary from 1/64th to continuous DC conditions during a field period.

Summary

The "Astrovision" Display System is unique in its capability to produce usable video images of extra ordinary dimensions under direct sunlight illumination. A contrast ratio of 10 to 1 can be achieved even under sunlight illumination as high as 5,000 foot candles.

Conclusions

The last and perhaps the most important link between the electronics world and human society is the image display devices and systems.

Information, data and entertainment materials, either transmitted and received, or retrieved from storage media must be displayed in a visible form to be useful.

Recent market introductions of large image size equipment described in this paper is the results of our recognition of the above mentioned facts by Matsushita Electric.

Acknowledgements

A. Takada and T. Ohashi of Matsushita Communication Industrial Co., Ltd. and Y. Wakahata of Matsushita Electroic Components, Ltd. have made significant contributions to the development of both large screen Liquid Crystal Display System and the Astrovision.

Visual Acuity

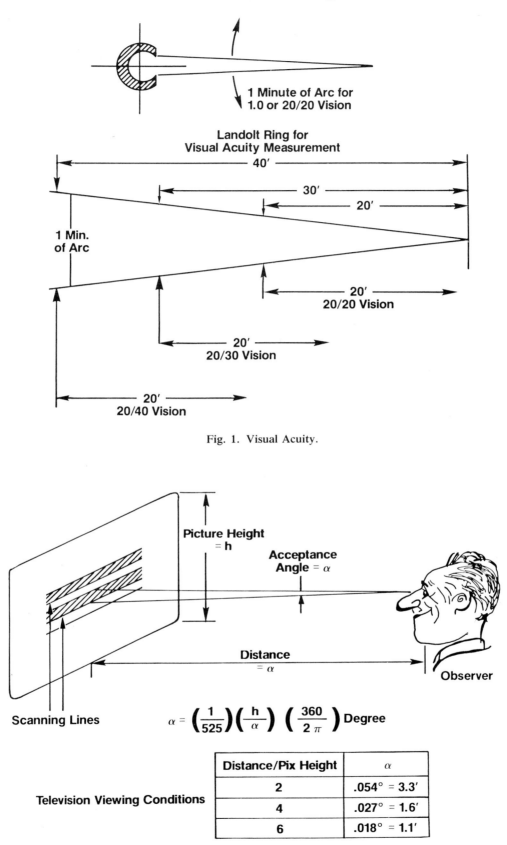

Fig. 1. Visual Acuity.

$$\alpha = \left(\frac{1}{525}\right)\left(\frac{h}{\alpha}\right)\left(\frac{360}{2\pi}\right) \text{Degree}$$

Television Viewing Conditions

Distance/Pix Height	α
2	.054° = 3.3'
4	.027° = 1.6'
6	.018° = 1.1'

Fig. 2.

Television Viewing in a Typical Living Room

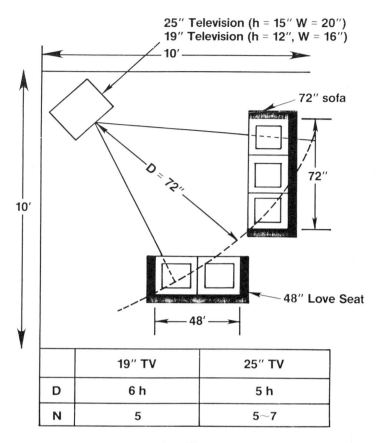

25″ Television (h = 15″ W = 20″)
19″ Television (h = 12″, W = 16″)

72″ sofa

D = 72″

72″

48″ Love Seat

48′

10′

10′

	19″ TV	25″ TV
D	6 h	5 h
N	5	5~7

Fig. 3. Television Viewing in a Typical Living Room.

Personal TV Viewing (Kitchen)

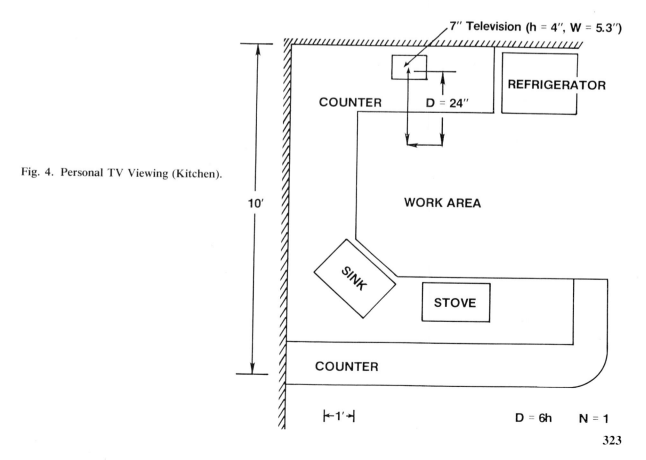

7″ Television (h = 4″, W = 5.3″)

REFRIGERATOR

COUNTER

D = 24″

WORK AREA

SINK

STOVE

COUNTER

10′

1′

Fig. 4. Personal TV Viewing (Kitchen).

D = 6h   N = 1

Small Auditorium TV Viewing Arrangement

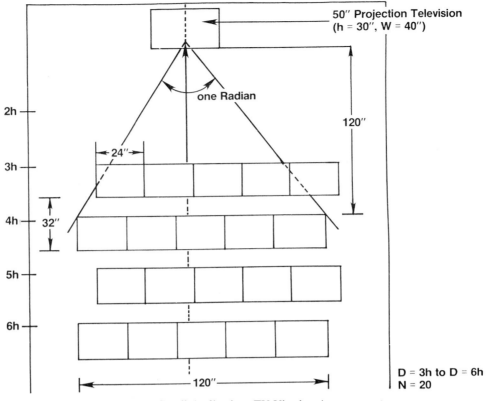

Fig. 5. Small Auditorium TV Viewing Arrangement.

Image Size vs Number of Viewers

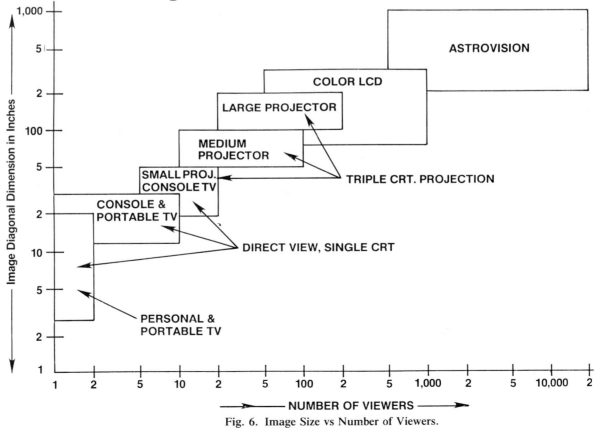

Fig. 6. Image Size vs Number of Viewers.

Applications of Various Video Display Systems

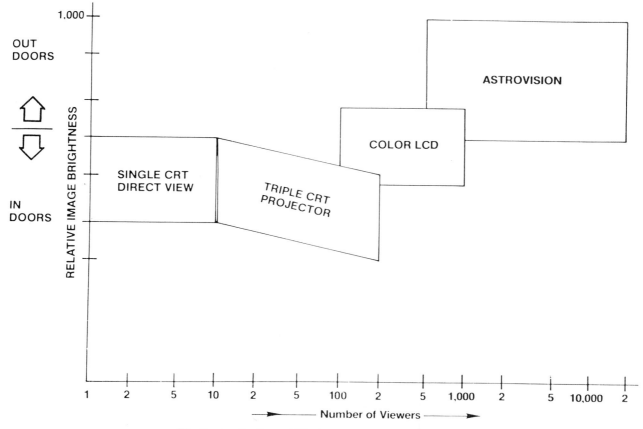

Fig. 7. Applications of Various Video Display Systems.

Color LCD Display System

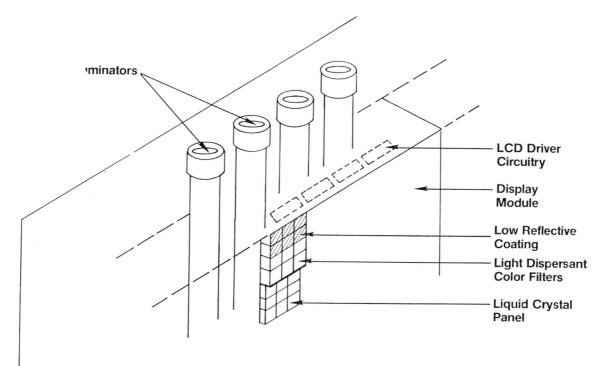

Fig. 8. Color LCD Display System.

LCD Panel Light transmission Characteristics

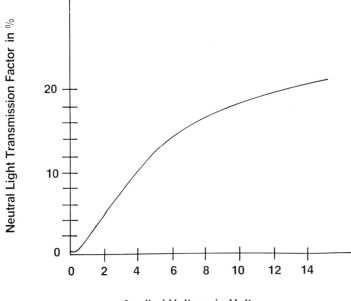

Fig. 9. LCD Panel Light Transmission Characteristics.

Display System Transfer Characteristics

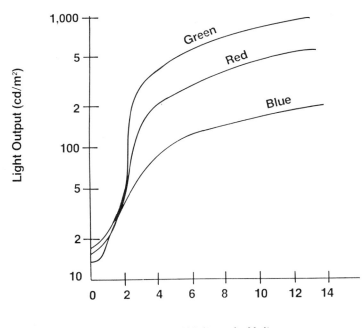

Fig. 10. Display System Transfer Characteristics.

Illuminator Spectrum Energy Distribution

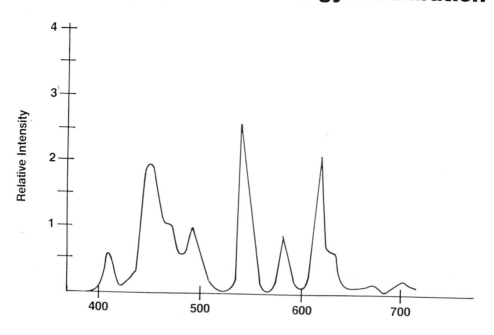

Wavelength (λ) in μm

Fig. 11. Illuminator Spectrum Energy Distribution.

Color Reproduction Zone, LCD Display

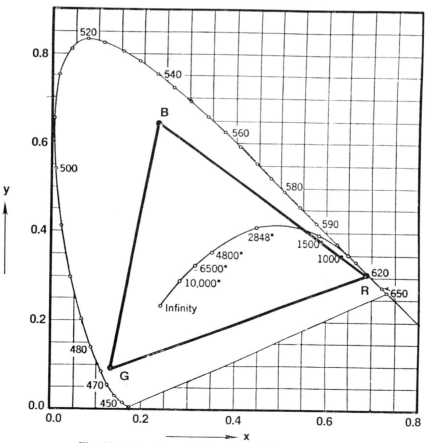

Fig. 12. Color Reproduction Zone, LCD Display.

Viewing Angle deviation from True Axis for 50% Brightness

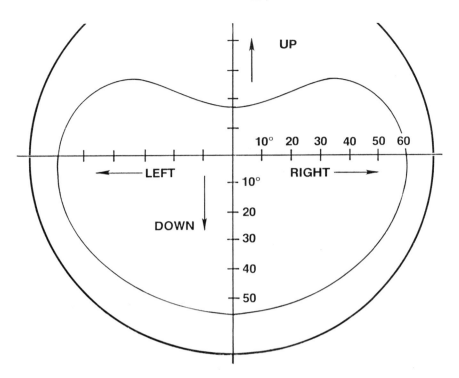

Fig. 13. Viewing Angle Deviation from True Axis for 50% Brightness.

Matrixed Pixcel Progression

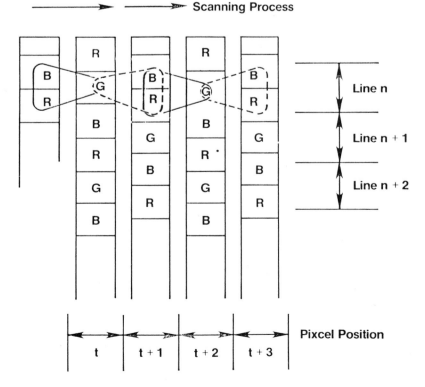

Fig. 14. Matrixed Pixel Progression.

Gamma Characteristics

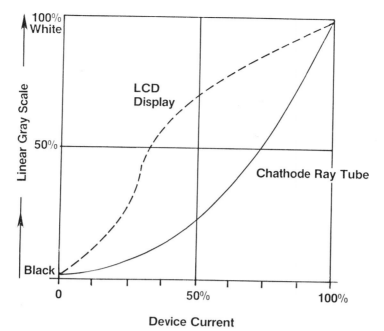

Fig. 15. Gamma Characteristics.

LCD Time Constant

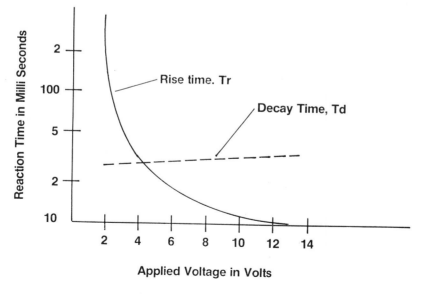

Fig. 16. LCD Time Constant.

Bulb Size and Configurations

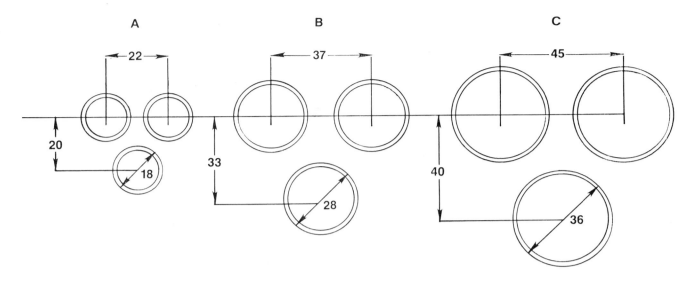

all dimensions in mm

Fig. 17. Bulb Size and Configurations.

Astrovision Configurations

Bulb Diameter	18 mm	28 mm	36mm
Image Dimensions Height (feet) Width (feet) Area (feet)	10~30 13~40 130~1200	17~51 23~70 390~3600	20~60 27~80 540~4800
Pixel Density number/(feet)²	41	25	17
Viewing Distance (feet)	> 130	> 230	> 300

Fig. 18. Astrovision Configurations.

Primary Color Light Source

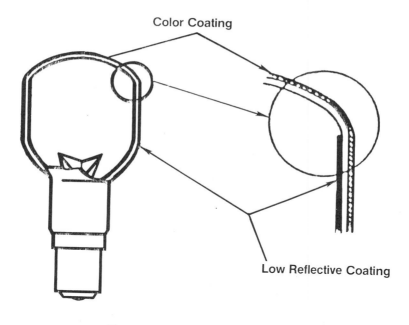

Color Coating

Low Reflective Coating

Fig. 19. Primary Color Light Source.

Energy Spectrum, Blue/Green/Red Light Sources

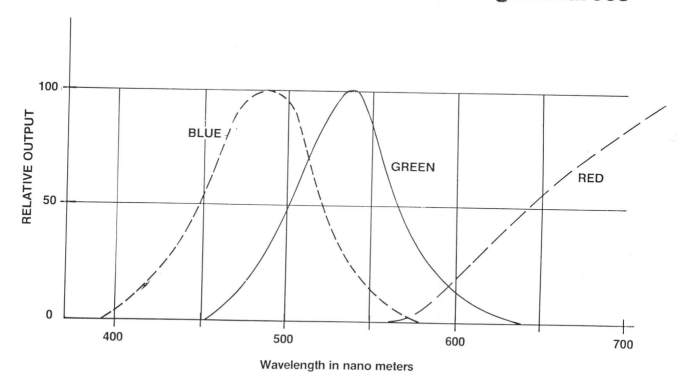

Fig. 20. Energy Spectrum, Blue/Green/Red Light Sources.

Light Source and Light Shield Assembly

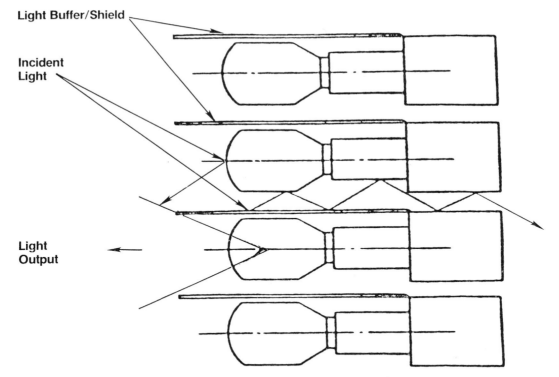

Light Buffer/Shield

Incident Light

Light Output

Fig. 21. Light Source and Light Shield Assembly.

Signal Processing and Lamp Driver Circuits

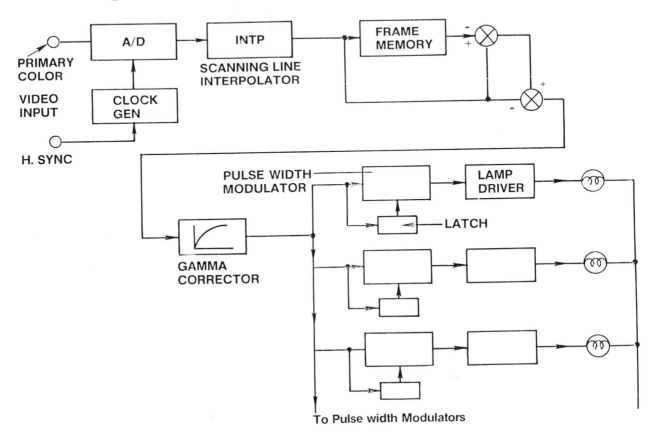

PRIMARY COLOR

VIDEO INPUT

H. SYNC

A/D

CLOCK GEN

INTP

SCANNING LINE INTERPOLATOR

FRAME MEMORY

PULSE WIDTH MODULATOR

GAMMA CORRECTOR

LAMP DRIVER

LATCH

To Pulse width Modulators

Fig. 22. Signal Processing and Lamp Driver Circuits.

Input/Output Transfer Characteristics (Gamma)

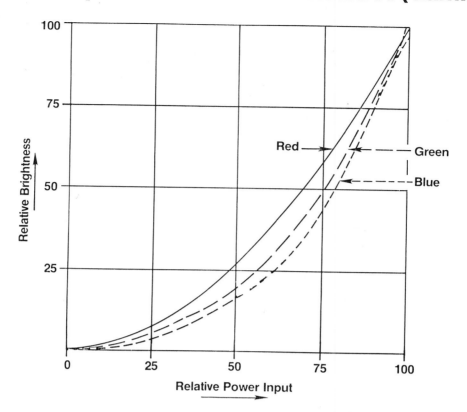

Fig. 23. Input/Output Transfer Characteristics (Gamma).

Fig. 24. An Example of a Large Screen Video Display.

Fig. 25. Another Example of a Large Screen Video Display.

Signal Processing for New HQTV Systems

Broder Wendland, Hartmut Schröder
Lehrstuhl für Nachrichtentechnik, Universität Dortmund
West Germany

1. Introduction

The present state of signal processing offers the possibility to achieve high television picture quality within a given standard. Particularly in new applications such as interactive videotex and still picture transmission or in cases where larger and brighter screens are used, there is a demand for improved picture quality with e. g. improved resolution of details and flicker free reproduction.

The first and simplest way to get better pictures may be to increase line numbers and bandwidth. In connection with new channels as e.g. satellite channels or optical fibres or coax tubes new high line number systems can be introduced.

This indeed is the Japanese approach with their 1125 line system. This system was demonstrated in several versions (NHK, Sony, Mitsubishi ..) and there is no doubt, that it works pretty good and gives excellent picture quality, although there are some problems left concerning moving blur and resolution depth.

On the other hand, this system ignores new signal processing facilities and the huge number of receivers, which are in use. So there is a good reason to think about improvements of TV-Systems which are compatible for standard receivers or at least give a chance for cheap conversion to standard receivers.

With respect to improved techniques of picture processing and the dramatic evolution of VLSI-techniques there are different possibilities for improving picture quality for tomorrow's TV. As it was pointed out in earlier papers /1/,/2/,/3/ the picture quality can be improved compatibly by motion adaptive pre- and postfiltering in combination with picture frame stores. This concept is based on the fact that with the application of digital signal processing and scan converters a picture transmission system can be divided into three parts: picture production, picture transmission and picture reproduction, wherein different standards can be applied.

Basing on this concept an effective pre- and postprocessing for an optimum picture quality is possible, whereas at the transmission channel the signals are still compatible (or "semicompatible") to standard receivers.

2. Compatible Improvements for Higher Picture Quality

Among the limitations and deficiencies of standard television systems we have

(1) poor horizontal and vertical resolution
(2) line flicker, line crawl

(3) frame and field aliasing
(4) irritating line structures (Kell's factor)
(5) large area flicker (50 Hz)
(6) crosscolour, crossluminance

Although some of these deficiencies may be reduced by a high line number system like the Japanese 1125 line-system there still remain several imperfections as e.g. reduced vertical resolution (Kell's factor, interlace factor /4/), flicker effects etc. This is all due to the basic concept illustrated in the block diagram of an early TV system of Fig.1 where just one line standard is used for production, transmission and reproduction.

But with respect to the high sophisticated techniques of signal processing - and especially in connection with picture frame stores - we can apply three different standards as it is shown in Fig. 2 namely

(1) High quality production standard
(2) Compatible or semi-compatible transmission standard
(3) Different independent reproduction standards

(1):
As it is pointed out in some more detail in previous papers /1/, /3/, /5/ a prefiltering process in connection with a high line number system at the production side can avoid frame aliasing. With a new concept, which is shown in section 3.2 also field aliasing in moving parts can be avoided. By this, with a suitable production standard in connection with signal preprocessing, an output signal can be constructed which fits within the transmission standard.

Beginning with a high quality production standard, suitable for direct HDTV-purposes and for HQ-video tape recording, the signal can be optimally preprocessed without any spatial aliasing and then transmitted over a channel in a HDTV- or in a DLT-format with 625ə, 50Hz, 2:1 interlace /3/.

(2):
At the transmission channel there can be applied a transmission standard which may be the hitherto used conventional standard. In this case a certain limited improvement is possible which is due to the signal pre- and postprocessing at the transmitter or receiver end respectively. So e.g. aliasing, Kell's factor and interlace factor can be overcome. Some first subjective judgements of these improvements will be presented in chapter 2.3.

With some more channel bandwidth as e.g. in the MAC-DBS-System the picture quality can be further increased in full compatibility with standard receivers. (MAC= Multiplexed Analogue Components, DBS = Direct Broadcast Satellite /6/) In addition there are some proposals for multiple channel systems in which one channel works in standard format - by this being compatible with standard receivers - whereas the other channels contain some information about additional resolution.

However, for channels with higher bandwidth like coax tubes or optical fibre systems the horizontal and vertical resolution can be increased. This can be done in a Dual Line Timeplex (DLT) format, pointed out in /3/. With this concept there are available all samples of a high line number system during the line time of a 625 line system. By this Timeplex format, within the same standard line number we get the resolution of a HDTV system. There is no real need for a high line number standard at the transmission channel /3/.

(3):
The reproduction standard can be chosen completely independent from the transmission standard if a picture frame store at the receiver is used. By this flicker free reproduction of pictures is possible. Some interesting solutions for flicker free picture reproduction are discussed in /8/ and /9/. Moreover, an interpolating postprocessing, combined with a high line number monitor, provides an impressive improvement of subjective picture quality /5/.

2.1 On Compatibility

Before going on in discussing compatible improvements some different cases of compatibility have to be distinguished:

(1): Direct compatibility
(2): Semi-compatibility

(1): Direct compatibility is given in cases where,

a) all improvements e.g. by signal processing at the receiver end do not affect the transmitted signal at all /7/,

b) signal preprocessing at the transmitter is done. Prefiltering for reduced frame or field aliasing improves signal quality and may improve picture quality of standard receivers slightly,

c) signal preprocessing as e.g. offset sampling at the transmitter is done. This produces new distortions or artifacts for the standard receiver which, however, can be reduced below a visibility level.

(2): In all cases, where some new transmission concepts within higher bandwidths are applicable, and in cases of more than one channel for just one service, there may be the necessity of a simple converter for the standard receiver. For example

a) for new DBS-channels in Europe the MAC-Concept is proposed /6/.

For this MAC concept, in which luminance, chrominance and sound signals are coded in time multiplex, for standard receivers a conversion is necessary from MAC-format to either PAL-format or Y,U,V-format, respectively. Applying 625 lines, 2:1 line interlace, with 50 Hz field frequency this MAC-standard can be translated by a cheap black box without changing the standard receiver.

For this MAC-channel with its higher bandwidth effective pre- and postfiltering can be applied without affecting the standard receiver. Thereby, horizontal and vertical resolution can be increased without any crosscolour, crossluminance, aliasing and flicker effects.

Moreover, with either more bandwidth or more channels further improvements of resolution are possible with the DLT-technique /3/. All these improvements are not really limited by the applied 625 line format at the transmission path.

b) With respect to new channels as e.g. coax tubes and optical fibres or in connection with the "digital studio" with its digital VTR's there will be applied "component coding".

Therefore, the different channels will be well separated without signal cross-talk. For these channels with a transmission standard of 625 lines/2:1 interlace compatible pre- and postprocessing is applicable, which can be matched to the given bandwidth or channel capacity and by this giving the optimum picture quality in either case.

2.2 Flicker Reduction with Picture Frame Stores

One of the most disturbing effects of TV systems depends on the applied line interlace technique in connection with 50 Hz field frequency. This causes the well known effects like line flicker, line crawl, heavy 25-Hz-flicker on horizontal contours of high contrast and large area flicker with 50 Hz.

Moreover, the subjective improvement of a line interlace system with 625 1/2:1 compared to a system of 312 lines without interlace is poor and does not exceed about 25 ... 30 %. This was already well known by Prof. Schröter, who first introduced line interlace into electronic video systems. In recent years also Dr. Fujio /4/ introduced a so called interlace factor of about 0.65, which corresponds to the improvement of line interlace of $2 \cdot 0,65 = 1,3$ compared with a non interlaced system of half the line number (e.g. for the same line frequency). Although the improvement is poor, the line interlace technique is applied all over the world and causes the above mentioned flicker effects.

To get rid of these disturbing effects picture frame stores can be applied. For this matter there are some different approaches which are described in e.g. /8/,/9/, /10/. One of the early concepts to overcome line interlace effects was developed at the University of Dortmund /11/. This basic concept is shown in Fig. 3a.

The incoming signal of one field (n-1) is delayed by a field store and then mixed with the undelayed signal of the next field (n). In Fig. 3b it is shown, how the interlaced lines of three sequential fields are added together to an output sequence with double line frequency. As it is obvious, the output sequence and consequently also the reproducing monitor work with progressive scanning. All flicker effects due to line interlace are overcome, and there is no more reason for an "interlace factor".

The subjectively tested improvement with this concept for still pictures is illustrated in Fig. 4 and explained in some more detail in /12/. It turns out, that with progressive scanned reproduction the subjectively weighted improvement compared to line interlace reproduction is impressive. Of course it has to be noted that the improvements depend on the structure of the reproduced picture.

At this point it should be mentioned, that the reduction of line interlace effects can be combined with reduction of large area flicker. This can be done by increasing frame frequency or applying e.g. 100 Hz field frequency at the output of a picture frame store and at the reproducing monitor. This will not be discussed here, but there are interesting concepts proposed in /8/,/9/.

A very important problem in connection with flicker reduction by frame or field stores comes up with moving pictures. For still pictures the above mentioned improvements are valid, however in moving parts of the picture moving blur occurs. This will be pointed out in chapter 3.1 in more detail.

2.3 Pre- and Postfiltering, First Results

As it is pointed out in /1/,/2/,/3/ and /5/ it can be shown, that with a proper prefiltering at the transmitter and an interpolating postfiltering at the receiver an error free picture scanning can be performed for still pictures. By this concept Kell's factor is overcome and the picture quality in vertical direction is improved. Moreover, with an offset sampling and suitable twodimensional pre- and postfiltering also the horizontal resolution can be improved.

By this technique in connection with picture frame stores and high line number monitors we can get

- flicker free reproduction
- flat field reproduction without irritating line structures
- optimally selected signals at the transmission channel without any aliasing
- well matched resolution to the picture content and to the human eye (high resolution in horizontal and vertical direction, less in diagonal direction)

This concept is basically shown in Fig. 5. We start with a high line number camera which may be a HDTV-Camera with 1249 lines, 2:1 line interlace. For still pictures we have by the scanning process periodic spectra in vertical direction of the twodimensional spatial frequency domain f^x, f^y.

Because of the high line number source with limited resolution we only get some aliasing (overlapping of spectra) at higher vertical frequencies in the fY domain. With a proper preprocessing and a scan conversion we can convert down to output signals of a 625 line /2:1 standard which are free of any aliasing /3/.

Consequently we can implement an upconversion at the receiver to e.g. again 1249 lines. By an interpolating postprocessing we get proper "high line number signals" which give a flat field reproduction with a matched HQ-Monitor.

By this concept we get an error free scanning, no aliasing and a flat field reproduction without irritating line structures or artifacts by aliasing effects. This concept of pre- and postprocessing overcomes the Kell-factor and gives an impressive improvement which, however, depends on the kind of transmitted picture.

In a further step, by offset sampling and diagonally orientated pre- and postfiltering, the horizontal resolution can be increased by approximately a factor of two. This is pointed out in some more detail in /3/.

In Fig. 6 the resolution bounds are shown for a HDTV-system and a standard system, wherein for the standard system also the resolution bounds are shown for a diagonal pre- and postfiltering. As it is obvious, for the diagonal filtering we get increased horizontal resolution but somewhat less diagonal resolution compared with the standard system.

To get a deeper insight into the subjective weighted improvements of picture quality with the different signal processing concepts a series of subjective tests were performed. Some of the results are shown in Fig. 7.

Fig. 7 shows the assessed improvements of picture quality (12 experts, CCIR comparison scale) for the different concepts:

    h: high line number system, 2:1 interlace,
    d: diagonal filtering,
    v: vertical filtering,
    p: progressive scanning,

all of them compared with the standard system, 2:1 interlace (s).

As the improvements depend to the picture content, results of two pictures with very different structures are shown for different criteria as sharpness, resolution, flicker reduction and total impression.

Results:

- It comes out, that in any case flicker reduction by picture frame store gives an impressive improvement.

- It further comes out, that vertical pre- and postfiltering - although giving an impressive improvement for the reproduction of horizontal contours or lines - gives a slightly less resolution and sharpness than in the case of progressive scanning.

This is an important point, because if we apply the same modulation transfer function in horizontal and in vertical direction, we get the same resolution or sharpness in these directions. And in a twodimensionally bandlimited system with the same cutoff frequencies $f_c{}^y = f_c{}^x$ there is no more sense for reducing $f_c{}^x$ by a Kellfactor.

But, because of this and the fact that without vertical pre- and postfiltering there is some more subjective impression of sharpness, we should never reduce the horizontal bandwidth by a "Kell-factor" if we apply progressive scanning (at the receiver!).

- In all cases diagonal pre- and postfiltering gives the best picture quality for a given standard and bandwidth.

3. A Concept for an Improved TV-System

As it was pointed out, the picture quality of the standard TV-systems suffers from the deficiencies (1)...(6) listed up in chapter 2. Whereas for still pictures the restrictions (1)...(5) can be overcome by pre- and postfiltering, crosscolour and crossluminance may be cancelled by some comb filter techniques /9/,,/10/. By this, picture quality can be impressively improved.

Moreover, by an early concept of a so called "spot wobble technique" /13/, /14/, /15/, /16/ the horizontal and vertical resolution can be increased for higher channel bandwidth within the same line standard at the transmission channel.

But most of these improvements suffer from line interlace technique at the transmission channel, because of some new moving blur at the contours of moving areas in the picture.

3.1 Motion Blur and Flicker Reduction

The flicker reduction discussed in chapter 2.2 is valid for still pictures. But in areas in which there is some moving in either horizontal or vertical direction, there comes up moving blur at the contours of the moving parts. This is pointed out in Fig. 8.

With Fig. 8a we have the input field sequence in which a black square may be scanned. Therefore we may get the dashed lines in any field with a movement of Δx in horizontal direction from one field to the next. As it is obvious, there is no real information about the picture content in the lines between the double spaced lines of one field at just the same time instant t_1 or t_2, respectively. The only information for the lines between the field lines of one field however comes from the offset lines of the next field at another time instant. So a mix up of two adjacent fields in this case leads to the situation in Fig. 8b, where at the vertical contours of the square we get some moving blur out of the pure addition of two fields.

So the proposed flicker reduction by combining two adjacent fields to one frame, and showing this frame with 50 Hz, 60 Hz or more at the monitor suffers from just this moving blur, for which the human eye is sensitiv. It may be surprising that the normal situation of a line interlace reproduction (Fig. 8a) does not create subjective moving blur. But it is a somewhat different situation in Fig. 8b, in which the different contours of two adjacent fields are shown <u>at the same time</u> and thereby giving the blur impression.

An approved concept to overcome this moving blur in horizontal direction (and later on in any direction) is given with Fig.9. The incoming field sequence is first fed into two field stores (Fig. 9b). Out of the difference of field (n-2) and field (n) we get a frame difference D, which indicates moving areas in the picture and which leads by some signal processing to a control function $ß = f(D)$.

On the other hand in Fig. 9a there may be given a situation, where at the output of frame (n-1) we need the line i, which is between the actual lines i-1 and i+1 of the actual given field (n-1) of the input signal. For still pictures - as it was described in chapter 2.2 -the output line i is correctly delivered by the line i of the (wrong) field (n-2) (line interlace).

But in case of a moving part (time variant content) in the line signal of line i, we should not take over the line signal i of field (n-2) into the output signal of line i in frame (n-1) because of their different time dependencies. In principle we do not have any information in this situation for the correct signal for the output line i. So the best we can do is the interpolation for this line out of the x, y and t direction (3-D-interpolation, wherein the time direction again may produce moving blur!).

For simplicity in this case we introduce a vertical interpolation out of just the field (n-1) which is actual for the output frame (n-1), which may be performed here by the weighted addition of the adjacent lines i-1 and i+1 of the input field (n-1). Now, controlled by the coefficient ß, for still pictures ($ß = 1$) we get the above described resolution of a full frame whereas for moving parts in the picture we get a controlled intrafield interpolation with less resolution in vertical direction but without moving blur. The control is thereby performed by the coefficient (soft decision) $ß(D)$, which is a function of weighted signal differences of adjacent frames /11/.

With this adaptive blur control it is possible to get rid of all flickering effects by picture frame stores at the monitor without loosing temporal resolution. This improvement can be done independently from the used standard in every receiver without loosing compatibility. And, because of performing full frames out of the incoming fields, the frame store content can be read out in principle with every speed we want to reduce large area flicker.

3.2 On Field Aliasing

One of the most annoying effects with line interlace techniques
is caused by the field aliasing in moving parts of a picture.
This comes up by the fact that the line distance in one field is
twice the line distance in a full frame. So, if we want a good
vertical resolution well matched to the line number of a full
frame, we get heavy field aliasing in every field. As it is
shown in /3/, for still pictures the field aliasing of two adjacent fields just cancel each other because of the line offset
position of adjacent fields.

However, if there is some time varying in the spatial spectrum
of the transmitted picture the field aliasing of adjacend fields
can no longer cancel each other exactly. Every field content
comes out of another time instant, and in a moving scene residual field aliasing arises.

This defect in a line interlaced picture is well known especially in connection with vertical moving parts in a picture
(line crawl, artifacts by field aliasing). Surprisingly there
is a high sensitivity of the human eye for this aliasing. So the
visibility already starts at a detail velocity of about 0.1 pel
per frame, which is a very low velocity.

This field aliasing in moving areas - caused by the line interlace - also takes place in case of offset sampling for increased
horizontal resolution /3/. Moreover, this case of offset sampling seems to be more critical, because of the same sensivity to
very low horizontal velocities leading to new artifacts, unknown
in the standard technique.

Anyway, also for the standard techniques with line interlace
there is a demand for a concept, avoiding field aliasing in
moving areas.

3.3 A Concept for a Motion Controlled Preprocessing

A new concept for a motion controlled preprocessing with error
free scanning for still pictures with high spatial resolution
but lower spatial resolution in moving parts without any field
aliasing is shown in Fig. 10.

Beginning with a HQ-Camera with e.g. 1249 lines, 2:1 interlace,
the video signal is stored in two field stores. Because of the
very limited resolution of the upcoming HDTV-Cameras we only
have small frame aliasing and limited field aliasing in moving
parts of the high line number signal. So we may implement a prefilter in the demultiplexer D to get input fields with 625 lines
without aliasing for still pictures or very slow motion. This
technique has been discussed before and is shown in more detail
in /1/,/3/.

This prefiltering allows a field scanning with 625 lines without
aliasing for still pictures or very slow motions, in moving
parts however this prefiltering will produce moving blur. There-

fore, for high temporal resolution the camera signal is also fed to a second path in which there is no interaction between adjacent fields by prefiltering, but there are interpolating lowpass filters, which - in connection with a multiplexer M - produce bandlimited output fields in $s_2(t)$. By this, out of the input fields of the 1249 lines /2:1 interlace signal we get output fields which produce standard signals $s_2(t)$ with 625 lines /2:1 which are free of field aliasing and moving blur. On the other hand this high temporal resolution for moving parts (50 Hz) is accompanied by reduced vertical resolution i.e. 312 lines per picture height of every output field.

To get a maximum spatial resolution for still pictures or for slowly moving parts of a picture in the upper path just one prefiltered field of the high line number system is used. Out of field 1 of the high resolution signal two synthetic output fields are performed by the selector S to build up a signal $s_1(t)$ with 625 lines/ 2:1 interlace.

For an optimum matching to the scene and for an optimum usage of the transmission channel, still avoiding moving blur and field aliasing, we can adaptively choose by the moving detector between

- an overall maximum spatial resolution within the standard with only 25 Hz temporal resolution for still pictures or slower moving parts in a picture. (Velocities up to about 2 pels per frame are allowed.)
- a maximum temporal resolution (50 Hz) with reduced spatial resolution (restricted to the resolution of just one field of the output signal)

It is important to note, that by this concept, because of the synthetic output fields out of one "high resolution" input field, we don't get any moving problems with cancelling of field aliasing in the output signal $s_1(t)$. Every two fields come just out of one single time instant and thereby "fit together". This also holds for the moving problems with increased horizontal resolution by offset sampling and diagonal spatial pre- and postfiltering. On the other hand, for heavy moving parts every output field is free of aliasing because of the interpolation (two-dimensional lowpass filtering) in the lower path in Fig. 10.

In Fig. 11 this concept is shown schematically with the construction of the signal $s_1(t)$ and $s_2(t)$ out of the fields of the incoming camera signal with 1249 lines/2:1 interlace.

3.4 Receiver Concept for Increased Picture Quality

At the receiver there is no real need for a certain reproduction standard, if a picture frame store is used as a scan converter. But it is obvious that, doubling the line number we get a very simple structure for the scan converter and by this an upconversion with nearly flat field reproduction.

Unfortunately, if we like to get in addition reduced large area flicker by increasing field frequency at the monitor (e.g. 100

Hz), this yields a line frequency of about 64 kHz. However, for countries with 60 Hz field frequencies there may be no real need for increasing field frequency. So for simplicity we will not discuss large area flicker and its reduction at this point, but the reduction of line interlace effects.

The receiver concept is principally shown in Fig. 12. The incoming video signal, produced by a transmitter shown in Fig. 11, is first splitted in a first (2n-1) and a second field (2n) of just the same frame n. By a twodimensional intraframe interpolation (2D-LP) combined with an upconversion (e.g. 1249 lines/2:1 interlace) we get a flat field reproduction without irritating line structures and artifacts by line interlace out of the upper path in Fig. 12.

By control of the moving detector MD the lower path in Fig. 12 will be switched on (soft decision) for moving areas. In this path the incoming signal - after proper delay - is transformed by an 2-D-interpolating lowpass LP_2, and then scanconverted to 1249 lines/ 2:1 interlace. This intrafield interpolation is done only between the lines out of the actual field at any time. By this, the resolution is reduced to the information content of just one field, but temporal resolution is increased to 50 Hz without any moving blur.

With this concept, the resolution is switched from

- high spatial resolution for still pictures or slowly moving areas and low temporal resolution (25 Hz)
- to high temporal resolution (50 Hz) for heavy moving parts with lower spatial resolution

5. Conclusions

With the application of digital signal processing in television systems, different standards can be applied for production, transmission and reproduction. By this the TV-signals can be well matched to different channels and services whereas at the receiver end the picture reproduction can be optimized for the human observer.

Basing on this signal processing a TV-system is proposed with two different steps of definition. In the first step a HDTV-standard is provided by high quality sources in the studio. The signals can be transmitted without any loss of information in a DLT-standard over suitable wideband channels. By this the High Quality Signals can be transmitted in an extended timeplex format, compatible to standard timeplex (MAC) receivers /3/.

In a second step by proper prefiltering these signals directly fit into standard 625ℓ, 50Hz, 2:1 channels as f.i. NTSC, PAL MAC etc. for broadcasting services. Depending on the rapid evolution of the microelectronics and its VLSI-techniques it will be possible and economic to implement picture frame stores into "high quality receivers". By this, and some signal processing at the transmitter and the receiver, an increased reproduction quality is possible which avoids line interlace defects and cancels Kell's factor.

Moreover with offset sampling and proper twodimensional filtering it is possible to match the transmission path to the spatial picture content and to the human eye. Furthermore, controlled by a moving detector, the transmission can adaptively switched from higher spatial resolution in any direction to higher temporal resolution with lower spatial resolution in moving areas. By these techniques an impressive improvement is possible within a given standard and bandwidth.

There is no real need for an incompatible high line number standard at the transmission channel. With new transmission channels and component coding (MAC, Timeplex, digital transmission) combined with higher channel bandwidth (or parallel channels) the same picture quality can be achieved. This can be done with still 625 lines /2:1 interlace at the transmission path.

Acknowledgement

The authors like to thank very much
- the german ministry of research (BMFT) for supporting these studies
- Dipl.-Ing. F. Stollenwerk and Dipl.-Ing. D. Uhlenkamp for some results out of their works and helpful discussions.

References

/1/ Wendland, B.: "HDTV Studies on Compatible Basis with Present Standards", in "Television Technology in the 80's" published by the SMPTE, Scarsdale, New York, 1981

/2/ Wendland, B.:"High Quality Television by Signal Processing" 2nd International Conference on new systems and services in telecommunications, Liège, 1983

/3/ Wendland, B.: "Extended Definition Television with High Picture Quality", SMPTE-Journal, Vol. 92 (1983), No. 10

/4/ Fujio, T.: "A Study on HDTV-Systems, IEEE Transactions on Broadcast", Vol. BC-24 (Dec. 1978) No. 4

/5/ Schröder, H.; Elsler, H.: "Planare Vor- und Nachfilterung für Fernsehsignale", ntz-Archiv, Band 4, (1982), H. 10, S. 303-312

/6/ Rawling, R.; Morcom, R.: "Multiplexed Analogue Components - A New Video Coding System for Satellite Broadcasting", Internat. Broadcasting Convention, Brighton, 1982, Conference Proceedings pp 158-164

/7/ Schönfelder,H.: "Möglichkeiten der Qualitätsverbesserungen beim heutigen Fernsehsystem", Fernseh- und Kinotechnik, Bd. 37 (1983), H. 5, pp 187-196

/8/ Sandbank, Moffat: "High Definition Television and Compatibility with Existing Standards" SMPTE-Journal, Vol. 9.2 (May 83) No. 5

/9/ Jackson, R.N.; Annegarn, M.J.J.C.: "Compatible Systems for High Quality Television", SMPTE Journal, Vol. 92, No. 7 (1983) pp 719 - 723

/10/ Clarke, C.K.P.: "High Quality Decoding for PAL Inputs to Digital YUV Studios", BBC Research Department, Report BBC RD 1982/12

/11/ Uhlenkamp, D.; Güttner, E.: "Verbesserte Wiedergabe von Norm-Fernsehsignalen", ntz-Archiv, Band 4, (1982), H. 10, S. 313-321

/12/ Stollenwerk, F.: "Qualitätsvergleich von Zeilensprung- und Vollbildwiedergabe" FREQUENZ 37 (1983) 11/12

/13/ Blümlein, A.D., British Patent No. 503555, October 1937

/14/ Jesty, L.C.; Phelp, N.R.: "The Evaluation of Picture Quality with Special Reference to Television Systems", Marcom Review, 1951, pp 113 and 156

/15/ Wendland, B.: "Kompatibles Bildfernsprechsystem", Deutsche Patentschrift DE 2551664 C3, 18. Nov. 1975

/16/ Powers, K.W.: "Compatibility Aspect of HDTV", same proceedings as in /2/.

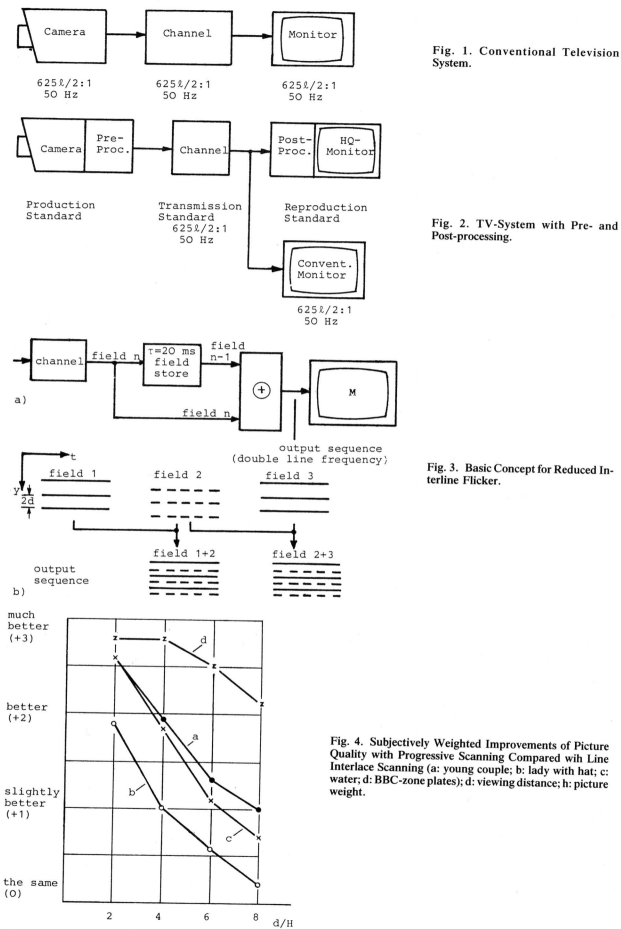

Fig. 1. Conventional Television System.

Fig. 2. TV-System with Pre- and Post-processing.

Fig. 3. Basic Concept for Reduced Interline Flicker.

Fig. 4. Subjectively Weighted Improvements of Picture Quality with Progressive Scanning Compared wih Line Interlace Scanning (a: young couple; b: lady with hat; c: water; d: BBC-zone plates); d: viewing distance; h: picture weight.

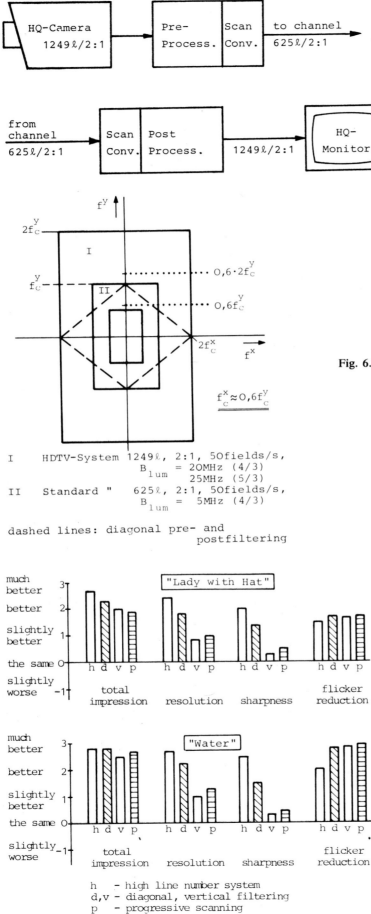

Fig. 5. Basic Concept for Compatible Improvement by Pre- and Post-filtering.

Fig. 6. Resolution Bounds for Different TV Systems.

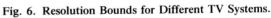

$$f_c^x \approx 0{,}6 f_c^y$$

I   HDTV-System 1249ℓ, 2:1, 50fields/s,
         B_{lum} = 20MHz (4/3)
                  25MHz (5/3)
II   Standard "   625ℓ, 2:1, 50fields/s,
         B_{lum} = 5MHz (4/3)

dashed lines: diagonal pre- and
                          postfiltering

Fig. 7. Comparison of Picture Quality of Improved Systems to the Standard System (Viewing distance: 3H).

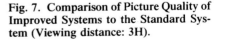

h   - high line number system
d,v - diagonal, vertical filtering
p   - progressive scanning

350

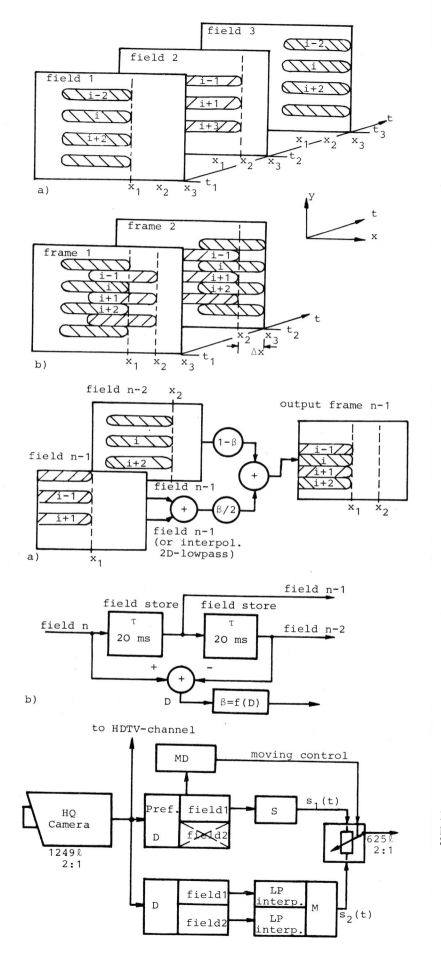

Fig. 8. On Moving Blur.

Fig. 9. Adaptive Controlled Interpolation for Flicker Reduction.

Fig. 10. Motion Controlled Preprocessing for Compatible Improved Standard Signals.

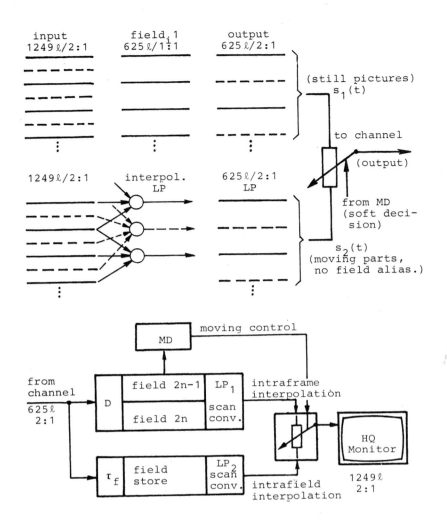

Fig. 11. Motion Controlled Pre-processing for Compatible Improved Standard Signals, Schematic.

Fig. 12. Receiver Concept with Moving Control.

Broder Wendland was born in Germany on May 16, 1934. He received the Ing. (grad) degree in electrical engineering from the Ingenieur School Berlin in 1957, the Diplom Ing. degree from the Technical University of Berlin in 1965. From 1965 to 1969 he was with the Heinrich Hertz Institute, Berlin, where he was concerned with data transmission techniques. In 1969 he received the Dr. Ing. degree. From 1969 to 1975 he worked at the research institute of AEG-Telefunken, Ulm, FRG, where he was engaged in commercial picturephone techniques. In 1975 he became full professor at the University of Dortmund. Since 1979 he is working in the field of High Picture Quality Television Systems and High Definition Television. In 1980 he got the Eduard Rhein Prize '79 for his proposals for compatible improvement of TV-systems. In 1982 he became chairman of a HQTV study group which was founded by the Nachrichtentechnische Gesellschaft (NTG) and the Fernseh-und Kinotechnische Gesellschaft (FKTG) to study all aspects of high quality television systems for the future.

Dr. Schröder received his Dipl.-Ing. degree in "Communication techniques" from the Technical University of Berlin in 1971 and his Dr.-Ing. degree in 1977 from the Technical University of Munich. From 1971—1977 he was with Siemens AG, Munich working in a research laboratory on video transmission and speech processing. In 1977 he joined the Institute for Communication Techniques, University of Dortmund (Leader: Prof. Dr.-Ing. B. Wendland) as a chief engineer. There he works in the field of "High Quality Television" and gives lectures on signal theory and communications systems.

Extended-Definition TV Fully Compatible with Existing Standards — Proposal and Experimental Results

Takahiko Fukinuki, Yasuhiro Hirano, and Hiroshi Yoshigi
Central Research Laboratory, Hitachi, Ltd.
Kokubunji, Tokyo, 185 Japan

ABSTRACT

Based on the new proposal/1/ for an Extended Definition TV system(EDTV) that is fully compatible with the existing standards, experiments have been done by computer simulation. Full compatibility implies that both existing and EDTV receivers can receive existing and EDTV signals which have the same bandwidth, without adaptors.

In order to insert high resolution information, vacant frequency bands are found. Resolution can be improved both vertically and horizontally, the former by progressive scanning and line interpolation, and the latter through insertion of horizontal high resolution information. This causes little degradation even when received by present TV receivers.

Experiments have been done on two kinds of schemes, which will be refered to as F and H schemes, hereafter.

These schemes are applicable to CATV, CCTV, video storage, broadcasting, and direct broadcasting satellites (DBS), without any modification of existing facilities.

(1) INTRODUCTION

The future of higher definition TV, which has been attracting great attention, is still technically uncertain, as to when and how it will be utilized in the world. There are a variety of ideas, for example, the methods for transmitting these extremely wide-band signals, or the importance of compatibility with today's TV standards.

Fully compatible Extended Definition TV(EDTV) has been proposed/1/, based on the authors' basic philosophies:
 i)   Receiver compatibility is very important,
 ii) Transmission compatibility is also very important. Utilization of a single channel is best,
 iii) Deficiencies inherent in the existing standards should be, and can be, removed or greatly reduced, and

----

* Presented orally at the 1984 Winter TV Conference under the title of "High Definition TV Fully Compatible with Existing Standards".

vi) Frame stores will be very inexpensive in the near future, and should be utilized fully in the new standards.

Full compatibility, i.e., both receiver- and transmission-compatibility, is best, if it is possible. This is almost the same situation as when today's color TV standards were being adopted: that is, such standards should allow both(monochrome and color) receivers to receive either(monochrome or color) TV signal without any adaptors.
Utilization of a single channel with the current bandwidth is best, considering the compatibility of transmission and/or storage facilities and in part the Japanese (and perhaps European and American) situation concerning DBSs.

The deficiencies inherent in the existing standards should be completely removed in the new standards. Such deficiencies include aliasing components when scanning is considered as temporal-vertical sampling and cross-signal interference between luminance and color components. Line flicker belongs to the former.
These deficiencies can be removed completely by temporal-vertical pre- and post-filters composed of a frame and/or field store. Time division multiplexing of luminance and color components is not the only way to eliminate them.

(2) FULLY-COMPATIBLE EDTV BY FIELD-TO-FIELD PROCESSING

2.1 REALIZATION OF FULLY COMPATIBLE EDTV

EDTV fully compatible with the current standards requires:
i) vacant frequency bands in which to insert high resolution information, and,
ii) no (or, little) picture degradation due to the inserted information when received by present TV receivers.

Similar efforts had been made in inserting color information when the present NTSC color TV standards were adopted. However, cross-signal interference was not taken into consideration sufficiently. This is an important aspect to remember.

2.2 IMPROVEMENT OF VERTICAL RESOLUTION

As is well known, vertical resolution can be greatly, e.g., 50%, improved by processing with progressive scanning, as is explained in Appendix-1 /3,4,5,7/. This processing is composed of
i) progressive scanning, pre-filtering in a temporal-vertical frequency domain, and 2:1 sub-sampling (interlaced scanning), at the camera end, and,
ii) interpolation of discarded scanning lines(post filtering) for display at the receiver end.

2.3 VACANT FREQUENCY BANDS(F SCHEME)

For ease of understanding, the proposed system will be explained in a one-dimensional frequency domain.

Figure 1 shows the frequency spectrum of a TV signal. Fig.1(a) is the frequency domain diagram familiar to every TV engineer. Fig.1(b) is simply magnification of part of Fig.1(a). Strictly speaking, this is the case for still pictures. As shown in that figure, in the current system, color components are inserted after every two luminance components and there are many slots that are vacant or not used effectively. These can be analyzed more precisely in a three-dimensional frequency domain, as explained in Appendix 2.

Therefore, it is suggested that these vacant frequency slots(bands) be used for inserting new information, Y ', as shown in Fig. 1(c). This scheme will be refered to as the F scheme(Field-to-field processing), hereafter.

In order for the new signal to have the frequency spectrum shown in Fig.1(c), the phase of the sub-carrier of the new signal should be controlled in the way shown in Fig.2. The phases of the new sub-carrier, ϕ and $\phi + \pi$, lower with every field, while those of the color sub-carrier, φ and $\varphi + \pi$, rise with every field.

2.4 UTILIZATION OF THE NEW COMPONENTS

As was explained before, vertical resolution can be greatly improved by processing with progressive scanning.

Therefore, it is desirable to utilize the new components for improvement of horizontal resolution. One possibility is shown in Fig.3, where the high frequency components of the luminance signal, Y_H', (e.g., 4.0-6.0 MHz) is shifted to 2.2-4.2 MHz, i.e., frequency band of the chrominance components. This will be refered to as the F1 scheme.

Another possibility is to shift high resolution luminance components(4.0-8.0 MHz) toward 0.0 MHz. One example is to shift 4.2-7.8 MHz to 0.6-4.2 MHz by modulating them with a modified color sub-carrier(the phase is inverted every field.). This will be refered to as the F2 scheme.

These high resolution components are detected at the receiver by field-to-field processing. In the simplest case, the color components are detected by a digital filter whose characteristics are $(1 - z^{-263H})$, and the high resolution components by one with $(1 - z^{-262H})$, as shown in Fig.4, utilizing the relationship of the phases of sub-carriers, f_{sc} and μ_0, as shown in Fig.2, where z^{-H} is a 1H delay operator.

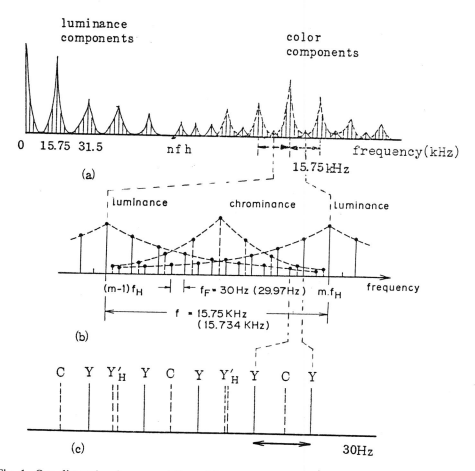

(a)

(b)

(c)

Fig. 1. One-dimensional representation of frequency spectrum in F scheme:
    (a) luminance and color components of an NTSC signal,
    (b) magnified spectrum of (a),
    (c) magnified spectrum of (b) and inserted high resolution components, Y_H'.

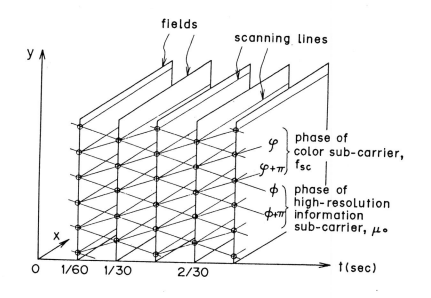

Fig. 2. Scanning line structure and phases of sub-carriers.

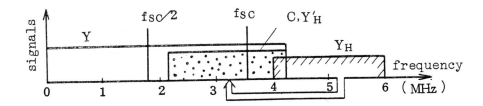

Fig. 3. Example of frequency shifting.

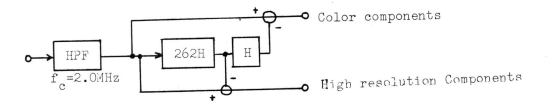

Fig. 4. Extraction of high resolution components and color components using field store.

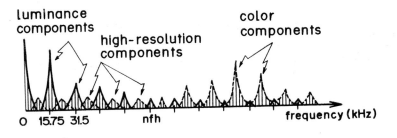

Fig. 5. One-dimensional representation of frequency spectrum in H scheme.

2.5 EXAMPLE OF FREQUENCY SHIFTING IN THE F SCHEME

Aspects to be determined for frequency shifting are:
  i)   method of modulation and modulation frequency,
  ii) phase control of the sub-carrier for modulation, and,
  iii) recovery of the sub-carrier at the receiver for demodulation (when synchronous detection is applied).

The method of modulation seems to be limited to AM, or more desirably, carrier-suppression AM, which takes into consideration power saving and disturbance to existing receivers. In this case, recovery of the carrier is necessary for synchronous detection.

For example, in the F1 scheme,, the carrier, μ_o, can be generated from a half-harmonic of the color sub-carrier, as

$$\mu_o = f_{sc}/2 = 1.8 \text{ MHz}.$$

Horizontal frequency components of 4.0-5.0 MHz are modulated by μ_o, and shifted to 2.2-4.2 MHz utilizing the lower side band. The phase of the carrier should be set as was shown in Fig.3.

2.6 PICTURE DEGRADATION

In the proposed system, high resolution information inserted in the NTSC signals might cause picture degradation in existing TV receivers. This is similar to the case where color information inserted in monochrome signals causes degradation in monochrome receivers.

Degradation induced by high resolution components, however, is expected to be much less than the color-component induced degradation, because the power of the former is much less than that of the latter around the color sub-carrier frequency. In addition, as with the color components, the phase of the high resolution component is inverted in every frame and line in a field.

2.7 APPLICATION TO PAL

This method is also applicable to the PAL system in the same way. High resolution information is inserted into the conjugate areas of the U and V signals in the temporal-vertical frequency domain.

(3) METHOD WHERE FIELD-TO-FIELD PROCESSING IS NOT INEVITABLE (H SCHEME)

In the method mentioned in the previous section, field-to-field processing was essential for extracting high resolution information. In this section, a method that does not require field-to-field processing is described. Picture quality is, nevertheless, improved greatly by such processing.

In this scheme, high resolution components are modulated by color sub-carrier, f_{sc}, and frequency-multiplexed in the lower portion in the same manner as color signals, as shown in Fig.5.

The high resolution components are demodulated in the TV receiver, either by intra-field or field-to-field processing. That is, both high resolution and color components are extracted by synchronous detection with the color sub-carrier, f_{sc}. This scheme will be refered to as the H scheme(High-resolution components in the same quadrants as color components. --see Fig. 11), hereafter. Three-dimensional representation is shown in Appendix 3.

Combination of both the F and H schemes is also possible. In this case, a high resolution luminance signal of 4.0-10.0 MHz is shifted to the existing frequency bandwidth(0.0-4.2 MHz).

(4) EXPERIMENTAL RESULTS

Experiments to prove this proposal must show:
i) improvement of horizontal resolution by inserted signals, and,
ii) no degradation of color and luminance representations in current TV receivers due to the inserted signals, and
iii) improvements and no degradation due to temporal-vertical processing, i.e., (progressive scanning)-(temporal-vertical filtering)-(interpolation of discarded scanning lines).

Item iii) has already been proved by other groups. In addition, these experiments were done by computer simulation, which makes it difficult to simulate moving pictures. Therefore, the experiments, i) and ii), were done.

4.1 IMPROVEMENT OF HORIZONTAL RESOLUTION DEFICIENCIES

Figure 5 shows processed pictures displayed on a 525-line, progressive-scanning CRT. Two schemes, F1 and H, were tried. Horizontal resolution was greatly improved by the inserted information.
Deficiencies in the existing TV standards, such as cross-interference and flicker, were removed completely.

4.2 DEGRADATION TO CURRENT TV RECEIVERS

Due to the current situation, only the case of color TV receivers has been tested. The experimental results, however, are very difficult to show in color photographs, since the distortion due to insertion is inverted every frame, except in one case. That case is color distortion in the F scheme mentioned in section 2. In this case, a little color distortion due to the inserted high resolution

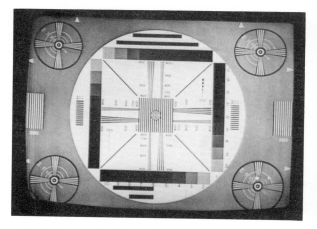

(a) Picture in NTSC standards.

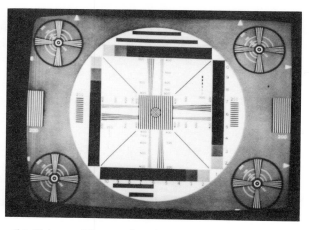

(b) Picture with reproduced high resolution information, Y_H.

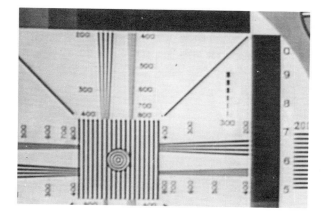

(c) Magnified picture of (a).

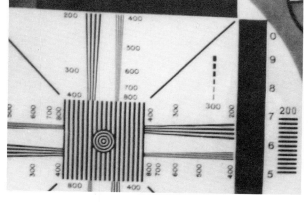

(d) Magnified picture of (b).

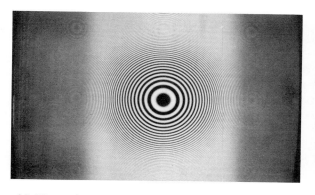

(e) Picture in NTSC standards (Y_L; low frequency components of luminance signal).

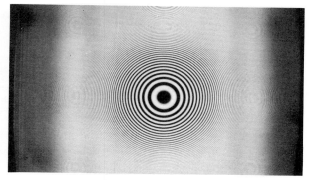

(f) Picture with reproduced high resolution information, Y_H.

Fig. 6. Experimental results; Pictures obtained by computer simulation with the F1 and H schemes.

information is steady in a still picture. On the other hand, in the H scheme, a little low frequency distortion caused by the insertion is visible.

In any case, however, the distortion is found to be too small for anyone to detect, unless the existence of such degradation is pointed out.

(5)APPLICATION EXAMPLES

The features of this system in practical application are:
i) The system is applicable to all the existing forms of video storage, including VTRs and Video Disks, since the video signal format and the audio signals can be exactly the same as in NTSC(PAL) standards.

ii) In the near future, picture quality in TV receivers for home use will be improved greatly by adaptive scanning-line interpolation, adaptive inter-field Y-C separation, and progressive scanning display through the use of field stores/2/. The system proposed here is well suited to these receivers. although this system is much simpler than TV sets that use the adaptive processing mentioned above. Post temporal-vertical processing will be done using one of the characteristics of adaptive processing. Only the extraction function of high resolution information should be added to receivers by using a part of the Y-C separation.

iii) The system can be used for CATV without any modification of existing facilities. It is especially suitable for introducing higher definition TV gradually to existing CATV systems.

iv) For direct broadcasting satellites(DBS), the bandwidth for a modulated signal is 27 MHz(in regions 1 and 2), which leaves almost 10 MHz available for the baseband signal. However, the narrower the bandwidth the better, in consideration of the triangular noise characteristics and transmission power of the FM link. This system can be applied to BS-2, the Japanese DBS, which uses exactly the same video signal format as NTSC, except for the sound signals, which are sent in DPSK modulated PCM around 5.7 MHz.

v) In this system, both cameras and receivers are assumed to have 525 progressive scanning lines and 60 frames. This is desirable for improving vertical resolution. Interlaced cameras and receivers, however, can be used if only improved horizontal resolution is desired.

(6)CONCLUSIONS

Experimental results on EDTV fully compatible with the NTSC(PAL) standards has been shown, based on a new proposal/1/. The system assumes that the specifications are the same as the existing ones in such areas as video signal format and transmission frequency bandwidth, for full compatibility in the strictest sense. It is also assumed that this EDTV receiver will be able to receive current signals and that ordinary receivers will be able to receive the new signals.

The high resolution information is inserted into the vacant frequency bands of existing TV signals.

It was already clear that vertical resolution can be greatly improved by progressive scanning at the camera and interpolation of discarded scanning lines through the use of field stores at the receiver/4,5,6/. In addition, due to the inserted information, it has become possible to improve horizontal resolution still further.

The attainable bandwidth(horizontal resolution) in each scheme is as follows:

(NTSC)	....	(4 MHz),
F1 scheme	....	6 MHz,
F2 scheme	....	8 MHz,
H scheme	....	6 MHz,
F2+H scheme	....	10 MHz.

Picture degradation caused by such insertion when received by an older receiver is found to be less than that due to the color subcarrier when received by a monochrome receiver.

REFERENCES

1) T. Fukinuki and Y. Hirano, "High-definition TV fully compatible with existing standards", presented at a domestic joint meeting of Technical Groups on Communication Systems and Image Engineering of the Institute of Electronics and Communication Engineers of Japan and the Technical Group on Image Communication Systems of the Institute of Television Engineers of Japan, July 1983, and now under review in IEEE Trans. on Communications.

2) (e.g.) M. Achiha, K. Ishikura and T. Fukinuki, "A motion adaptive high-definition converter for NTSC color TV signals", The 13th Intern'l Television Symp. (in Montreux), May 1983.

3) (e.g.) D. Nishizawa and Y. Tanaka, "Conversion of interlaced pictures to non-interlaced pictures" (in Japanese), Record of the Technical Group on Image Engineering of the Inst. of Electronics and Communication Engineers of Japan, No.IE82-6, April 1982.

4) K. Lucus and M. D. Windram, "Direct television broadcast by satellite, desirability of a new transmission standard", IBA R.& D. Report,116/81, Sept. 1981.

5) B. Wendland, "High-definition television studies on compatible basis with present standards", in "Television Technology in the 80's", SMPTE (1981, New York).

6) E. Dubois, M. S. Sabri and J.-Y. Ouellet, "Three-dimensional spectrum and processing of digital NTSC signals", SMPTE Journal, vol. 91, No. 4, pp. 372-378.

7) T. S. Rzeszewski, "A compatible High-Definition Television system", Bell Syst. Tech. J., vol. 62, No. 7, pp. 2091-2111, Sept. 1983.

Appendix 1   IMPROVEMENT OF VERTICAL RESOLUTION BY TEMPORAL-VERTICAL PROCESSING

Fields, scanning lines and the phases of the color sub-carrier were shown in Fig. 2 in the temporal-vertical domain. Scanning here is taken as sampling in the domain. This sampling is understood to be sub-Nyquist sampling (offset sampling or frequency interleaved sampling), in analogy to two-dimensional (vertical and horizontal) sampling /4,5,6/.

Transformed into a temporal-vertical frequency domain, these components are plotted as shown in Fig. 7. To avoid aliasing, the temporal-vertical frequency components of a luminance signal, Y, should be limited in the diamond-shaped region, as shown in the figure. However, no filtering is done in today's TV cameras. Therefore, aliasing occurs due to the spectrum centered at the sampling frequency, f_{IS}, which causes such picture degradation as line flicker.

Color signals, C, occupy two small diamond-shaped regions around f_{SC} as depicted in Fig. 7. In the NTSC standards, however, their frequency components are not prefiltered, except in the horizontal frequency domain. This also causes picture degradation. The luminance signal, Y, and color signals, C, should not overlap. Otherwise, cross-signal interference, such as cross-color and cross-luminance, takes place.

The method shown in Fig. 8 overcomes this problem. That is, the picture signal is first taken using a TV camera with progressive scanning, as shown in Fig. 8(a). This is then filtered by a temporal-vertical filter, as in (b), and sub-sampled (interlaced) at a 2:1 ratio, as in (c).

For current NTSC TV signals, vertical resolution theoretically attainable with the present number of scanning lines has not been achieved mainly because of:
(i) picture degradation due to aliasing, as mentioned above, and
(ii) spot size of the scanning electron beam which is so wide it causes one scanning line to overlap with adjacent lines which results in reduced resolution.

364

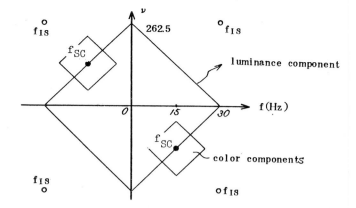

Fig. 7. NTSC signal in temporal-vertical frequency domain.

μ; horizontal
    frequency

ν; vertical frequency

f; temporal frequency

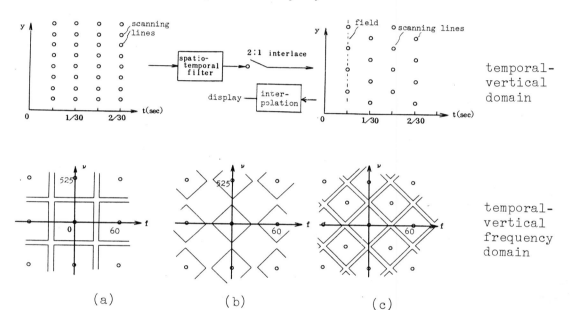

(a)   (b)   (c)

Fig. 8. Aliasing-free scanning.
(a) 525 lines/60 fields/60 frames progressive scanning.
(b) output of temporal-vertical filter and input of display.
(c) 525 lines/60 fields/30 frames interlaced scanning.

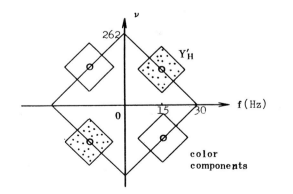

Fig. 9. High resolution and color components in temporal-vertical frequency domain in F scheme.

In other words, vertical resolution can be greatly improved even with the same number of scanning lines, if the method shown in Fig. 8 is adopted/7/.

Usually, vertical resolution is related to the so-called Kell factor, K(K=0.7). In the case of interlaced scanning, the line structure becomes visible. This effectively decreases the factor to K', and,

K' = K x (Interlace Factor).

According to some experiments,

K' = 0.42 ～ 0.6, and,

Interlace factor = 0.6 ～ 0.8

Therefore, interpolation would improve vertical resolution by 1/(interlace factor), i.e., $1/0.6 (\doteqdot 1.7) \sim 1/0.8 (\doteqdot 1.3)$.

Appendix 2 AVAILABLE VACANT FREQUENCY BANDS IN THE THREE-DIMENSIONAL FREQUENCY DOMAIN IN THE F SCHEME

In section 2, vacant frequency bands were explained in a one-dimensional frequency domain. Here, the concept is clarified by analyzing TV signals in a three-dimensional frequency domain.

Re-examining Fig. 7, which shows the cross section of a temporal-vertical frequency domain, makes it clear that color signals exist in the second and fourth quadrants and there are no signals in the first and third quadrants/5/. It is into these unused quadrants that the authors propose inserting the high resolution information.

Figure 9(a) shows the temporal-vertical frequency spectrum when new information, Y_H', is inserted into the vacant quadrants. These signals, transformed from the frequency domain to the real domain, were plotted in Fig. 2.

Figure 10(a) is a front view in the F1 scheme, and Figs. 10(b) and (c) are cross-sections at the horizontal frequency $\mu < 2.2$MHz and at 2.2MHz$< \mu < 4.2$MHz, respectively. The high-frequency component, Y_H, is frequency shifted and inserted as Y_H'.

Appendix 3 AVAILABLE VACANT FREQUENCY BANDS IN THE THREE-DIMENSIONAL FREQUENCY DOMAIN IN THE H SCHEME

In section 3, another scheme, called the H scheme, was proposed. This is also shown in a three-dimensional frequency domain in Fig. 11.

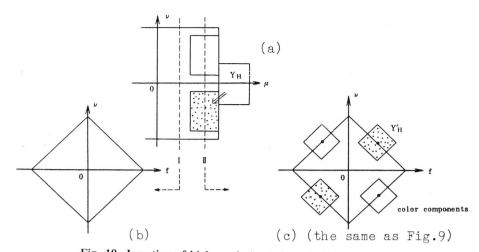

Fig. 10. Insertion of high resolution information in three-dimensional frequency domain in F1 scheme.
  (a) front view.
  (b) cross section at I.
  (c) cross section at II (the same as Fig. 9).

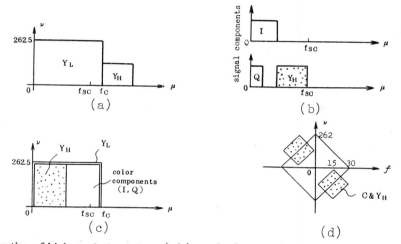

Fig. 11. Insertion of high resolution information in three-dimensional frequency domain in H scheme.
  (a) two-dimensional frequency band of luminance signal, Y_L and Y_H.
  (b) base band color components, I and Q, and modulated high resolution information Y_H'.
  (c) Y_L, Y_H, I and Q in horizontal-vertical frequency domain.
  (d) Y_L, Y_H, I and Q in temporal-vertical frequency domain.

Takahiko Fukinuki was born in Osaka, Japan, on December 26, 1936. He received the B.E. and M.E. degrees in electronics and the Ph.D. degree in information engineering all from Kyoto University, Japan, in 1959, 1961 and 1975, respectively.
Since 1961, he has been with Central Research Laboratory, Hitachi, Ltd., working on signal processing, especially on picture processing since 1968. From 1969 to 1970, he was Visiting Scientist at MIT. Currently he is Chief Researcher and Leader of Signal Processing of Pictures Group. He has authored books entitled "Digital Signal Processing of Pictures" (Author's Award of Inst. TV engineers of Japan) and "Signal Processing of Pictures for FAX and OA" (both in Japanese).

Yasuhiro Hirano was born in 1947 in Aichi, Japan. He received the M.S. degree in Electrical Engineering from Tokyo Institute of Technology in 1973. He joined the Central Research Laboratory, Hitachi Ltd. in 1973. He has been engaged in the development of a facsimile modem, digital VTR and digital signal processing of video signal.

Hiroshi Yoshigi was born in Shimane prefecture, Japan, on November 17, 1946. He graduated from Matsue Technical High School, Japan, in 1965.
Since 1965, he has been with Central Research Laboratory, Hitachi, Ltd., working on signal processing for digital communications and its applications.

New Aspects and Experiences in Stereoscopic Television

Ruediger Sand
Institut fuer Rundfunktechnik (IRT)
Munich, Fed. Rep. of Germany

INTRODUCTION

During the conference you have had the opportunity to see our 3D-television demonstration program "An evening magazine in 3D", in true stereoscopy, in color and with stereophonic sound, produced for the International Audio and Video Fair 1983 in Berlin. In addition we displayed some sequences of a conventional TV program in "quasi-stereoscopic" mode. The following paper gives supplementary background information to our presentation.

In 1982, in Germany and in some other European countries a series of stereoscopic TV programs in simple anaglyphic technology were transmitted. The broadcasts found an unexpected public response: Fourty millions of red/green filter glasses were sold. Similar experiences are known from USA. In 1983, the Thomson-Brandt group introduced color television sets equipped with a circuitry which, by wearing color filter glasses, adds spatial impression to normal TV broadcasts. Worldwide there is an apparent renaissance of interest for three dimensional imaging in other media too, as in cinematography, photography and printing.

This indicates that the old idea of perfectioning pictorial presentation by spatial depth has not yet lost its attractiveness. But up to now the success of all 3D efforts always was of short duration. One of the crucial reasons was unsatisfactory quality, especially in TV. Most viewers obviously are not willing to accept different colorfilters for either eye, lack or reduction of natural color as well as reduction of picture sharpness or of other quality parameters as a trade-off for the 3D impression.

Our institute, the IRT in Munich, the research and development centre of the broadcasting organizations in the Federal Republic of Germany, had started investigations on 3DTV fifteen years ago already, after color TV had been introduced in Germany. Meanwhile the technical prerequisites have increased and it seems that now, or at least in the near future, the technical basis will be available to achieve an attractive high quality 3DTV as a real improvement of today's picture quality. Especially in combination with research and standardization of new TV systems - providing enhanced quality and sense of realism - we believe that 3DTV should be taken into consideration.

3D STUDIO EQUIPMENT

The basis of 3D reproduction is to copy human binocular vision as perfectly as possible. Today, some ENG-cameras even of high quality are sufficiently slim to be mounted side by side closely within the interaxial distance of the human eyes, which is 65 mm in average. Fig. 1 shows a 3D-camera we used for our 3DTV production, consisting of two Hitachi SK 81. The interaxial distance, however, is 100 mm and this causes a somewhat exaggerated perspective perceptible in some scenes of our demonstration program. Nevertheless, it is a very handy equipment for outdoor shooting. In more complex arrangements (Fig. 2) by means of semi-transparent mirrors, as known from 3D-cinematography, one can obtain interaxial distances down to zero for close-up shootings. Fig. 3 presents a camera of this kind developed by Philips, Netherlands. Further necessary or desirable features are devices for converging the optical axis to position the so-called "stereo window", as well as for simultaneous operation of the lenses and camera controls. This can be achieved by means of servos and micro-processors. A much simpler construction we used in our 3D-camera: the zoom lenses were controlled by cords, wrapped around both lenses. Sufficient mechanical and electrical stability to avoid misregistration between both cameras - expecially in vertical direction, which causes eye strain to the viewer - can be achieved by modern technology. Altogether it can be summarized that today 3D-productions are only a matter of cost.

Slide and film scanning presents no fundamental problems either. Fig. 4 shows the scheme of a 3D slide scanner in flying spot technology which we developed in the beginning of our 3D-investigations. It is still in operation and was used for the still pictures in our demonstration program. For film scanning in separate-reel technique it is recommendable to scan both reels with the same film scanner storing one reel on a VTR in order to avoid geometrical differences.

3D RECORDING AND TRANSMISSION

For high quality 3DTV two channel recording and transmission is a practicable method and up to now the most efficient one.

Our demonstration program was recorded on two B-format VTRs from Bosch-Fernseh, using time code for synchronisation (Fig. 5). 3D editing can be accomplished by most of the modern editing systems. We used the MOSAIC system developed in the IRT. As we did not have enough machines for simultaneous editing of the "left" and the "right" recordings, we edited both in sequence. This was carried out automatically, under the control of the stored data. For synchronous play back, with the necessary accuracy of one field, normal editing systems can be used, but it is also possible to synchronize both machines manually by means of a suitable synchron-leader and the tape-speed-override mode, as done for our demonstration at this conference.

For home application twin-track VTRs seem to be possible, e.g. using the Video 2000 format manufactured by Grundig and Philips. This format uses a reversing cassette on which only one half of the tape is recorded per run. Sony presented a prototype of a twin-track VTR recently. A 3D demonstration system consisting of two locked video disc players was shown by Philips. Experiments with a single-disc two-track player are carried out in the laboratories of the same manufacturer.

For 3D transmissions, now and in the near future, a two-channel system by cable and satellites could be an imaginable and practicable solution. It would be advantageous that both channels are evidently compatible with conventional TV. Recently, a range of HDTV systems using two-channel technology have been proposed, considering that there are no transmission channels offering the adequate high bandwith for one-channel HDTV. It seems to be obvious to combine a two-channel HDTV system with a two-channel 3DTV system allowing alternative services.

If compatibility with conventional TV can be ignored, sequential one-channel 3D systems could be conceived by means of frame stores, which are becoming cheaper and are expected to appear in home receivers in the near future. It is impossible to discuss all the various methods in this paper in detail, but it is obvious that also in the field of transmission today or in the near future the technical basis is available for high quality 3DTV.

3D DISPLAY DEVICES

For 3D display the polarization technology, using the almost neutral-grey polarizing glasses, is the favourite method. A simple and well-known arrangement consisting of two picture tubes, polarizing filters in front of the screens and a semi-transparent mirror is illustrated in Fig. 6. The viewer wears corresponding filter glasses. Plane polarizers (90°-V) are commonly used, but bicircularly polarized systems allowing more freedom for head movement are possible too. In the future, it is imaginable to build a combined 3D-tube or a flat-panel-display offering a screen with alternately polarized pixels. Instead of polarizing filters, technology may allow the use of an arrangement of lenticular lenses (Fig. 7) for glassless viewing. At a conference of the International Society for Optical Engineering in Geneva, Switzerland, last year, excellent lenticular sheets in large dimensions for photographic purposes were presented.

The most convincing 3D-display device today is TV projection. The larger screen size in TV projection supports the 3D impression considerably. Fig. 8 shows the 3D-projector, which we use for our demonstration, consisting of two Barco "Data"-Projectors with polarizing filters in front of the projection lenses. The customary metallized screen causes no depolarization. By means of an additional convergence circuit the registration of the two pictures for left and right is quite well all over the screen. The reversed color sequence in the second row compensates in the resultant picture the typical color shading to be found in that kind of projectors. This principle also can be applied in rear projection. On the International Audio and Video Fair in Berlin last year, the German manufacturer Grundig presented a prototype of a 3DTV rear-projector.

QUASI STEREOSCOPY

At the end of our survey on true stereoscopic devices I would like to mention a method which adds a 3D impression to any conventional TV program, shot two-dimensionally. It has been developed at the IRT and we call it "Quasi stereoscopy". In 3D displays as described, the picture for one eye only needs to be shifted somewhat horizontally (up to 9 percent picture height) (Fig. 9). Viewed by the polarizing glasses, this displacement creates the impression that the picture is in some distance behind the screen, but moreover, the two-dimensional picture itself appears three-dimensional. This astonishing phenomenon can be explained by stimulation of spatial vision and by visual experience. Of course, it can not offer real depth information or typical 3D effects like objects protruding out of the screen, but nevertheless the spatial impression is surprising. We feel that this could be an interim solution prior to true stereoscopy.

The principle of "Quasi stereoscopy" is also the basis for the 3D television sets by the Thomson-Brandt group mentioned before. With conventional color TV sets, only the red picture component is shifted by means of a 600 nsec delay line. The viewer has to wear color filter glasses. This method also creates the three-dimensional impression, but with the drawbacks of the anaglyphic technology.

In our 3D-demonstration we present "Quasi stereoscopy" in polarizing technology, thus providing natural color. The demonstration program is a conventional TV program music show.

CONCLUSION

The purpose of our 3D demonstration and of this paper is to stimulate a discussion. We have seen the great public interest in the 3DTV broadcasts in the simple and hardly satisfying anaglyph technology. At the presentation of our 3D demonstration program in full color and full sharpness at the International Audio and Video Fair 1983 in Berlin, people were nearly enthusiastic: 12 000 visitors have taken the opportunity to attend the presentation and many people had to be sent away because of shortage of space.

Not only the feeling of spatial depth is the advantage of a stereoscopic system, but also the impression of a generally increased picture quality. The reasons for this phenomenon are not yet fully explicable and should be further investigated. It could be compared with stereophony, where not mainly true sound location, but the over-all transparency of sound adds the attractiveness to monophonic sound. In 3D display, the impression of resolution increases remarkably; the picture looks more crisp. Distortions as jitter, noise (especially color noise), conspicuous in a one-channel picture, appear to be significantly reduced in 3D.

The demonstration may have shown that high quality 3DTV can be achieved with conventional studio equipment. However, we are aware of the technical, economical and last but not least psychological problems which have to be solved prior to a public introduction of 3DTV. An important question would be, whether people will accept to wear glasses - shurely not in primitive cardboard mounts - or whether technologies dispensing with glasses have to be found. On the economical side it has to be taken into account that up to now for 3DTV only a limited number of 3D films are available.

Nevertheless, we believe that high quality 3D television is attractive enough and worth to think about it. Let me end with an optimistic quotation from Charles W. Smith, a well-known British expert in 3DTV: "Future generations will be astonished that for a few decades in the 20th century we were happy to accept these small flat images as a representation of the real three-dimensional world".

ACKNOWLEDGEMENTS

The IRT wishes to thank Barco Electronics N.V., Kuurne, Belgium, for supporting transportation of the 3DTV equipment to Montreal and to thank Refeka, Kirchheim/Munich, W.-Germany, for the donation of the polarizing glasses.

Fig. 1. 3D camera consisting of two Hitachi "SK 81" cameras (IRT).

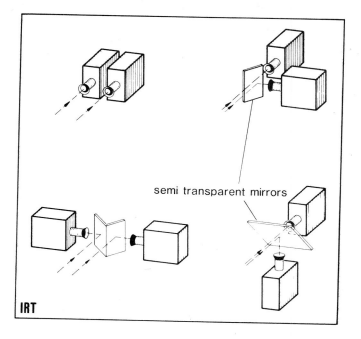

semi transparent mirrors

IRT

Fig. 2. Design principles of 3D cameras.

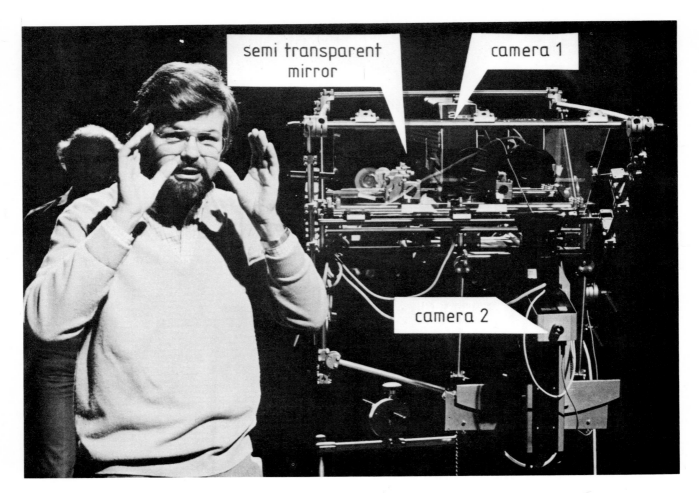

Fig. 3. 3D camera using a semi-transparent mirror for reduced interaxis distances (Philips).

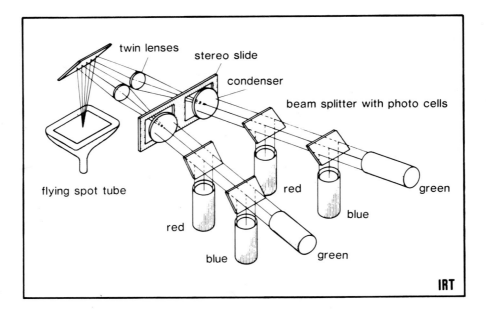

Fig. 4. Scheme of a flying-spot 3D slide scanner (IRT).

Fig. 5. 3D recording and display equipment consisting of two B-format VTRs (Bosch-Fernseh) and the MOSAIC editing system (IRT).

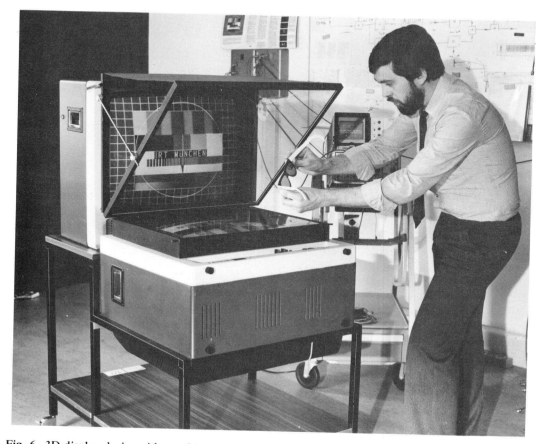

Fig. 6. 3D display device with two 26-in. monitors, polarizing filters and a semi-transparent mirror (IRT).

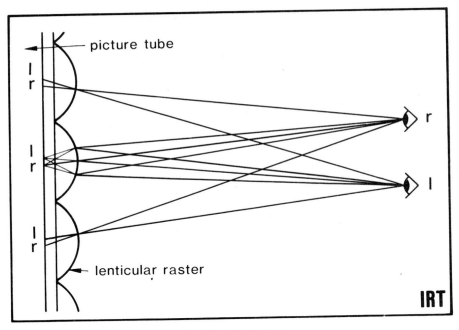

Fig. 7. Principle of a lenticular screen.

Fig. 8. 3D projector consisting of two TV Barco "DATA" projectors with polarizing filters (IRT).

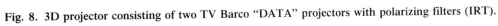

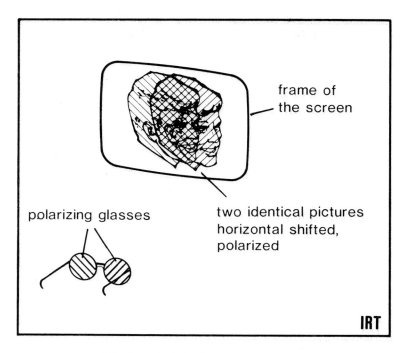

Fig. 9. Principle of "Quasi stereoscopy".

Ruediger Sand was born in 1931 in Koenigsberg, Germany. He studied Telecommunication Engineering at the Ohm-Polytechnikum in Nuremberg until 1958 and received the degree of Diplom-Ingenieur (FH). That year he joined the IRT (Institute of Broadcasting Engineering) in Munich, where he worked in the department for Advanced Technologies on television systems and studio equipment. Since 1975 he is head of the TV Display Technology department. He is a member of the FKTG in Germany.